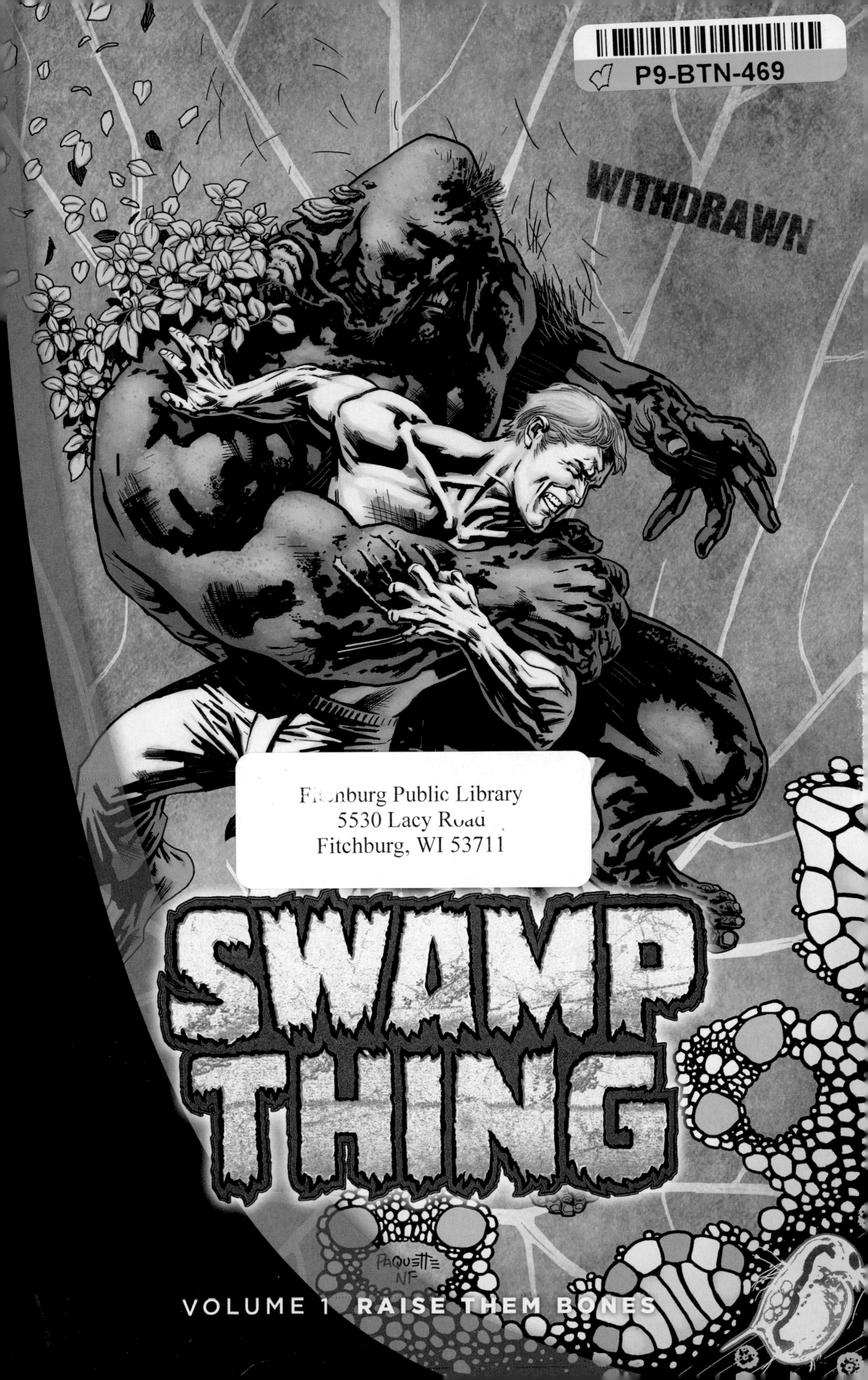
SWAMP THING
PAQUETTE NF
VOLUME 1 RAISE THEM BONES

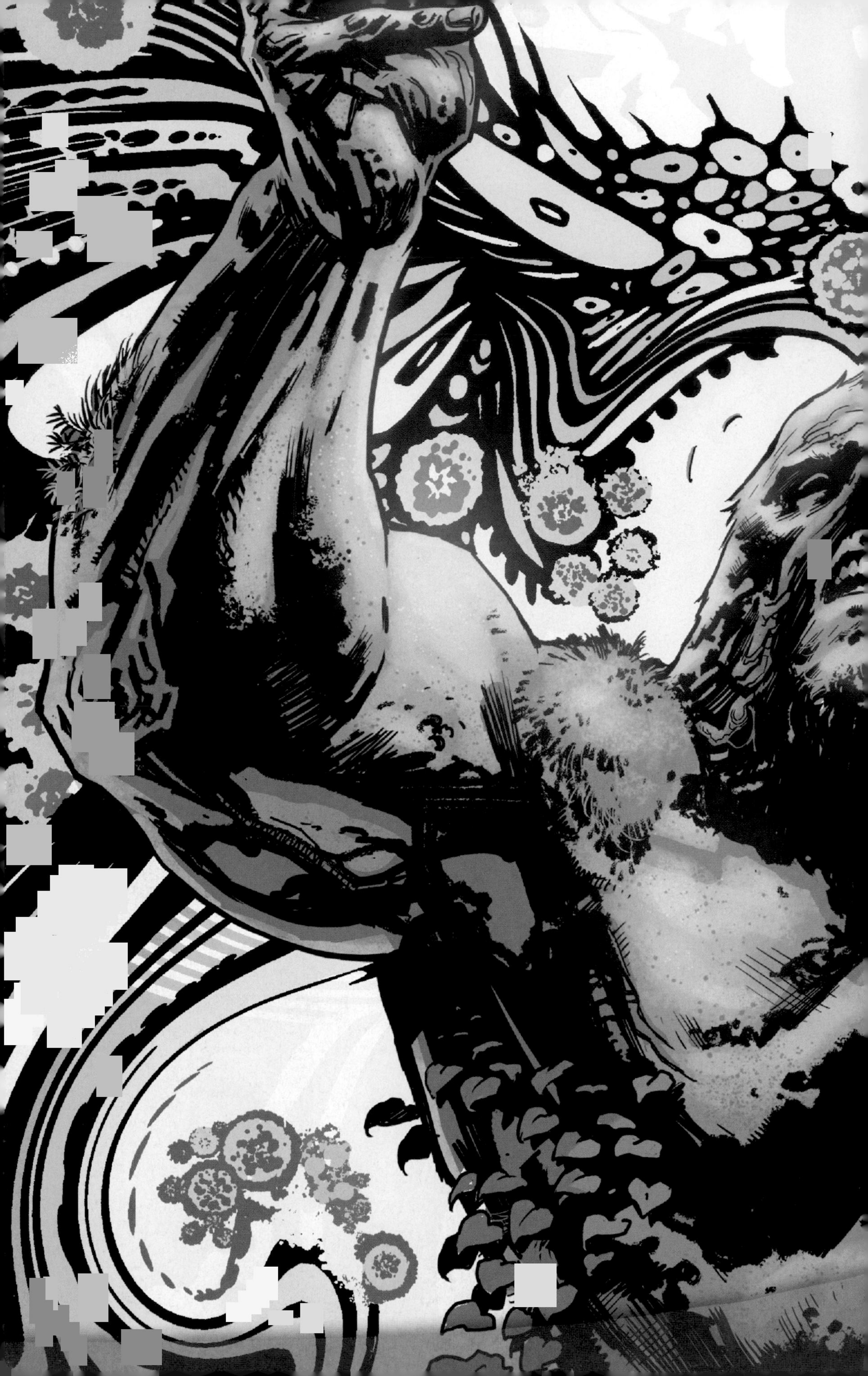

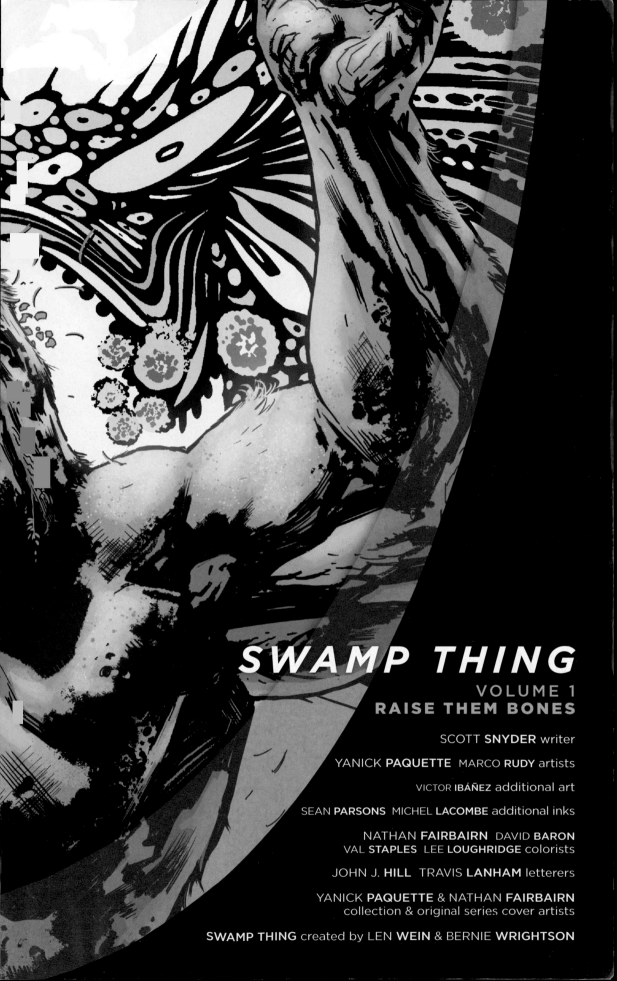

SWAMP THING

VOLUME 1
RAISE THEM BONES

SCOTT **SNYDER** writer

YANICK **PAQUETTE** MARCO **RUDY** artists

VICTOR **IBÁÑEZ** additional art

SEAN **PARSONS** MICHEL **LACOMBE** additional inks

NATHAN **FAIRBAIRN** DAVID **BARON**
VAL **STAPLES** LEE **LOUGHRIDGE** colorists

JOHN J. **HILL** TRAVIS **LANHAM** letterers

YANICK **PAQUETTE** & NATHAN **FAIRBAIRN**
collection & original series cover artists

SWAMP THING created by LEN **WEIN** & BERNIE **WRIGHTSON**

MATT IDELSON Editor – Original Series CHRIS CONROY Associate Editor – Original Series
PETER HAMBOUSSI Editor ROBBIN BROSTERMAN Design Director – Books ROBBIE BIEDERMAN Publication Design

BOB HARRAS VP – Editor-in-Chief

DIANE NELSON President DAN DIDIO and JIM LEE Co-Publishers GEOFF JOHNS Chief Creative Officer
JOHN ROOD Executive VP – Sales, Marketing and Business Development AMY GENKINS Senior VP – Business and Legal Affairs
NAIRI GARDINER Senior VP – Finance JEFF BOISON VP – Publishing Operations
MARK CHIARELLO VP – Art Direction and Design JOHN CUNNINGHAM VP – Marketing
TERRI CUNNINGHAM VP – Talent Relations and Services ALISON GILL Senior VP – Manufacturing and Operations
HANK KANALZ Senior VP – Digital JAY KOGAN VP – Business and Legal Affairs, Publishing
JACK MAHAN VP – Business Affairs, Talent NICK NAPOLITANO VP – Manufacturing Administration
SUE POHJA VP – Book Sales COURTNEY SIMMONS Senior VP – Publicity BOB WAYNE Senior VP – Sales

SWAMP THING VOLUME 1: RAISE THEM BONES

DC Comics, 1700 Broadway, New York, NY 10019
A Warner Bros. Entertainment Company.
Printed by RR Donnelley, Salem, VA, USA. 3/20/13. Second Printing.

ISBN: 978-1-4012-3462-1

Library of Congress Cataloging-in-Publication Data

Snyder, Scott.
Swamp thing volume 1 : raise them bones / Scott Snyder, Yanick Paquette, Marco Rudy.
p. cm.
"Originally published in single magazine form in SWAMP THING 1-7."
ISBN 978-1-4012-3462-1
1. Graphic novels. I. Paquette, Yanick. II. Rudy, Marco. III. Title. IV. Title: Raise them bones.
PN6728.S93S69 2012
741.5'973 — dc23
2012015245

SUSTAINABLE FORESTRY INITIATIVE
Certified Chain of Custody
At Least 20% Certified Forest Content
www.sfiprogram.org
SFI-01042
APPLIES TO TEXT STOCK ONLY

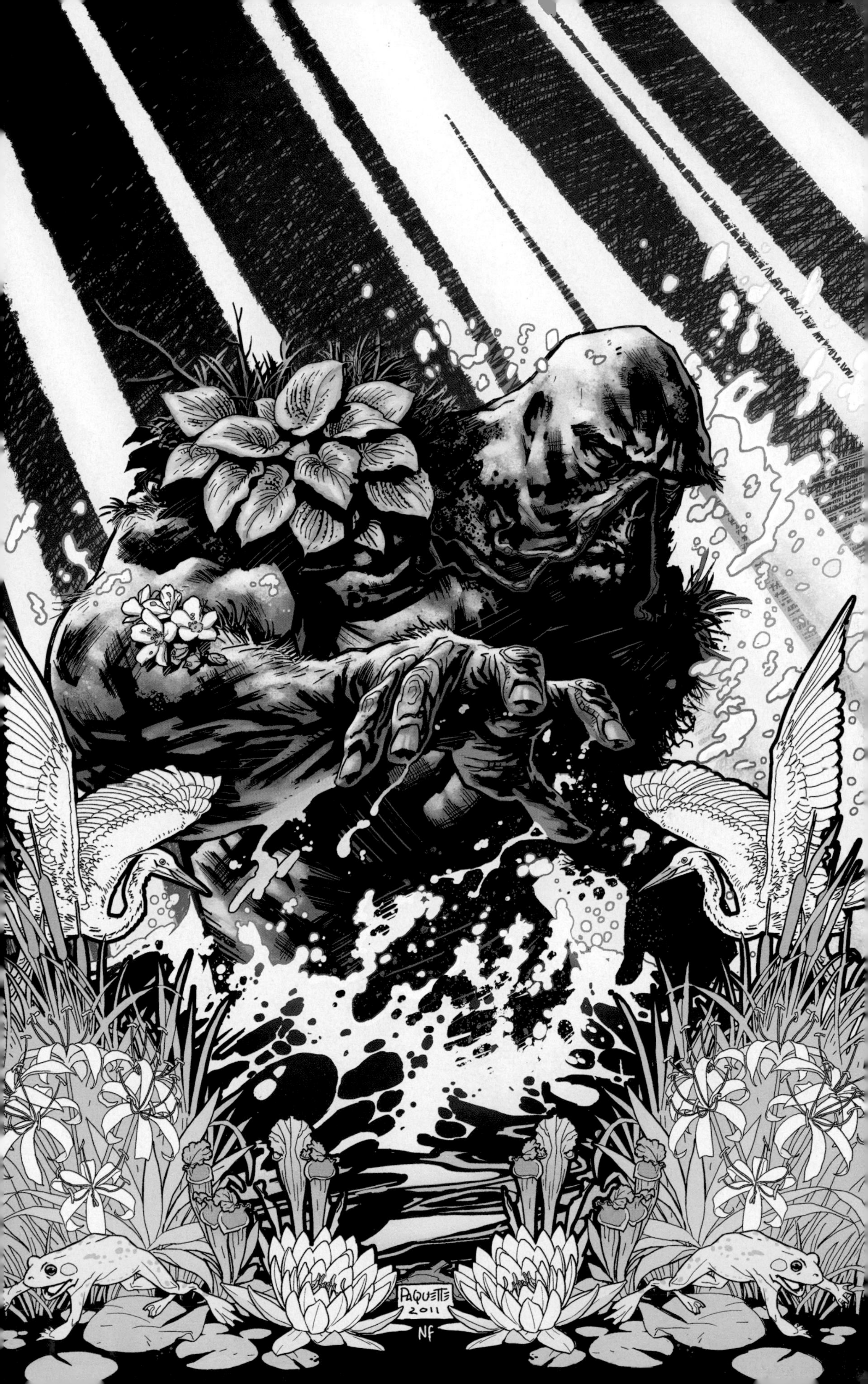
PAQUETTE
2011
NF

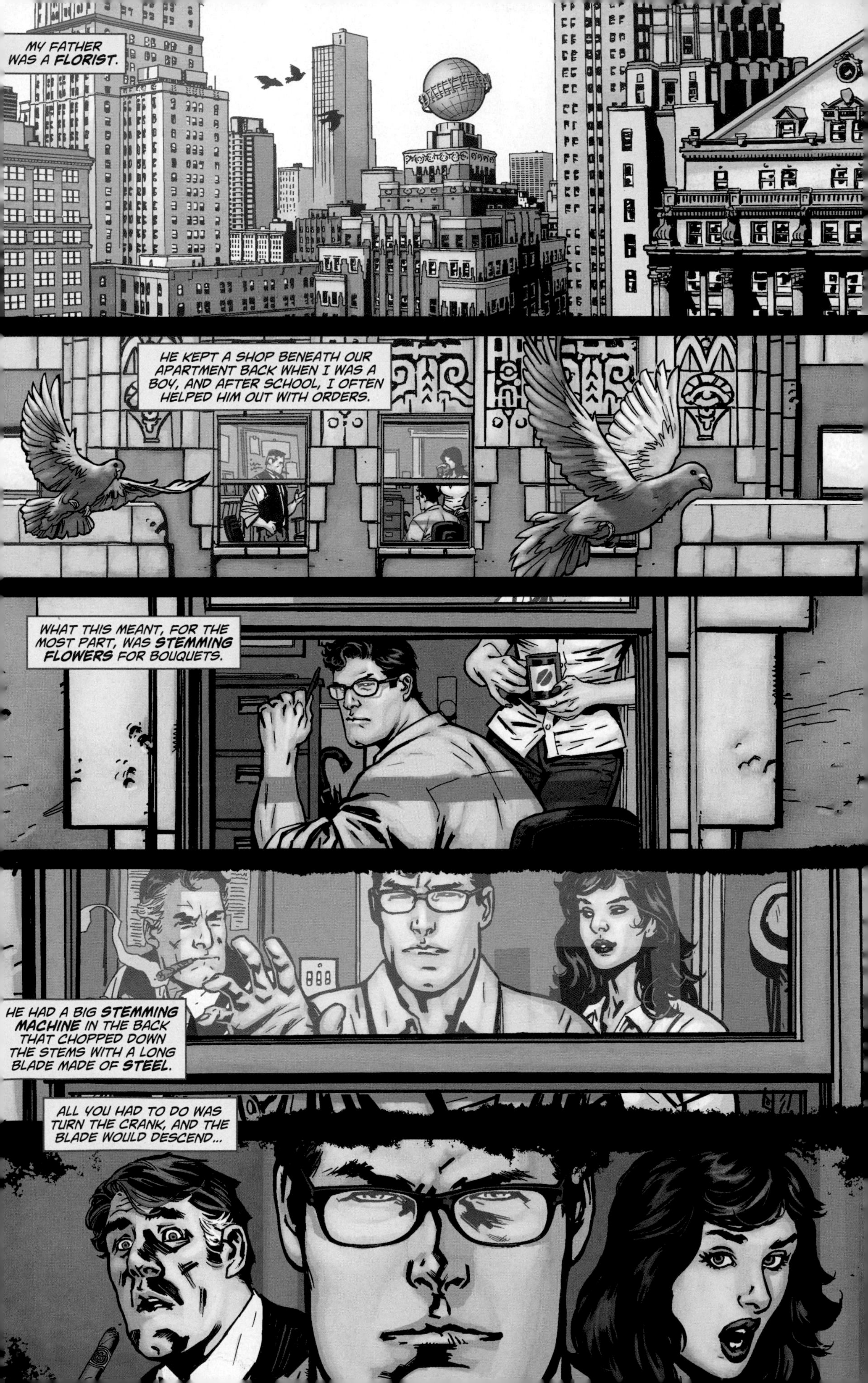
MY FATHER WAS A FLORIST.
HE KEPT A SHOP BENEATH OUR APARTMENT BACK WHEN I WAS A BOY, AND AFTER SCHOOL, I OFTEN HELPED HIM OUT WITH ORDERS.
WHAT THIS MEANT, FOR THE MOST PART, WAS STEMMING FLOWERS FOR BOUQUETS.
HE HAD A BIG STEMMING MACHINE IN THE BACK THAT CHOPPED DOWN THE STEMS WITH A LONG BLADE MADE OF STEEL.
ALL YOU HAD TO DO WAS TURN THE CRANK, AND THE BLADE WOULD DESCEND...

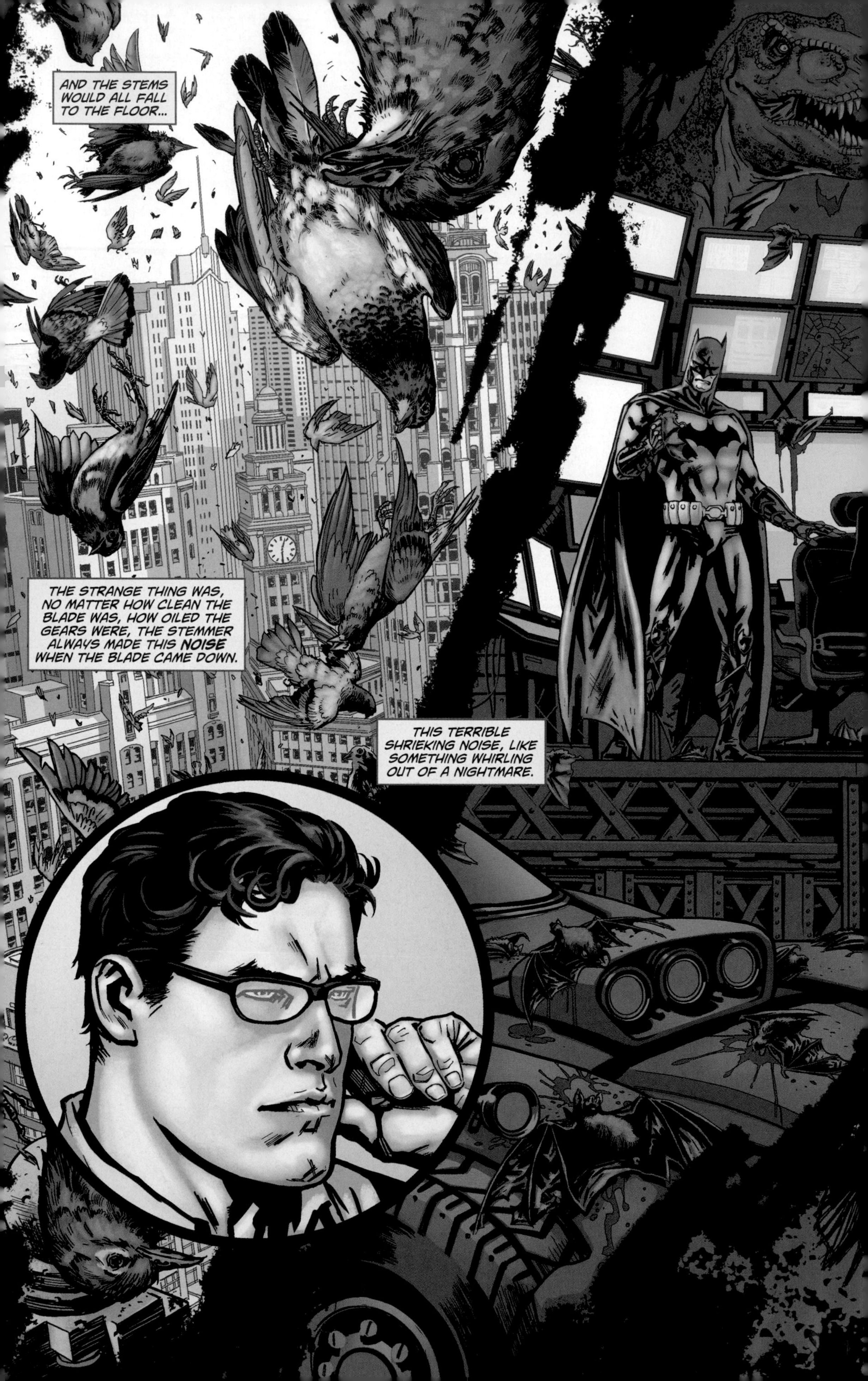
AND THE STEMS WOULD ALL FALL TO THE FLOOR...
THE STRANGE THING WAS, NO MATTER HOW CLEAN THE BLADE WAS, HOW OILED THE GEARS WERE, THE STEMMER ALWAYS MADE THIS NOISE WHEN THE BLADE CAME DOWN.
THIS TERRIBLE SHRIEKING NOISE, LIKE SOMETHING WHIRLING OUT OF A NIGHTMARE.

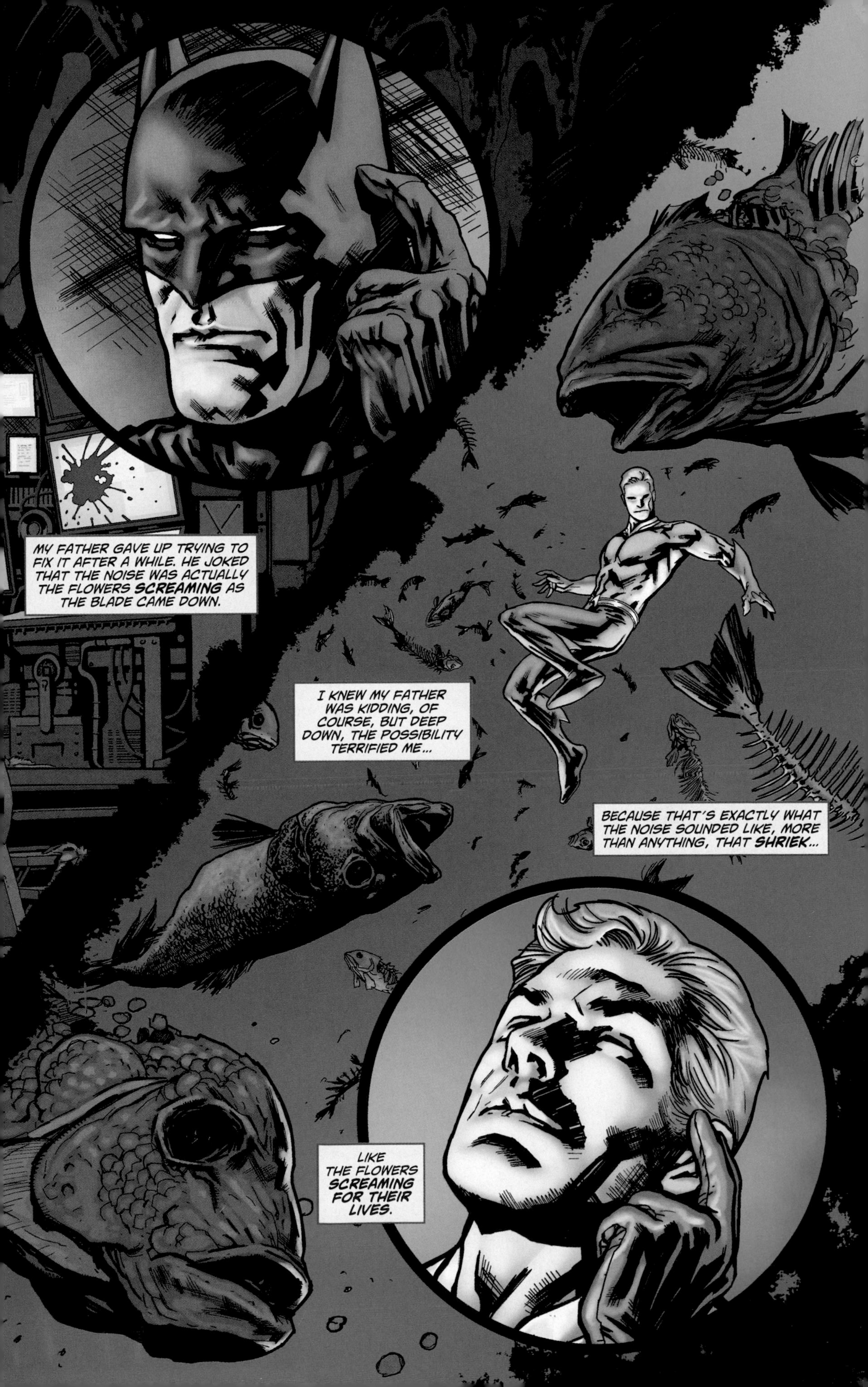
MY FATHER GAVE UP TRYING TO FIX IT AFTER A WHILE. HE JOKED THAT THE NOISE WAS ACTUALLY THE FLOWERS **SCREAMING** AS THE BLADE CAME DOWN.
I KNEW MY FATHER WAS KIDDING, OF COURSE, BUT DEEP DOWN, THE POSSIBILITY TERRIFIED ME...
BECAUSE THAT'S EXACTLY WHAT THE NOISE SOUNDED LIKE, MORE THAN ANYTHING, THAT **SHRIEK**...
LIKE THE FLOWERS **SCREAMING FOR THEIR LIVES.**

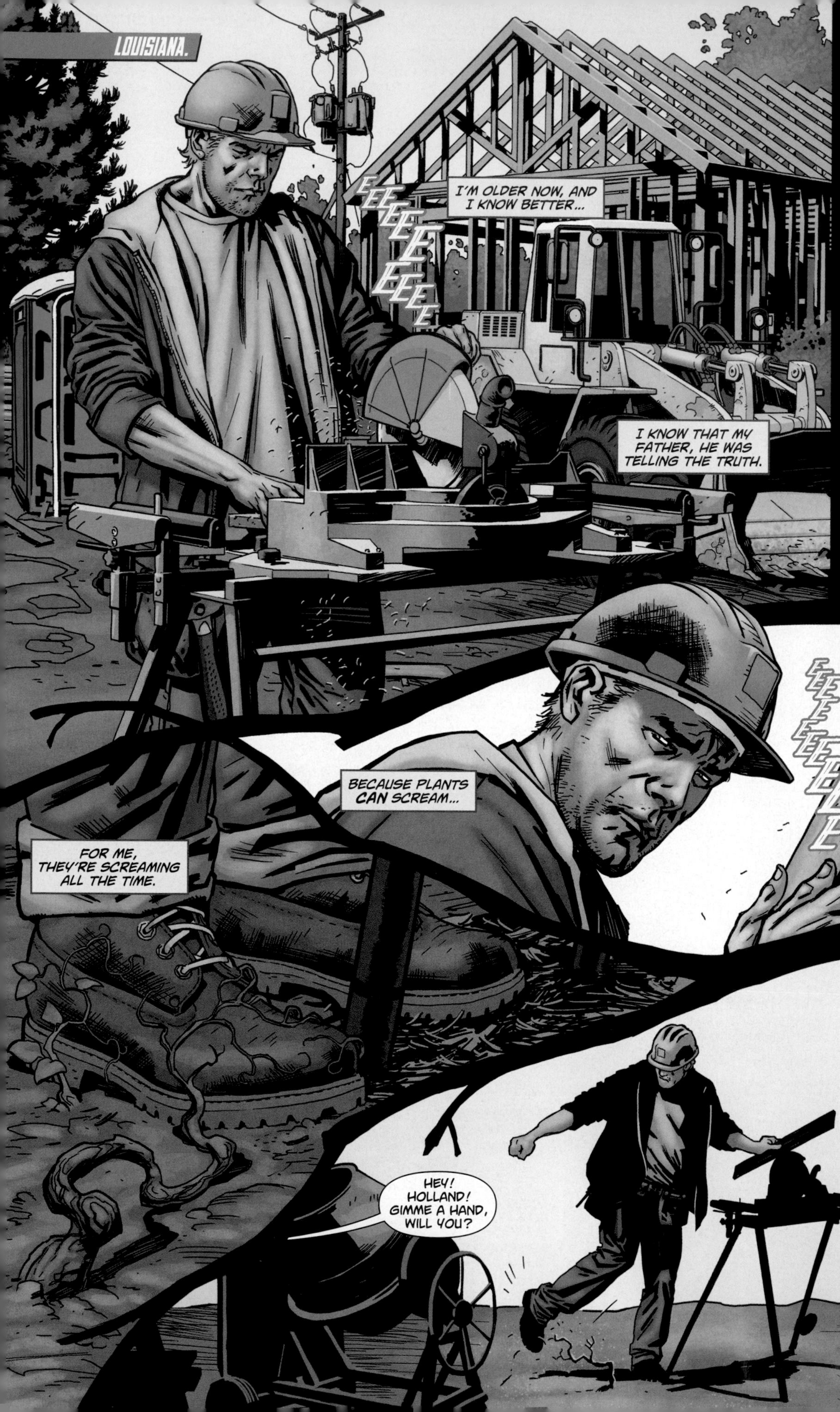
LOUISIANA.
EEEEEEEEEEEE
I'M OLDER NOW, AND I KNOW BETTER...
I KNOW THAT MY FATHER, HE WAS TELLING THE TRUTH.
BECAUSE PLANTS CAN SCREAM...
EEEEEEEEEEE
FOR ME, THEY'RE SCREAMING ALL THE TIME.
HEY! HOLLAND! GIMME A HAND, WILL YOU?

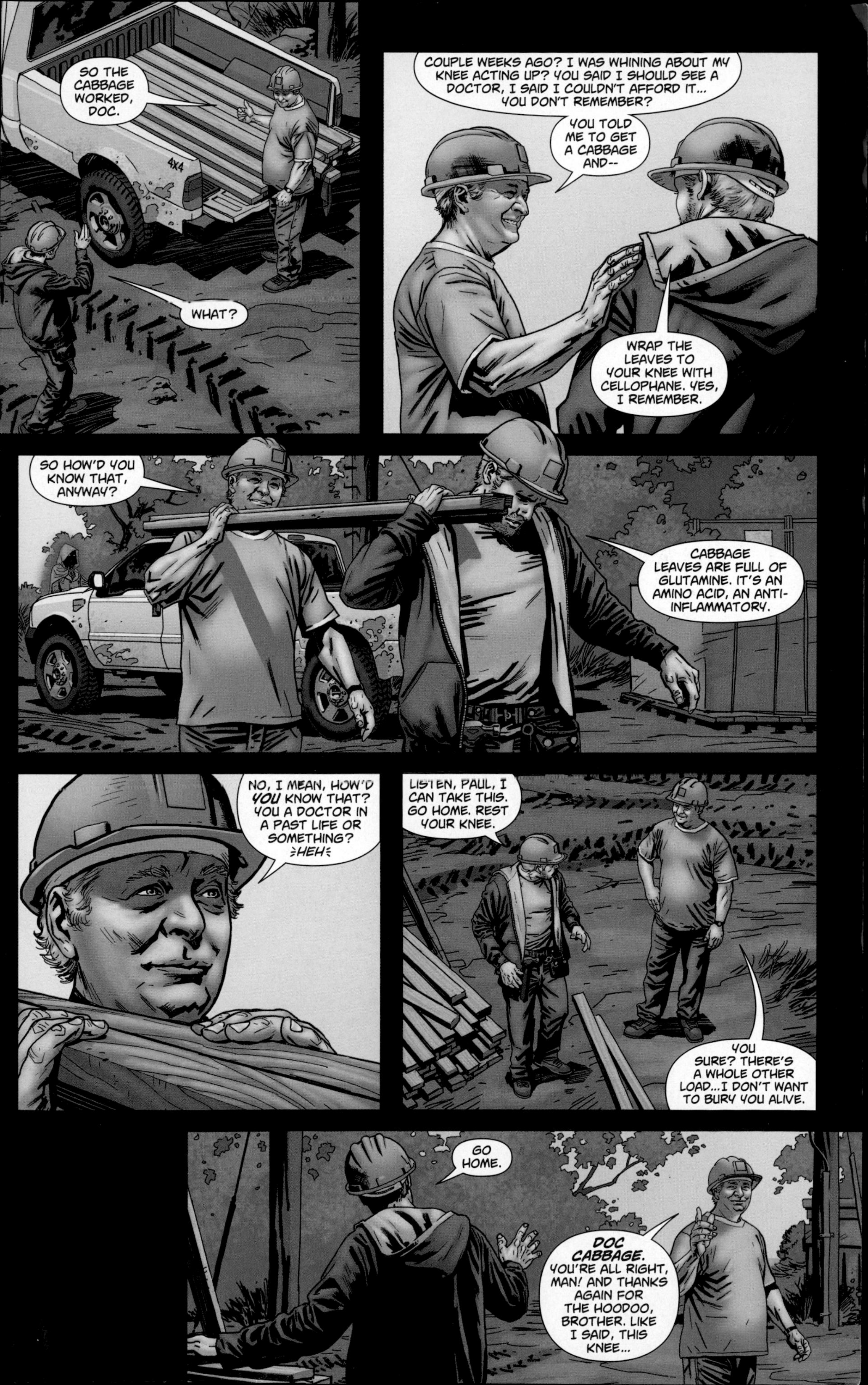
SO THE CABBAGE WORKED, DOC.
WHAT?
COUPLE WEEKS AGO? I WAS WHINING ABOUT MY KNEE ACTING UP? YOU SAID I SHOULD SEE A DOCTOR, I SAID I COULDN'T AFFORD IT... YOU DON'T REMEMBER?
YOU TOLD ME TO GET A CABBAGE AND--
WRAP THE LEAVES TO YOUR KNEE WITH CELLOPHANE. YES, I REMEMBER.
SO HOW'D YOU KNOW THAT, ANYWAY?
CABBAGE LEAVES ARE FULL OF GLUTAMINE. IT'S AN AMINO ACID, AN ANTI-INFLAMMATORY.
NO, I MEAN, HOW'D YOU KNOW THAT? YOU A DOCTOR IN A PAST LIFE OR SOMETHING? HEH
LISTEN, PAUL, I CAN TAKE THIS. GO HOME. REST YOUR KNEE.
YOU SURE? THERE'S A WHOLE OTHER LOAD...I DON'T WANT TO BURY YOU ALIVE.
GO HOME.
DOC CABBAGE. YOU'RE ALL RIGHT, MAN! AND THANKS AGAIN FOR THE HOODOO, BROTHER. LIKE I SAID, THIS KNEE...

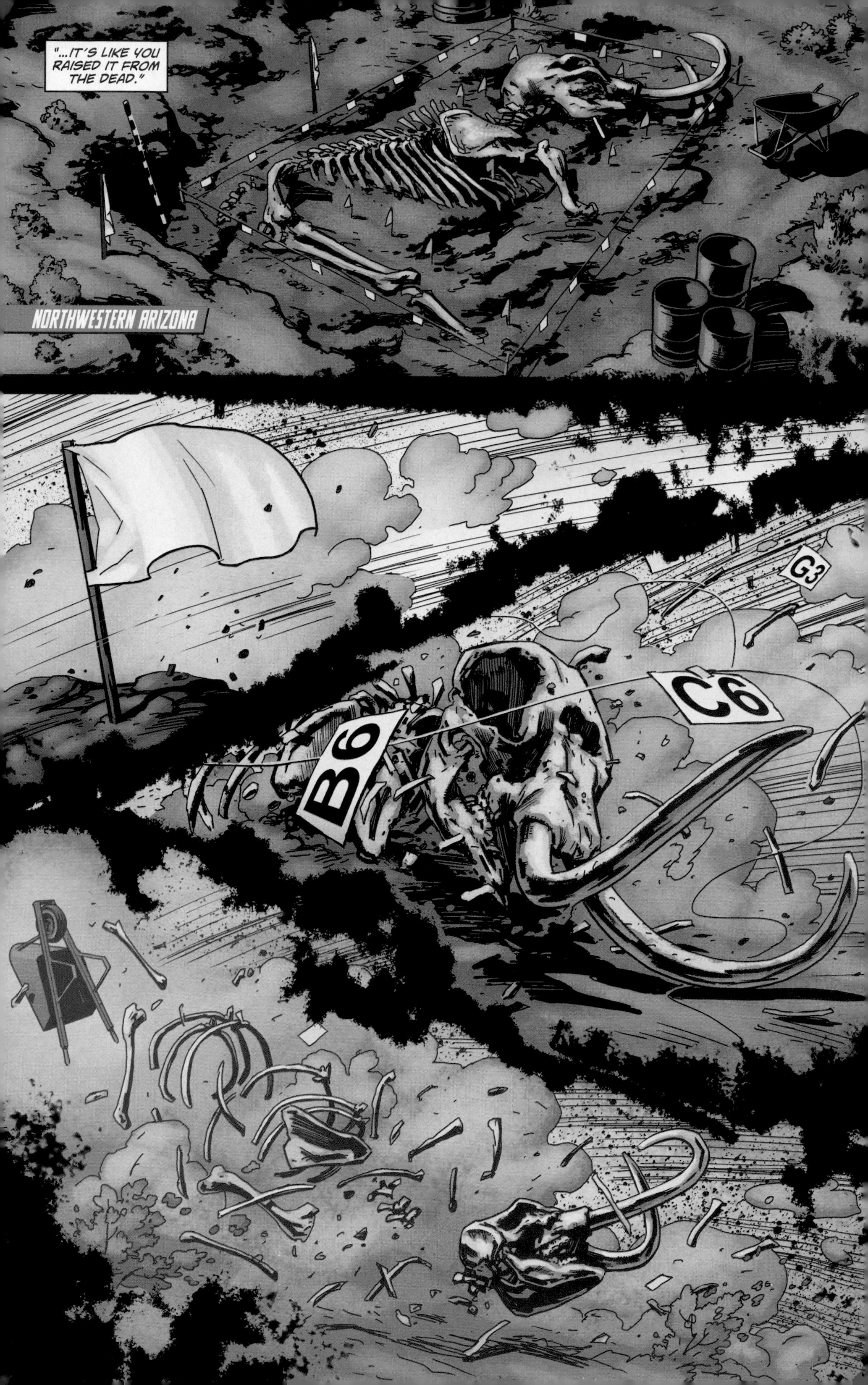
"...IT'S LIKE YOU RAISED IT FROM THE DEAD."
NORTHWESTERN ARIZONA
G3
C6
B6

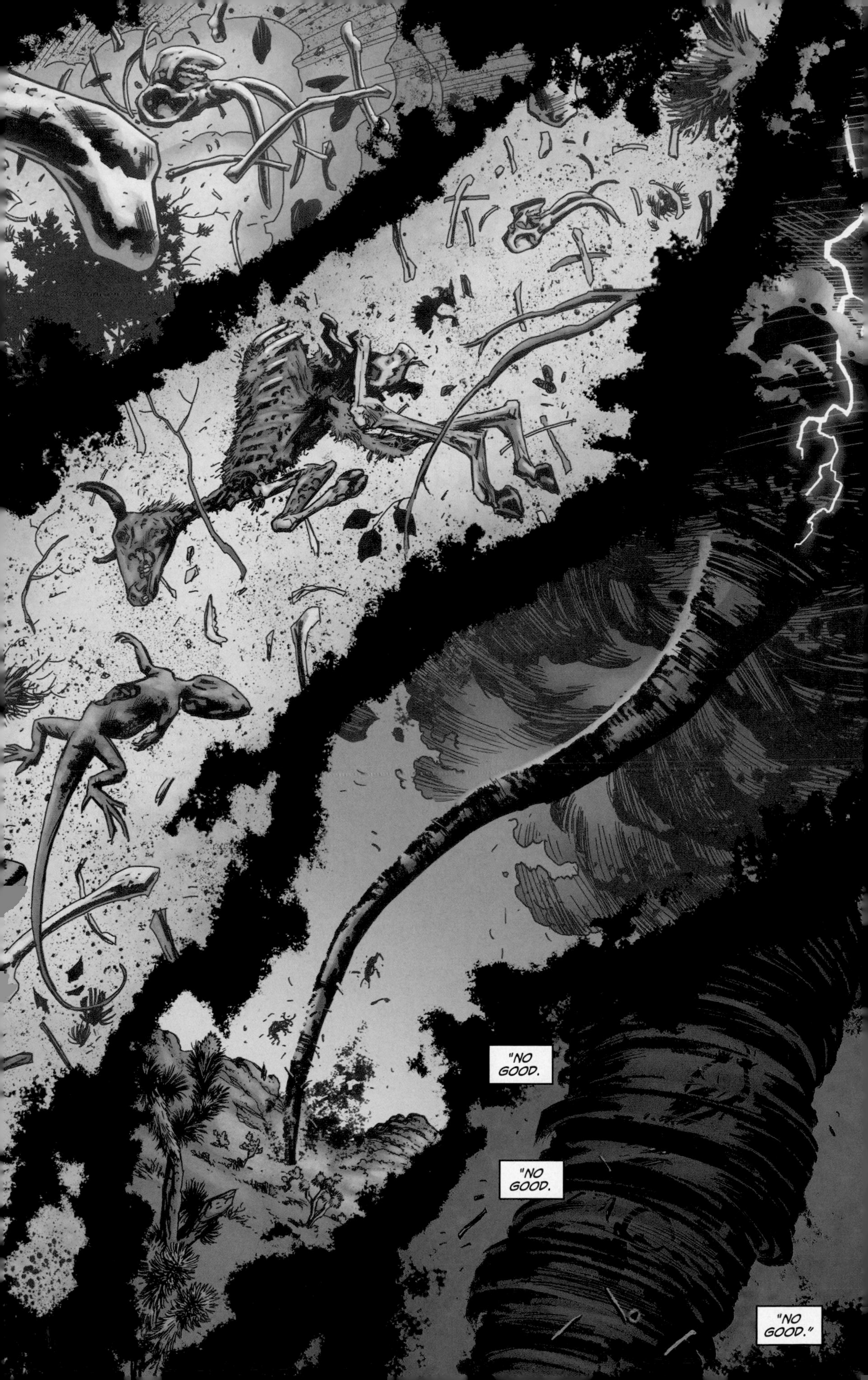
"NO GOOD.
"NO GOOD.
"NO GOOD."

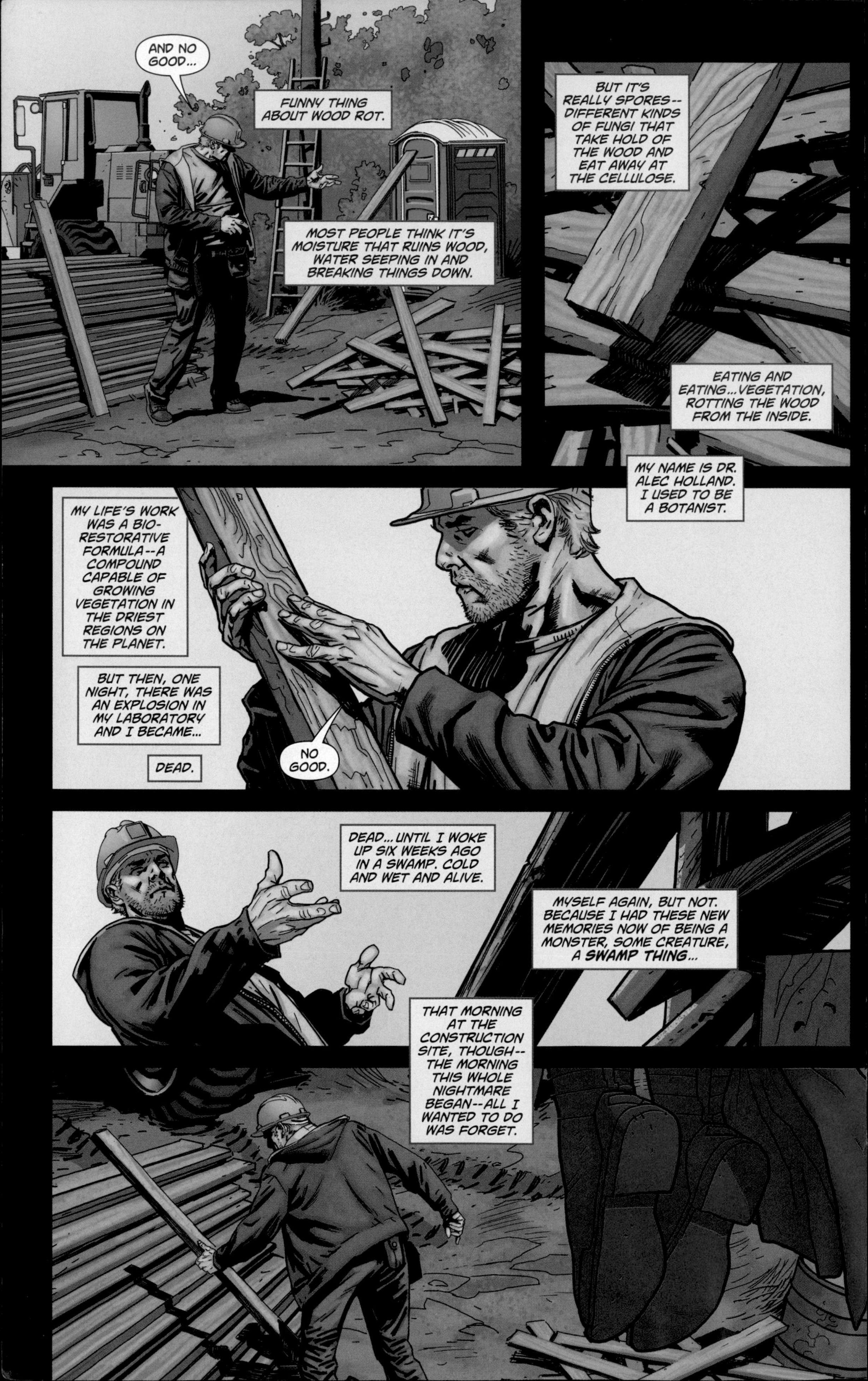
AND NO GOOD...
FUNNY THING ABOUT WOOD ROT.
MOST PEOPLE THINK IT'S MOISTURE THAT RUINS WOOD, WATER SEEPING IN AND BREAKING THINGS DOWN.
BUT IT'S REALLY SPORES--DIFFERENT KINDS OF FUNGI THAT TAKE HOLD OF THE WOOD AND EAT AWAY AT THE CELLULOSE.
EATING AND EATING...VEGETATION, ROTTING THE WOOD FROM THE INSIDE.
MY NAME IS DR. ALEC HOLLAND. I USED TO BE A BOTANIST.
MY LIFE'S WORK WAS A BIO-RESTORATIVE FORMULA--A COMPOUND CAPABLE OF GROWING VEGETATION IN THE DRIEST REGIONS ON THE PLANET.
BUT THEN, ONE NIGHT, THERE WAS AN EXPLOSION IN MY LABORATORY AND I BECAME...
DEAD.
NO GOOD.
DEAD... UNTIL I WOKE UP SIX WEEKS AGO IN A SWAMP. COLD AND WET AND ALIVE.
MYSELF AGAIN, BUT NOT. BECAUSE I HAD THESE NEW MEMORIES NOW OF BEING A MONSTER, SOME CREATURE, A SWAMP THING...
THAT MORNING AT THE CONSTRUCTION SITE, THOUGH--THE MORNING THIS WHOLE NIGHTMARE BEGAN--ALL I WANTED TO DO WAS FORGET.

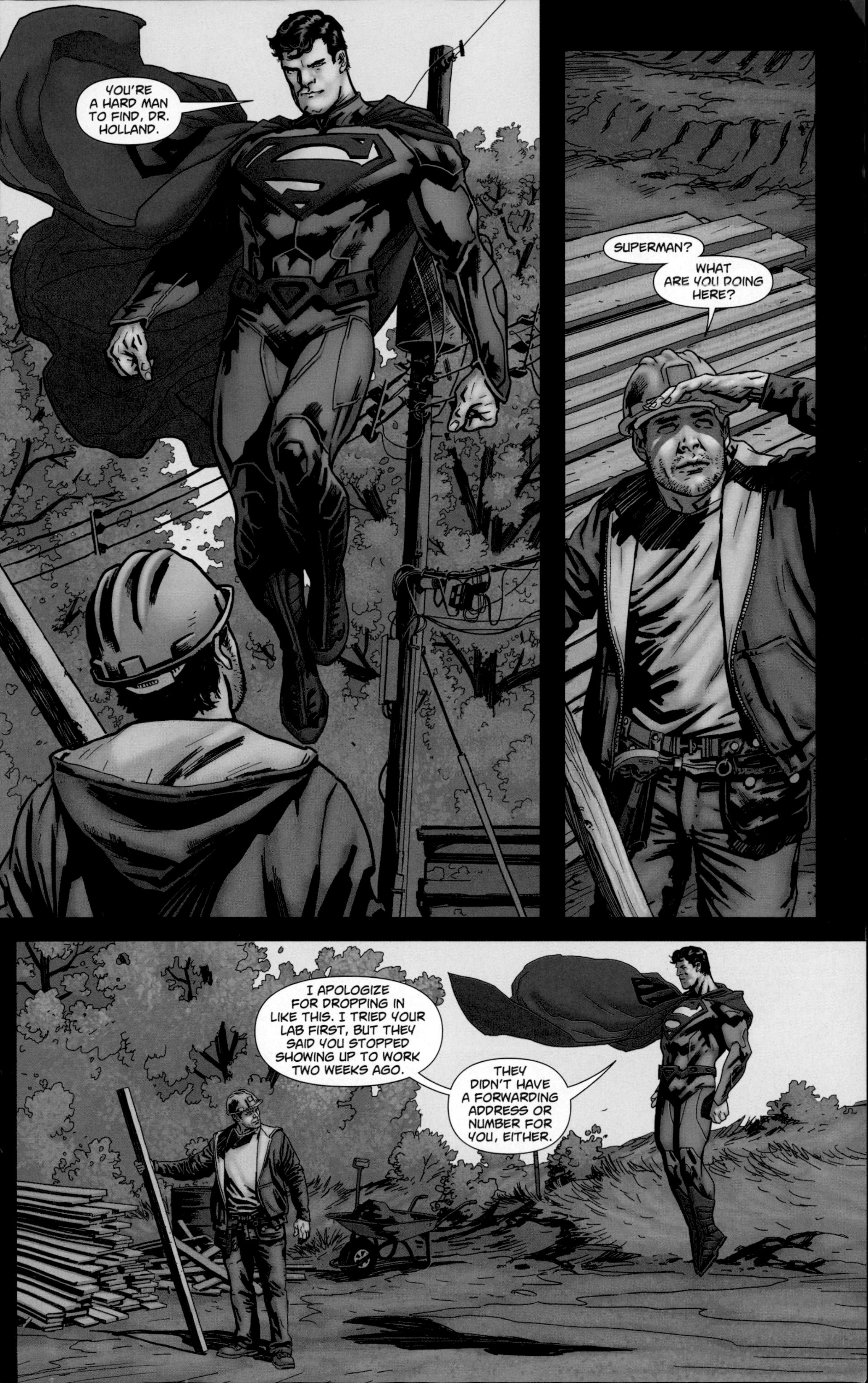
YOU'RE A HARD MAN TO FIND, DR. HOLLAND.
SUPERMAN?
WHAT ARE YOU DOING HERE?
I APOLOGIZE FOR DROPPING IN LIKE THIS. I TRIED YOUR LAB FIRST, BUT THEY SAID YOU STOPPED SHOWING UP TO WORK TWO WEEKS AGO.
THEY DIDN'T HAVE A FORWARDING ADDRESS OR NUMBER FOR YOU, EITHER.

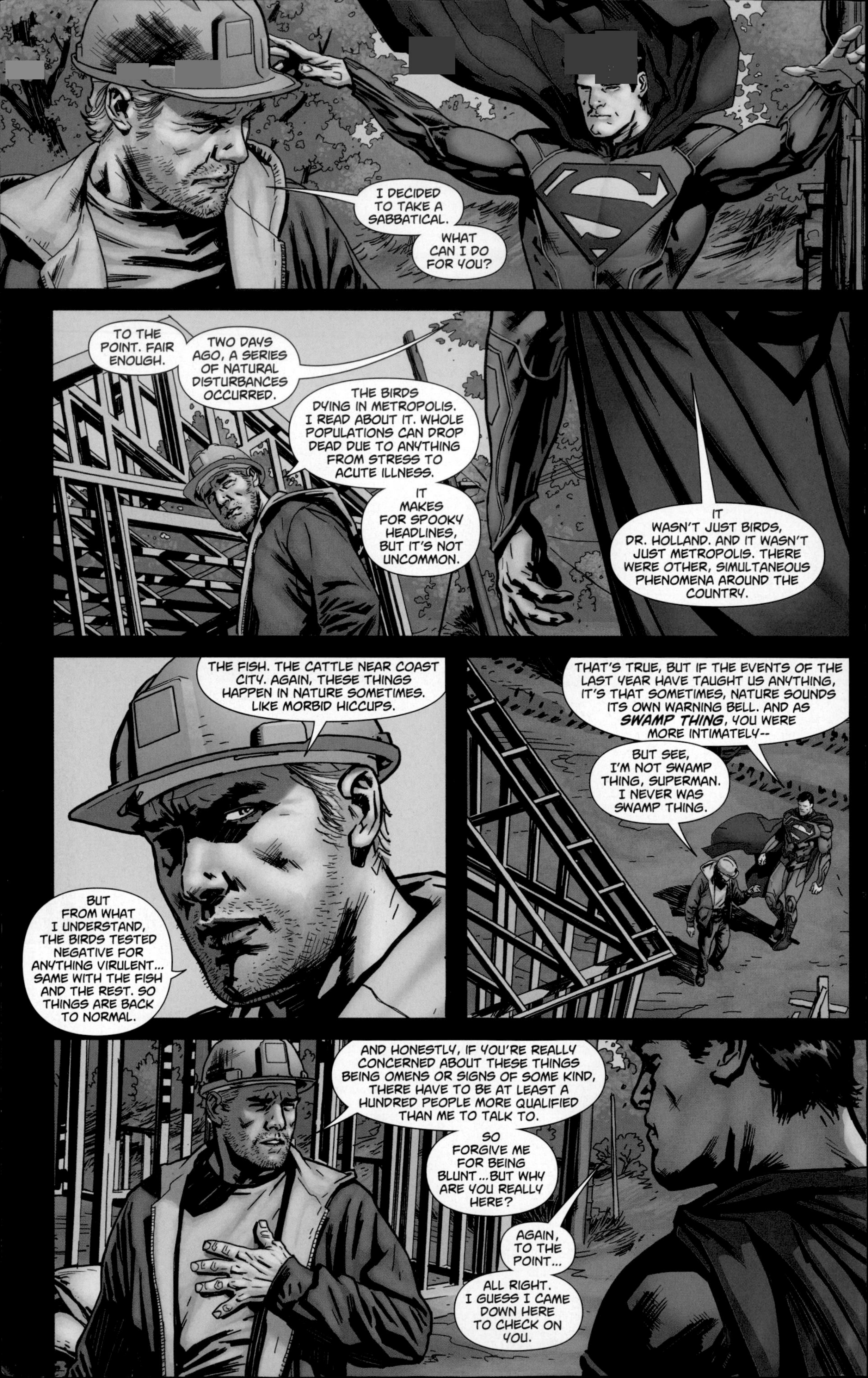
I DECIDED TO TAKE A SABBATICAL.
WHAT CAN I DO FOR YOU?
TO THE POINT. FAIR ENOUGH.
TWO DAYS AGO, A SERIES OF NATURAL DISTURBANCES OCCURRED.
THE BIRDS DYING IN METROPOLIS. I READ ABOUT IT. WHOLE POPULATIONS CAN DROP DEAD DUE TO ANYTHING FROM STRESS TO ACUTE ILLNESS.
IT MAKES FOR SPOOKY HEADLINES, BUT IT'S NOT UNCOMMON.
IT WASN'T JUST BIRDS, DR. HOLLAND. AND IT WASN'T JUST METROPOLIS. THERE WERE OTHER, SIMULTANEOUS PHENOMENA AROUND THE COUNTRY.
THE FISH. THE CATTLE NEAR COAST CITY. AGAIN, THESE THINGS HAPPEN IN NATURE SOMETIMES. LIKE MORBID HICCUPS.
BUT FROM WHAT I UNDERSTAND, THE BIRDS TESTED NEGATIVE FOR ANYTHING VIRULENT... SAME WITH THE FISH AND THE REST. SO THINGS ARE BACK TO NORMAL.
THAT'S TRUE, BUT IF THE EVENTS OF THE LAST YEAR HAVE TAUGHT US ANYTHING, IT'S THAT SOMETIMES, NATURE SOUNDS ITS OWN WARNING BELL. AND AS SWAMP THING, YOU WERE MORE INTIMATELY--
BUT SEE, I'M NOT SWAMP THING, SUPERMAN. I NEVER WAS SWAMP THING.
AND HONESTLY, IF YOU'RE REALLY CONCERNED ABOUT THESE THINGS BEING OMENS OR SIGNS OF SOME KIND, THERE HAVE TO BE AT LEAST A HUNDRED PEOPLE MORE QUALIFIED THAN ME TO TALK TO.
SO FORGIVE ME FOR BEING BLUNT...BUT WHY ARE YOU REALLY HERE?
AGAIN, TO THE POINT...
ALL RIGHT. I GUESS I CAME DOWN HERE TO CHECK ON YOU.

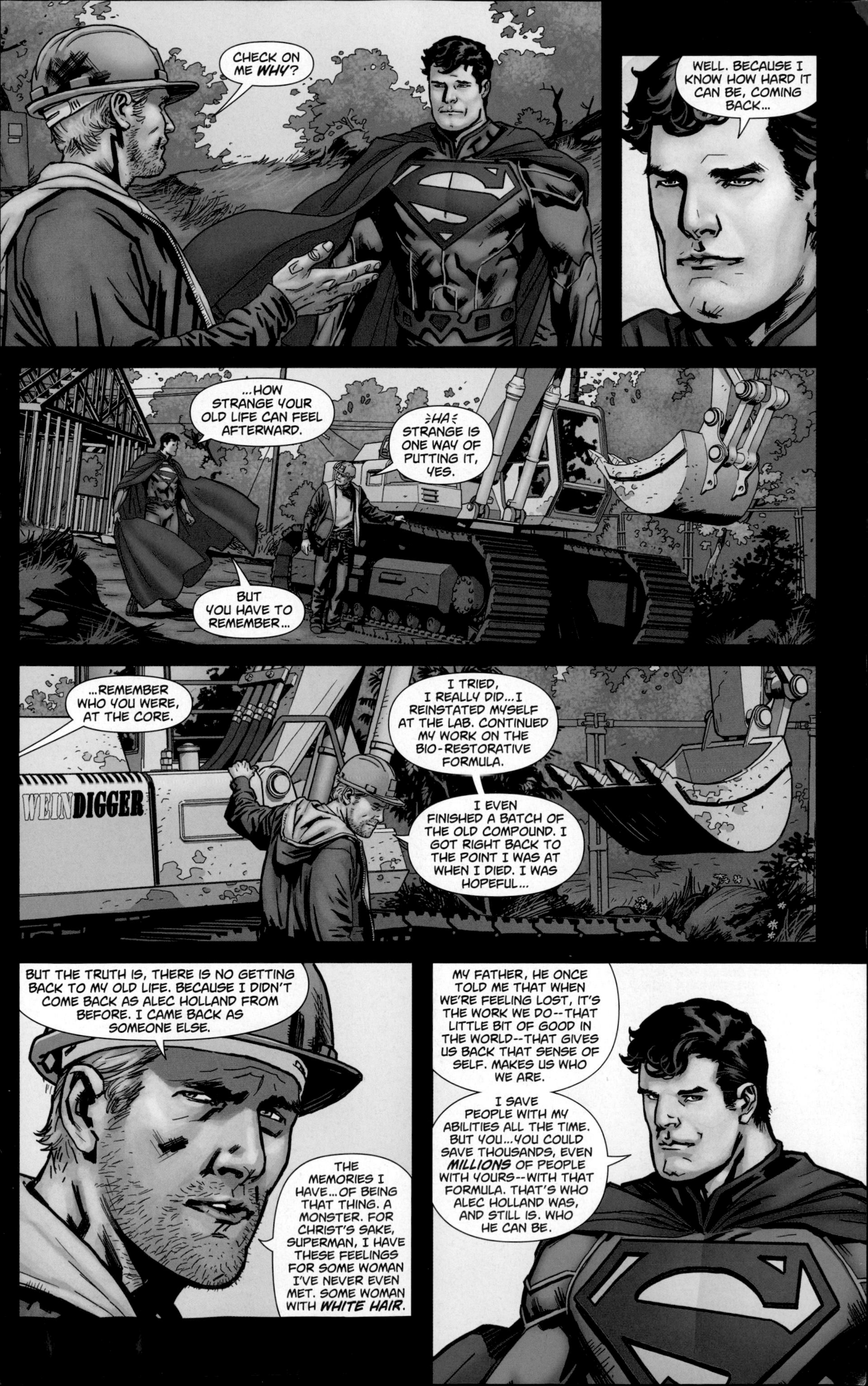
CHECK ON ME *WHY*?
WELL. BECAUSE I KNOW HOW HARD IT CAN BE, COMING BACK...
...HOW STRANGE YOUR OLD LIFE CAN FEEL AFTERWARD.
HA STRANGE IS ONE WAY OF PUTTING IT, YES.
BUT YOU HAVE TO REMEMBER...
...REMEMBER WHO YOU WERE, AT THE CORE.
WEINDIGGER
I TRIED, I REALLY DID...I REINSTATED MYSELF AT THE LAB. CONTINUED MY WORK ON THE BIO-RESTORATIVE FORMULA.
I EVEN FINISHED A BATCH OF THE OLD COMPOUND. I GOT RIGHT BACK TO THE POINT I WAS AT WHEN I DIED. I WAS HOPEFUL...
BUT THE TRUTH IS, THERE IS NO GETTING BACK TO MY OLD LIFE. BECAUSE I DIDN'T COME BACK AS ALEC HOLLAND FROM BEFORE. I CAME BACK AS SOMEONE ELSE.
THE MEMORIES I HAVE...OF BEING THAT THING. A MONSTER. FOR CHRIST'S SAKE, SUPERMAN, I HAVE THESE FEELINGS FOR SOME WOMAN I'VE NEVER EVEN MET. SOME WOMAN WITH *WHITE HAIR*.
MY FATHER, HE ONCE TOLD ME THAT WHEN WE'RE FEELING LOST, IT'S THE WORK WE DO--THAT LITTLE BIT OF GOOD IN THE WORLD--THAT GIVES US BACK THAT SENSE OF SELF. MAKES US WHO WE ARE.
I SAVE PEOPLE WITH MY ABILITIES ALL THE TIME. BUT YOU...YOU COULD SAVE THOUSANDS, EVEN *MILLIONS* OF PEOPLE WITH YOURS--WITH THAT FORMULA. THAT'S WHO ALEC HOLLAND WAS, AND STILL IS. WHO HE CAN BE.

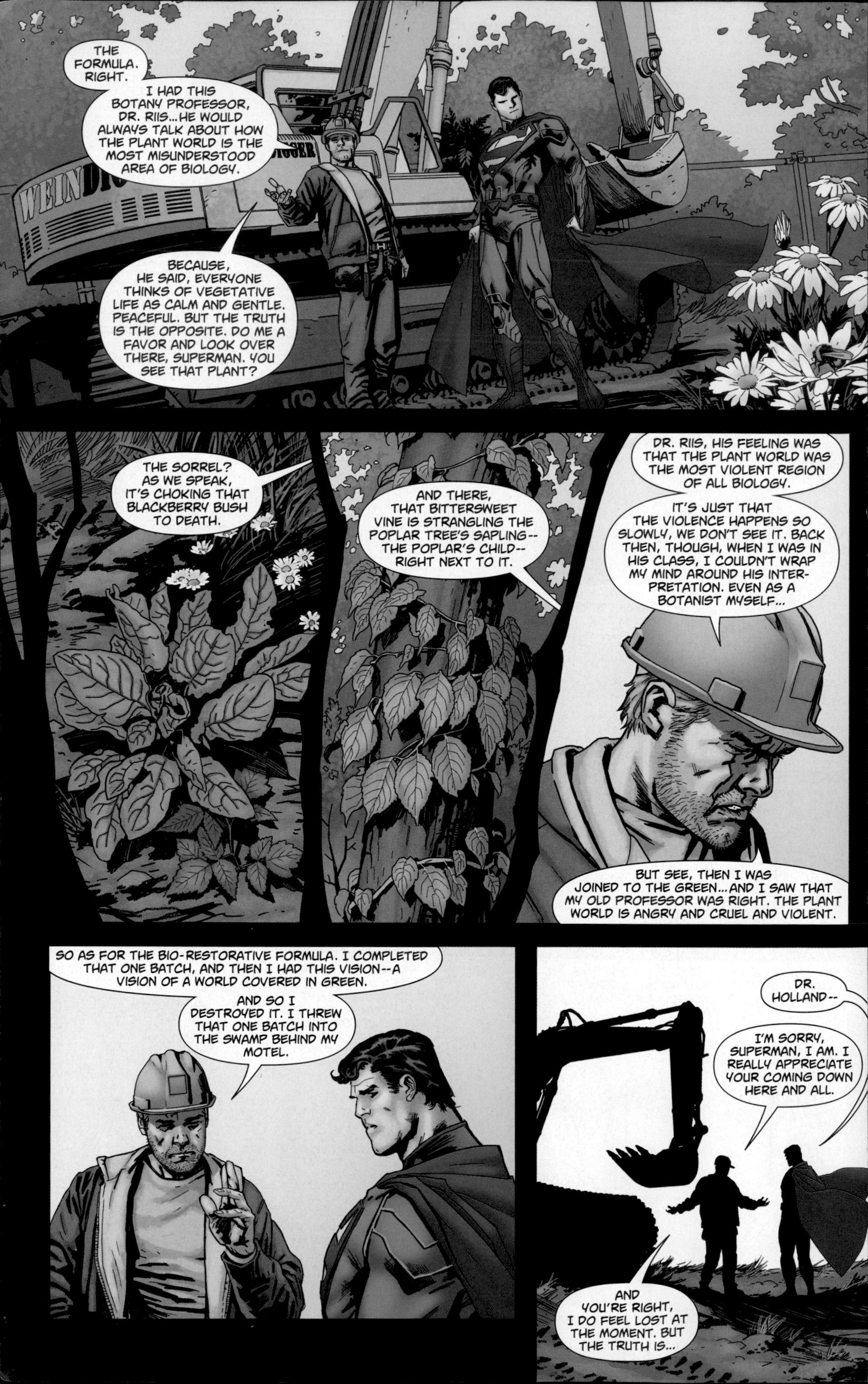
THE FORMULA. RIGHT.
I HAD THIS BOTANY PROFESSOR, DR. RIIS...HE WOULD ALWAYS TALK ABOUT HOW THE PLANT WORLD IS THE MOST MISUNDERSTOOD AREA OF BIOLOGY.
BECAUSE, HE SAID, EVERYONE THINKS OF VEGETATIVE LIFE AS CALM AND GENTLE. PEACEFUL. BUT THE TRUTH IS THE OPPOSITE. DO ME A FAVOR AND LOOK OVER THERE, SUPERMAN. YOU SEE THAT PLANT?
THE SORREL? AS WE SPEAK, IT'S CHOKING THAT BLACKBERRY BUSH TO DEATH.
AND THERE, THAT BITTERSWEET VINE IS STRANGLING THE POPLAR TREE'S SAPLING-- THE POPLAR'S CHILD-- RIGHT NEXT TO IT.
DR. RIIS, HIS FEELING WAS THAT THE PLANT WORLD WAS THE MOST VIOLENT REGION OF ALL BIOLOGY.
IT'S JUST THAT THE VIOLENCE HAPPENS SO SLOWLY, WE DON'T SEE IT. BACK THEN, THOUGH, WHEN I WAS IN HIS CLASS, I COULDN'T WRAP MY MIND AROUND HIS INTER-PRETATION. EVEN AS A BOTANIST MYSELF...
BUT SEE, THEN I WAS JOINED TO THE GREEN...AND I SAW THAT MY OLD PROFESSOR WAS RIGHT. THE PLANT WORLD IS ANGRY AND CRUEL AND VIOLENT.
SO AS FOR THE BIO-RESTORATIVE FORMULA. I COMPLETED THAT ONE BATCH, AND THEN I HAD THIS VISION--A VISION OF A WORLD COVERED IN GREEN.
AND SO I DESTROYED IT. I THREW THAT ONE BATCH INTO THE SWAMP BEHIND MY MOTEL.
DR. HOLLAND--
I'M SORRY, SUPERMAN, I AM. I REALLY APPRECIATE YOUR COMING DOWN HERE AND ALL.
AND YOU'RE RIGHT, I DO FEEL LOST AT THE MOMENT. BUT THE TRUTH IS...

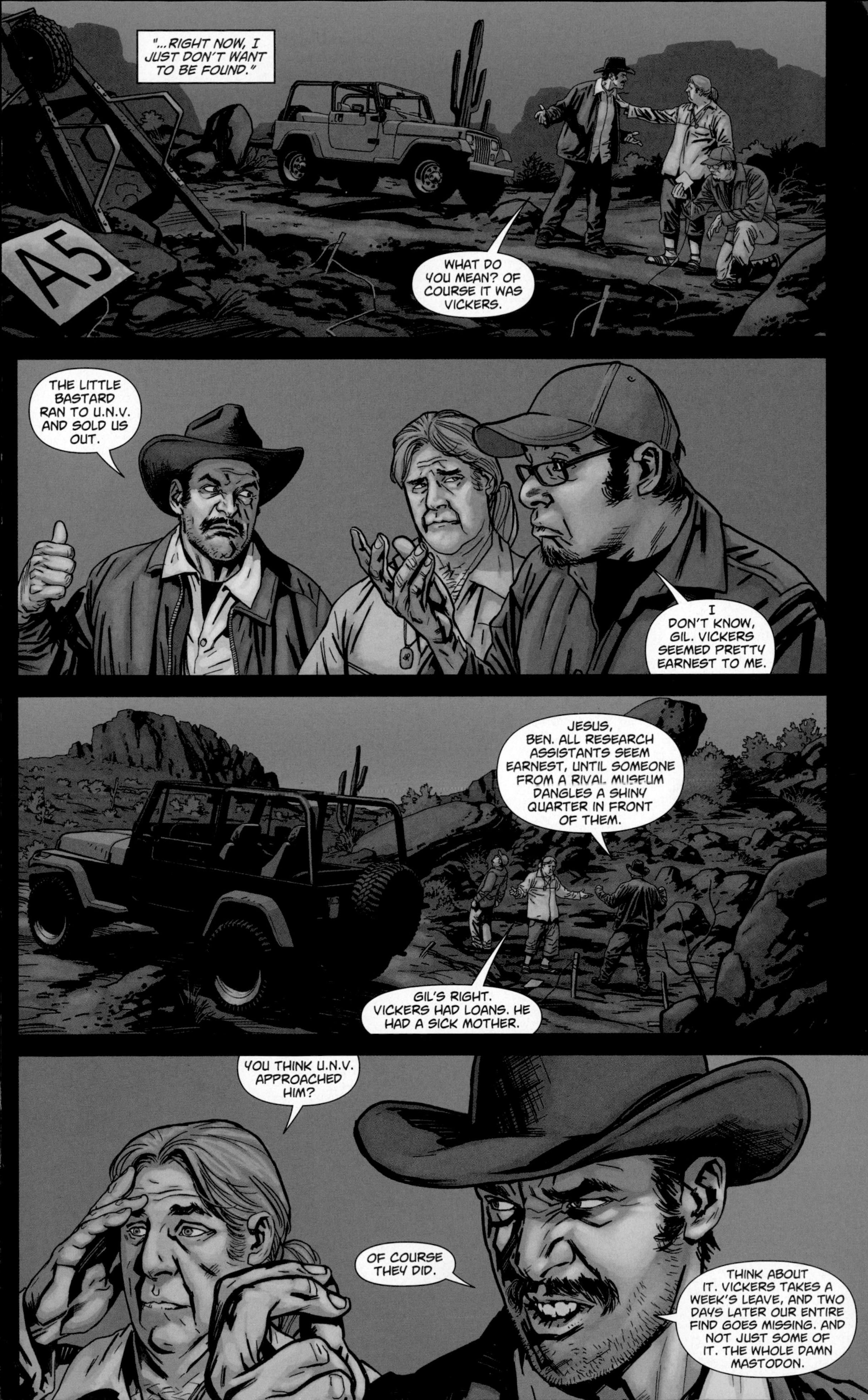
"...RIGHT NOW, I JUST DON'T WANT TO BE FOUND."
A5
WHAT DO YOU MEAN? OF COURSE IT WAS VICKERS.
THE LITTLE BASTARD RAN TO U.N.V. AND SOLD US OUT.
I DON'T KNOW, GIL. VICKERS SEEMED PRETTY EARNEST TO ME.
JESUS, BEN. ALL RESEARCH ASSISTANTS SEEM EARNEST, UNTIL SOMEONE FROM A RIVAL MUSEUM DANGLES A SHINY QUARTER IN FRONT OF THEM.
GIL'S RIGHT. VICKERS HAD LOANS. HE HAD A SICK MOTHER.
YOU THINK U.N.V. APPROACHED HIM?
OF COURSE THEY DID.
THINK ABOUT IT. VICKERS TAKES A WEEK'S LEAVE, AND TWO DAYS LATER OUR ENTIRE FIND GOES MISSING. AND NOT JUST SOME OF IT. THE WHOLE DAMN MASTODON.

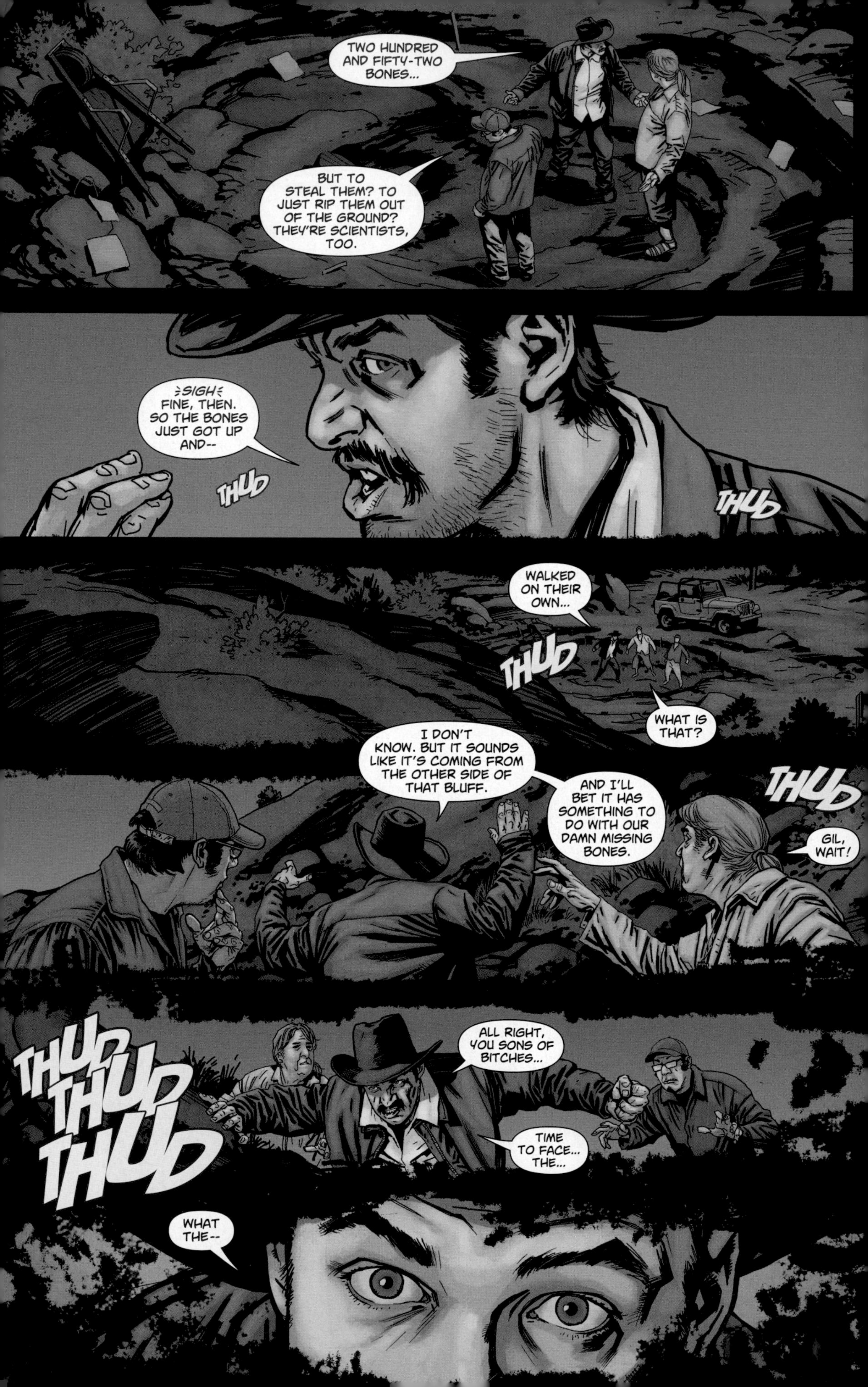
TWO HUNDRED AND FIFTY-TWO BONES...
BUT TO STEAL THEM? TO JUST RIP THEM OUT OF THE GROUND? THEY'RE SCIENTISTS, TOO.
SIGH FINE, THEN. SO THE BONES JUST GOT UP AND--
THUD
THUD
WALKED ON THEIR OWN...
THUD
WHAT IS THAT?
I DON'T KNOW. BUT IT SOUNDS LIKE IT'S COMING FROM THE OTHER SIDE OF THAT BLUFF.
AND I'LL BET IT HAS SOMETHING TO DO WITH OUR DAMN MISSING BONES.
THUD
GIL, WAIT!
THUD THUD THUD
ALL RIGHT, YOU SONS OF BITCHES...
TIME TO FACE... THE...
WHAT THE--

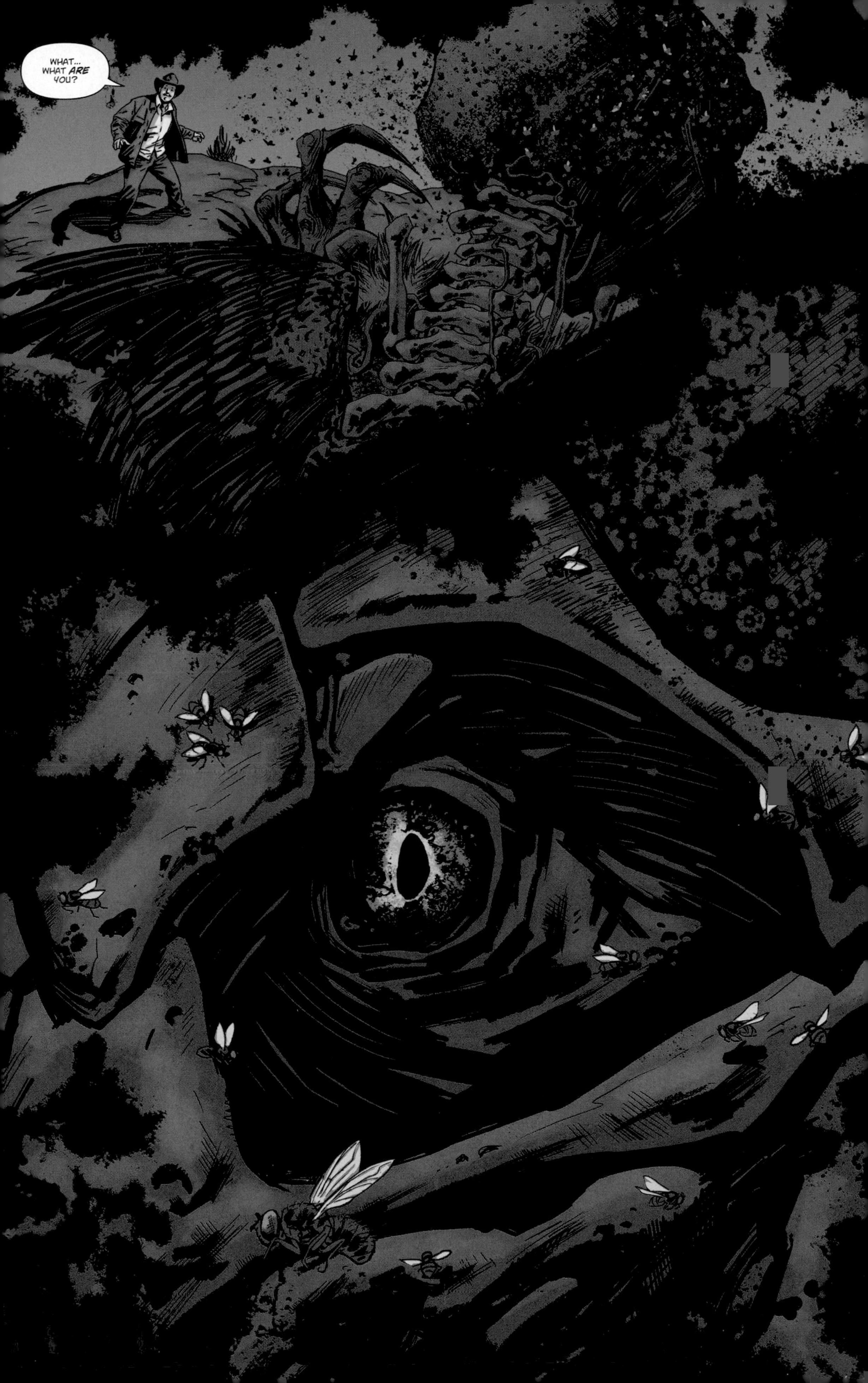
WHAT... WHAT ARE YOU?

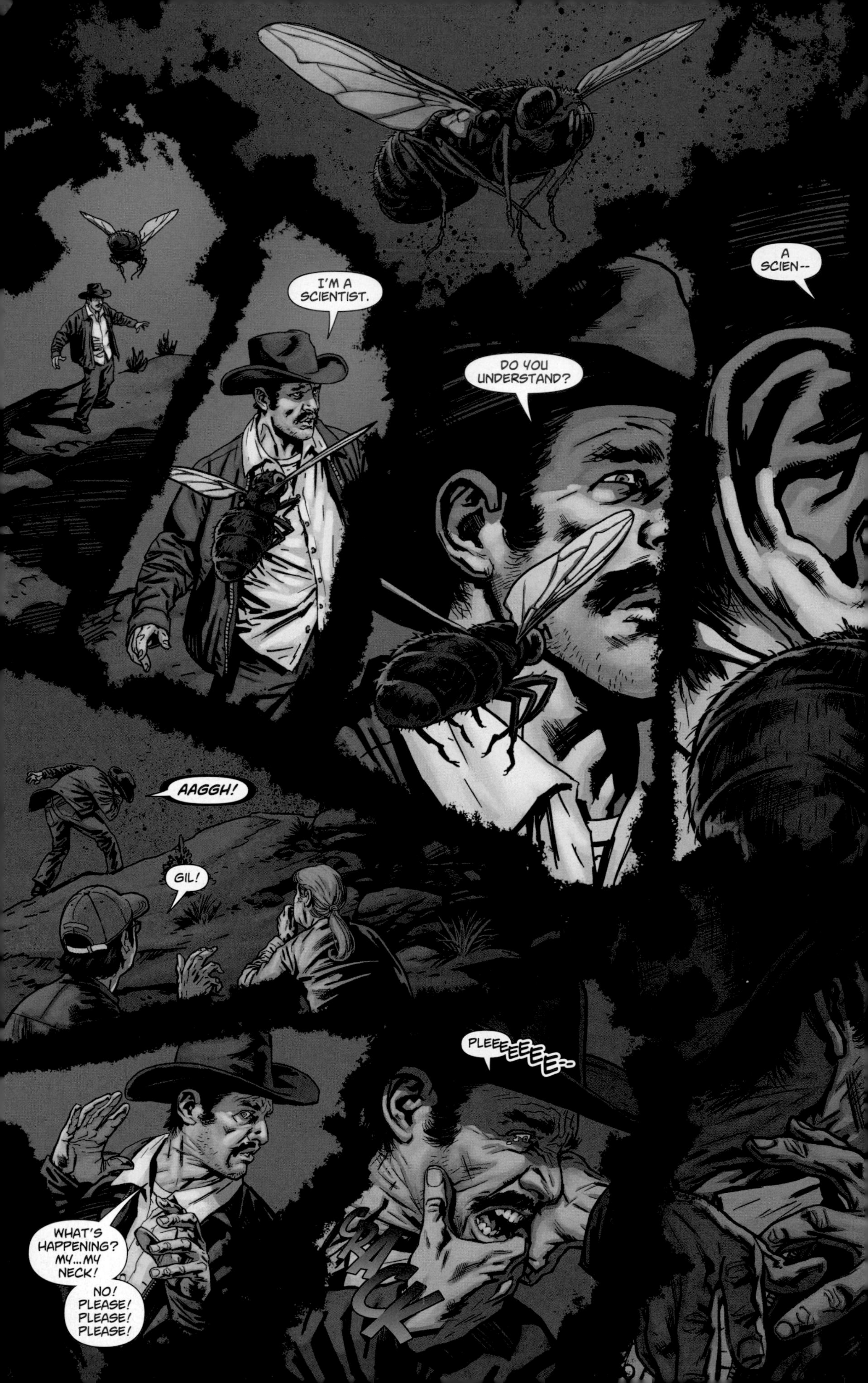
I'M A SCIENTIST.
DO YOU UNDERSTAND?
A SCIEN--
AAGGH!
GIL!
WHAT'S HAPPENING? MY...MY NECK!
NO! PLEASE! PLEASE! PLEASE!
PLEEEEEEE--
CRACK

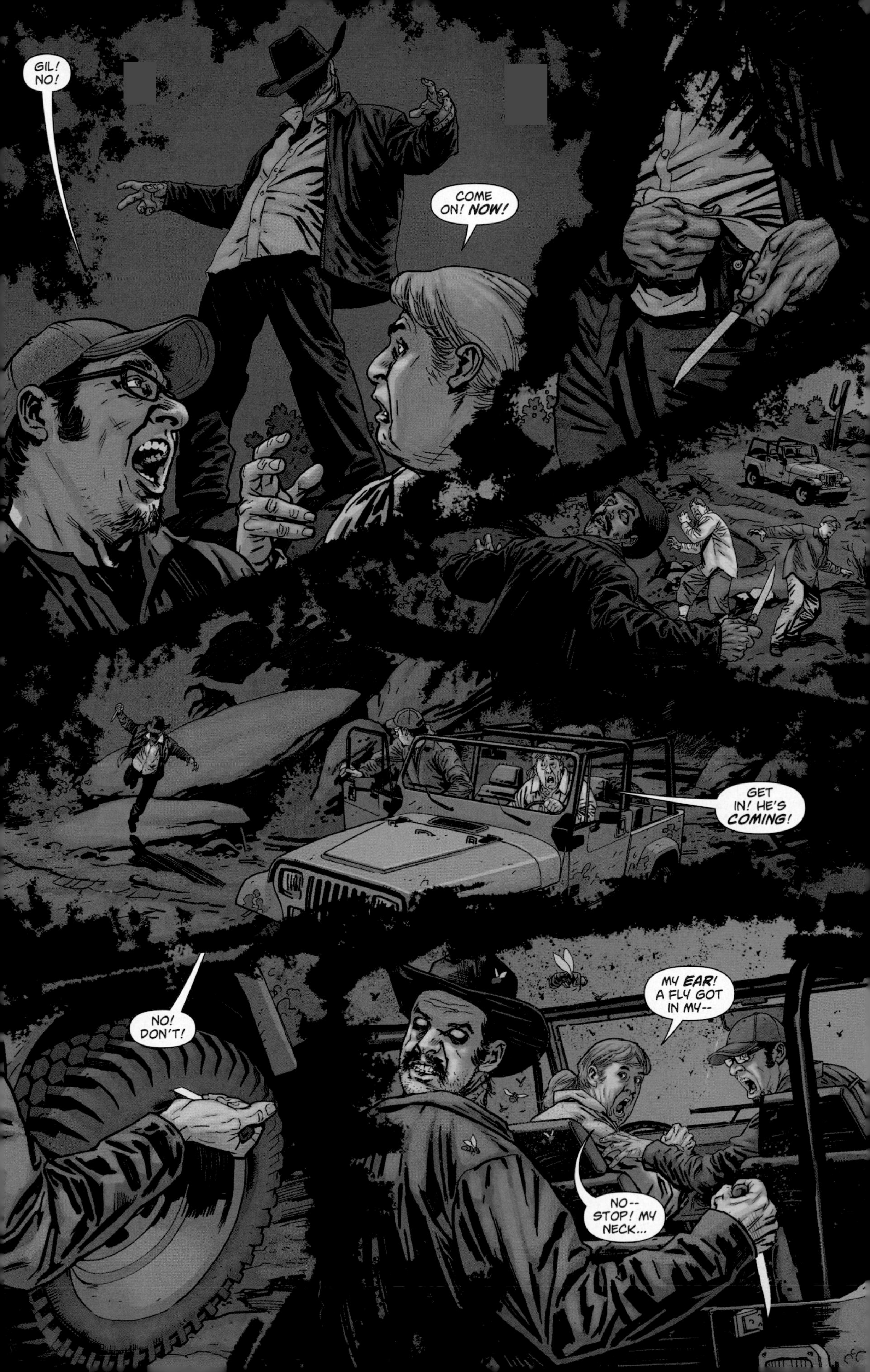
GIL! NO!
COME ON! NOW!
GET IN! HE'S COMING!
NO! DON'T!
MY EAR! A FLY GOT IN MY--
NO-- STOP! MY NECK...

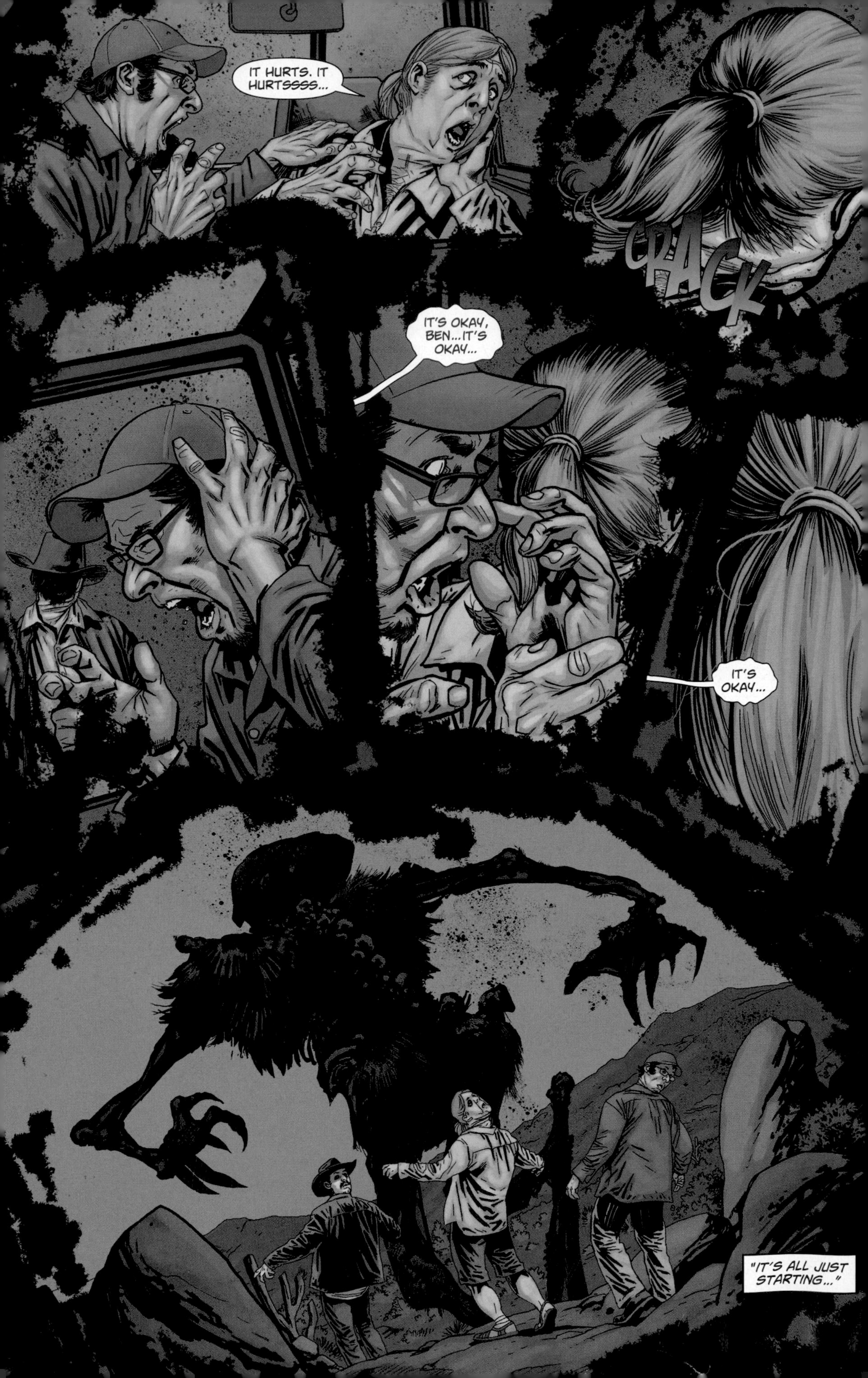
IT HURTS. IT HURTSSSS...
CRACK
IT'S OKAY, BEN...IT'S OKAY...
IT'S OKAY...
"IT'S ALL JUST STARTING..."

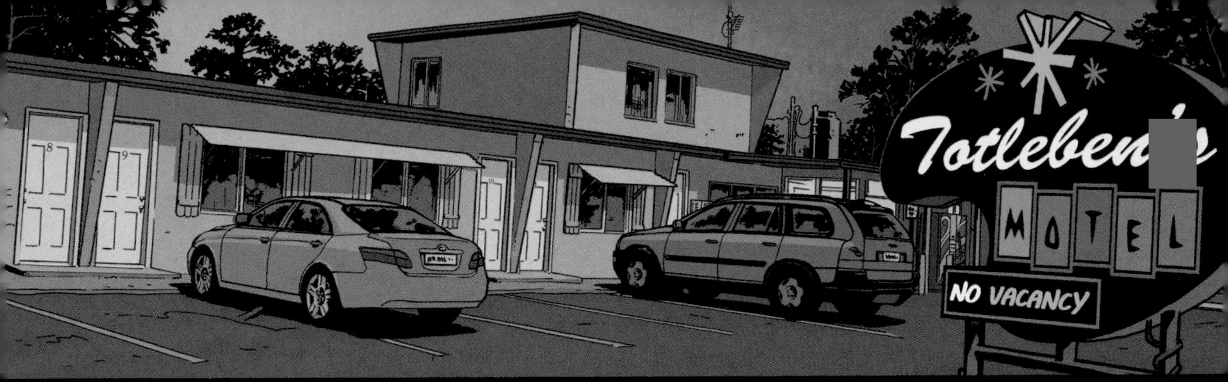
Totleben
MOTEL
NO VACANCY

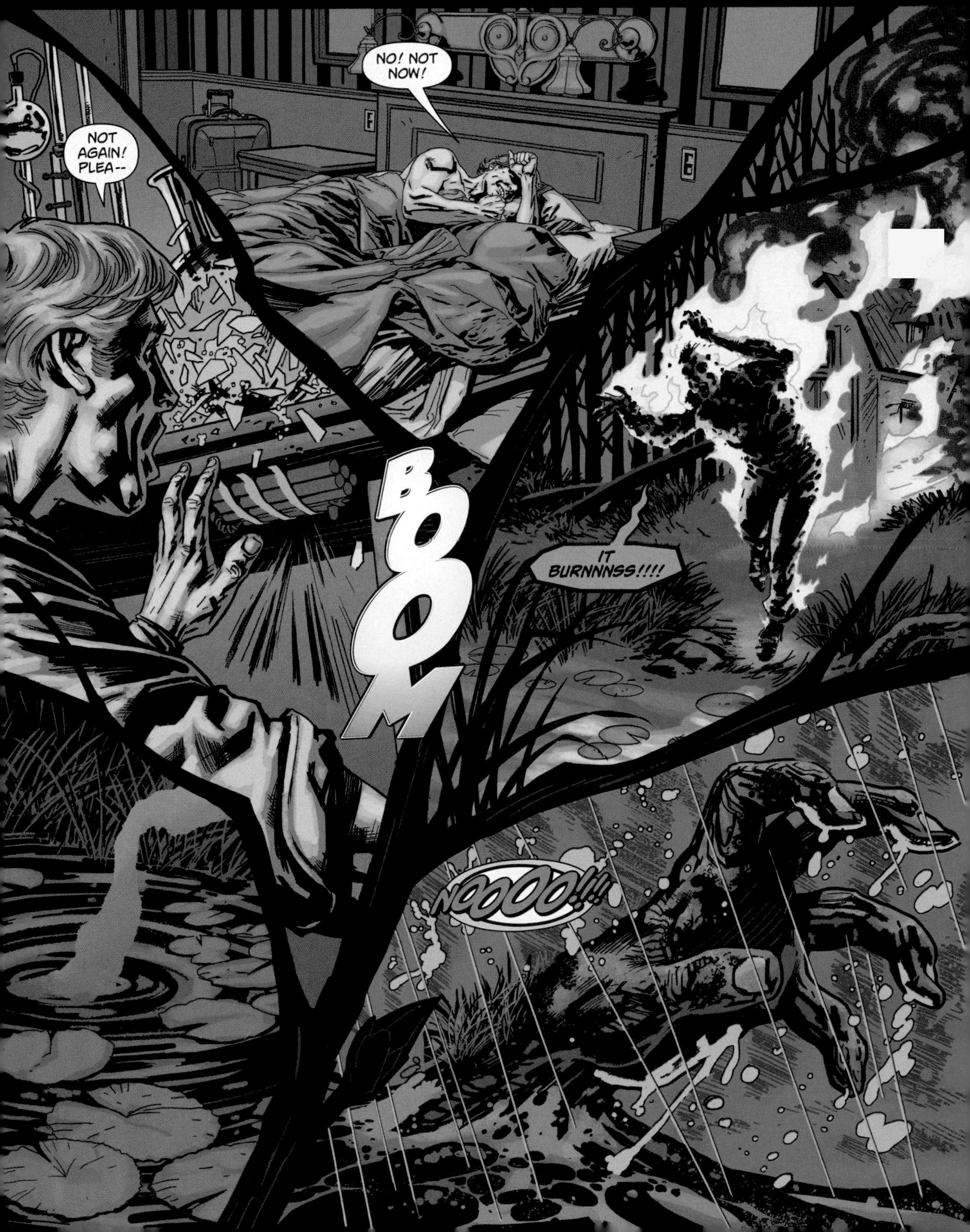
NOT AGAIN! PLEA--
NO! NOT NOW!
BOOM
IT BURNNNSS!!!!
NOOOOO!!!

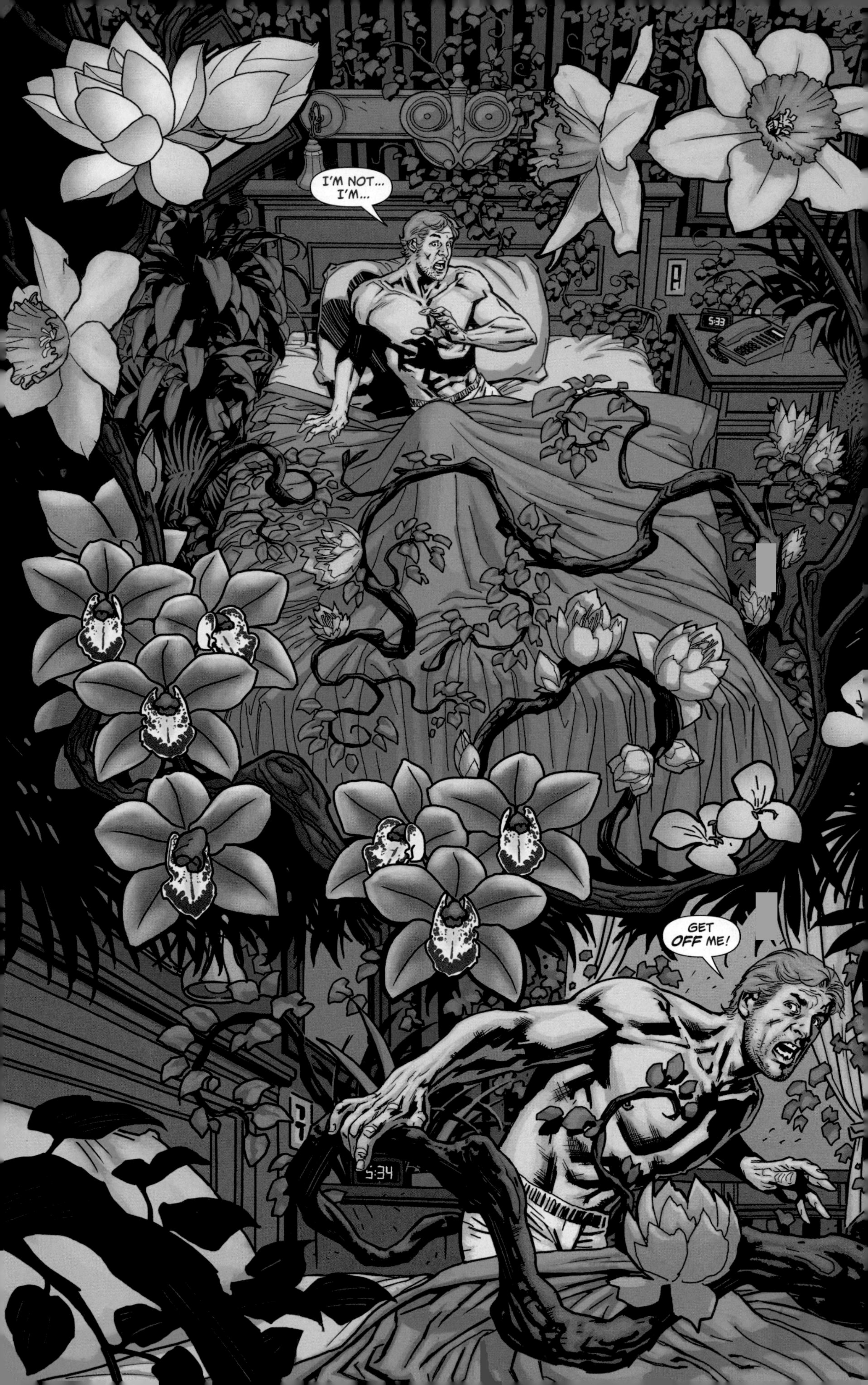
I'M NOT... I'M...
5:33
GET OFF ME!
5:34

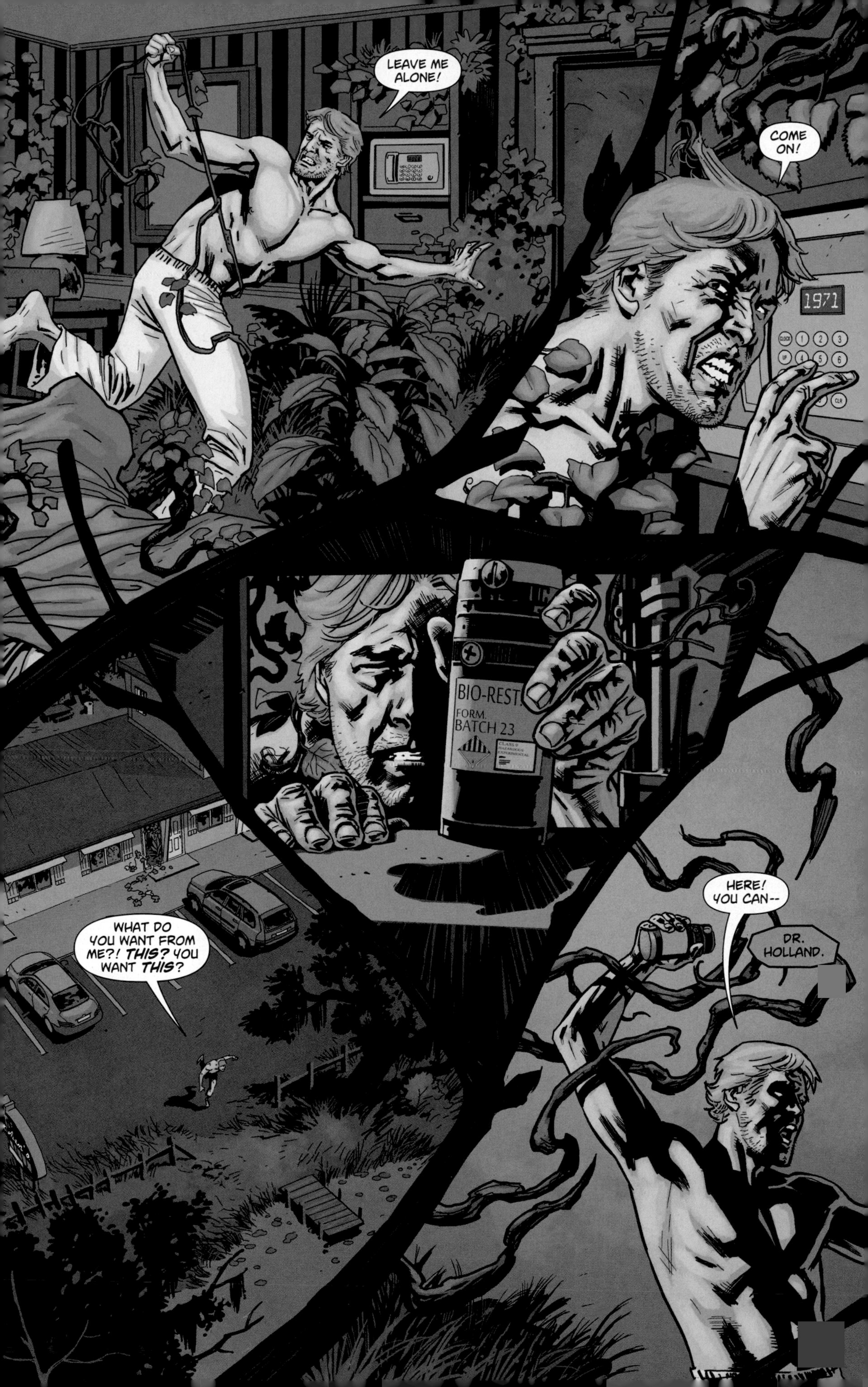
LEAVE ME ALONE!
COME ON!
1971
BIO-REST
FORM. BATCH 23
WHAT DO YOU WANT FROM ME?! THIS? YOU WANT THIS?
HERE! YOU CAN--
DR. HOLLAND.

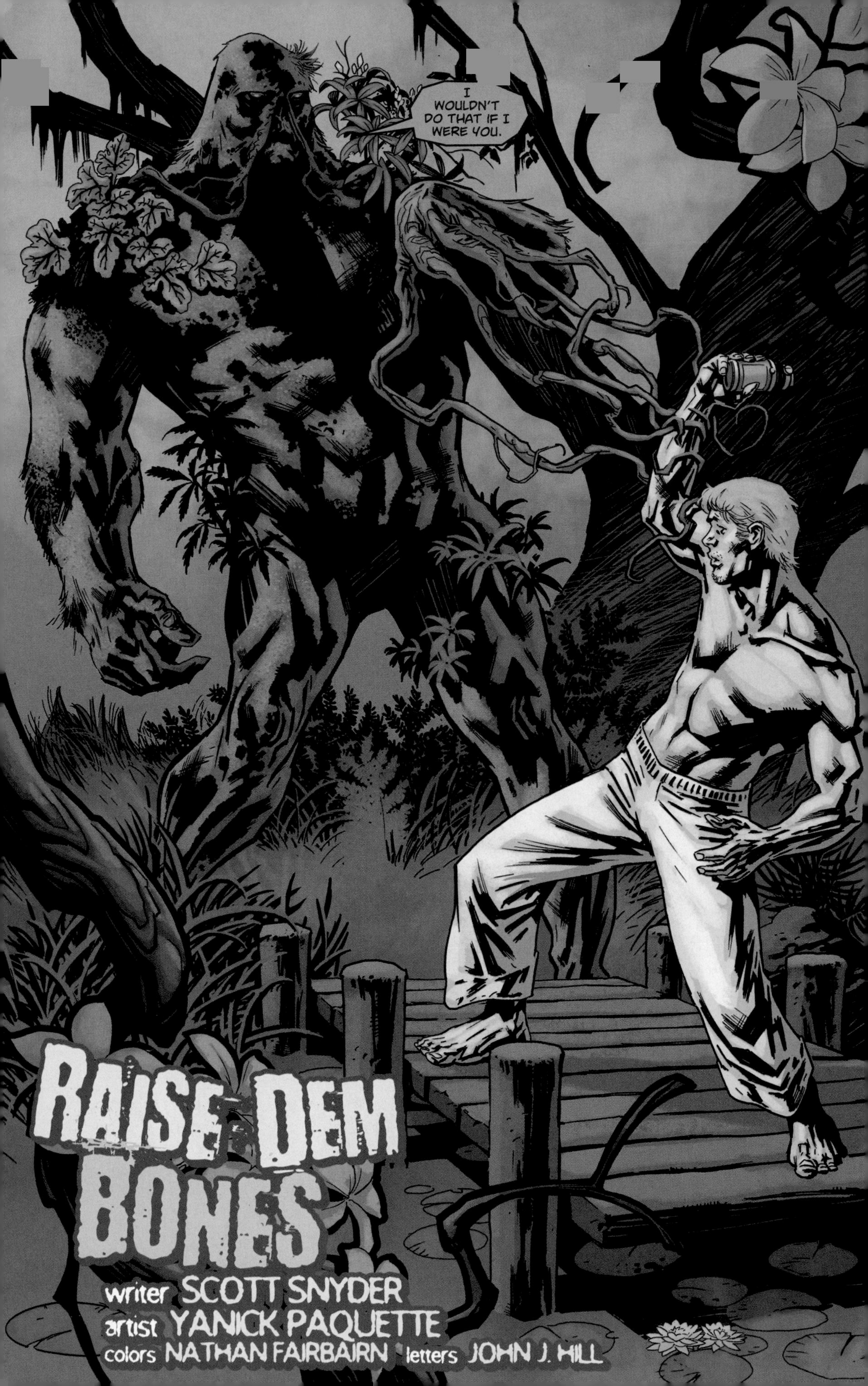
I WOULDN'T DO THAT IF I WERE YOU.
RAISE DEM BONES
writer SCOTT SNYDER
artist YANICK PAQUETTE
colors NATHAN FAIRBAIRN letters JOHN J. HILL

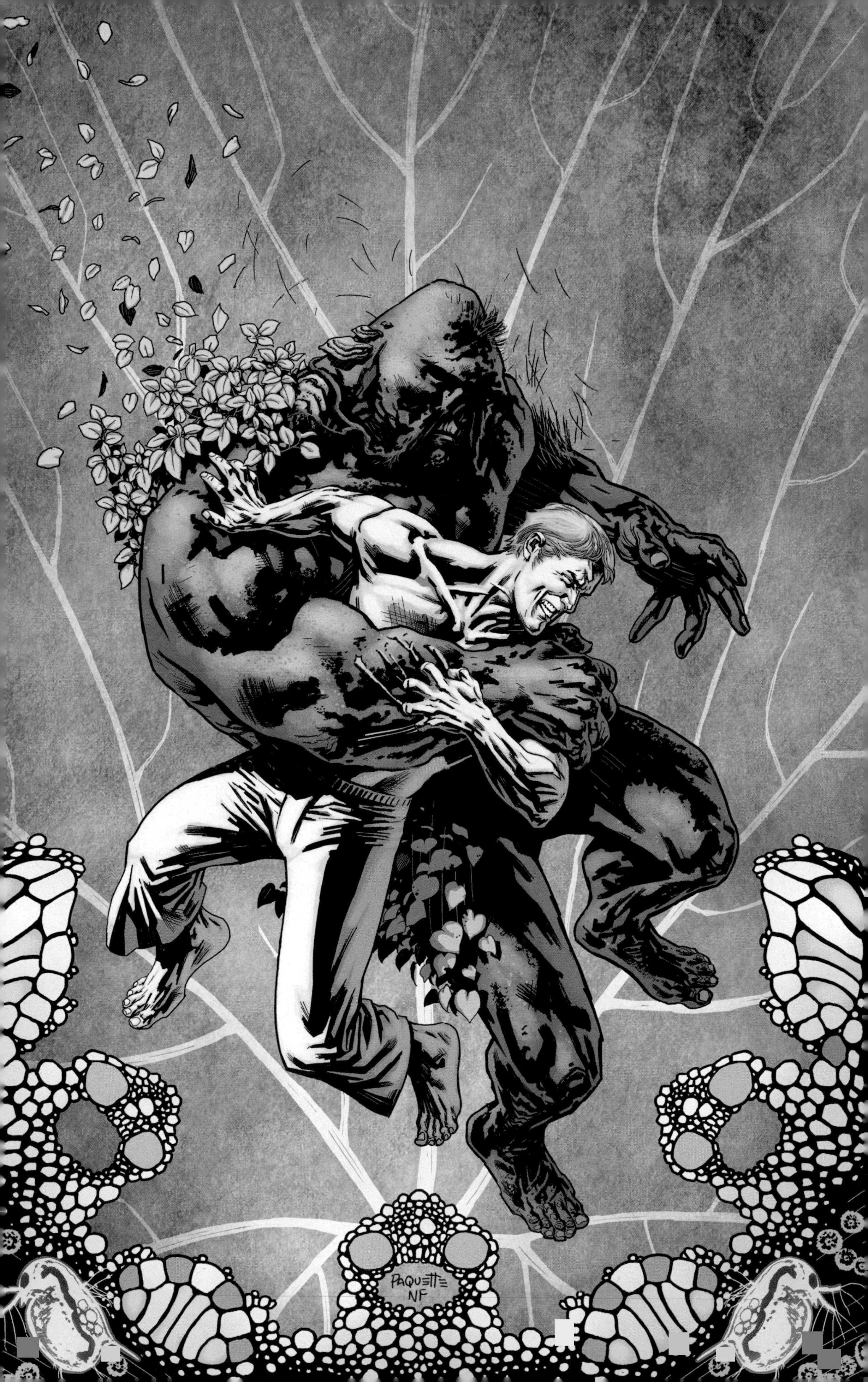
PAQUETTE
NF

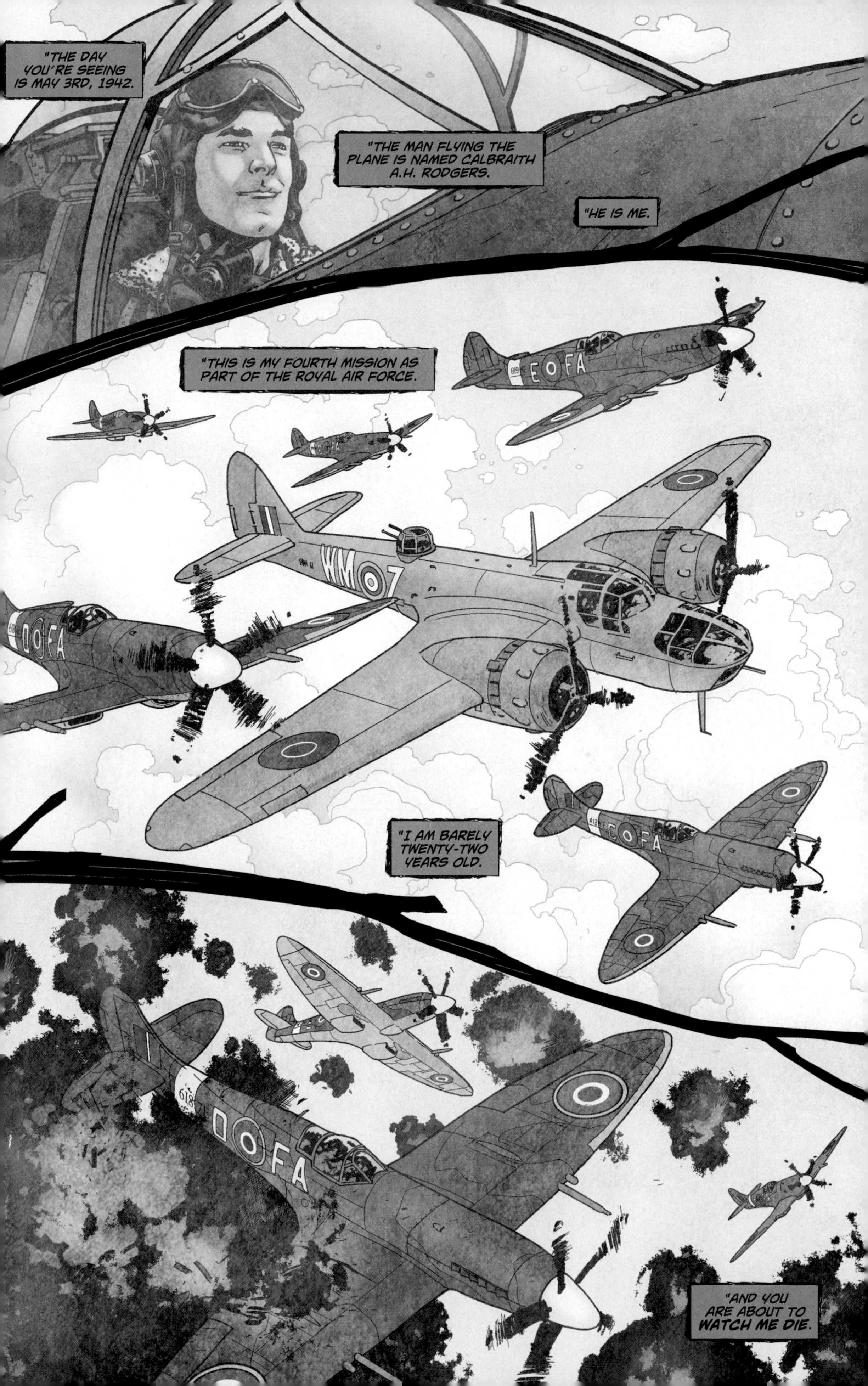
"THE DAY YOU'RE SEEING IS MAY 3RD, 1942.
"THE MAN FLYING THE PLANE IS NAMED CALBRAITH A.H. RODGERS.
"HE IS ME.
"THIS IS MY FOURTH MISSION AS PART OF THE ROYAL AIR FORCE.
"I AM BARELY TWENTY-TWO YEARS OLD.
"AND YOU ARE ABOUT TO WATCH ME DIE.

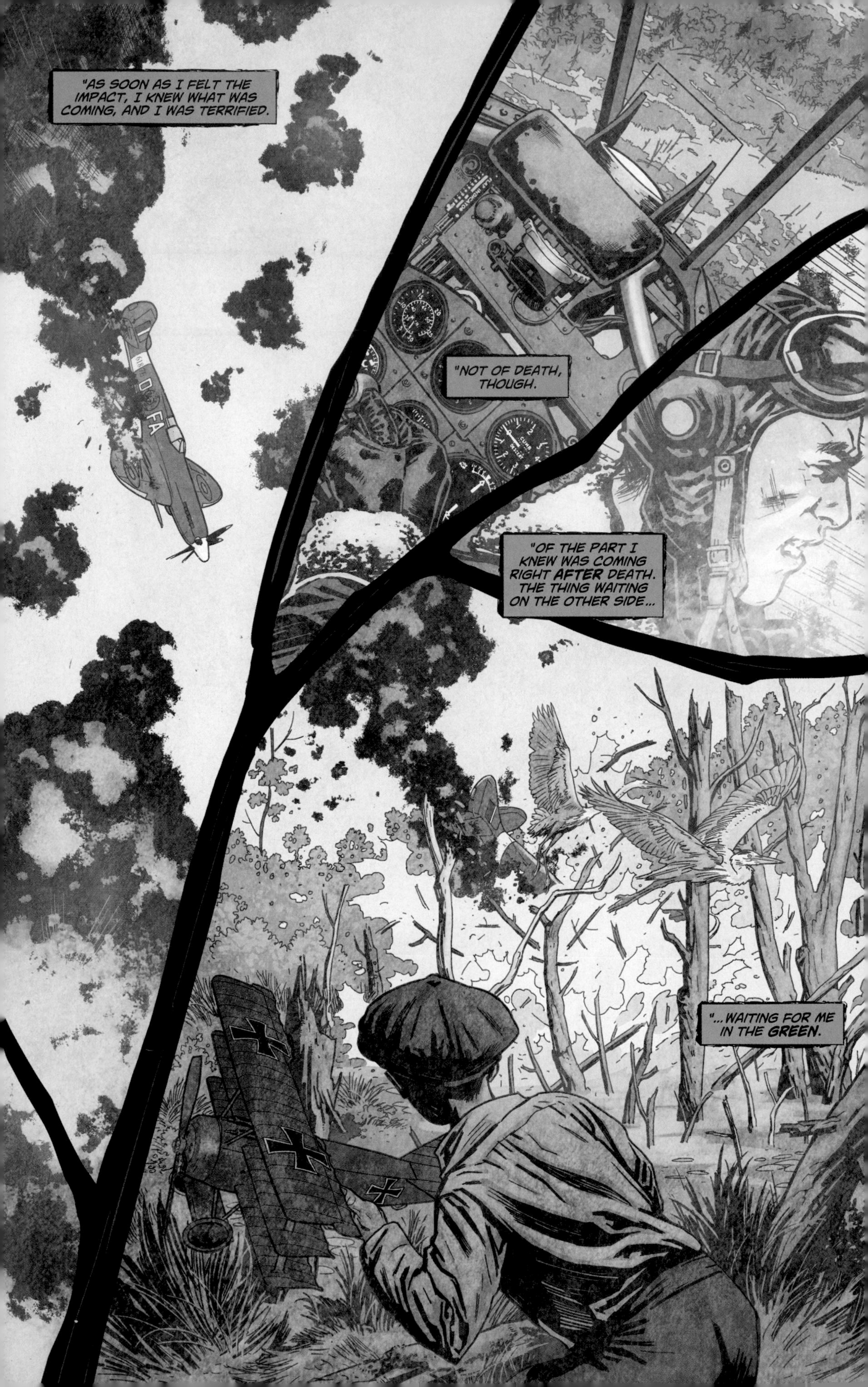
"AS SOON AS I FELT THE IMPACT, I KNEW WHAT WAS COMING, AND I WAS TERRIFIED.
"NOT OF DEATH, THOUGH.
"OF THE PART I KNEW WAS COMING RIGHT AFTER DEATH. THE THING WAITING ON THE OTHER SIDE...
"...WAITING FOR ME IN THE GREEN.

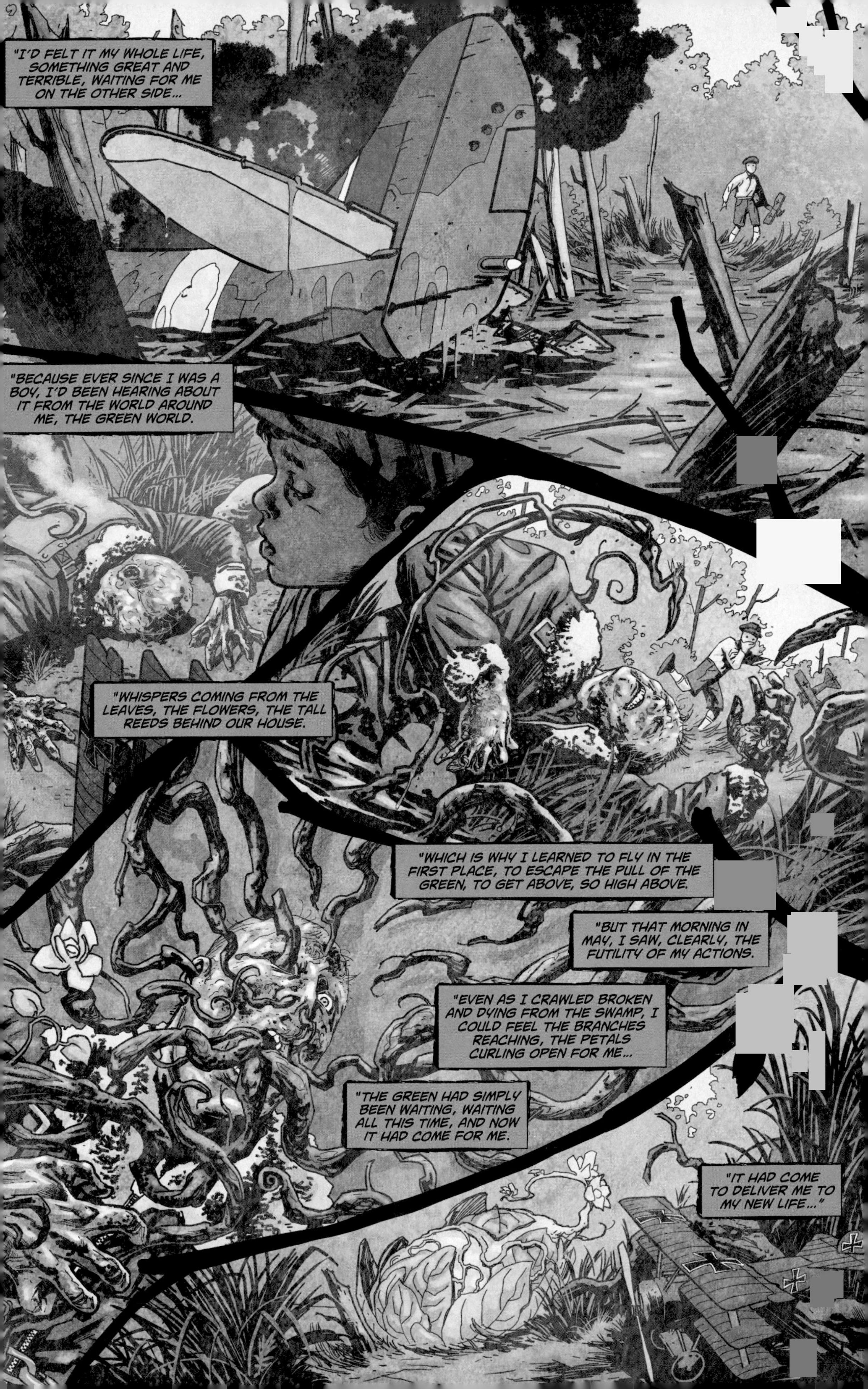
"I'D FELT IT MY WHOLE LIFE, SOMETHING GREAT AND TERRIBLE, WAITING FOR ME ON THE OTHER SIDE...
"BECAUSE EVER SINCE I WAS A BOY, I'D BEEN HEARING ABOUT IT FROM THE WORLD AROUND ME, THE GREEN WORLD.
"WHISPERS COMING FROM THE LEAVES, THE FLOWERS, THE TALL REEDS BEHIND OUR HOUSE.
"WHICH IS WHY I LEARNED TO FLY IN THE FIRST PLACE, TO ESCAPE THE PULL OF THE GREEN, TO GET ABOVE, SO HIGH ABOVE.
"BUT THAT MORNING IN MAY, I SAW, CLEARLY, THE FUTILITY OF MY ACTIONS.
"EVEN AS I CRAWLED BROKEN AND DYING FROM THE SWAMP, I COULD FEEL THE BRANCHES REACHING, THE PETALS CURLING OPEN FOR ME...
"THE GREEN HAD SIMPLY BEEN WAITING, WAITING ALL THIS TIME, AND NOW IT HAD COME FOR ME.
"IT HAD COME TO DELIVER ME TO MY NEW LIFE..."

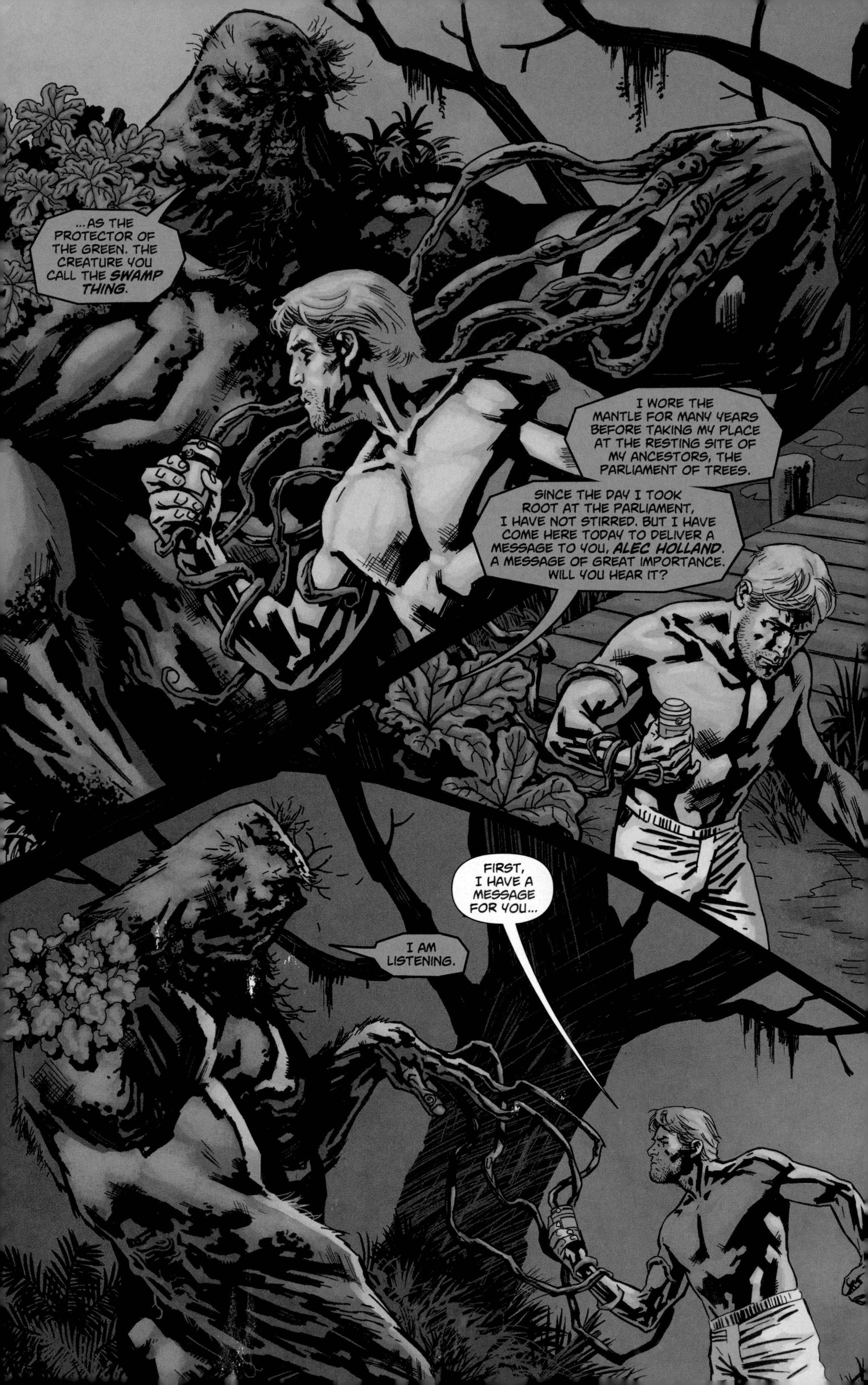
...AS THE PROTECTOR OF THE GREEN. THE CREATURE YOU CALL THE SWAMP THING.
I WORE THE MANTLE FOR MANY YEARS BEFORE TAKING MY PLACE AT THE RESTING SITE OF MY ANCESTORS, THE PARLIAMENT OF TREES.
SINCE THE DAY I TOOK ROOT AT THE PARLIAMENT, I HAVE NOT STIRRED. BUT I HAVE COME HERE TODAY TO DELIVER A MESSAGE TO YOU, ALEC HOLLAND. A MESSAGE OF GREAT IMPORTANCE. WILL YOU HEAR IT?
FIRST, I HAVE A MESSAGE FOR YOU...
I AM LISTENING.

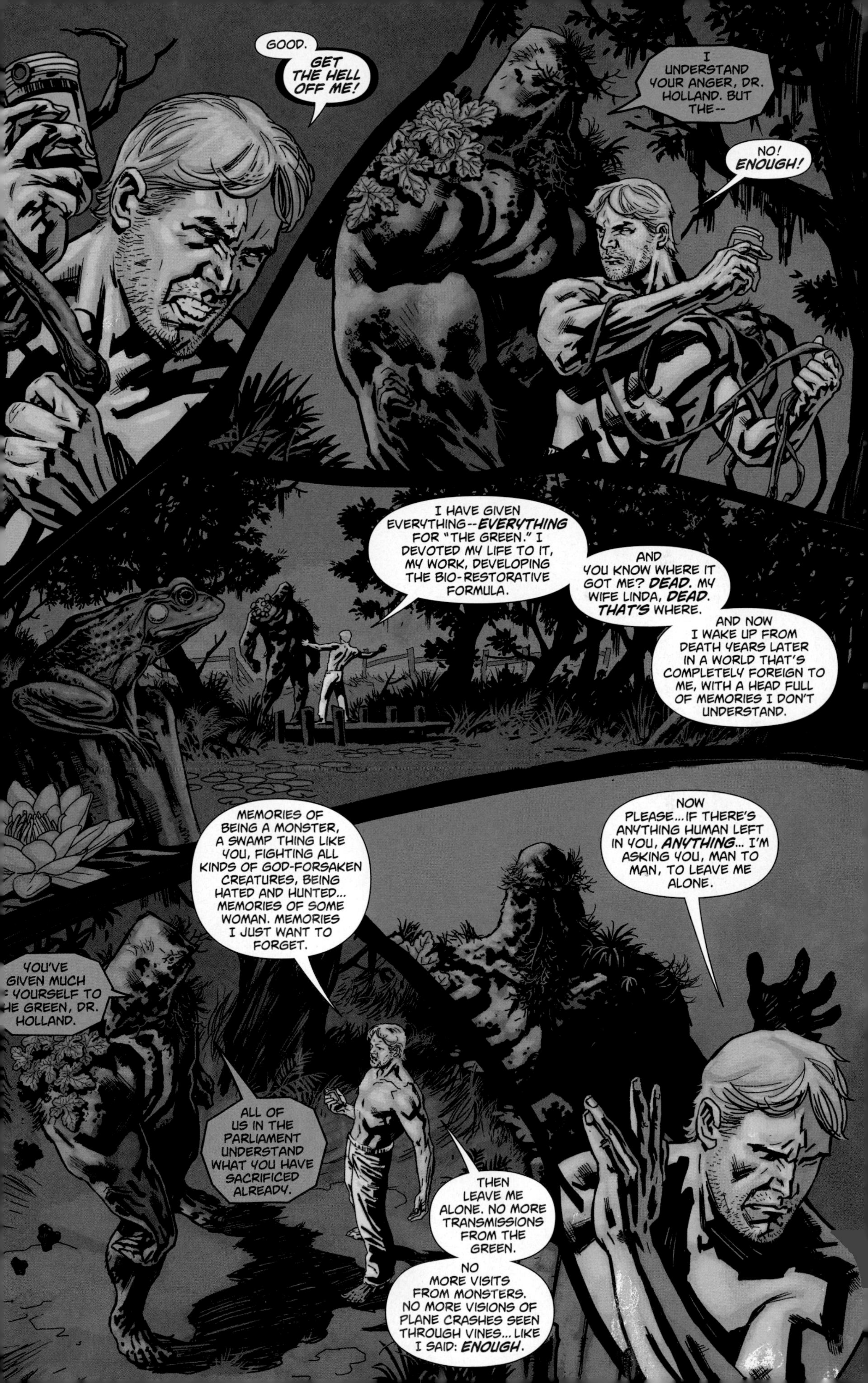
GOOD. GET THE HELL OFF ME!
I UNDERSTAND YOUR ANGER, DR. HOLLAND. BUT THE--
NO! ENOUGH!
I HAVE GIVEN EVERYTHING--EVERYTHING FOR "THE GREEN." I DEVOTED MY LIFE TO IT, MY WORK, DEVELOPING THE BIO-RESTORATIVE FORMULA.
AND YOU KNOW WHERE IT GOT ME? DEAD. MY WIFE LINDA, DEAD. THAT'S WHERE.
AND NOW I WAKE UP FROM DEATH YEARS LATER IN A WORLD THAT'S COMPLETELY FOREIGN TO ME, WITH A HEAD FULL OF MEMORIES I DON'T UNDERSTAND.
MEMORIES OF BEING A MONSTER, A SWAMP THING LIKE YOU, FIGHTING ALL KINDS OF GOD-FORSAKEN CREATURES, BEING HATED AND HUNTED... MEMORIES OF SOME WOMAN. MEMORIES I JUST WANT TO FORGET.
YOU'VE GIVEN MUCH YOURSELF TO HE GREEN, DR. HOLLAND.
ALL OF US IN THE PARLIAMENT UNDERSTAND WHAT YOU HAVE SACRIFICED ALREADY.
THEN LEAVE ME ALONE. NO MORE TRANSMISSIONS FROM THE GREEN.
NO MORE VISITS FROM MONSTERS. NO MORE VISIONS OF PLANE CRASHES SEEN THROUGH VINES... LIKE I SAID: ENOUGH.
NOW PLEASE... IF THERE'S ANYTHING HUMAN LEFT IN YOU, ANYTHING... I'M ASKING YOU, MAN TO MAN, TO LEAVE ME ALONE.

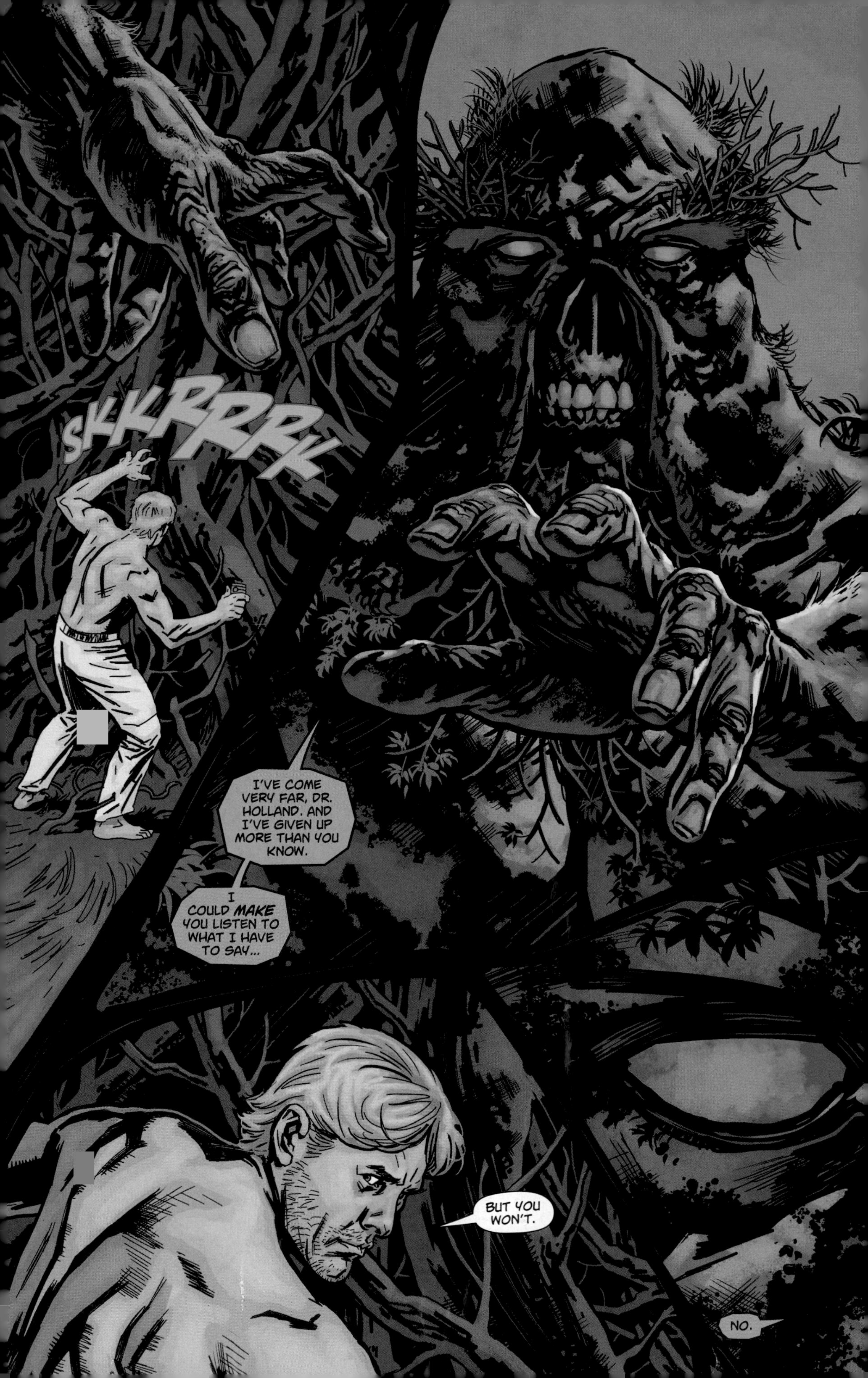
SKKRRRK
I'VE COME VERY FAR, DR. HOLLAND. AND I'VE GIVEN UP MORE THAN YOU KNOW.
I COULD MAKE YOU LISTEN TO WHAT I HAVE TO SAY...
BUT YOU WON'T.
NO.

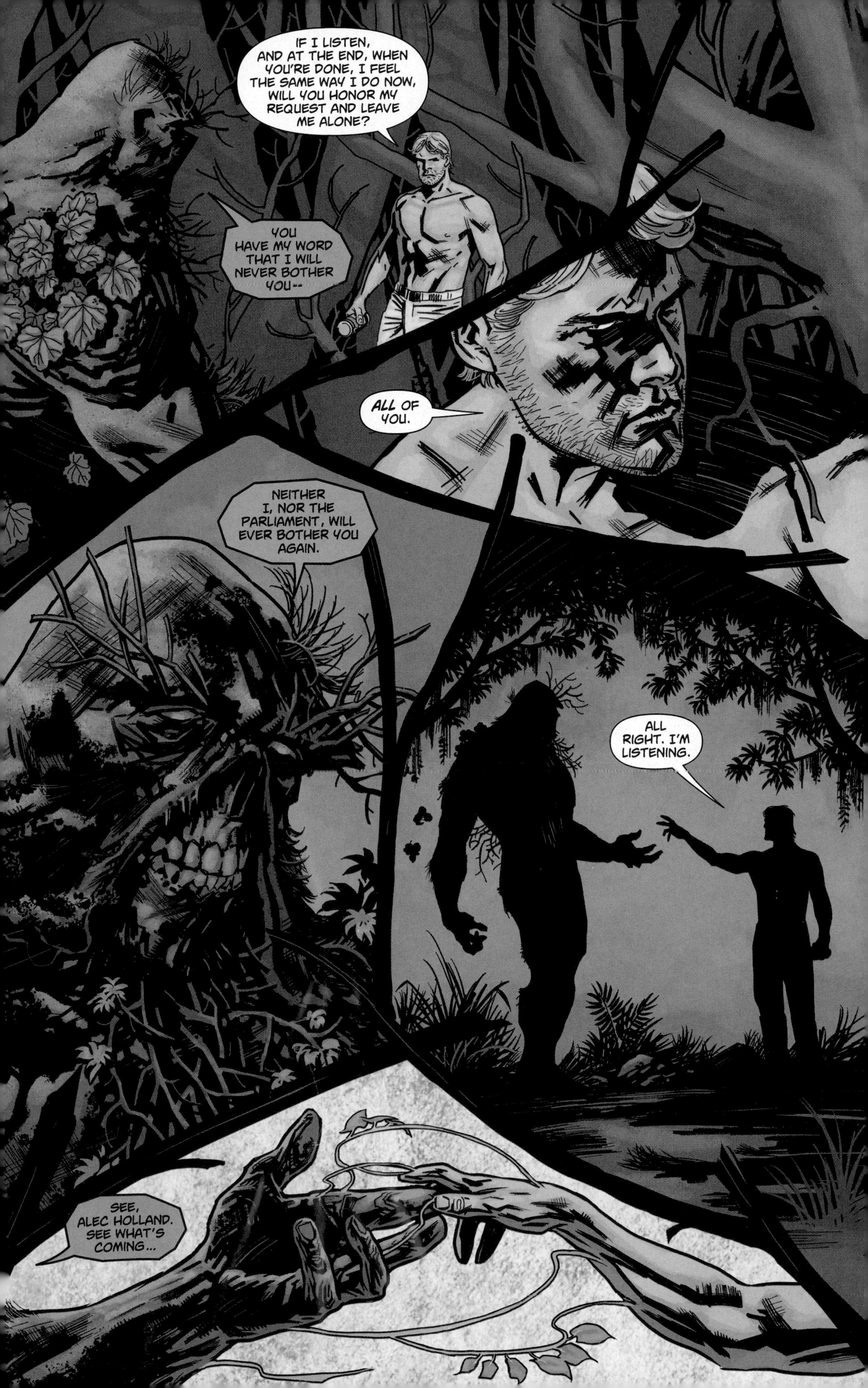
IF I LISTEN, AND AT THE END, WHEN YOU'RE DONE, I FEEL THE SAME WAY I DO NOW, WILL YOU HONOR MY REQUEST AND LEAVE ME ALONE?
YOU HAVE MY WORD THAT I WILL NEVER BOTHER YOU--
ALL OF YOU.
NEITHER I, NOR THE PARLIAMENT, WILL EVER BOTHER YOU AGAIN.
ALL RIGHT. I'M LISTENING.
SEE, ALEC HOLLAND. SEE WHAT'S COMING...

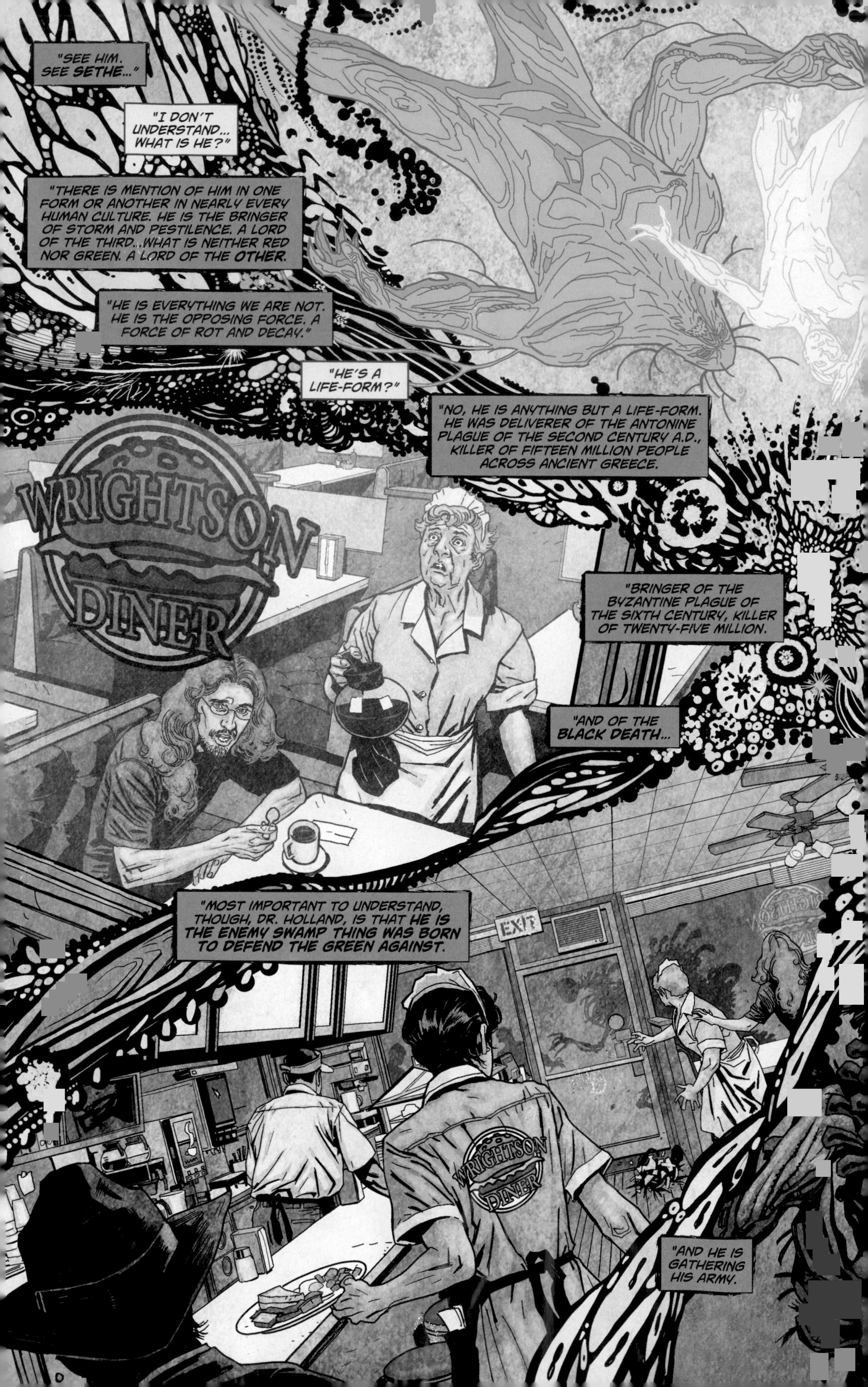
"SEE HIM. SEE SETHE..."
"I DON'T UNDERSTAND... WHAT IS HE?"
"THERE IS MENTION OF HIM IN ONE FORM OR ANOTHER IN NEARLY EVERY HUMAN CULTURE. HE IS THE BRINGER OF STORM AND PESTILENCE. A LORD OF THE THIRD...WHAT IS NEITHER RED NOR GREEN. A LORD OF THE OTHER.
"HE IS EVERYTHING WE ARE NOT. HE IS THE OPPOSING FORCE. A FORCE OF ROT AND DECAY."
"HE'S A LIFE-FORM?"
"NO, HE IS ANYTHING BUT A LIFE-FORM. HE WAS DELIVERER OF THE ANTONINE PLAGUE OF THE SECOND CENTURY A.D., KILLER OF FIFTEEN MILLION PEOPLE ACROSS ANCIENT GREECE.
WRIGHTSON DINER
"BRINGER OF THE BYZANTINE PLAGUE OF THE SIXTH CENTURY, KILLER OF TWENTY-FIVE MILLION.
"AND OF THE BLACK DEATH...
"MOST IMPORTANT TO UNDERSTAND, THOUGH, DR. HOLLAND, IS THAT HE IS THE ENEMY SWAMP THING WAS BORN TO DEFEND THE GREEN AGAINST.
EXIT
WRIGHTSON DINER
"AND HE IS GATHERING HIS ARMY.

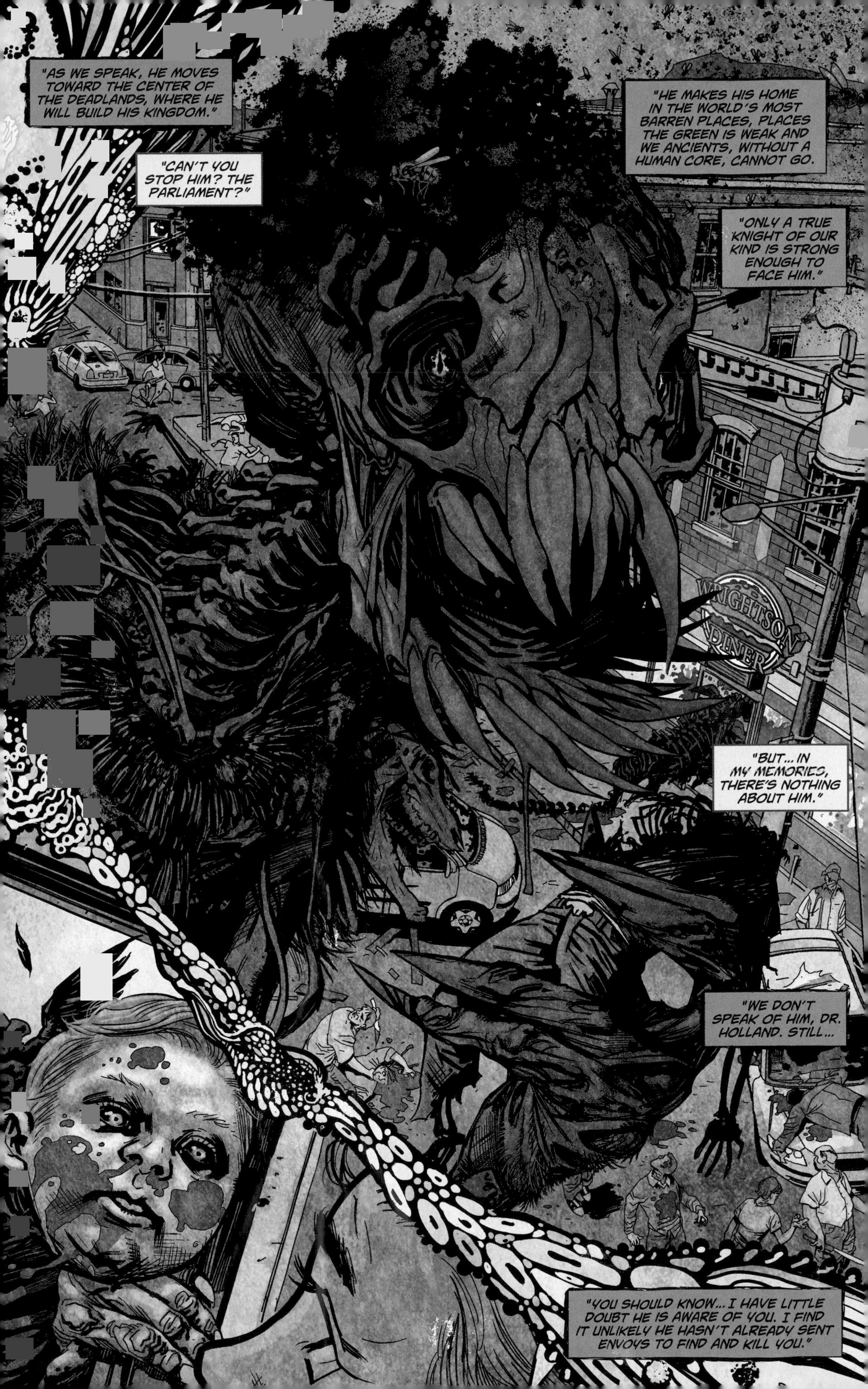
"AS WE SPEAK, HE MOVES TOWARD THE CENTER OF THE DEADLANDS, WHERE HE WILL BUILD HIS KINGDOM."
"CAN'T YOU STOP HIM? THE PARLIAMENT?"
"HE MAKES HIS HOME IN THE WORLD'S MOST BARREN PLACES, PLACES THE GREEN IS WEAK AND WE ANCIENTS, WITHOUT A HUMAN CORE, CANNOT GO.
"ONLY A TRUE KNIGHT OF OUR KIND IS STRONG ENOUGH TO FACE HIM."
WRIGHTSON DINER
"BUT... IN MY MEMORIES, THERE'S NOTHING ABOUT HIM."
"WE DON'T SPEAK OF HIM, DR. HOLLAND. STILL...
"YOU SHOULD KNOW... I HAVE LITTLE DOUBT HE IS AWARE OF YOU. I FIND IT UNLIKELY HE HASN'T ALREADY SENT ENVOYS TO FIND AND KILL YOU."

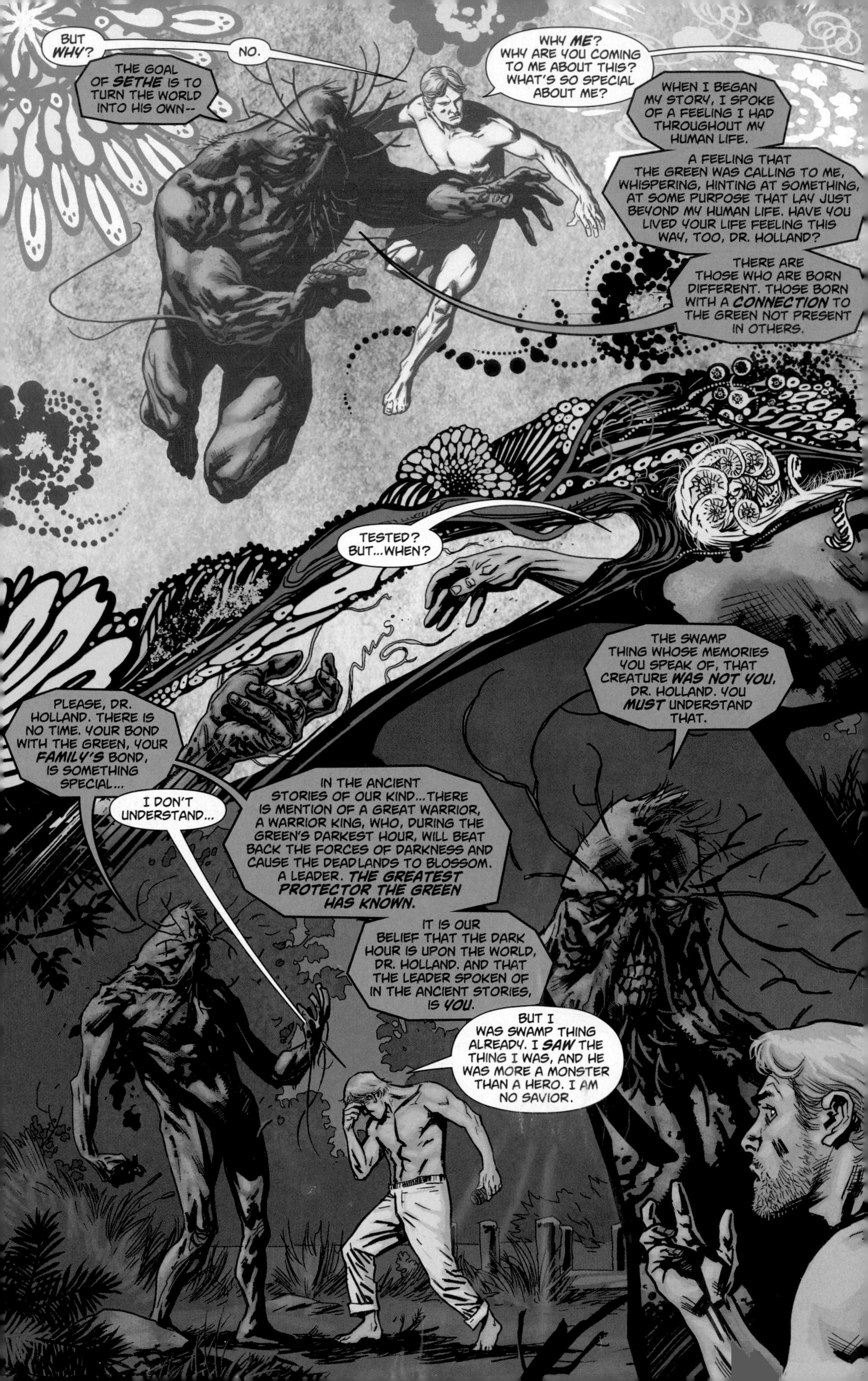
BUT WHY?
NO.
THE GOAL OF SETHE IS TO TURN THE WORLD INTO HIS OWN--
WHY ME? WHY ARE YOU COMING TO ME ABOUT THIS? WHAT'S SO SPECIAL ABOUT ME?
WHEN I BEGAN MY STORY, I SPOKE OF A FEELING I HAD THROUGHOUT MY HUMAN LIFE.
A FEELING THAT THE GREEN WAS CALLING TO ME, WHISPERING, HINTING AT SOMETHING, AT SOME PURPOSE THAT LAY JUST BEYOND MY HUMAN LIFE. HAVE YOU LIVED YOUR LIFE FEELING THIS WAY, TOO, DR. HOLLAND?
THERE ARE THOSE WHO ARE BORN DIFFERENT. THOSE BORN WITH A CONNECTION TO THE GREEN NOT PRESENT IN OTHERS.
TESTED? BUT...WHEN?
THE SWAMP THING WHOSE MEMORIES YOU SPEAK OF, THAT CREATURE WAS NOT YOU, DR. HOLLAND. YOU MUST UNDERSTAND THAT.
PLEASE, DR. HOLLAND. THERE IS NO TIME. YOUR BOND WITH THE GREEN, YOUR FAMILY'S BOND, IS SOMETHING SPECIAL...
I DON'T UNDERSTAND...
IN THE ANCIENT STORIES OF OUR KIND...THERE IS MENTION OF A GREAT WARRIOR, A WARRIOR KING, WHO, DURING THE GREEN'S DARKEST HOUR, WILL BEAT BACK THE FORCES OF DARKNESS AND CAUSE THE DEADLANDS TO BLOSSOM. A LEADER. THE GREATEST PROTECTOR THE GREEN HAS KNOWN.
IT IS OUR BELIEF THAT THE DARK HOUR IS UPON THE WORLD, DR. HOLLAND. AND THAT THE LEADER SPOKEN OF IN THE ANCIENT STORIES, IS YOU.
BUT I WAS SWAMP THING ALREADY. I SAW THE THING I WAS, AND HE WAS MORE A MONSTER THAN A HERO. I AM NO SAVIOR.

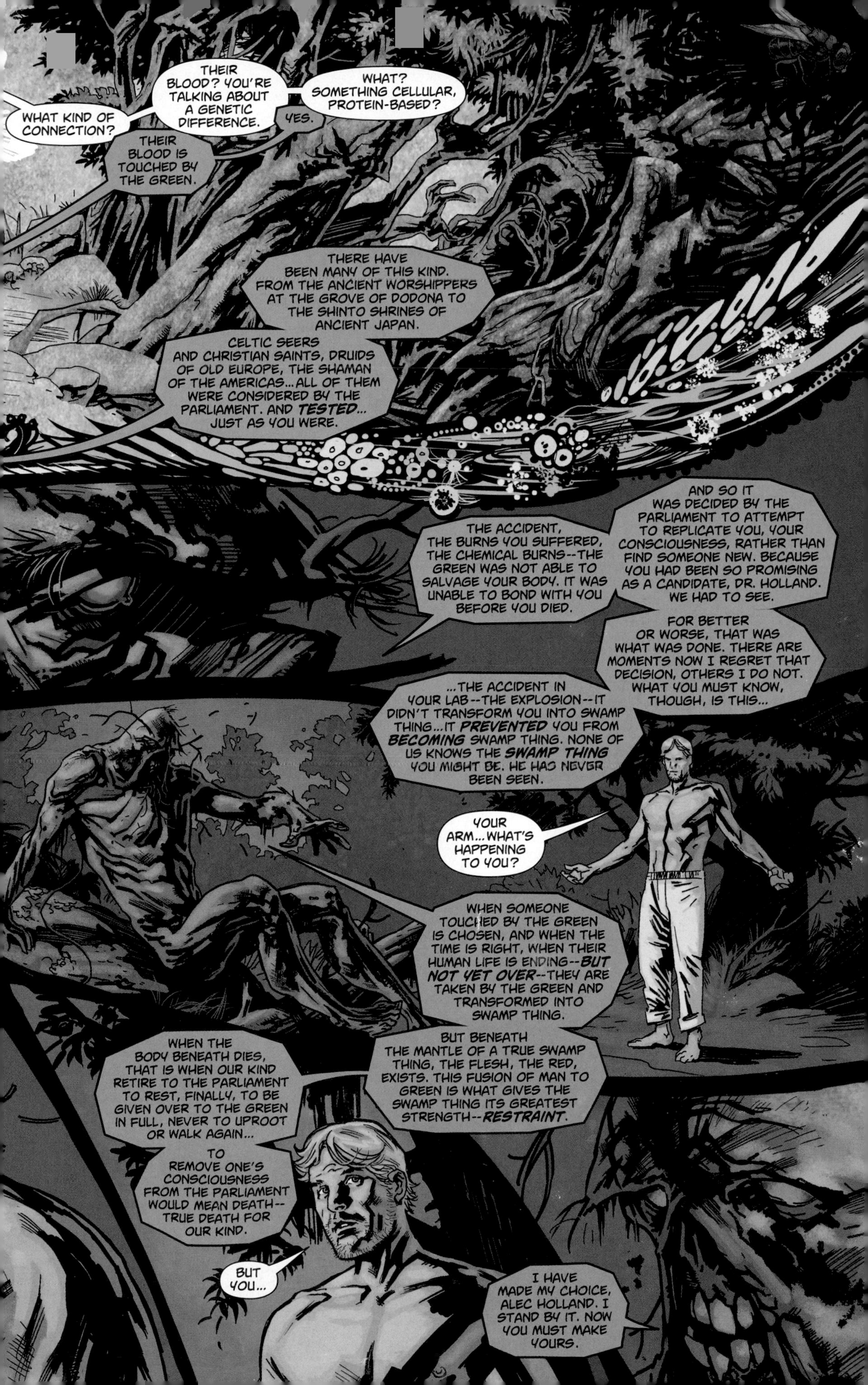
WHAT KIND OF CONNECTION?
THEIR BLOOD? YOU'RE TALKING ABOUT A GENETIC DIFFERENCE.
YES.
WHAT? SOMETHING CELLULAR, PROTEIN-BASED?
THEIR BLOOD IS TOUCHED BY THE GREEN.
THERE HAVE BEEN MANY OF THIS KIND. FROM THE ANCIENT WORSHIPPERS AT THE GROVE OF DODONA TO THE SHINTO SHRINES OF ANCIENT JAPAN.
CELTIC SEERS AND CHRISTIAN SAINTS, DRUIDS OF OLD EUROPE, THE SHAMAN OF THE AMERICAS...ALL OF THEM WERE CONSIDERED BY THE PARLIAMENT. AND TESTED... JUST AS YOU WERE.
THE ACCIDENT, THE BURNS YOU SUFFERED, THE CHEMICAL BURNS--THE GREEN WAS NOT ABLE TO SALVAGE YOUR BODY. IT WAS UNABLE TO BOND WITH YOU BEFORE YOU DIED.
AND SO IT WAS DECIDED BY THE PARLIAMENT TO ATTEMPT TO REPLICATE YOU, YOUR CONSCIOUSNESS, RATHER THAN FIND SOMEONE NEW. BECAUSE YOU HAD BEEN SO PROMISING AS A CANDIDATE, DR. HOLLAND. WE HAD TO SEE.
FOR BETTER OR WORSE, THAT WAS WHAT WAS DONE. THERE ARE MOMENTS NOW I REGRET THAT DECISION, OTHERS I DO NOT. WHAT YOU MUST KNOW, THOUGH, IS THIS...
...THE ACCIDENT IN YOUR LAB--THE EXPLOSION--IT DIDN'T TRANSFORM YOU INTO SWAMP THING...IT PREVENTED YOU FROM BECOMING SWAMP THING. NONE OF US KNOWS THE SWAMP THING YOU MIGHT BE. HE HAS NEVER BEEN SEEN.
YOUR ARM...WHAT'S HAPPENING TO YOU?
WHEN SOMEONE TOUCHED BY THE GREEN IS CHOSEN, AND WHEN THE TIME IS RIGHT, WHEN THEIR HUMAN LIFE IS ENDING--BUT NOT YET OVER--THEY ARE TAKEN BY THE GREEN AND TRANSFORMED INTO SWAMP THING.
BUT BENEATH THE MANTLE OF A TRUE SWAMP THING, THE FLESH, THE RED, EXISTS. THIS FUSION OF MAN TO GREEN IS WHAT GIVES THE SWAMP THING ITS GREATEST STRENGTH--RESTRAINT.
WHEN THE BODY BENEATH DIES, THAT IS WHEN OUR KIND RETIRE TO THE PARLIAMENT TO REST, FINALLY, TO BE GIVEN OVER TO THE GREEN IN FULL, NEVER TO UPROOT OR WALK AGAIN...
TO REMOVE ONE'S CONSCIOUSNESS FROM THE PARLIAMENT WOULD MEAN DEATH--TRUE DEATH FOR OUR KIND.
BUT YOU...
I HAVE MADE MY CHOICE, ALEC HOLLAND. I STAND BY IT. NOW YOU MUST MAKE YOURS.

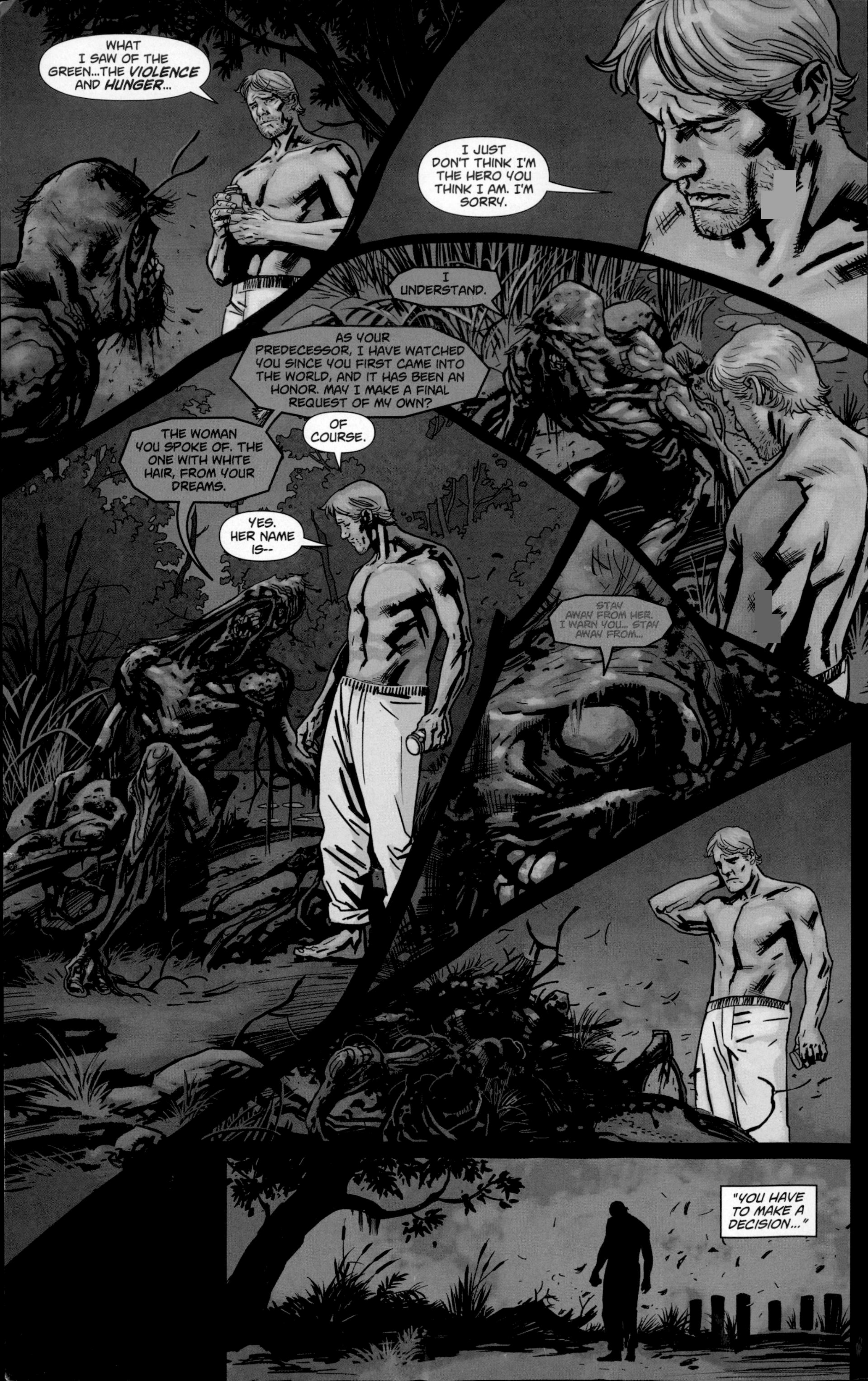
WHAT I SAW OF THE GREEN...THE *VIOLENCE* AND *HUNGER*...
I JUST DON'T THINK I'M THE HERO YOU THINK I AM. I'M SORRY.
I UNDERSTAND.
AS YOUR PREDECESSOR, I HAVE WATCHED YOU SINCE YOU FIRST CAME INTO THE WORLD, AND IT HAS BEEN AN HONOR. MAY I MAKE A FINAL REQUEST OF MY OWN?
OF COURSE.
THE WOMAN YOU SPOKE OF. THE ONE WITH WHITE HAIR, FROM YOUR DREAMS.
YES. HER NAME IS--
STAY AWAY FROM HER. I WARN YOU... STAY AWAY FROM...
"YOU HAVE TO MAKE A DECISION..."

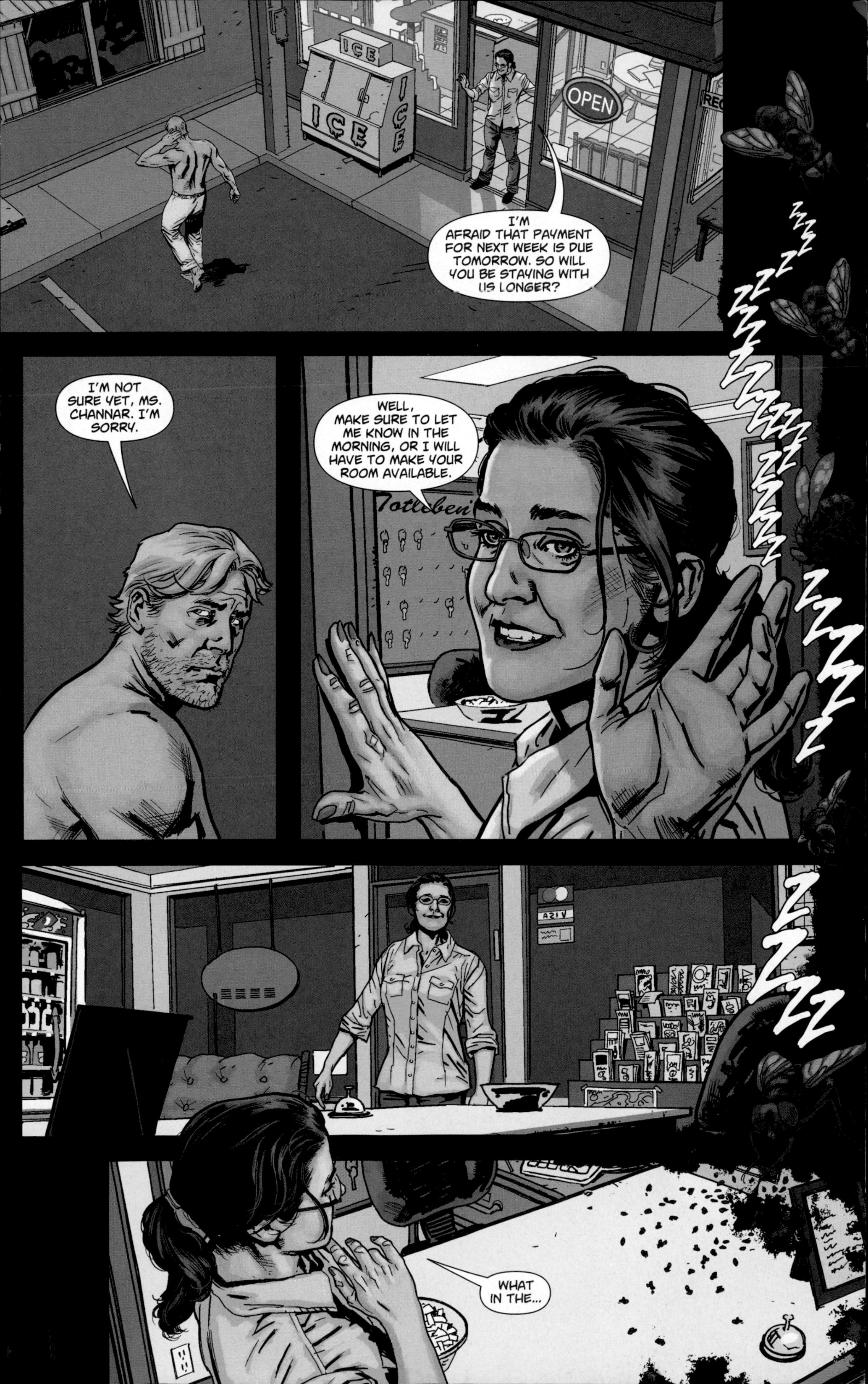
ICE
ICE
ICE
OPEN
I'M AFRAID THAT PAYMENT FOR NEXT WEEK IS DUE TOMORROW. SO WILL YOU BE STAYING WITH US LONGER?
I'M NOT SURE YET, MS. CHANNAR. I'M SORRY.
WELL, MAKE SURE TO LET ME KNOW IN THE MORNING, OR I WILL HAVE TO MAKE YOUR ROOM AVAILABLE.
Totleben
VISA
WHAT IN THE...

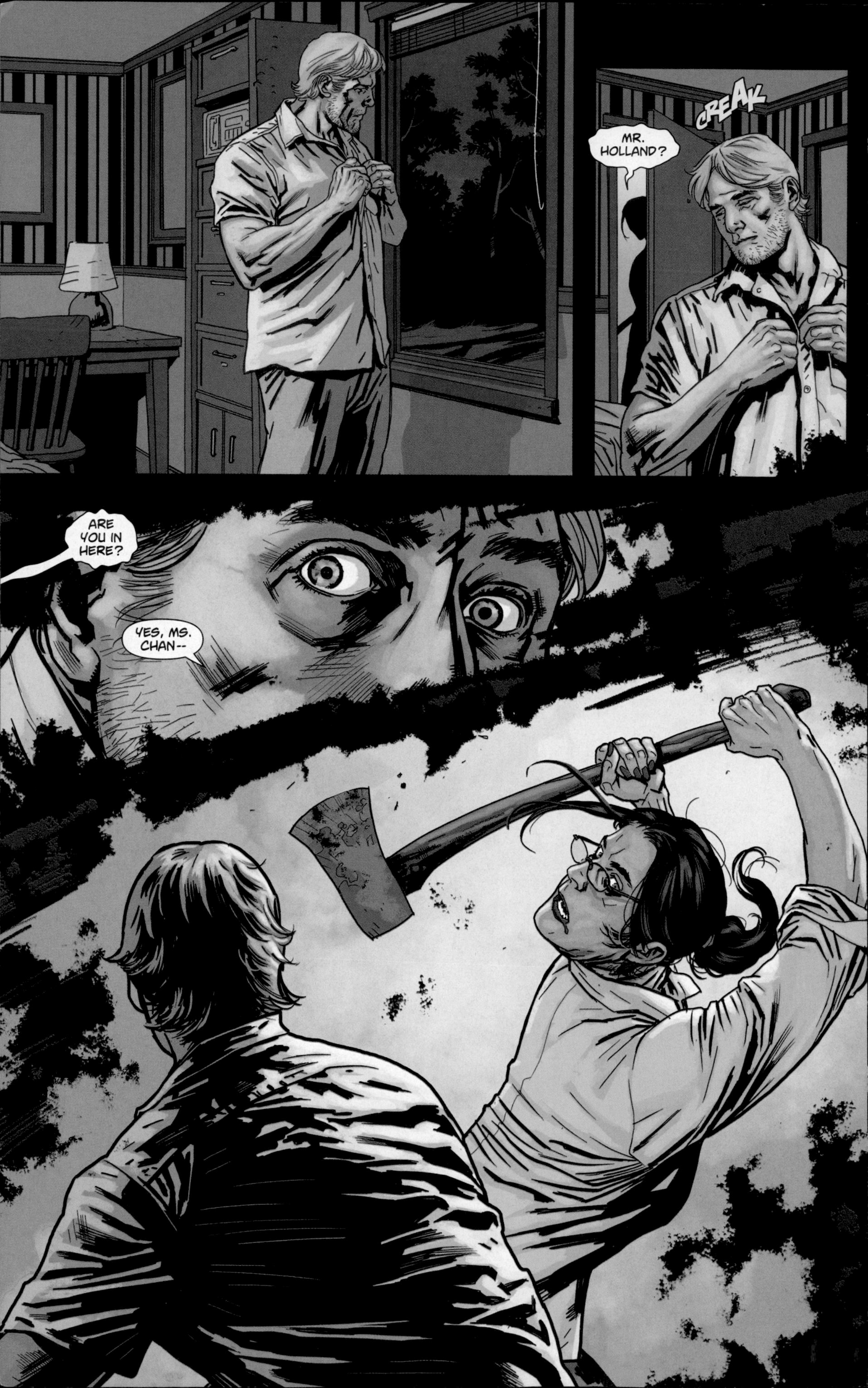
CREAK
MR. HOLLAND?
ARE YOU IN HERE?
YES, MS. CHAN--

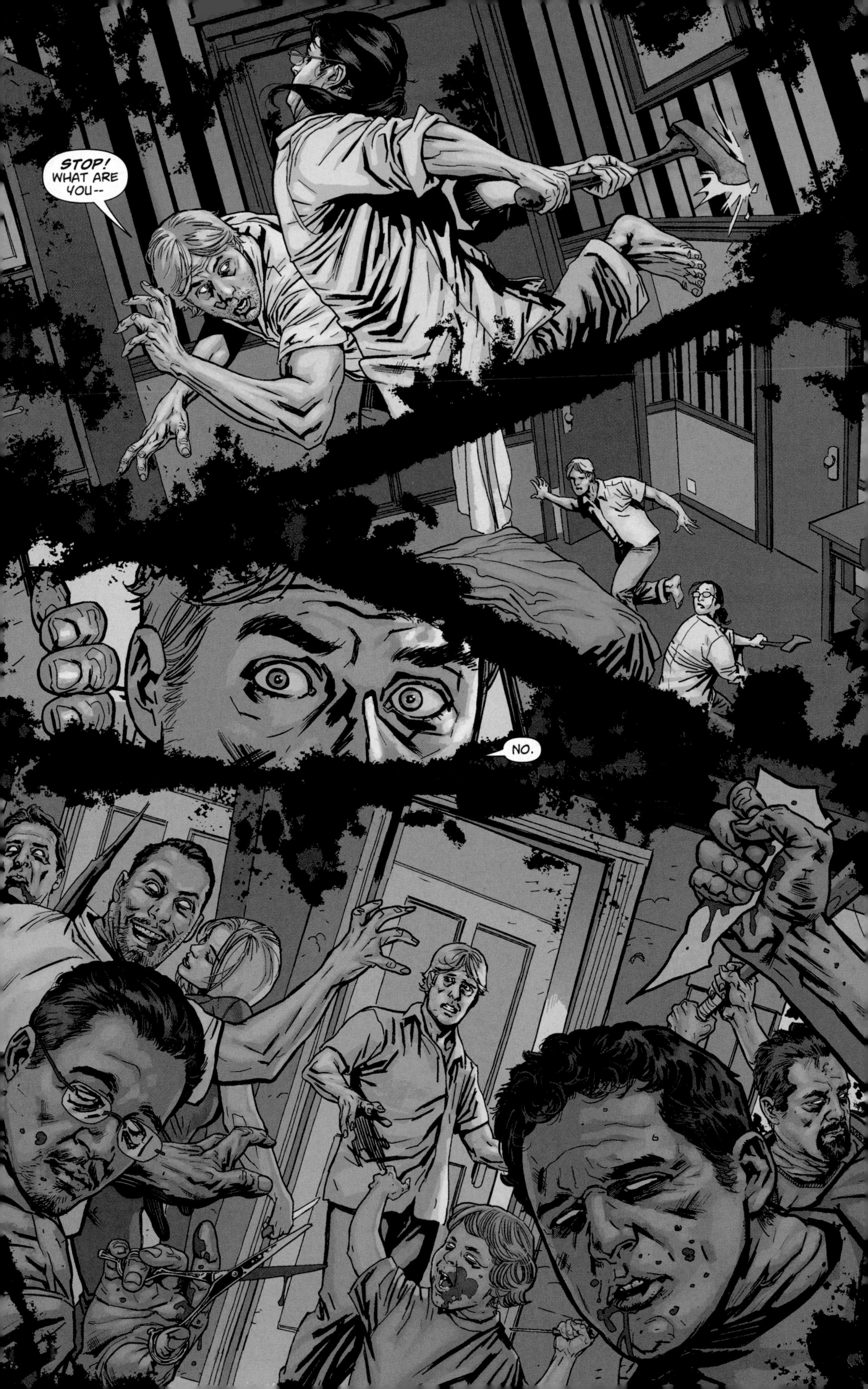
STOP! WHAT ARE YOU--
NO.

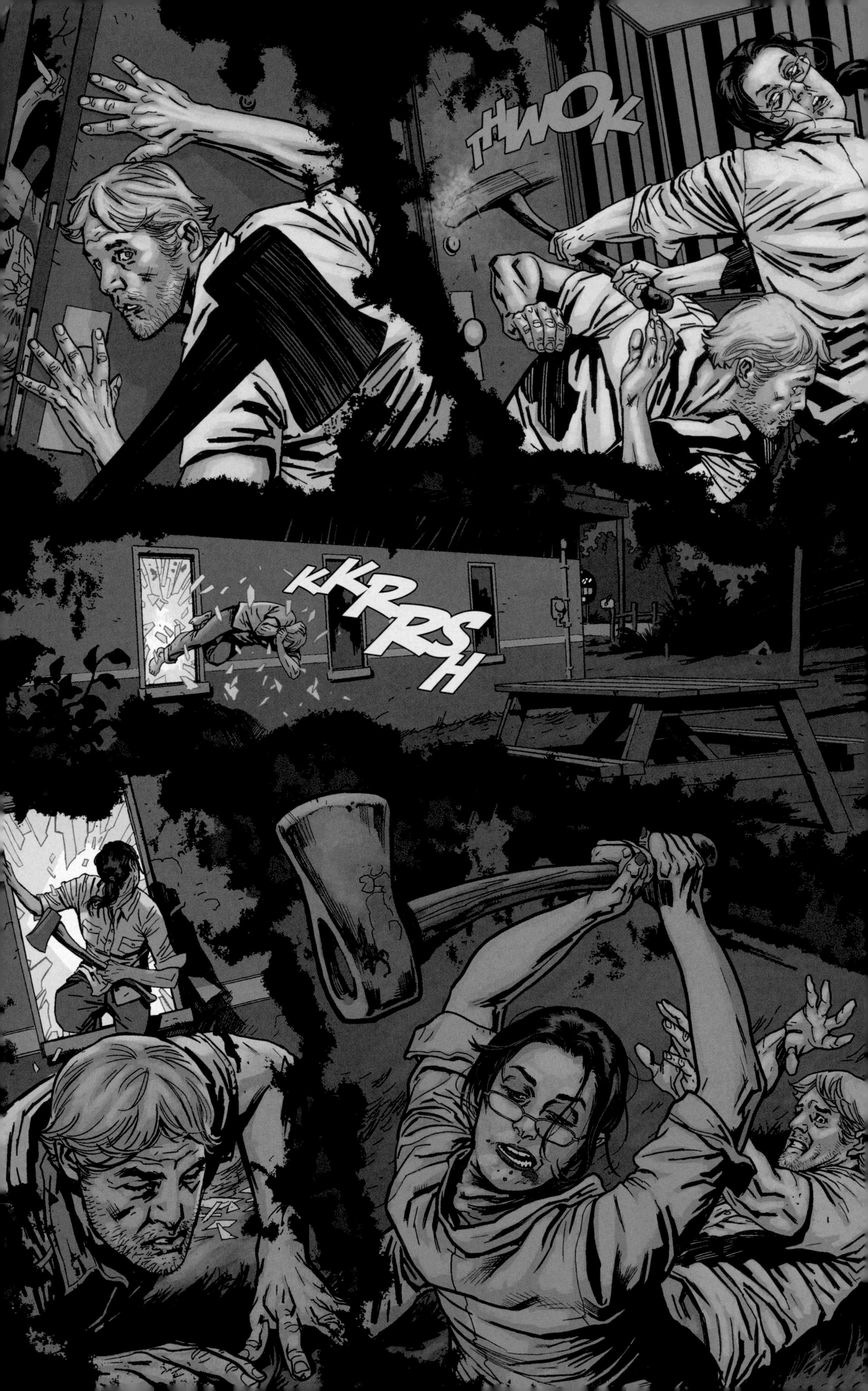
THWOK
KKRRSH

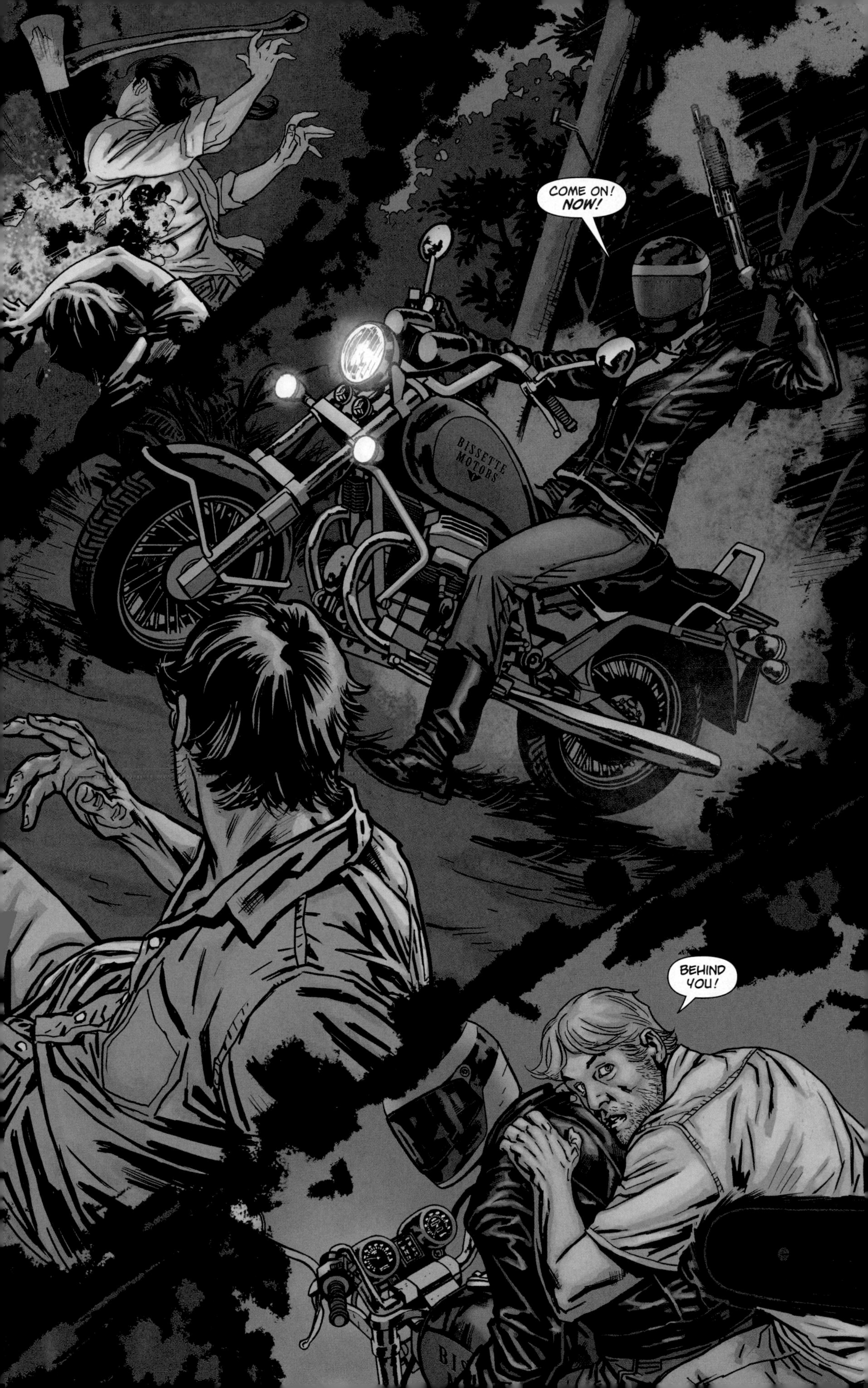
COME ON! NOW!
BISSETTE MOTORS
BEHIND YOU!

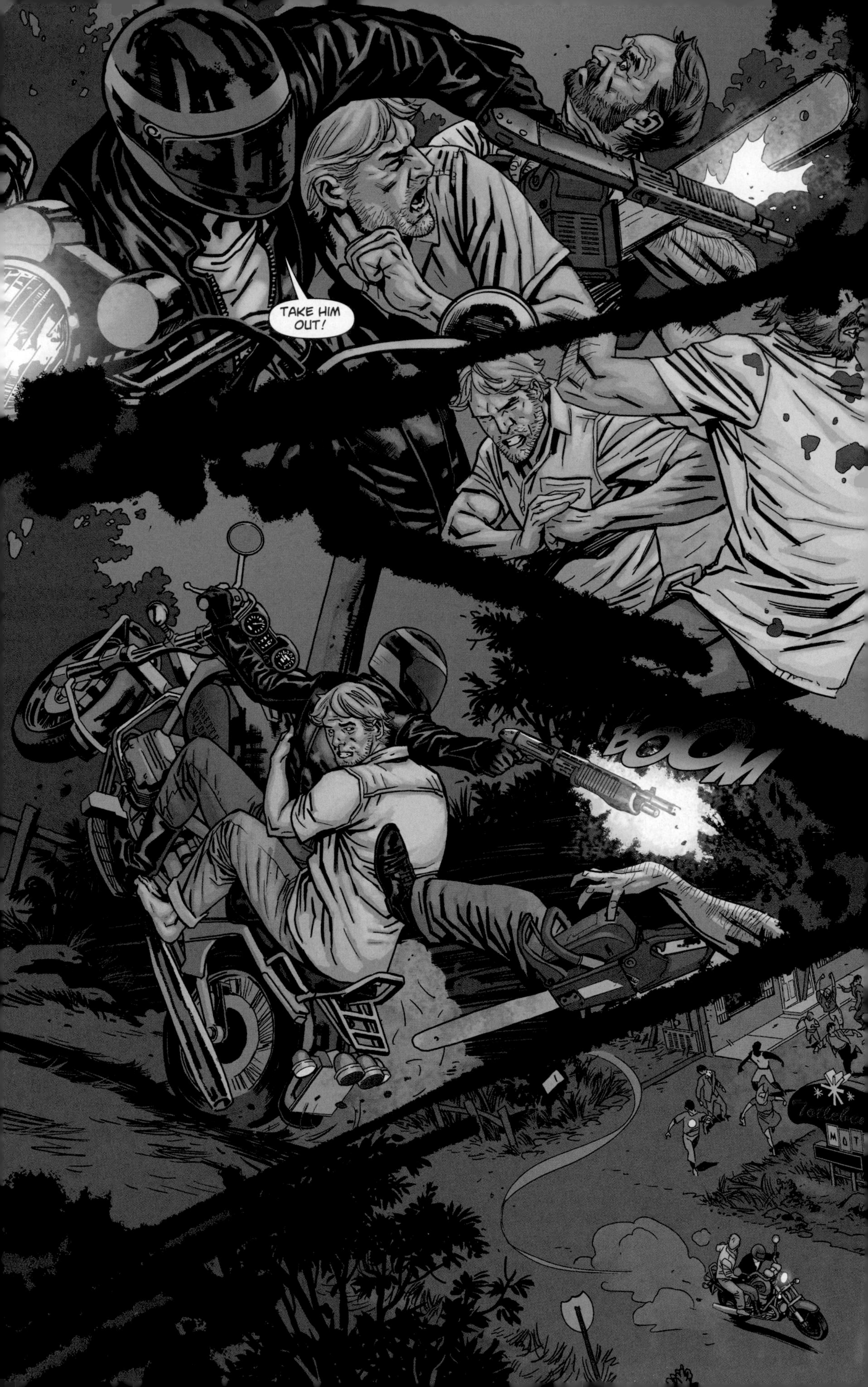
TAKE HIM OUT!
BOOM

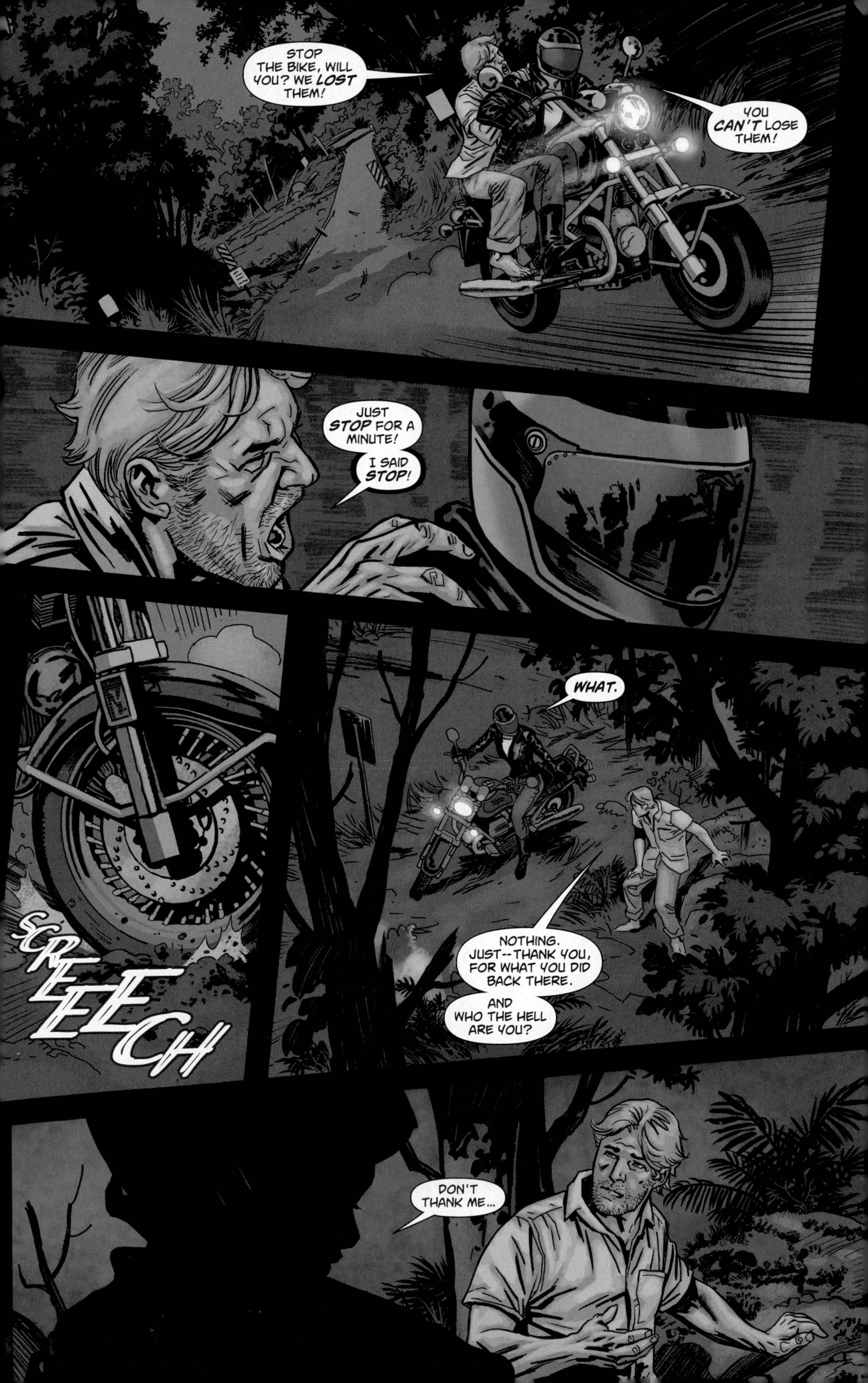
STOP THE BIKE, WILL YOU? WE LOST THEM!
YOU CAN'T LOSE THEM!
JUST STOP FOR A MINUTE!
I SAID STOP!
SCREEECH
WHAT.
NOTHING. JUST--THANK YOU, FOR WHAT YOU DID BACK THERE.
AND WHO THE HELL ARE YOU?
DON'T THANK ME...

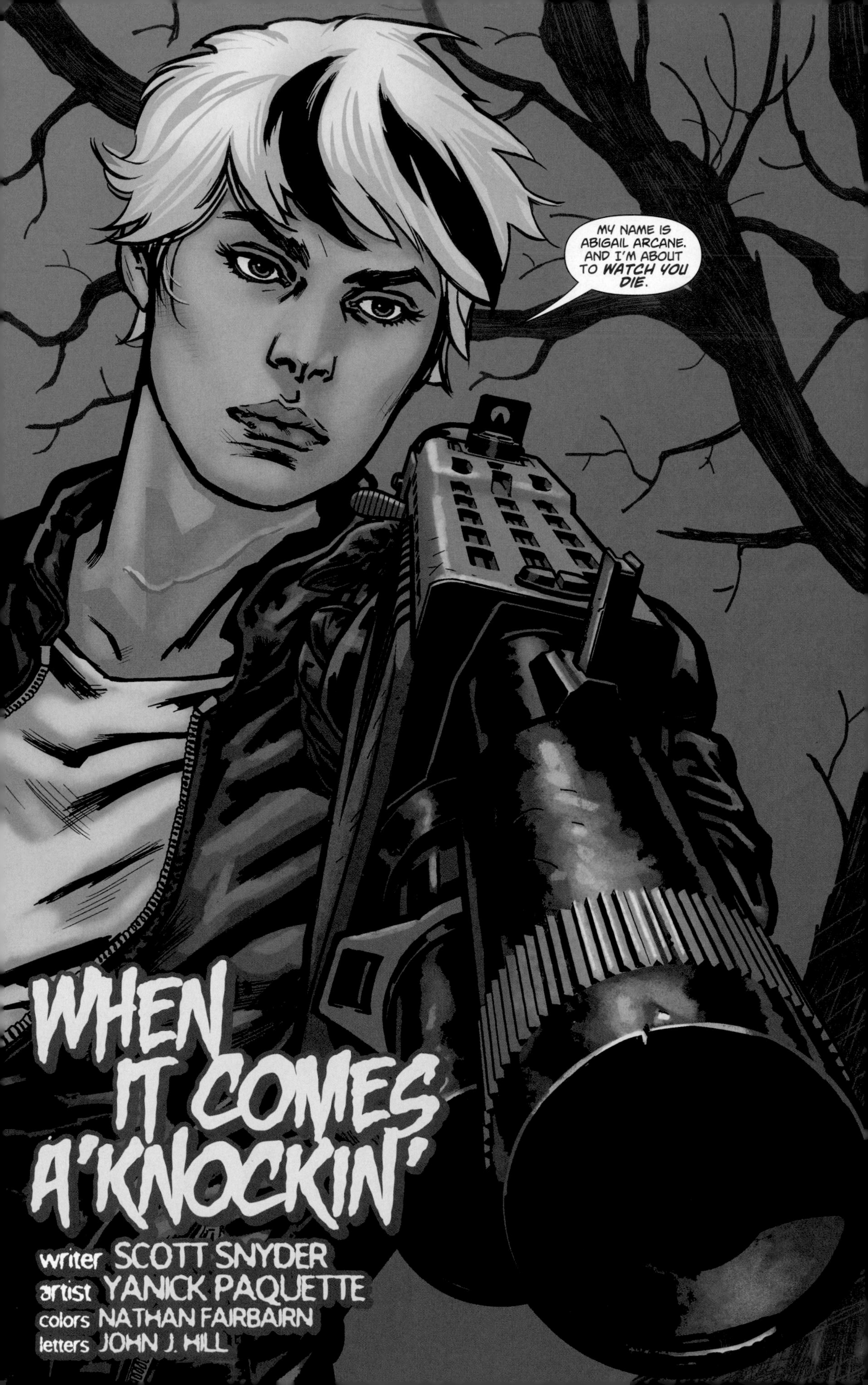
MY NAME IS ABIGAIL ARCANE. AND I'M ABOUT TO WATCH YOU DIE.
WHEN IT COMES A'KNOCKIN'
writer SCOTT SNYDER
artist YANICK PAQUETTE
colors NATHAN FAIRBAIRN
letters JOHN J. HILL

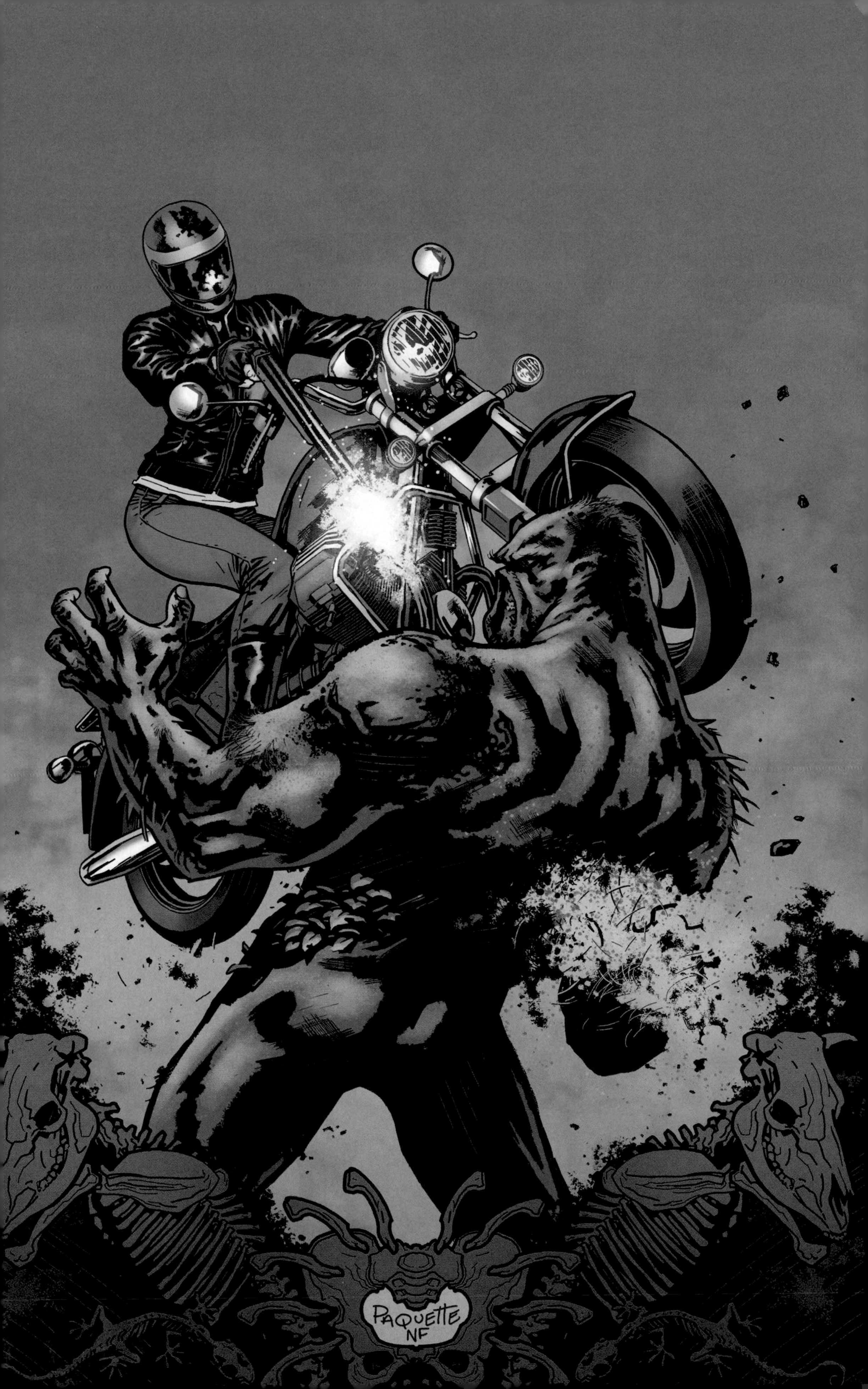
PAQUETTE
NF

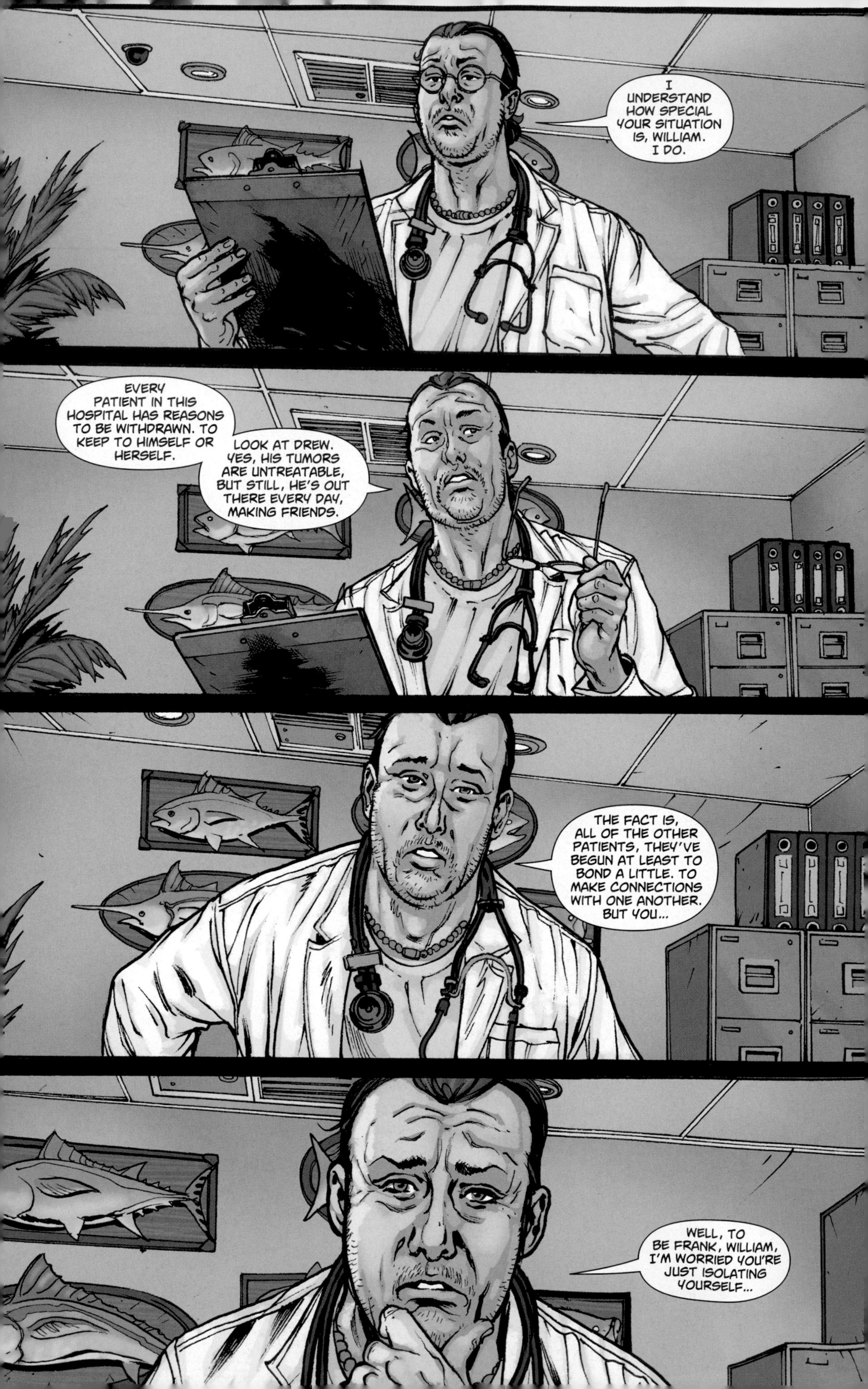
I UNDERSTAND HOW SPECIAL YOUR SITUATION IS, WILLIAM. I DO.
EVERY PATIENT IN THIS HOSPITAL HAS REASONS TO BE WITHDRAWN. TO KEEP TO HIMSELF OR HERSELF.
LOOK AT DREW. YES, HIS TUMORS ARE UNTREATABLE, BUT STILL, HE'S OUT THERE EVERY DAY, MAKING FRIENDS.
THE FACT IS, ALL OF THE OTHER PATIENTS, THEY'VE BEGUN AT LEAST TO BOND A LITTLE. TO MAKE CONNECTIONS WITH ONE ANOTHER. BUT YOU...
WELL, TO BE FRANK, WILLIAM, I'M WORRIED YOU'RE JUST ISOLATING YOURSELF...

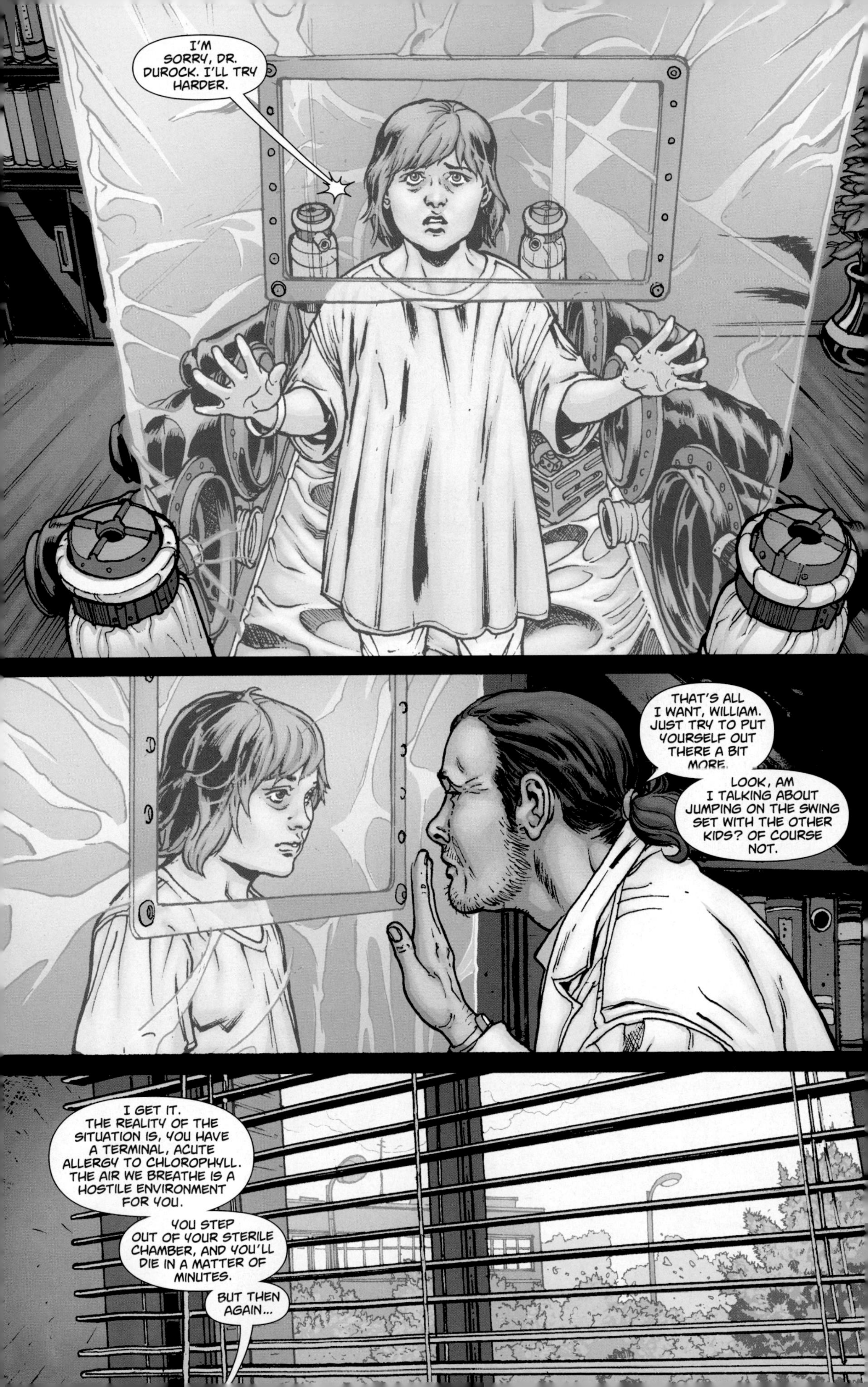
I'M SORRY, DR. DUROCK. I'LL TRY HARDER.
THAT'S ALL I WANT, WILLIAM. JUST TRY TO PUT YOURSELF OUT THERE A BIT MORE.
LOOK, AM I TALKING ABOUT JUMPING ON THE SWING SET WITH THE OTHER KIDS? OF COURSE NOT.
I GET IT. THE REALITY OF THE SITUATION IS, YOU HAVE A TERMINAL, ACUTE ALLERGY TO CHLOROPHYLL. THE AIR WE BREATHE IS A HOSTILE ENVIRONMENT FOR YOU.
YOU STEP OUT OF YOUR STERILE CHAMBER, AND YOU'LL DIE IN A MATTER OF MINUTES.
BUT THEN AGAIN...

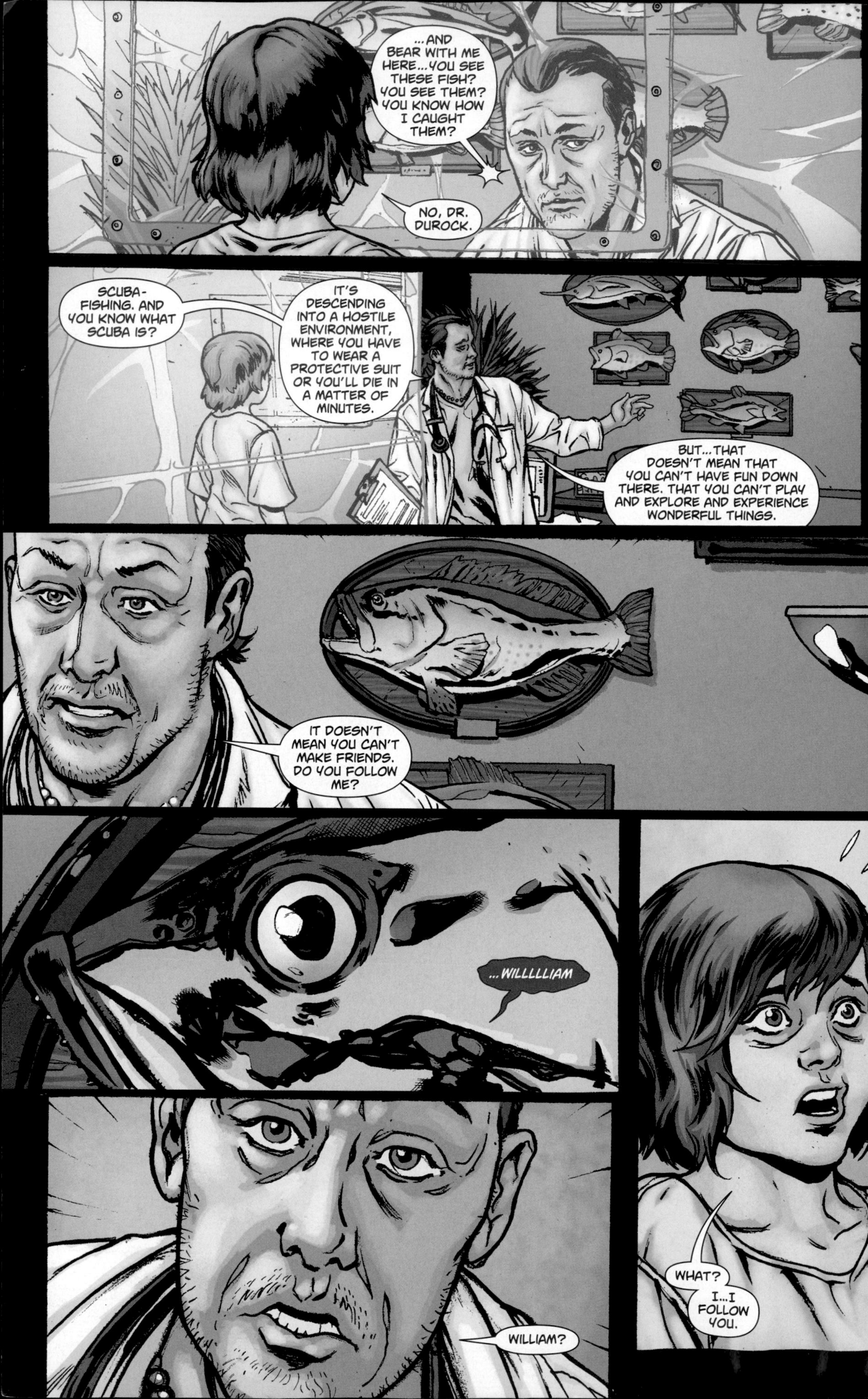

...AND BEAR WITH ME HERE...YOU SEE THESE FISH? YOU SEE THEM? YOU KNOW HOW I CAUGHT THEM?
NO, DR. DUROCK.
SCUBA-FISHING. AND YOU KNOW WHAT SCUBA IS?
IT'S DESCENDING INTO A HOSTILE ENVIRONMENT, WHERE YOU HAVE TO WEAR A PROTECTIVE SUIT OR YOU'LL DIE IN A MATTER OF MINUTES.
BUT...THAT DOESN'T MEAN THAT YOU CAN'T HAVE FUN DOWN THERE. THAT YOU CAN'T PLAY AND EXPLORE AND EXPERIENCE WONDERFUL THINGS.
IT DOESN'T MEAN YOU CAN'T MAKE FRIENDS. DO YOU FOLLOW ME?
...WILLLLLIAM
WILLIAM?
WHAT?
I...I FOLLOW YOU.

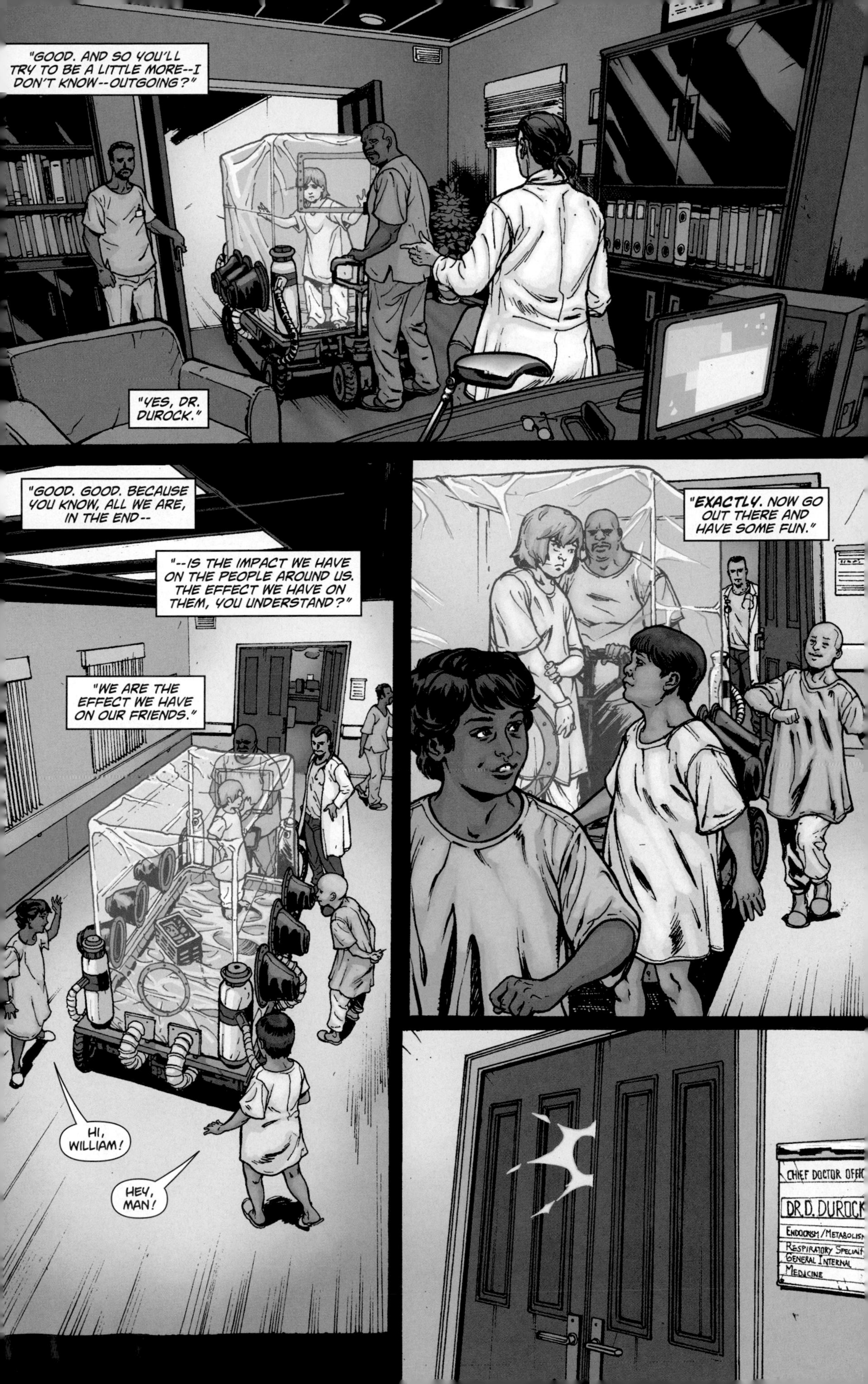
"GOOD. AND SO YOU'LL TRY TO BE A LITTLE MORE--I DON'T KNOW--OUTGOING?"
"YES, DR. DUROCK."
"GOOD. GOOD. BECAUSE YOU KNOW, ALL WE ARE, IN THE END--
"--IS THE IMPACT WE HAVE ON THE PEOPLE AROUND US. THE EFFECT WE HAVE ON THEM, YOU UNDERSTAND?"
"WE ARE THE EFFECT WE HAVE ON OUR FRIENDS."
HI, WILLIAM!
HEY, MAN!
"EXACTLY. NOW GO OUT THERE AND HAVE SOME FUN."
CHIEF DOCTOR OFFIC
DR. D. DUROCK
ENDOCRINISM / METABOLISM
RESPIRATORY SPECIALI
GENERAL INTERNAL MEDICINE

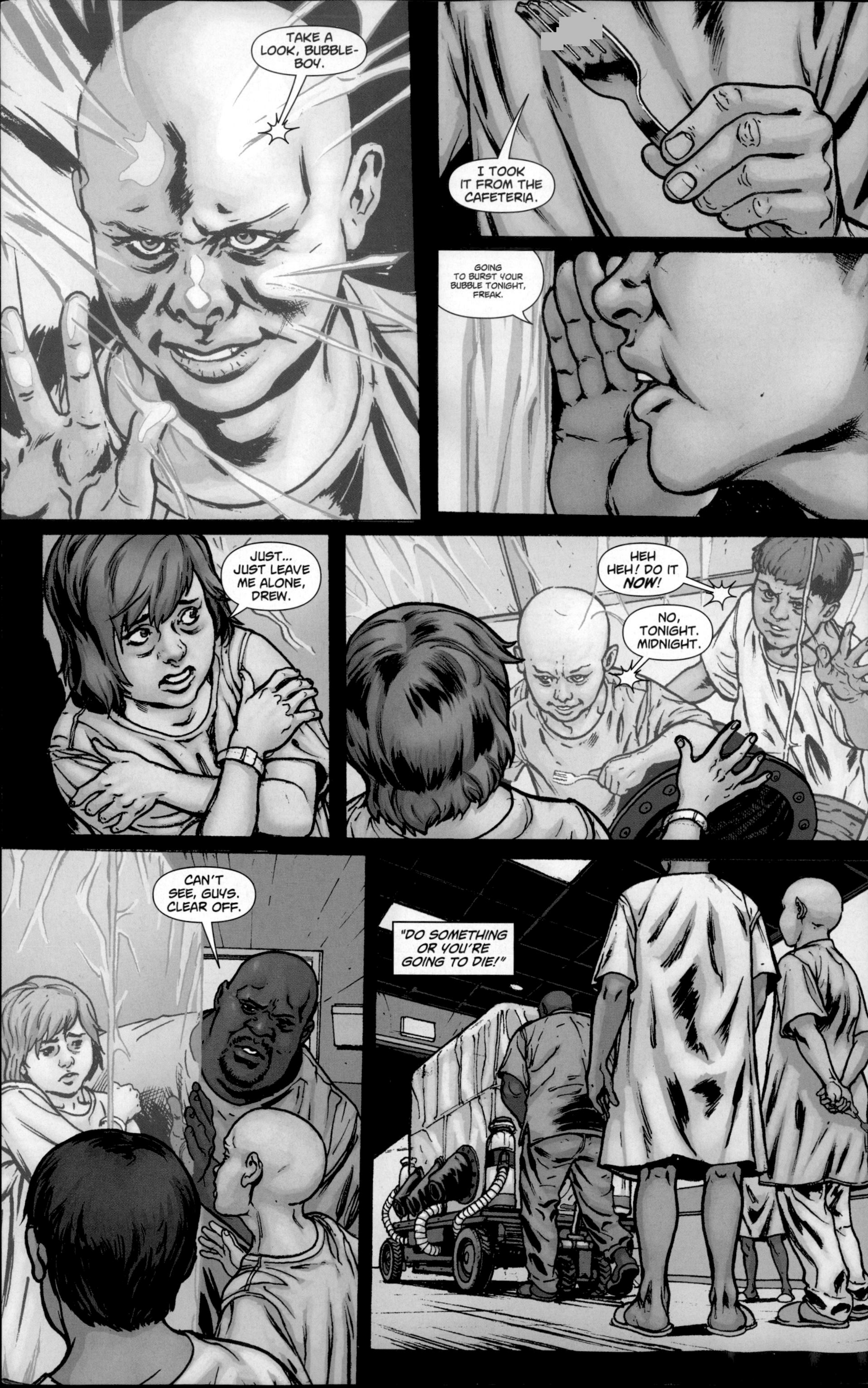
TAKE A LOOK, BUBBLE-BOY.
I TOOK IT FROM THE CAFETERIA.
GOING TO BURST YOUR BUBBLE TONIGHT, FREAK.
JUST... JUST LEAVE ME ALONE, DREW.
HEH HEH! DO IT *NOW*!
NO, TONIGHT. MIDNIGHT.
CAN'T SEE, GUYS. CLEAR OFF.
"DO SOMETHING OR YOU'RE GOING TO DIE!"

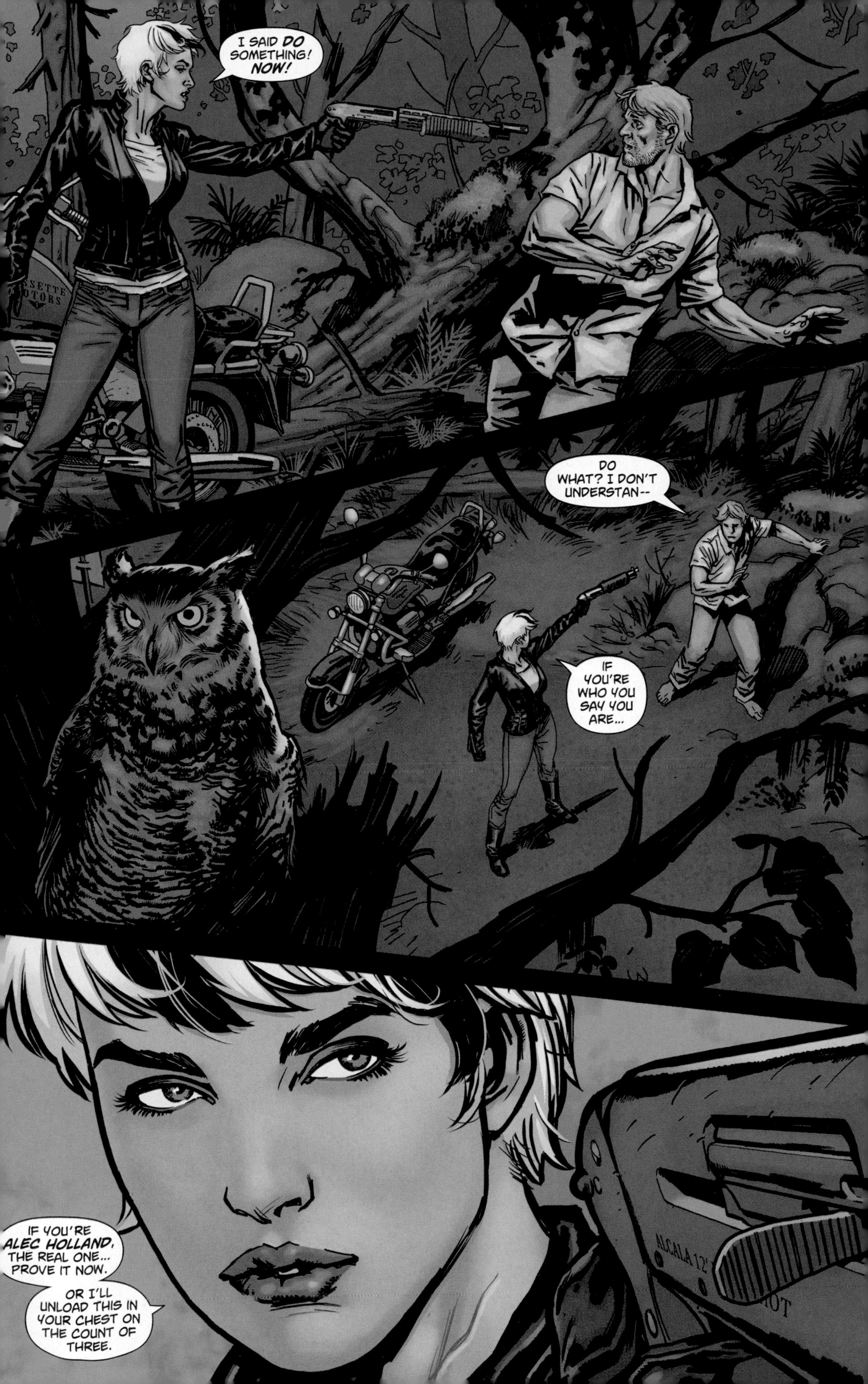
I SAID **DO** SOMETHING! **NOW!**
DO WHAT? I DON'T UNDERSTAN--
IF YOU'RE WHO YOU SAY YOU ARE...
IF YOU'RE ***ALEC HOLLAND***, THE REAL ONE... PROVE IT NOW.
OR I'LL UNLOAD THIS IN YOUR CHEST ON THE COUNT OF THREE.

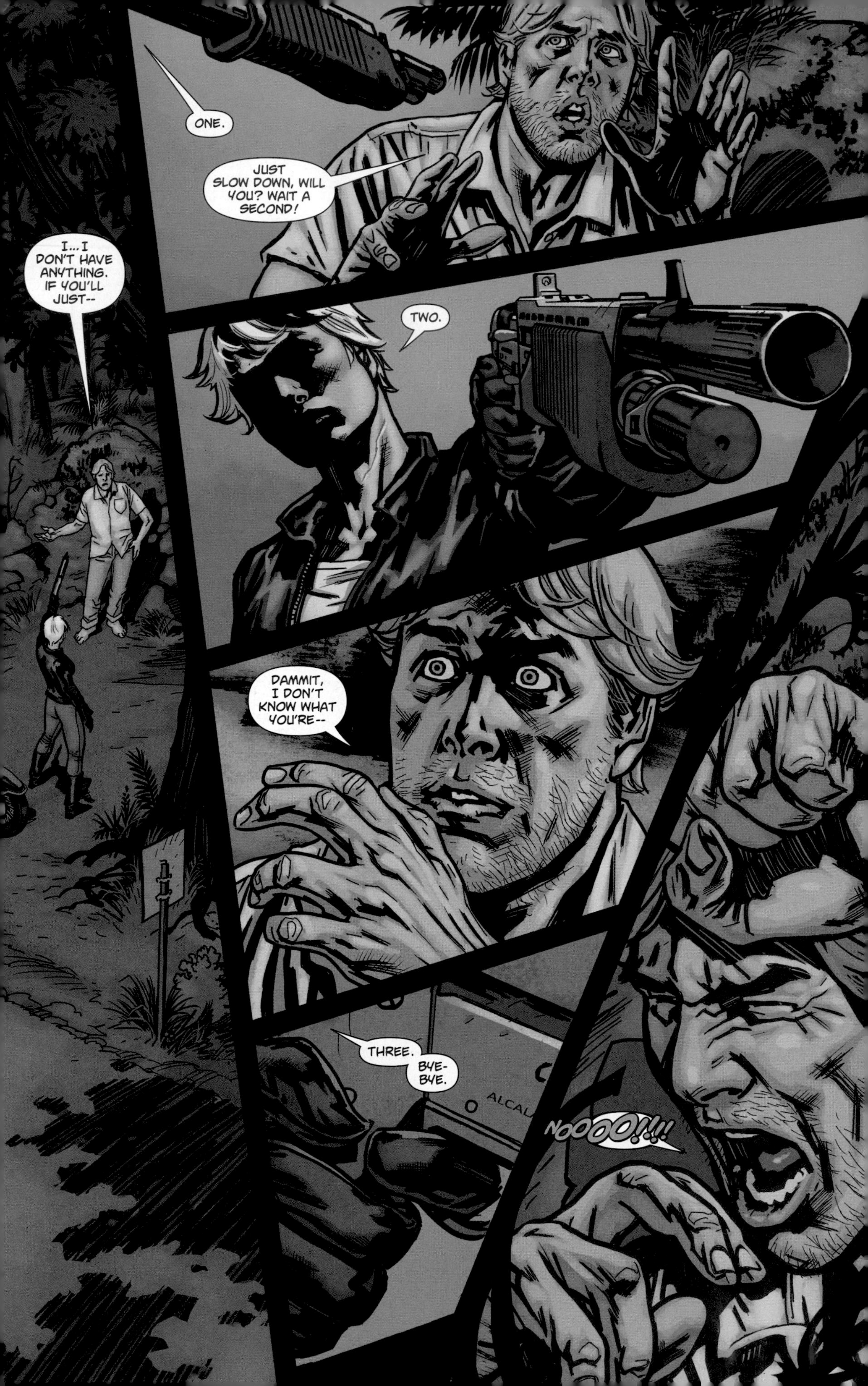
ONE.
JUST SLOW DOWN, WILL YOU? WAIT A SECOND!
I... I DON'T HAVE ANYTHING. IF YOU'LL JUST--
TWO.
DAMMIT, I DON'T KNOW WHAT YOU'RE--
THREE.
BYE-BYE.
NOOOO!!!!

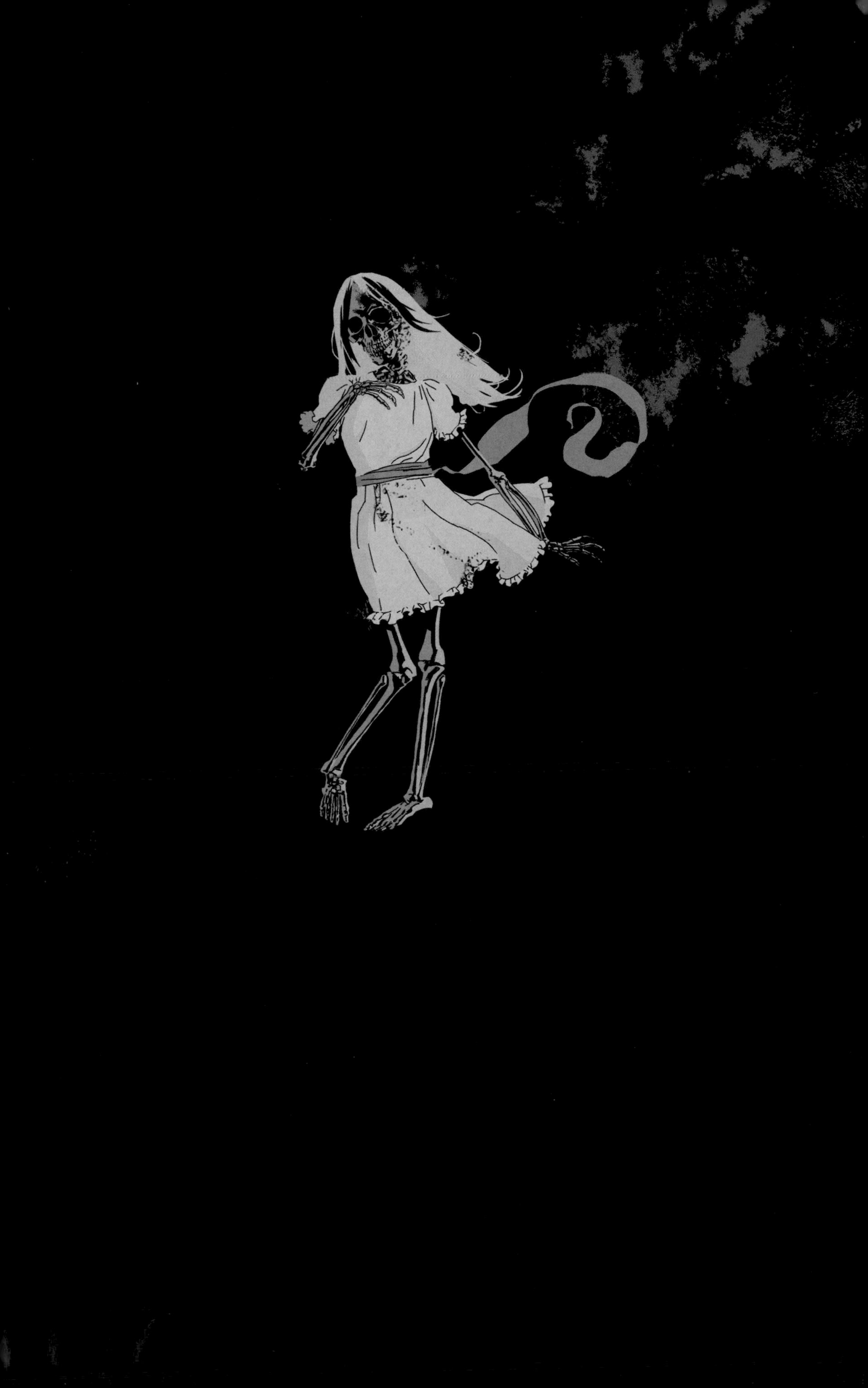

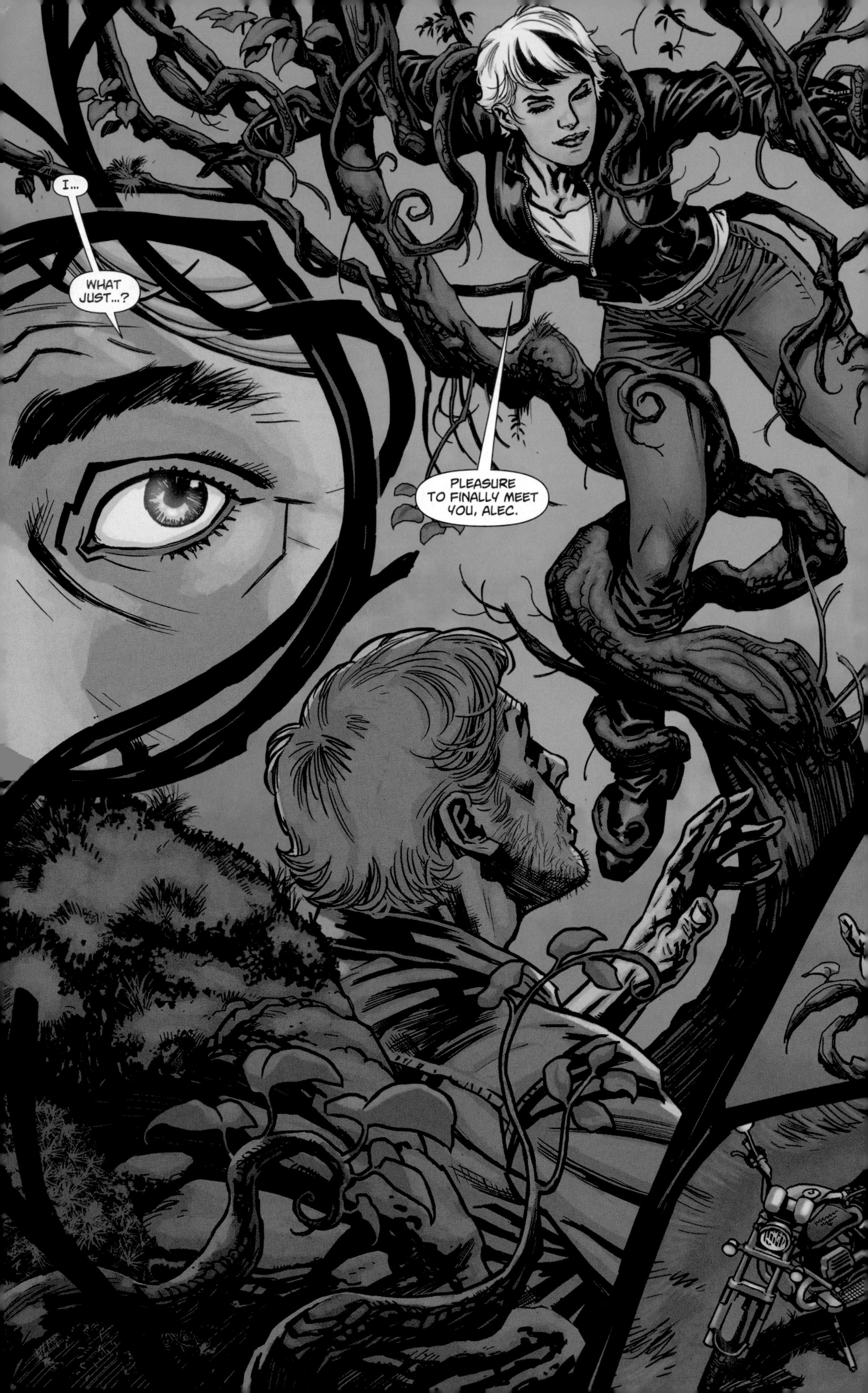
I...
WHAT JUST...?
PLEASURE TO FINALLY MEET YOU, ALEC.

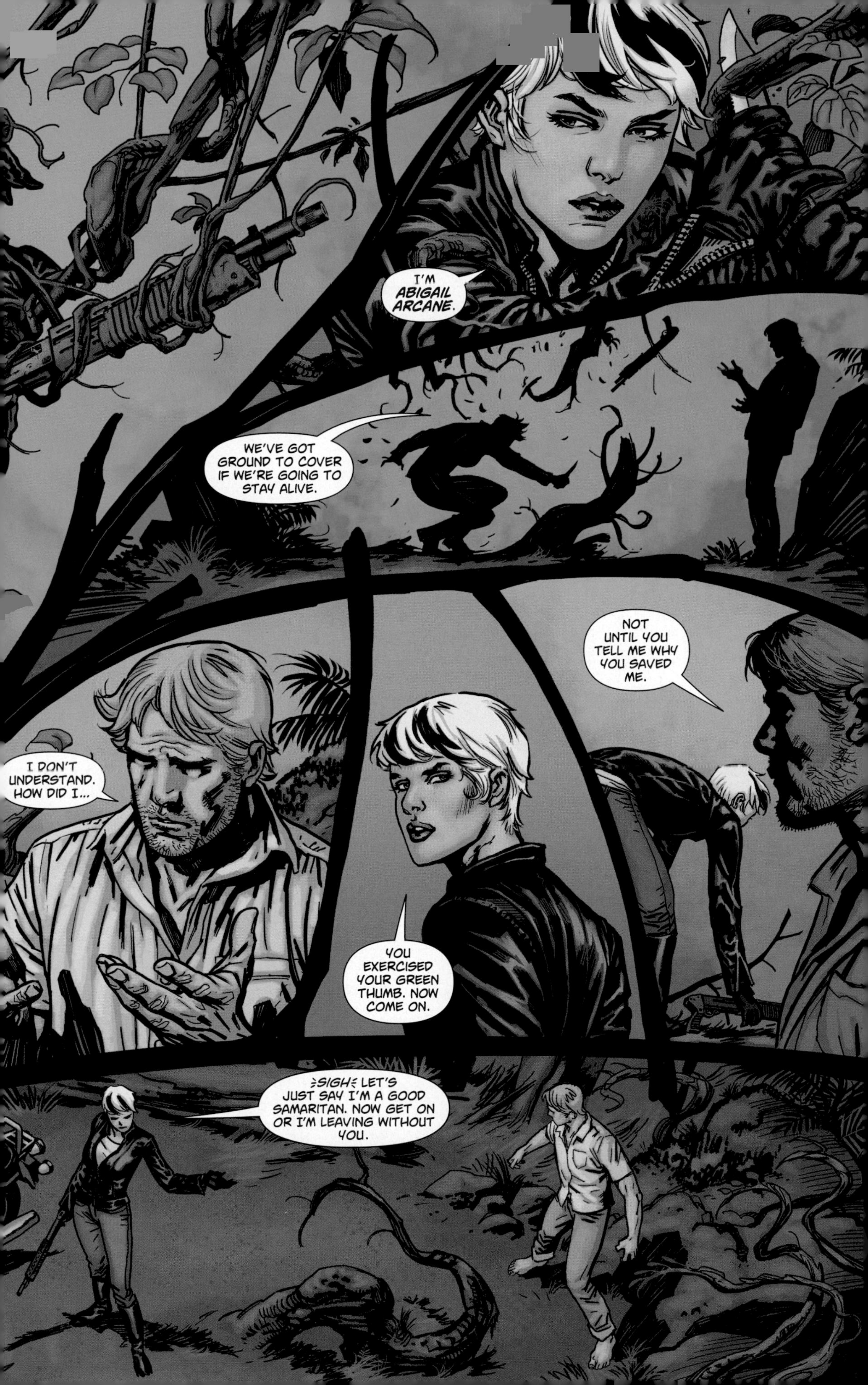
I'M ABIGAIL ARCANE.
WE'VE GOT GROUND TO COVER IF WE'RE GOING TO STAY ALIVE.
I DON'T UNDERSTAND. HOW DID I...
YOU EXERCISED YOUR GREEN THUMB. NOW COME ON.
NOT UNTIL YOU TELL ME WHY YOU SAVED ME.
SIGH LET'S JUST SAY I'M A GOOD SAMARITAN. NOW GET ON OR I'M LEAVING WITHOUT YOU.

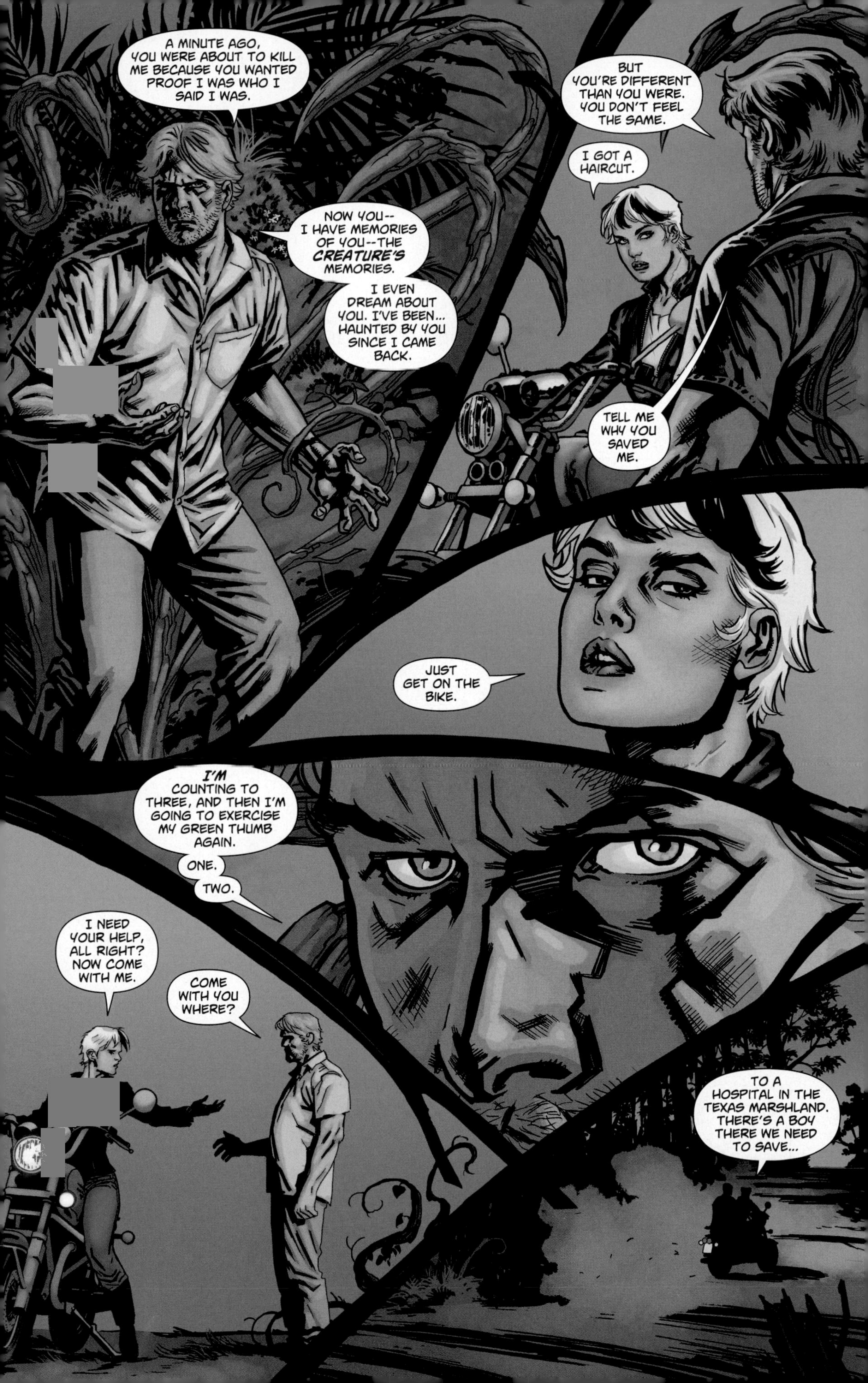
A MINUTE AGO, YOU WERE ABOUT TO KILL ME BECAUSE YOU WANTED PROOF I WAS WHO I SAID I WAS.
NOW YOU-- I HAVE MEMORIES OF YOU--THE CREATURE'S MEMORIES.
I EVEN DREAM ABOUT YOU. I'VE BEEN... HAUNTED BY YOU SINCE I CAME BACK.
BUT YOU'RE DIFFERENT THAN YOU WERE. YOU DON'T FEEL THE SAME.
I GOT A HAIRCUT.
TELL ME WHY YOU SAVED ME.
JUST GET ON THE BIKE.
I'M COUNTING TO THREE, AND THEN I'M GOING TO EXERCISE MY GREEN THUMB AGAIN.
ONE.
TWO.
I NEED YOUR HELP, ALL RIGHT? NOW COME WITH ME.
COME WITH YOU WHERE?
TO A HOSPITAL IN THE TEXAS MARSHLAND. THERE'S A BOY THERE WE NEED TO SAVE...

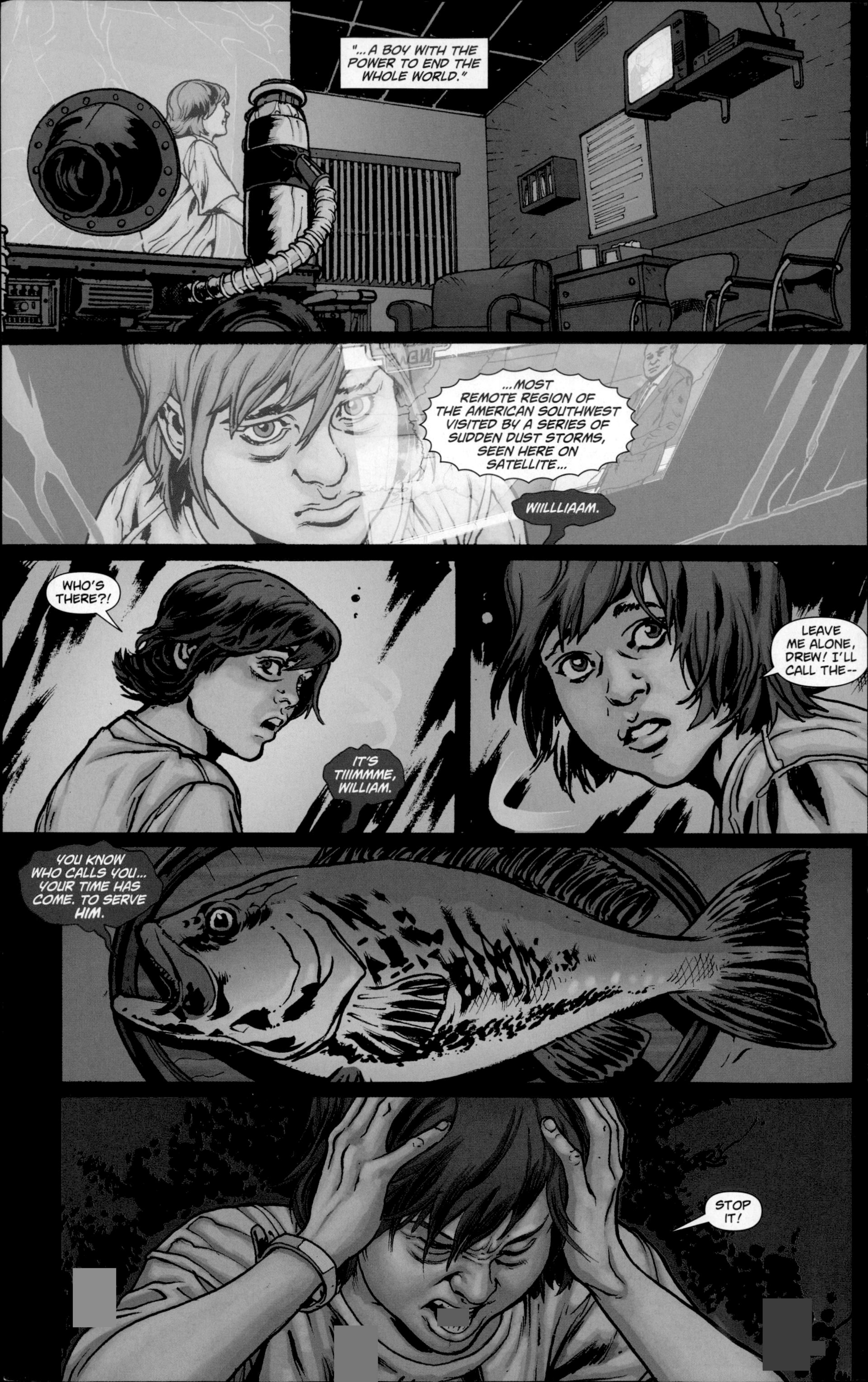
"...A BOY WITH THE POWER TO END THE WHOLE WORLD."
...MOST REMOTE REGION OF THE AMERICAN SOUTHWEST VISITED BY A SERIES OF SUDDEN DUST STORMS, SEEN HERE ON SATELLITE...
WIILLLIAAM.
WHO'S THERE?!
IT'S TIIIMMME, WILLIAM.
LEAVE ME ALONE, DREW! I'LL CALL THE--
YOU KNOW WHO CALLS YOU... YOUR TIME HAS COME. TO SERVE HIM.
STOP IT!

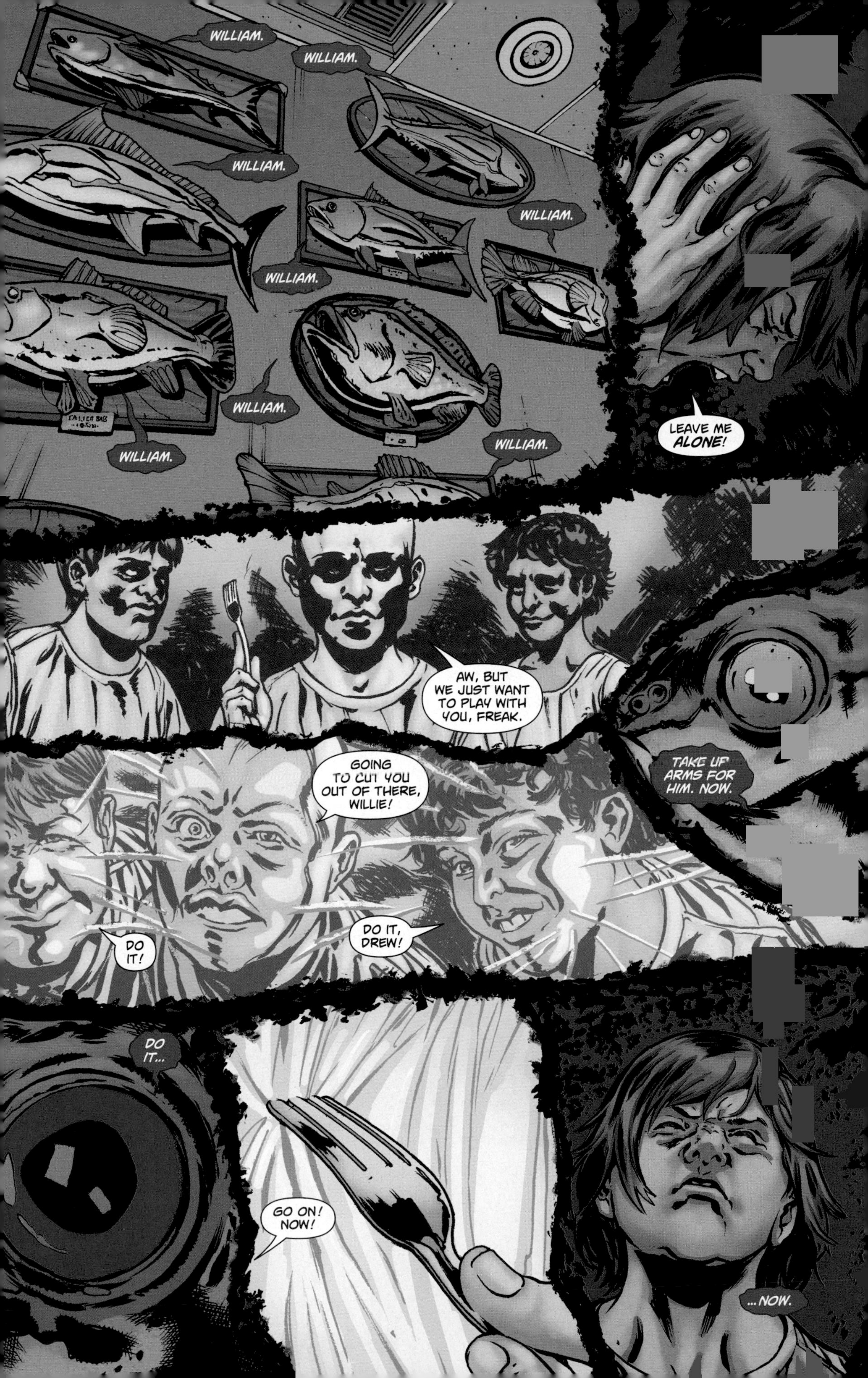
WILLIAM.
WILLIAM.
WILLIAM.
WILLIAM.
WILLIAM.
WILLIAM.
WILLIAM.
WILLIAM.
LEAVE ME ALONE!
AW, BUT WE JUST WANT TO PLAY WITH YOU, FREAK.
TAKE UP ARMS FOR HIM. NOW.
GOING TO CUT YOU OUT OF THERE, WILLIE!
DO IT!
DO IT, DREW!
DO IT...
GO ON! NOW!
...NOW.

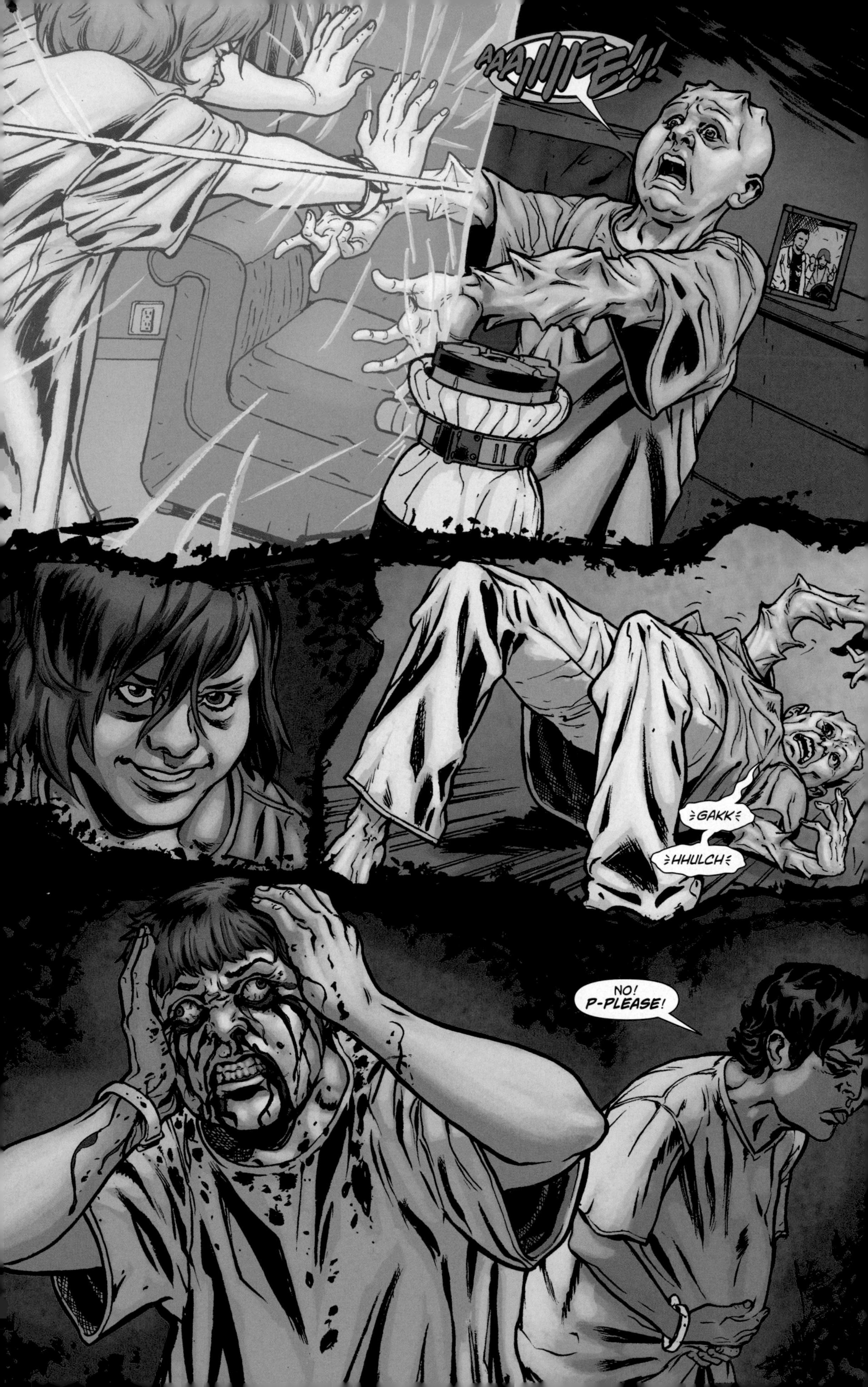
AAAIIIIEEE!!!
GAKK
HHULCH
NO! P-PLEASE!

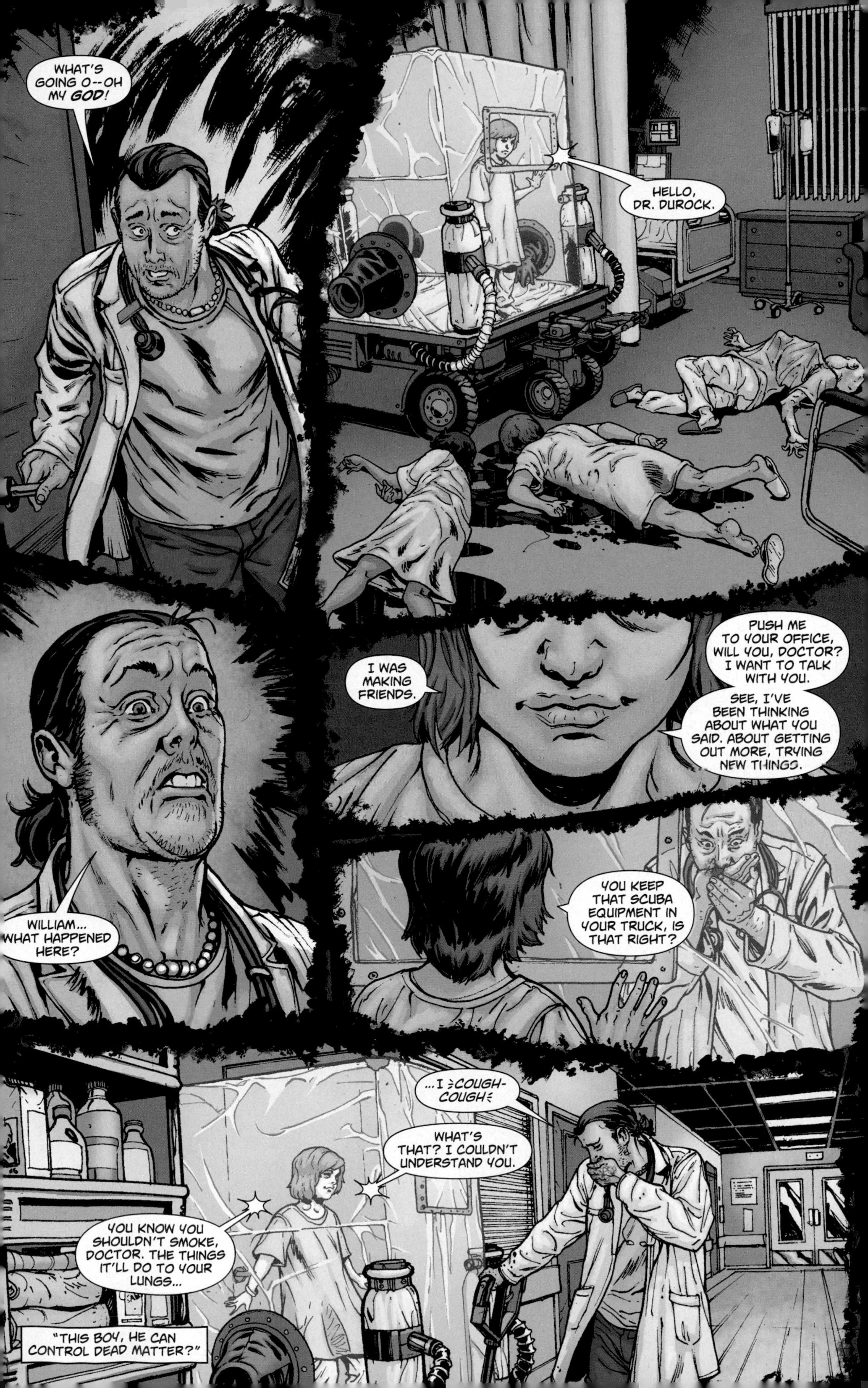
WHAT'S GOING O--OH MY *GOD*!
HELLO, DR. DUROCK.
WILLIAM... WHAT HAPPENED HERE?
I WAS MAKING FRIENDS.
PUSH ME TO YOUR OFFICE, WILL YOU, DOCTOR? I WANT TO TALK WITH YOU.
SEE, I'VE BEEN THINKING ABOUT WHAT YOU SAID. ABOUT GETTING OUT MORE, TRYING NEW THINGS.
YOU KEEP THAT SCUBA EQUIPMENT IN YOUR TRUCK, IS THAT RIGHT?
...I *COUGH-COUGH*
WHAT'S THAT? I COULDN'T UNDERSTAND YOU.
YOU KNOW YOU SHOULDN'T SMOKE, DOCTOR. THE THINGS IT'LL DO TO YOUR LUNGS...
"THIS BOY, HE CAN CONTROL DEAD MATTER?"

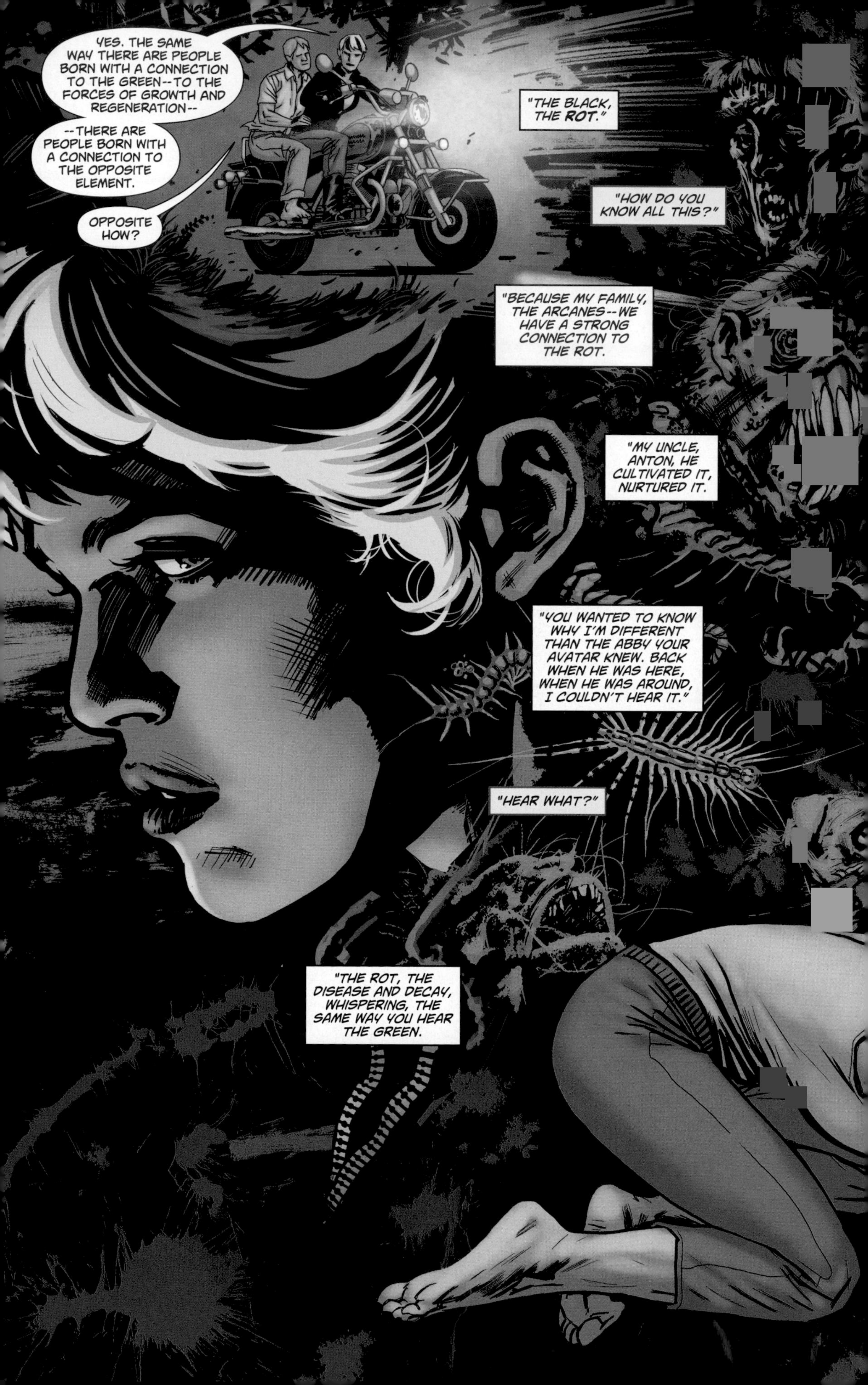
YES. THE SAME WAY THERE ARE PEOPLE BORN WITH A CONNECTION TO THE GREEN--TO THE FORCES OF GROWTH AND REGENERATION--
--THERE ARE PEOPLE BORN WITH A CONNECTION TO THE OPPOSITE ELEMENT.
OPPOSITE HOW?
"THE BLACK, THE ROT."
"HOW DO YOU KNOW ALL THIS?"
"BECAUSE MY FAMILY, THE ARCANES--WE HAVE A STRONG CONNECTION TO THE ROT.
"MY UNCLE, ANTON, HE CULTIVATED IT, NURTURED IT.
"YOU WANTED TO KNOW WHY I'M DIFFERENT THAN THE ABBY YOUR AVATAR KNEW. BACK WHEN HE WAS HERE, WHEN HE WAS AROUND, I COULDN'T HEAR IT."
"HEAR WHAT?"
"THE ROT, THE DISEASE AND DECAY, WHISPERING, THE SAME WAY YOU HEAR THE GREEN.

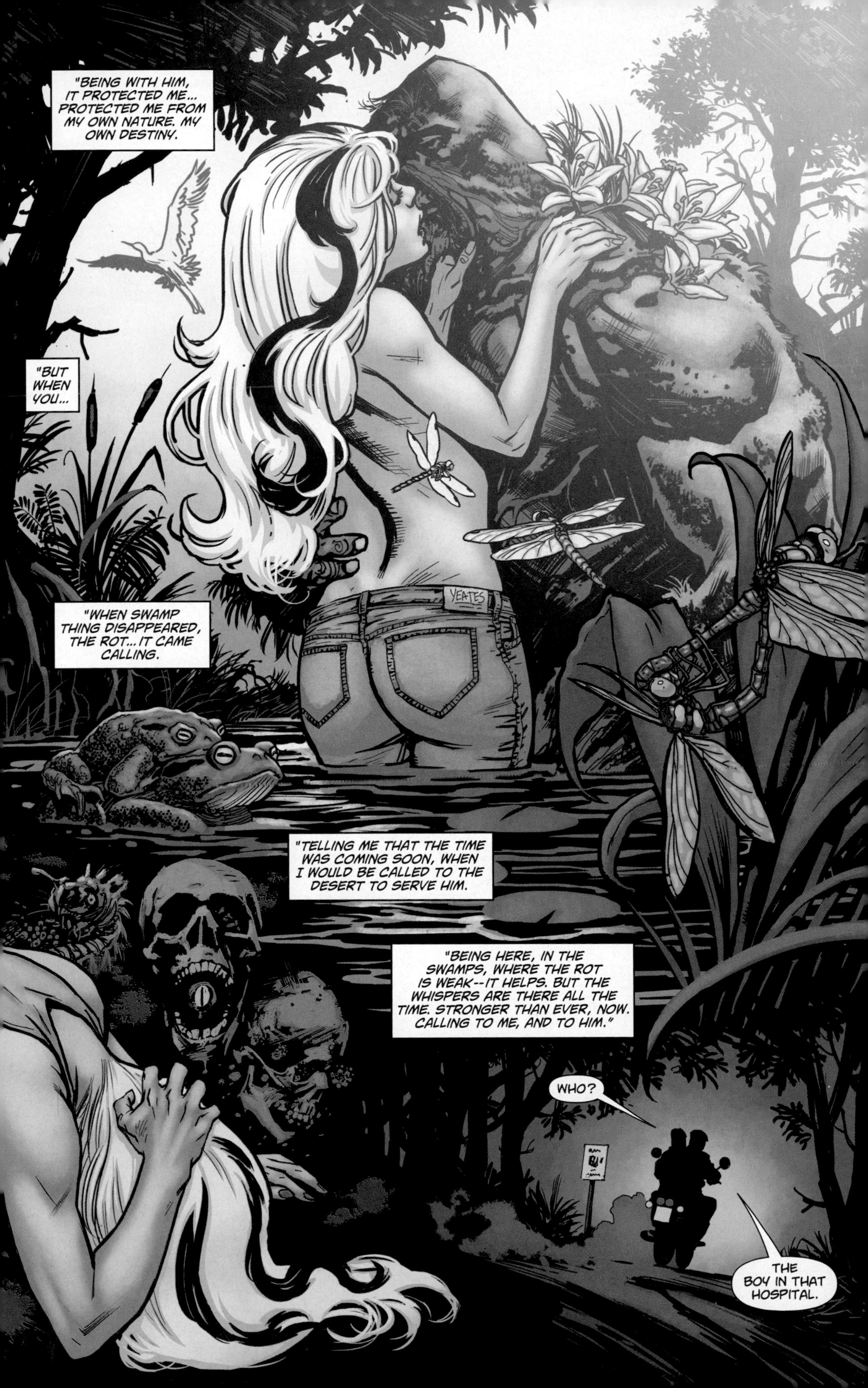
"BEING WITH HIM, IT PROTECTED ME... PROTECTED ME FROM MY OWN NATURE. MY OWN DESTINY.
"BUT WHEN YOU...
"WHEN SWAMP THING DISAPPEARED, THE ROT... IT CAME CALLING.
"TELLING ME THAT THE TIME WAS COMING SOON, WHEN I WOULD BE CALLED TO THE DESERT TO SERVE HIM.
"BEING HERE, IN THE SWAMPS, WHERE THE ROT IS WEAK--IT HELPS. BUT THE WHISPERS ARE THERE ALL THE TIME. STRONGER THAN EVER, NOW. CALLING TO ME, AND TO HIM."
WHO?
THE BOY IN THAT HOSPITAL.
YEATES

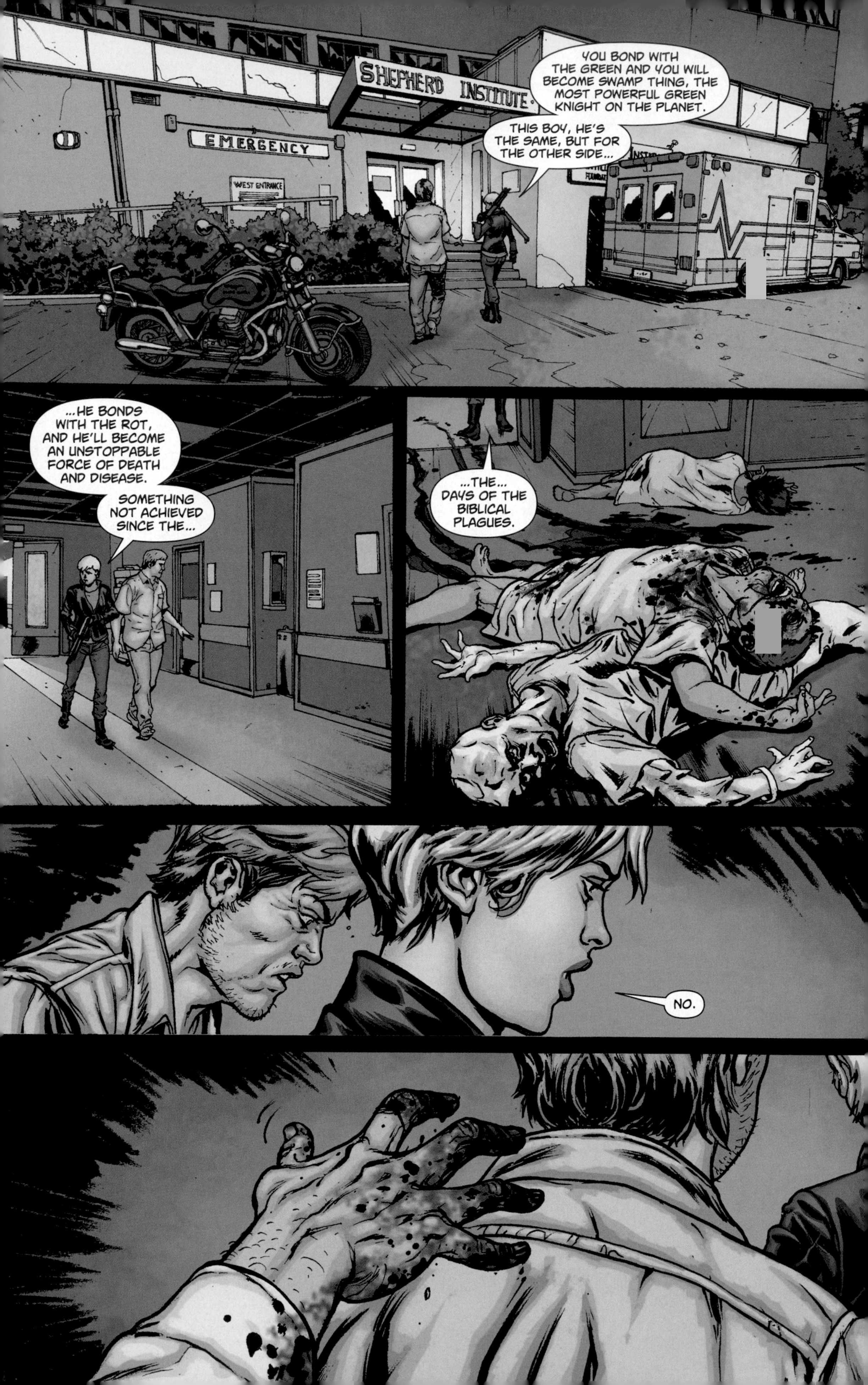
SHEPHERD INSTITUTE
EMERGENCY
WEST ENTRANCE
YOU BOND WITH THE GREEN AND YOU WILL BECOME SWAMP THING, THE MOST POWERFUL GREEN KNIGHT ON THE PLANET.
THIS BOY, HE'S THE SAME, BUT FOR THE OTHER SIDE...
...HE BONDS WITH THE ROT, AND HE'LL BECOME AN UNSTOPPABLE FORCE OF DEATH AND DISEASE.
SOMETHING NOT ACHIEVED SINCE THE...
...THE... DAYS OF THE BIBLICAL PLAGUES.
NO.

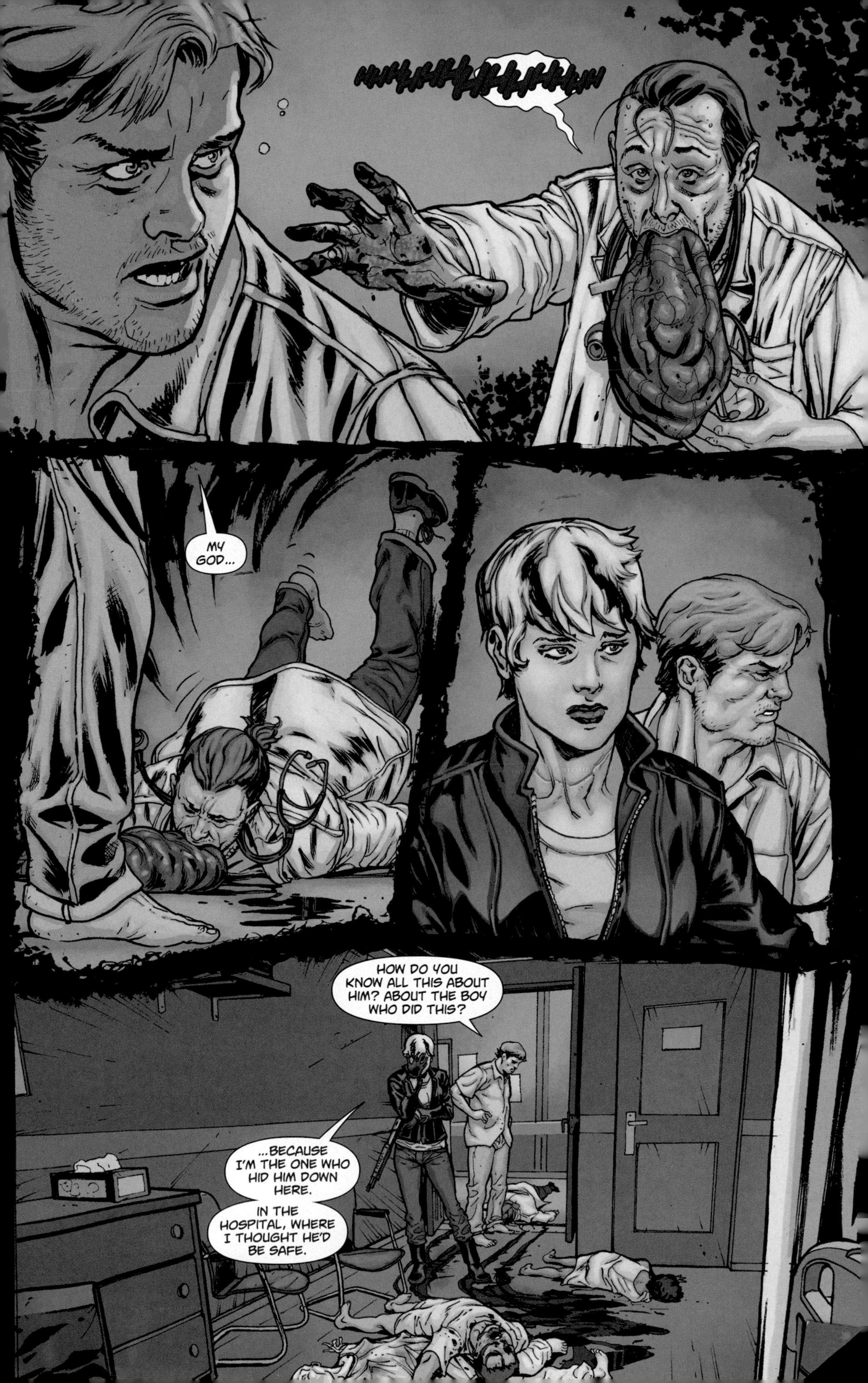
HUHLHHHHHHHHHHHHHHH
MY GOD...
HOW DO YOU KNOW ALL THIS ABOUT HIM? ABOUT THE BOY WHO DID THIS?
...BECAUSE I'M THE ONE WHO HID HIM DOWN HERE.
IN THE HOSPITAL, WHERE I THOUGHT HE'D BE SAFE.

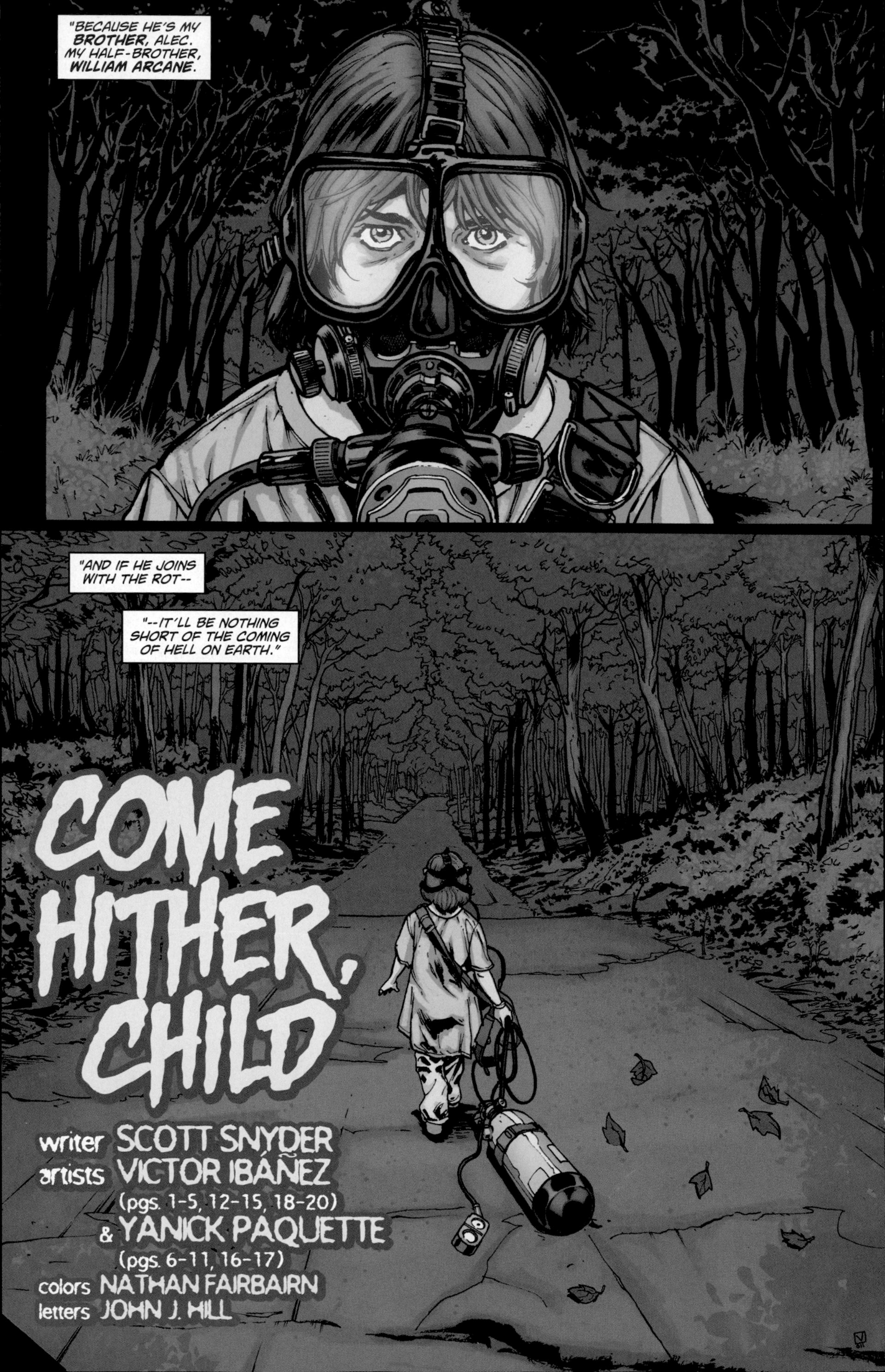
"BECAUSE HE'S MY BROTHER, ALEC. MY HALF-BROTHER, WILLIAM ARCANE.
"AND IF HE JOINS WITH THE ROT--
"--IT'LL BE NOTHING SHORT OF THE COMING OF HELL ON EARTH."
COME HITHER, CHILD
writer SCOTT SNYDER
artists VICTOR IBÁÑEZ (pgs. 1-5, 12-15, 18-20) & YANICK PAQUETTE (pgs. 6-11, 16-17)
colors NATHAN FAIRBAIRN
letters JOHN J. HILL

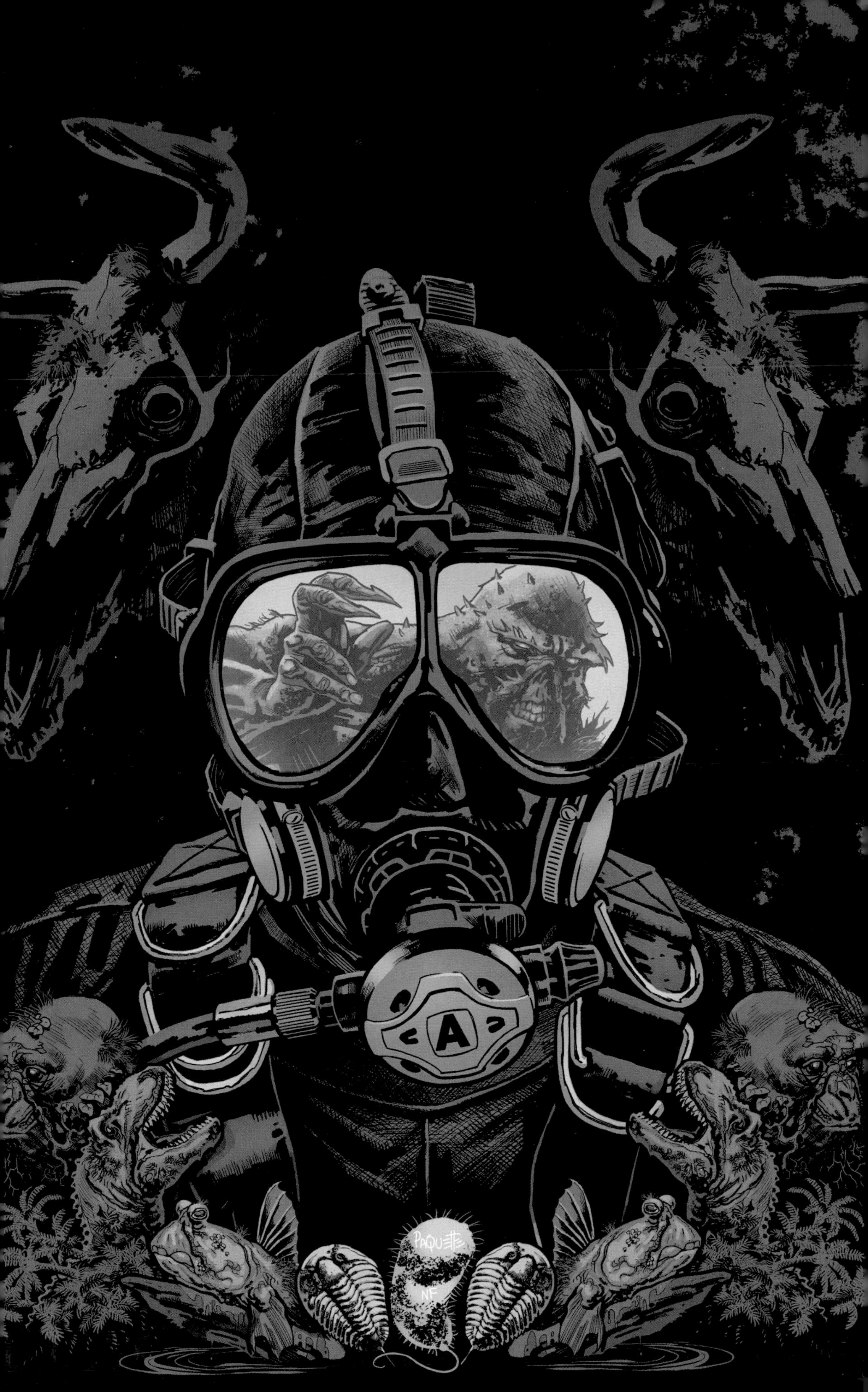
A
PAQUETTE
NF

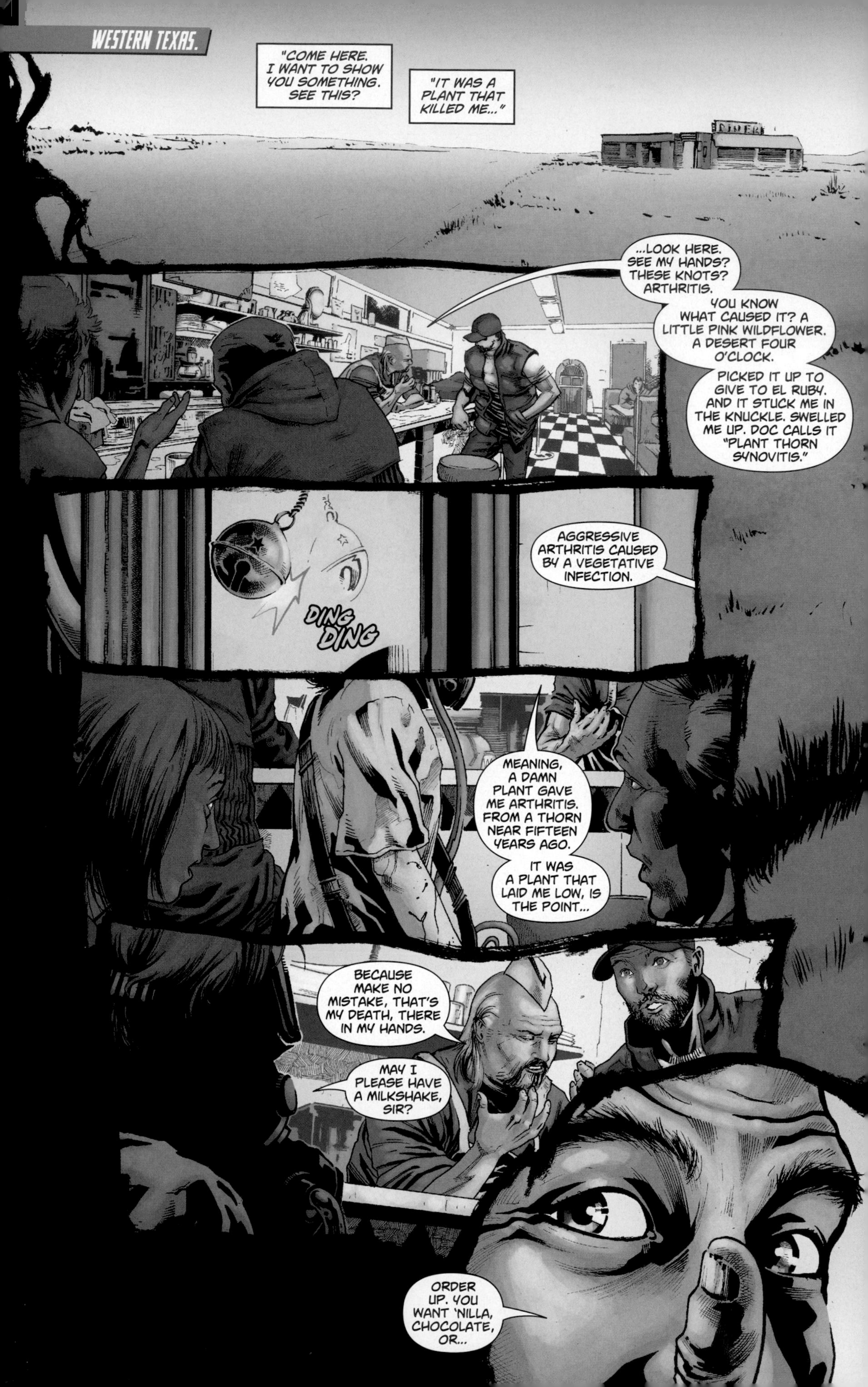
WESTERN TEXAS.
"COME HERE. I WANT TO SHOW YOU SOMETHING. SEE THIS?
"IT WAS A PLANT THAT KILLED ME..."
DINER
...LOOK HERE. SEE MY HANDS? THESE KNOTS? ARTHRITIS.
YOU KNOW WHAT CAUSED IT? A LITTLE PINK WILDFLOWER. A DESERT FOUR O'CLOCK.
PICKED IT UP TO GIVE TO EL RUBY. AND IT STUCK ME IN THE KNUCKLE. SWELLED ME UP. DOC CALLS IT "PLANT THORN SYNOVITIS."
AGGRESSIVE ARTHRITIS CAUSED BY A VEGETATIVE INFECTION.
DING DING
MEANING, A DAMN PLANT GAVE ME ARTHRITIS. FROM A THORN NEAR FIFTEEN YEARS AGO.
IT WAS A PLANT THAT LAID ME LOW, IS THE POINT...
BECAUSE MAKE NO MISTAKE, THAT'S MY DEATH, THERE IN MY HANDS.
MAY I PLEASE HAVE A MILKSHAKE, SIR?
ORDER UP. YOU WANT 'NILLA, CHOCOLATE, OR...

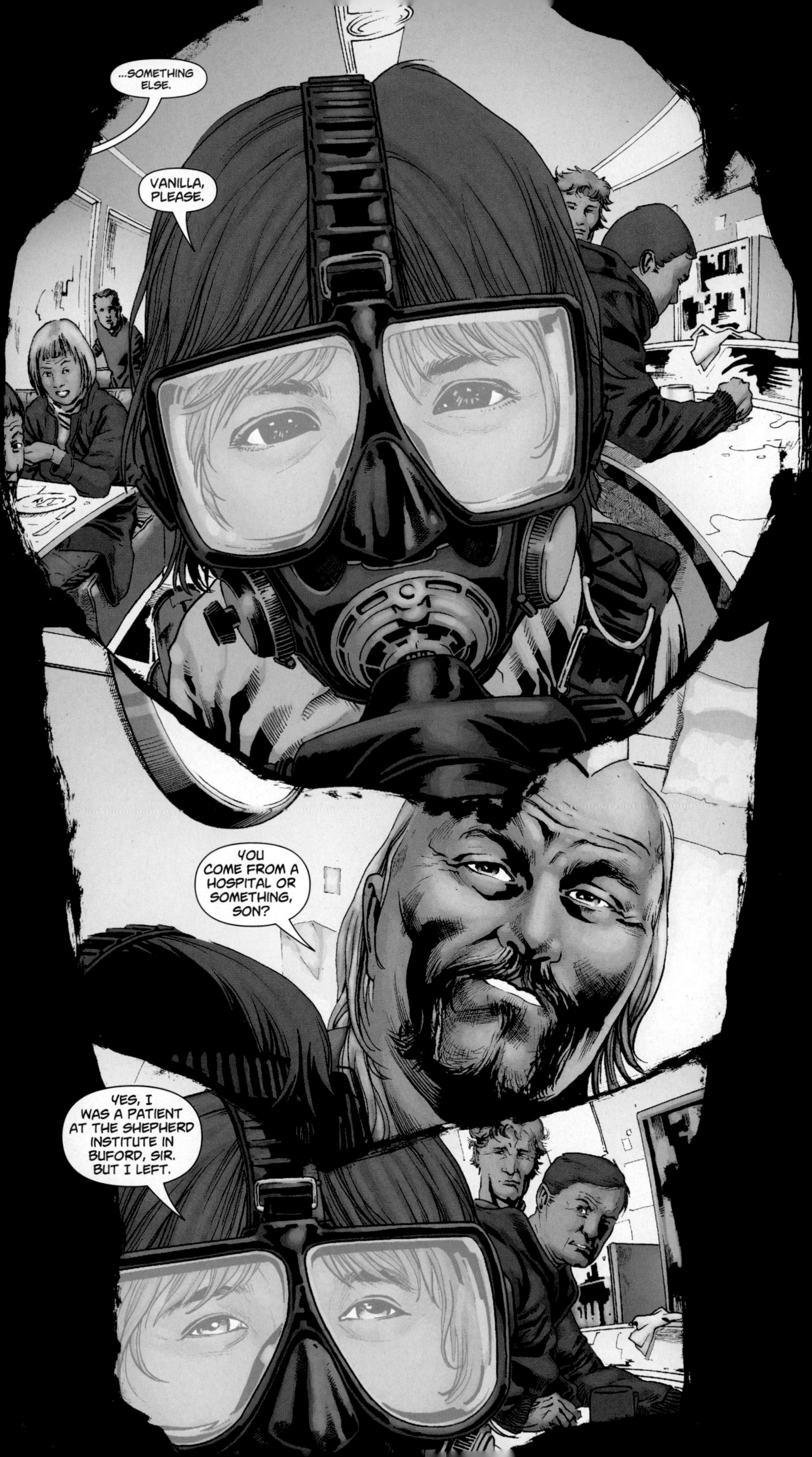
...SOMETHING ELSE.
VANILLA, PLEASE.
YOU COME FROM A HOSPITAL OR SOMETHING, SON?
YES, I WAS A PATIENT AT THE SHEPHERD INSTITUTE IN BUFORD, SIR. BUT I LEFT.

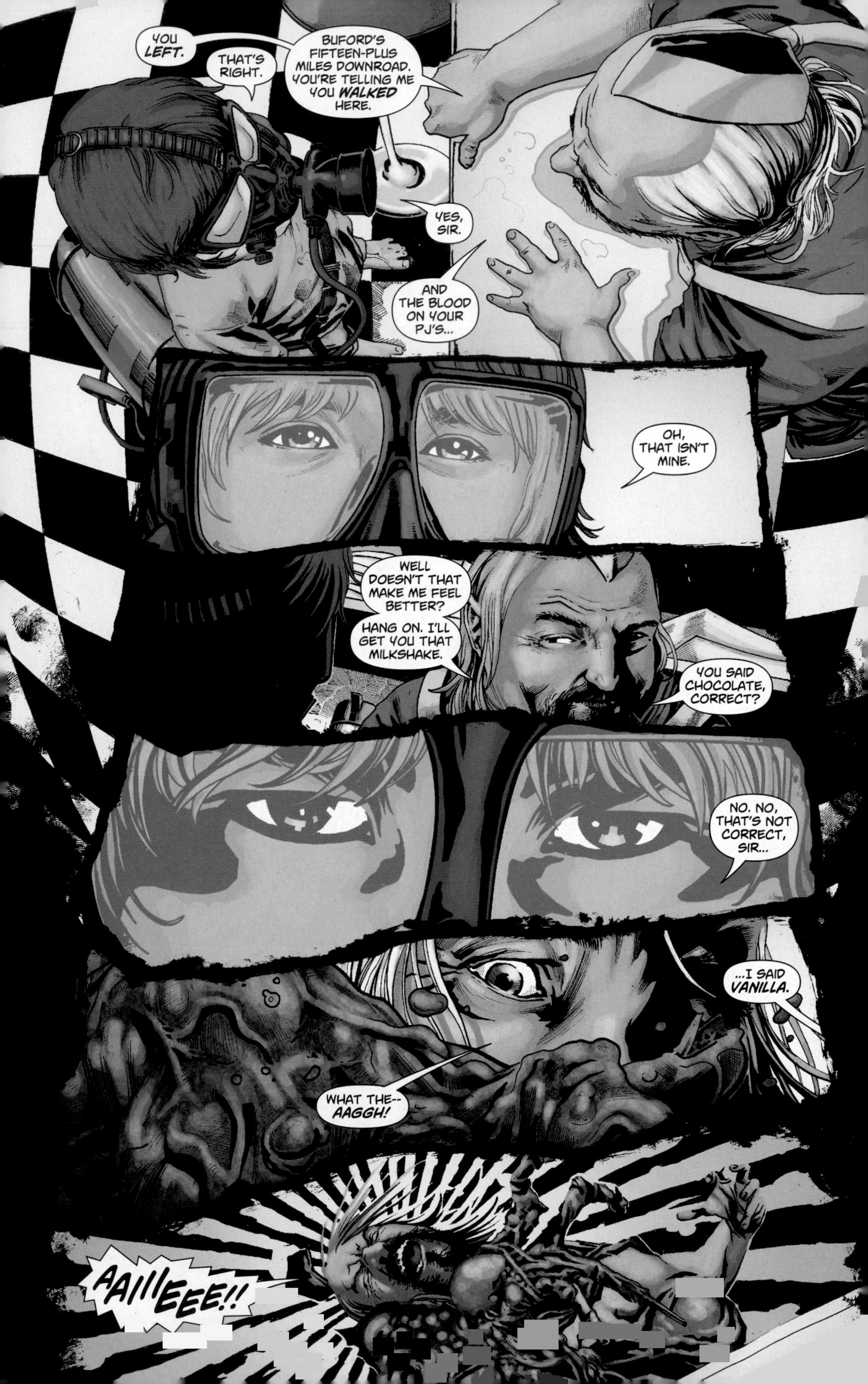
YOU LEFT.
THAT'S RIGHT.
BUFORD'S FIFTEEN-PLUS MILES DOWNROAD. YOU'RE TELLING ME YOU WALKED HERE.
YES, SIR.
AND THE BLOOD ON YOUR PJ'S...
OH, THAT ISN'T MINE.
WELL DOESN'T THAT MAKE ME FEEL BETTER?
HANG ON. I'LL GET YOU THAT MILKSHAKE.
YOU SAID CHOCOLATE, CORRECT?
NO. NO, THAT'S NOT CORRECT, SIR...
...I SAID VANILLA.
WHAT THE-- AAGGH!
AAIIIEEE!!

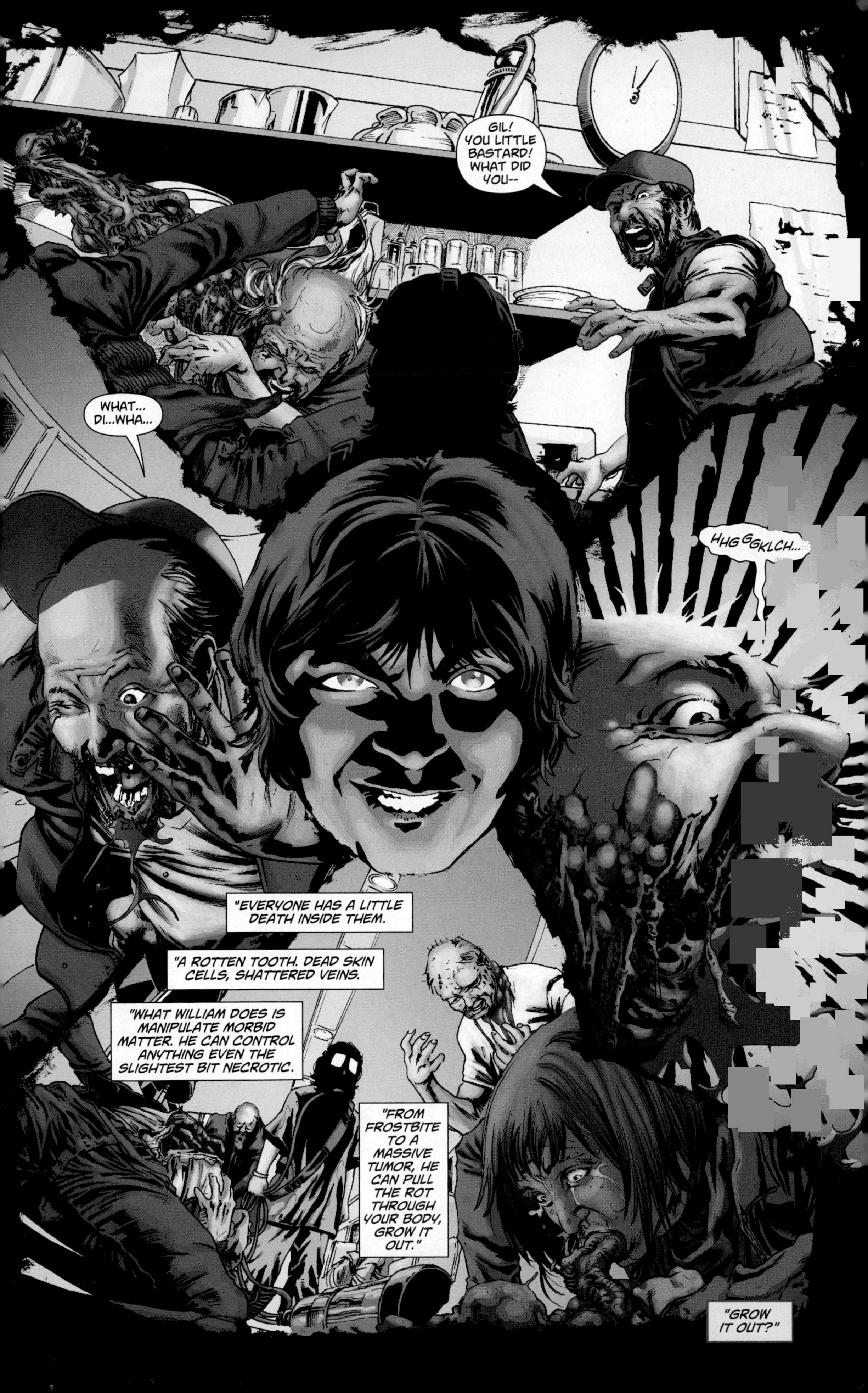
GIL! YOU LITTLE BASTARD! WHAT DID YOU--
WHAT... DI...WHA...
HHGGGKLCH...
"EVERYONE HAS A LITTLE DEATH INSIDE THEM.
"A ROTTEN TOOTH. DEAD SKIN CELLS, SHATTERED VEINS.
"WHAT WILLIAM DOES IS MANIPULATE MORBID MATTER. HE CAN CONTROL ANYTHING EVEN THE SLIGHTEST BIT NECROTIC.
"FROM FROSTBITE TO A MASSIVE TUMOR, HE CAN PULL THE ROT THROUGH YOUR BODY, GROW IT OUT."
"GROW IT OUT?"

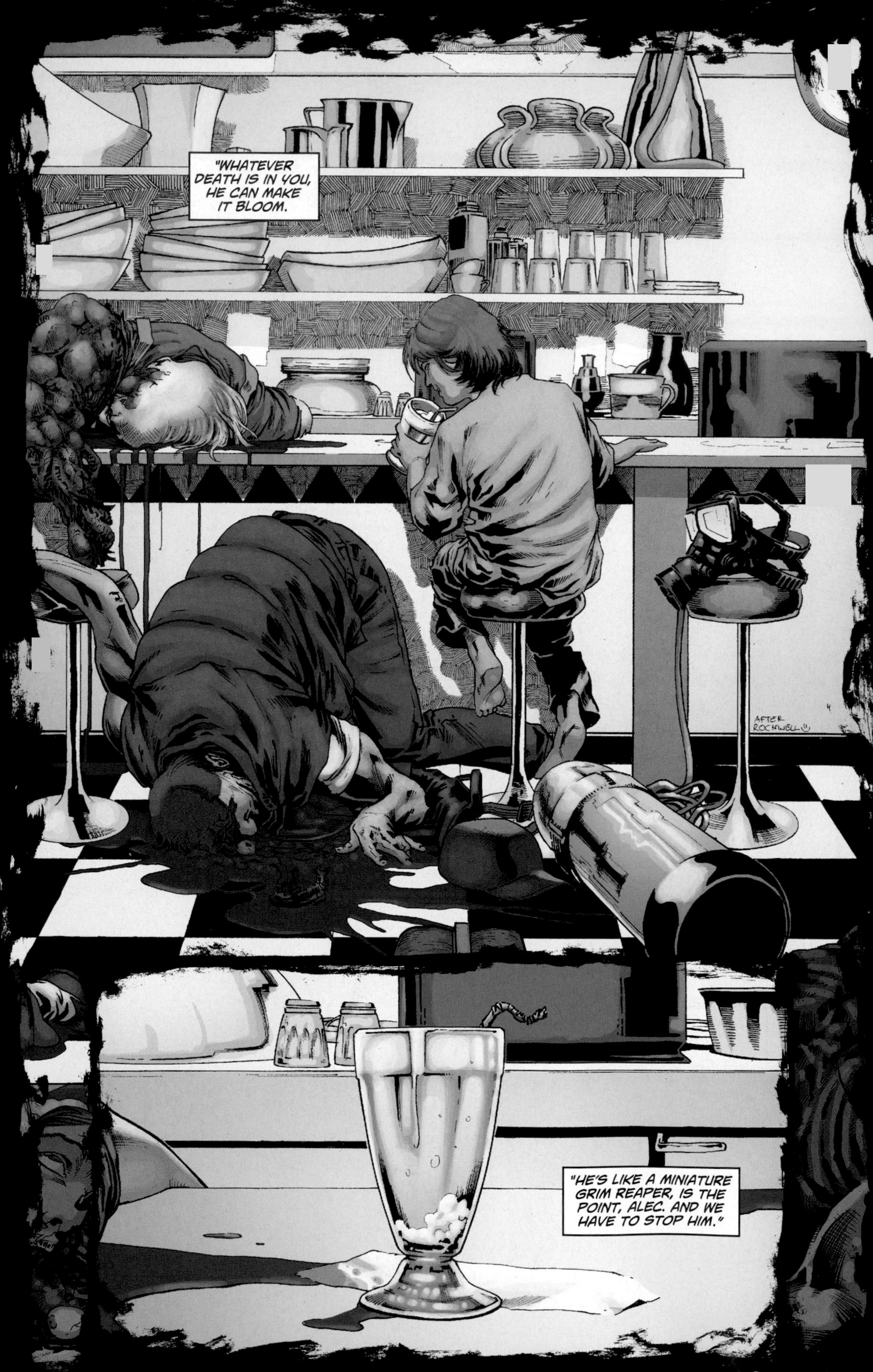
"WHATEVER DEATH IS IN YOU, HE CAN MAKE IT BLOOM.
AFTER ROCKWELL
"HE'S LIKE A MINIATURE GRIM REAPER, IS THE POINT, ALEC. AND WE HAVE TO STOP HIM."

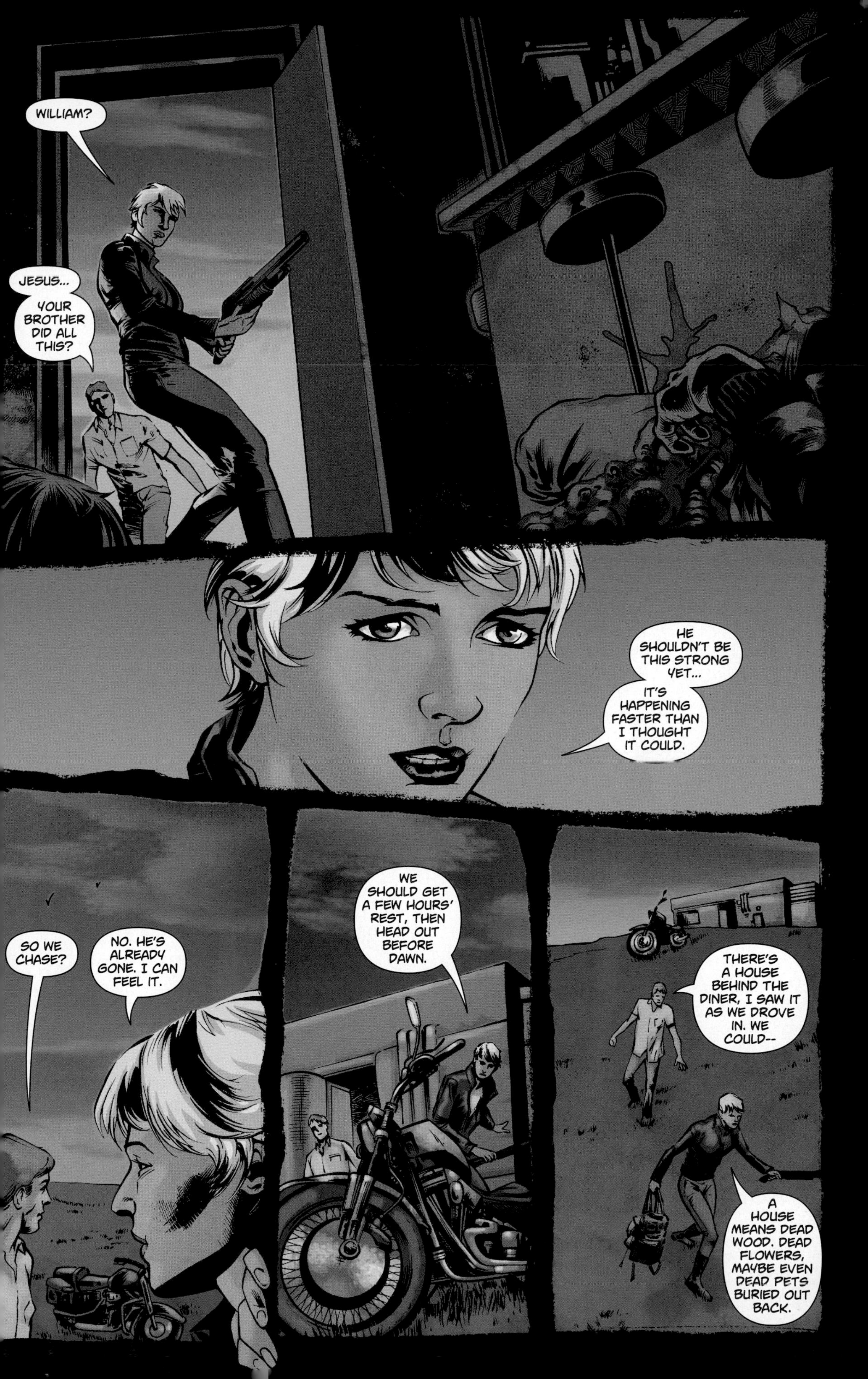
WILLIAM?
JESUS... YOUR BROTHER DID ALL THIS?
HE SHOULDN'T BE THIS STRONG YET...
IT'S HAPPENING FASTER THAN I THOUGHT IT COULD.
SO WE CHASE?
NO. HE'S ALREADY GONE. I CAN FEEL IT.
WE SHOULD GET A FEW HOURS' REST, THEN HEAD OUT BEFORE DAWN.
THERE'S A HOUSE BEHIND THE DINER, I SAW IT AS WE DROVE IN. WE COULD--
A HOUSE MEANS DEAD WOOD. DEAD FLOWERS, MAYBE EVEN DEAD PETS BURIED OUT BACK.

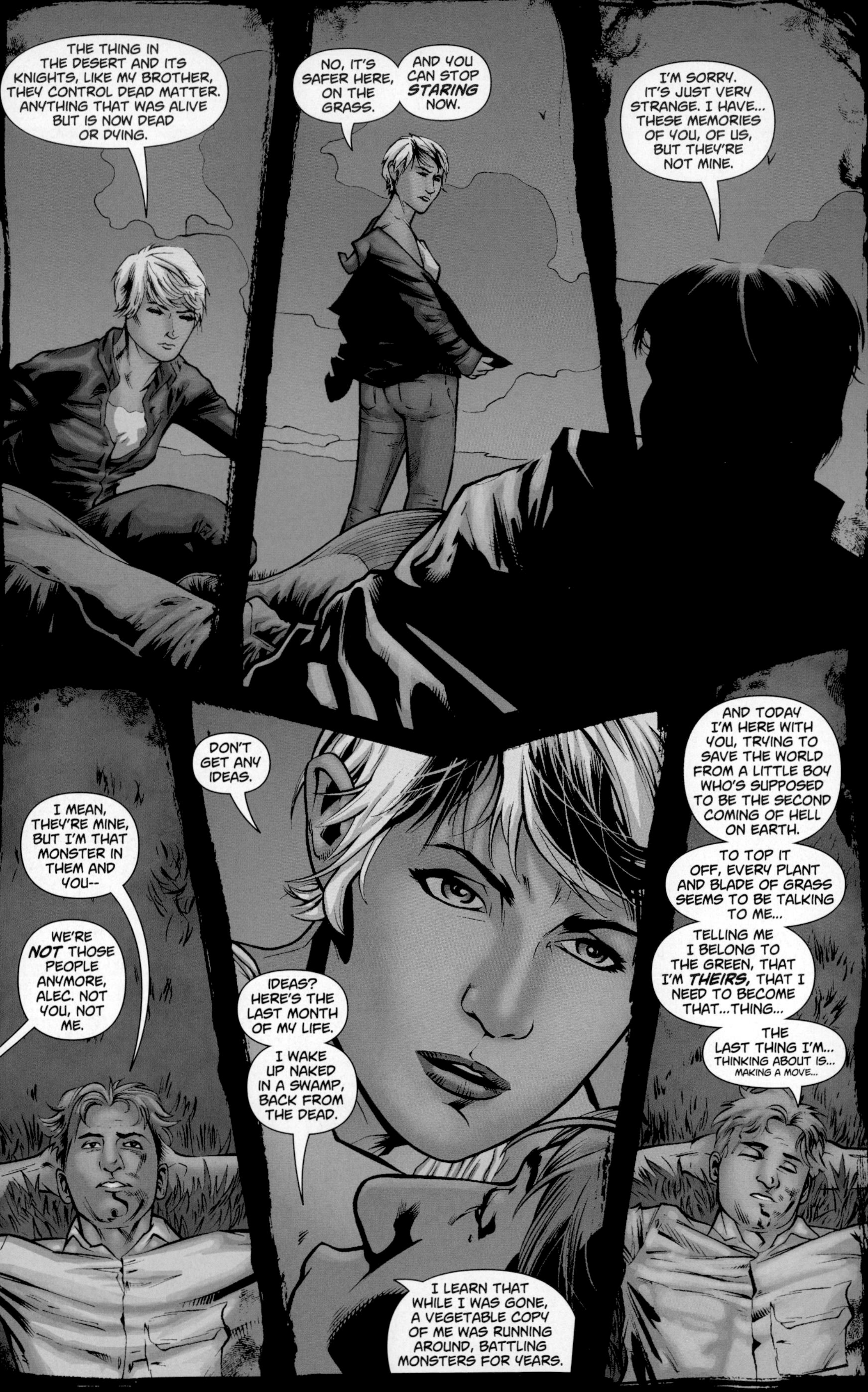
THE THING IN THE DESERT AND ITS KNIGHTS, LIKE MY BROTHER, THEY CONTROL DEAD MATTER. ANYTHING THAT WAS ALIVE BUT IS NOW DEAD OR DYING.
NO, IT'S SAFER HERE, ON THE GRASS.
AND YOU CAN STOP STARING NOW.
I'M SORRY. IT'S JUST VERY STRANGE. I HAVE... THESE MEMORIES OF YOU, OF US, BUT THEY'RE NOT MINE.
I MEAN, THEY'RE MINE, BUT I'M THAT MONSTER IN THEM AND YOU--
WE'RE NOT THOSE PEOPLE ANYMORE, ALEC. NOT YOU, NOT ME.
DON'T GET ANY IDEAS.
IDEAS? HERE'S THE LAST MONTH OF MY LIFE.
I WAKE UP NAKED IN A SWAMP, BACK FROM THE DEAD.
I LEARN THAT WHILE I WAS GONE, A VEGETABLE COPY OF ME WAS RUNNING AROUND, BATTLING MONSTERS FOR YEARS.
AND TODAY I'M HERE WITH YOU, TRYING TO SAVE THE WORLD FROM A LITTLE BOY WHO'S SUPPOSED TO BE THE SECOND COMING OF HELL ON EARTH.
TO TOP IT OFF, EVERY PLANT AND BLADE OF GRASS SEEMS TO BE TALKING TO ME...
TELLING ME I BELONG TO THE GREEN, THAT I'M THEIRS, THAT I NEED TO BECOME THAT...THING...
THE LAST THING I'M... THINKING ABOUT IS... MAKING A MOVE...

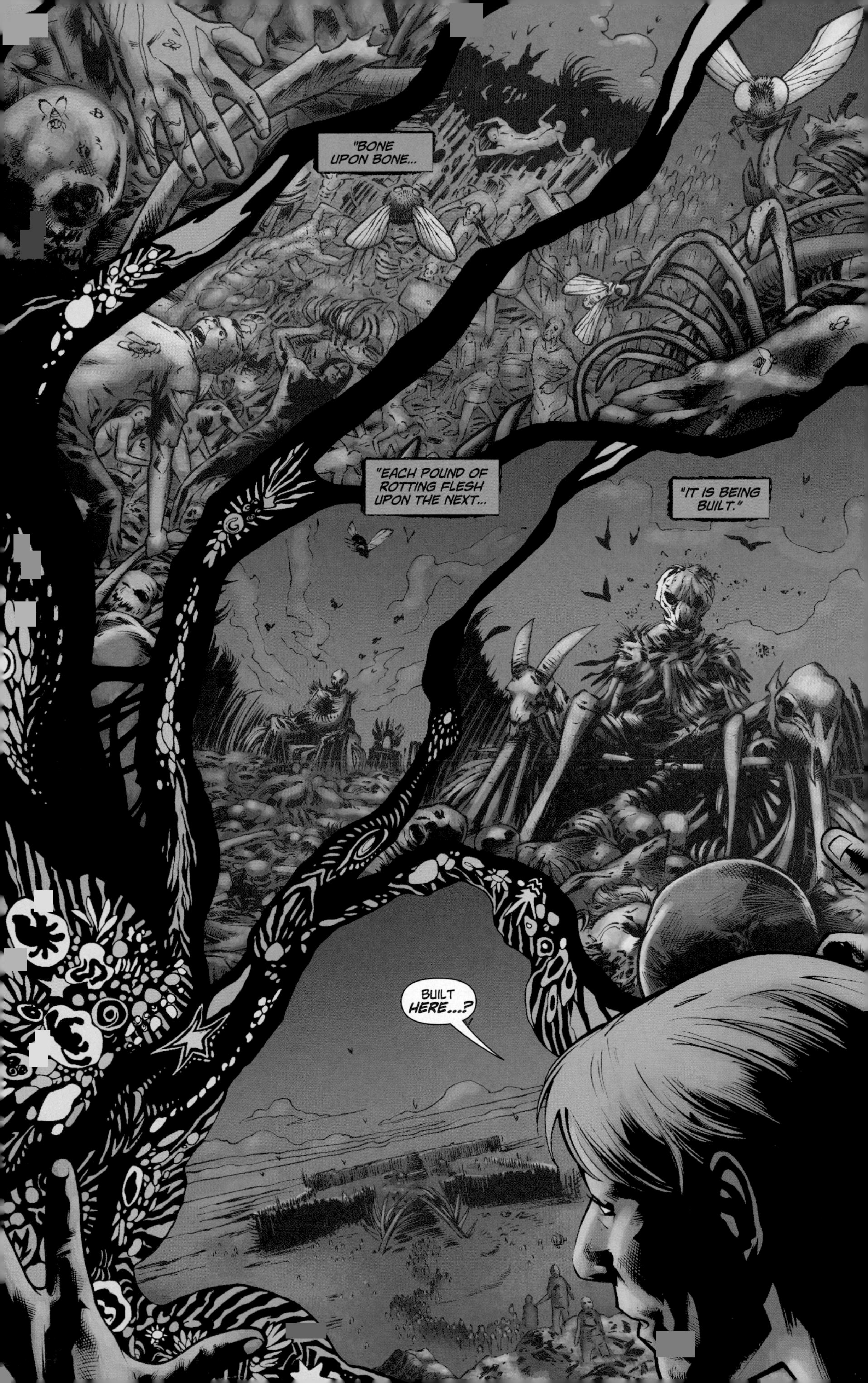
"BONE UPON BONE...
"EACH POUND OF ROTTING FLESH UPON THE NEXT...
"IT IS BEING BUILT."
BUILT HERE...?

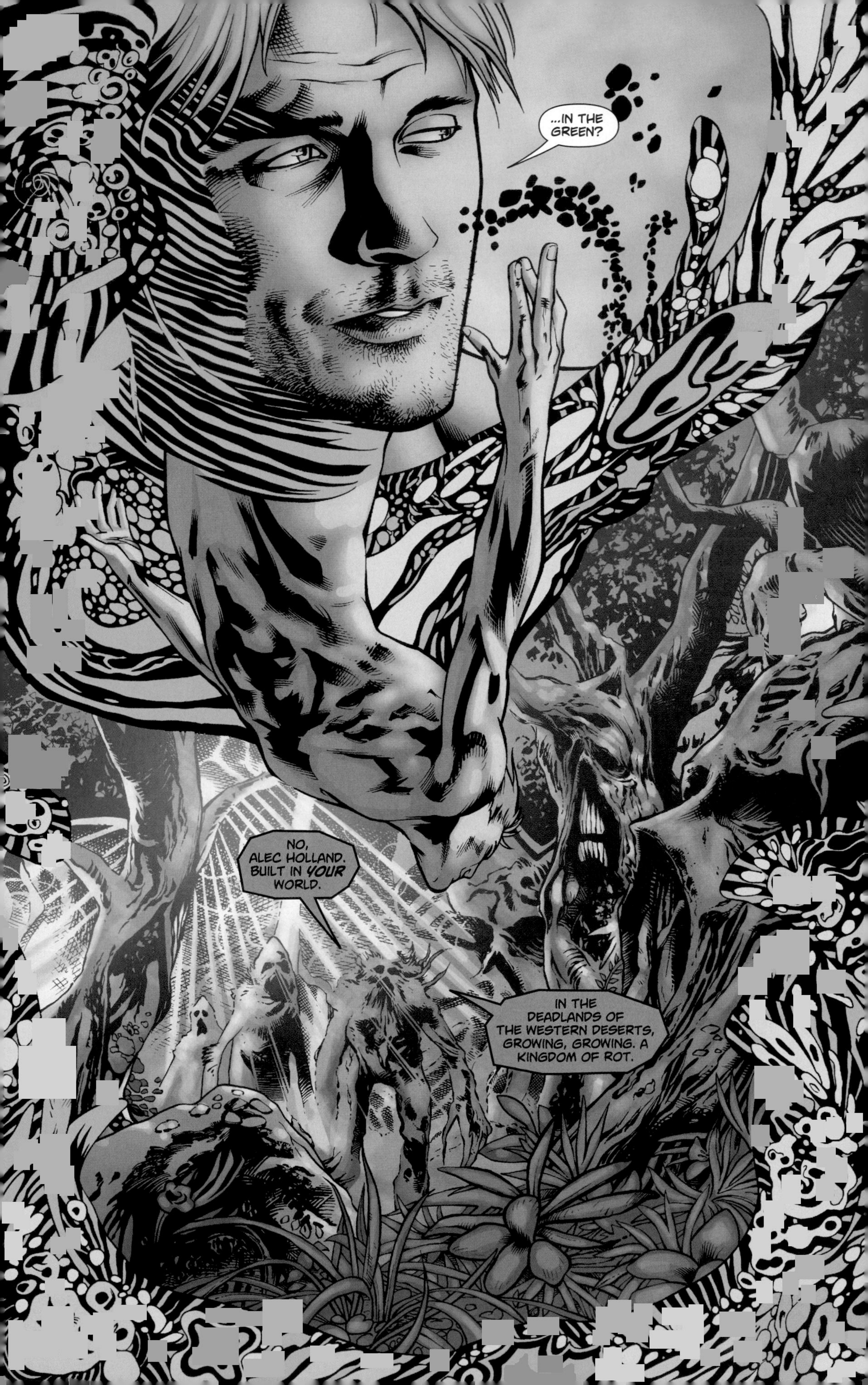
...IN THE GREEN?
NO, ALEC HOLLAND. BUILT IN YOUR WORLD.
IN THE DEADLANDS OF THE WESTERN DESERTS, GROWING, GROWING. A KINGDOM OF ROT.

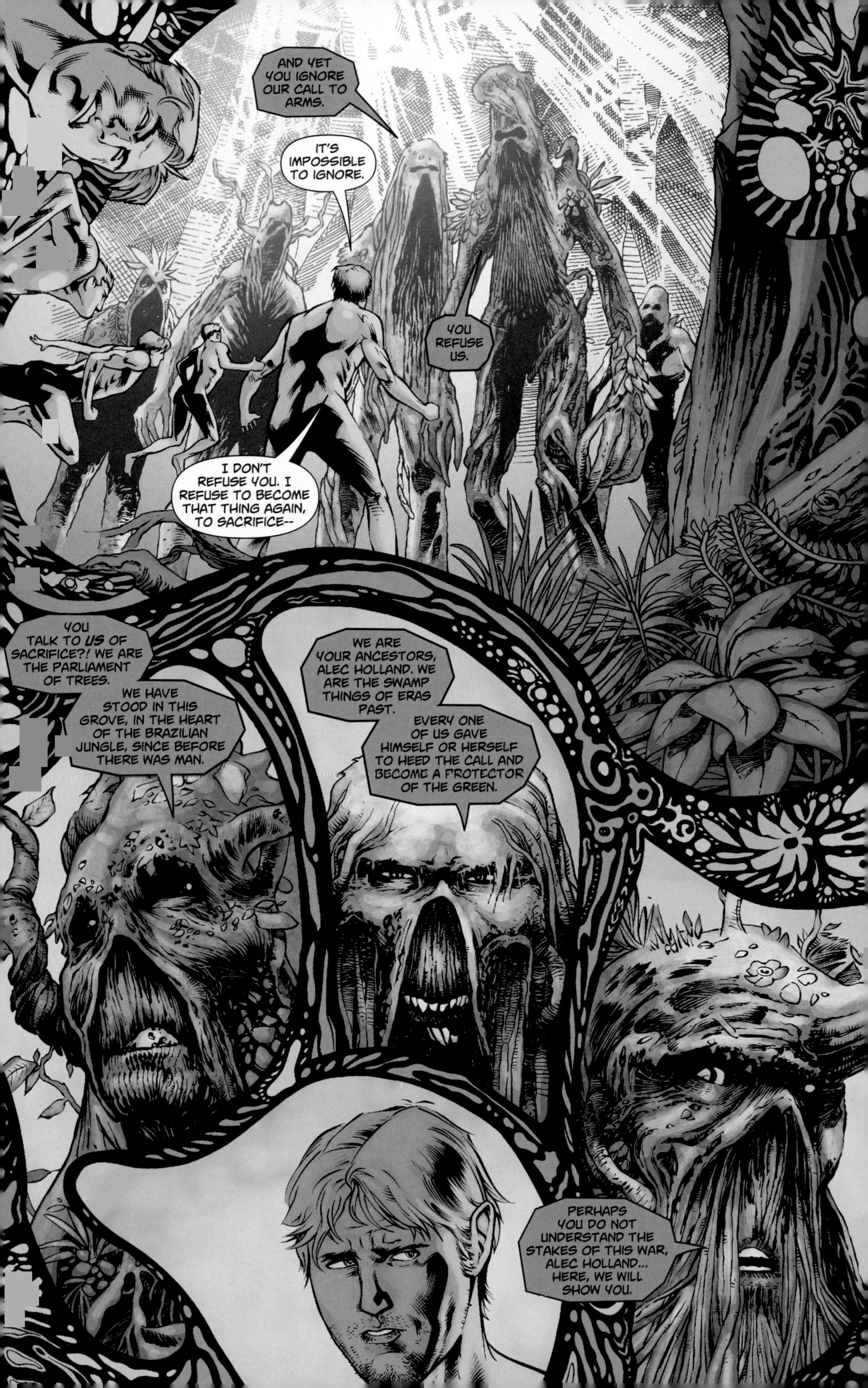
AND YET YOU IGNORE OUR CALL TO ARMS.
IT'S IMPOSSIBLE TO IGNORE.
YOU REFUSE US.
I DON'T REFUSE YOU. I REFUSE TO BECOME THAT THING AGAIN, TO SACRIFICE--
YOU TALK TO US OF SACRIFICE?! WE ARE THE PARLIAMENT OF TREES.
WE HAVE STOOD IN THIS GROVE, IN THE HEART OF THE BRAZILIAN JUNGLE, SINCE BEFORE THERE WAS MAN.
WE ARE YOUR ANCESTORS, ALEC HOLLAND. WE ARE THE SWAMP THINGS OF ERAS PAST.
EVERY ONE OF US GAVE HIMSELF OR HERSELF TO HEED THE CALL AND BECOME A PROTECTOR OF THE GREEN.
PERHAPS YOU DO NOT UNDERSTAND THE STAKES OF THIS WAR, ALEC HOLLAND... HERE, WE WILL SHOW YOU.

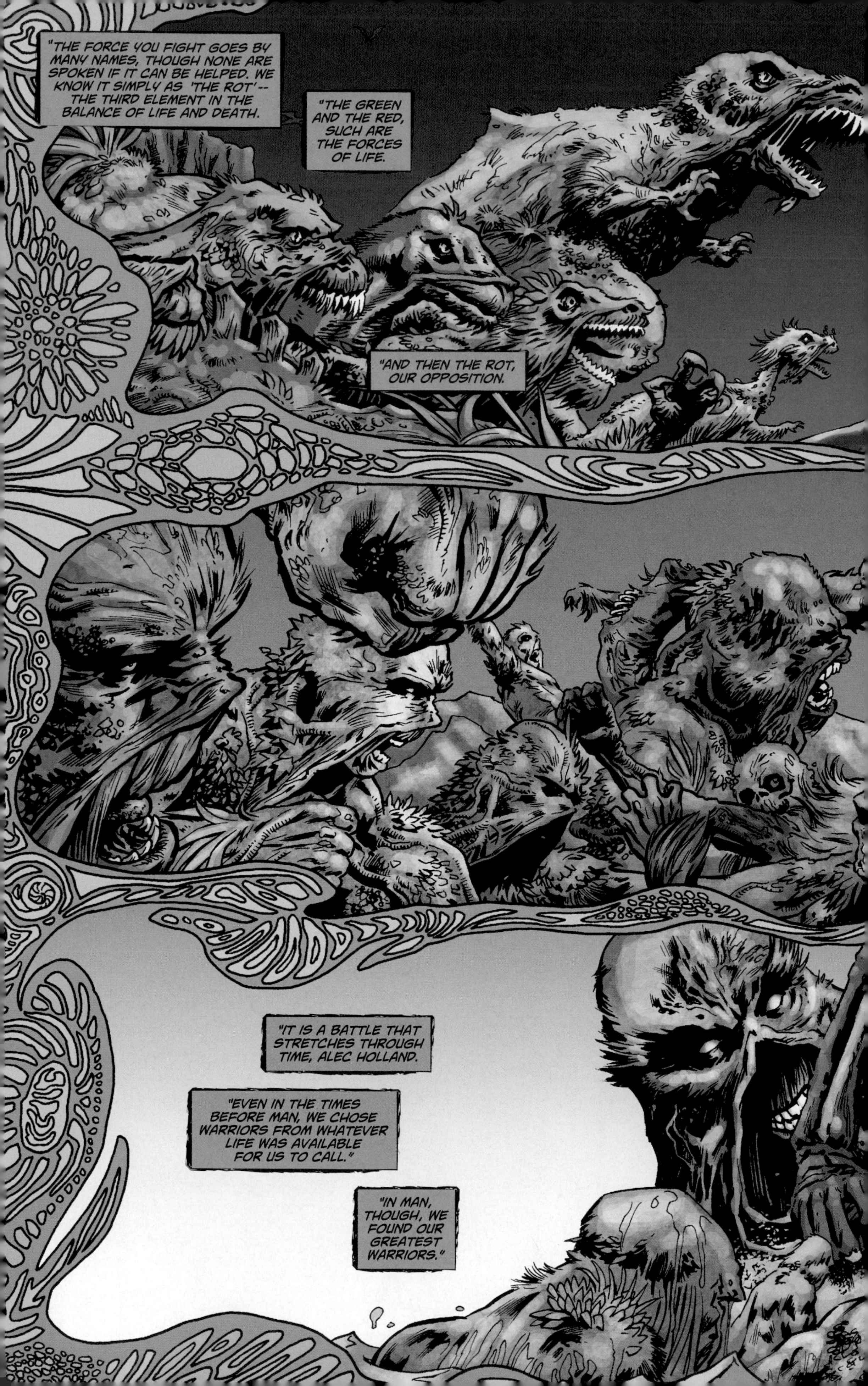
"THE FORCE YOU FIGHT GOES BY MANY NAMES, THOUGH NONE ARE SPOKEN IF IT CAN BE HELPED. WE KNOW IT SIMPLY AS 'THE ROT'-- THE THIRD ELEMENT IN THE BALANCE OF LIFE AND DEATH.
"THE GREEN AND THE RED, SUCH ARE THE FORCES OF LIFE.
"AND THEN THE ROT, OUR OPPOSITION.
"IT IS A BATTLE THAT STRETCHES THROUGH TIME, ALEC HOLLAND.
"EVEN IN THE TIMES BEFORE MAN, WE CHOSE WARRIORS FROM WHATEVER LIFE WAS AVAILABLE FOR US TO CALL."
"IN MAN, THOUGH, WE FOUND OUR GREATEST WARRIORS."

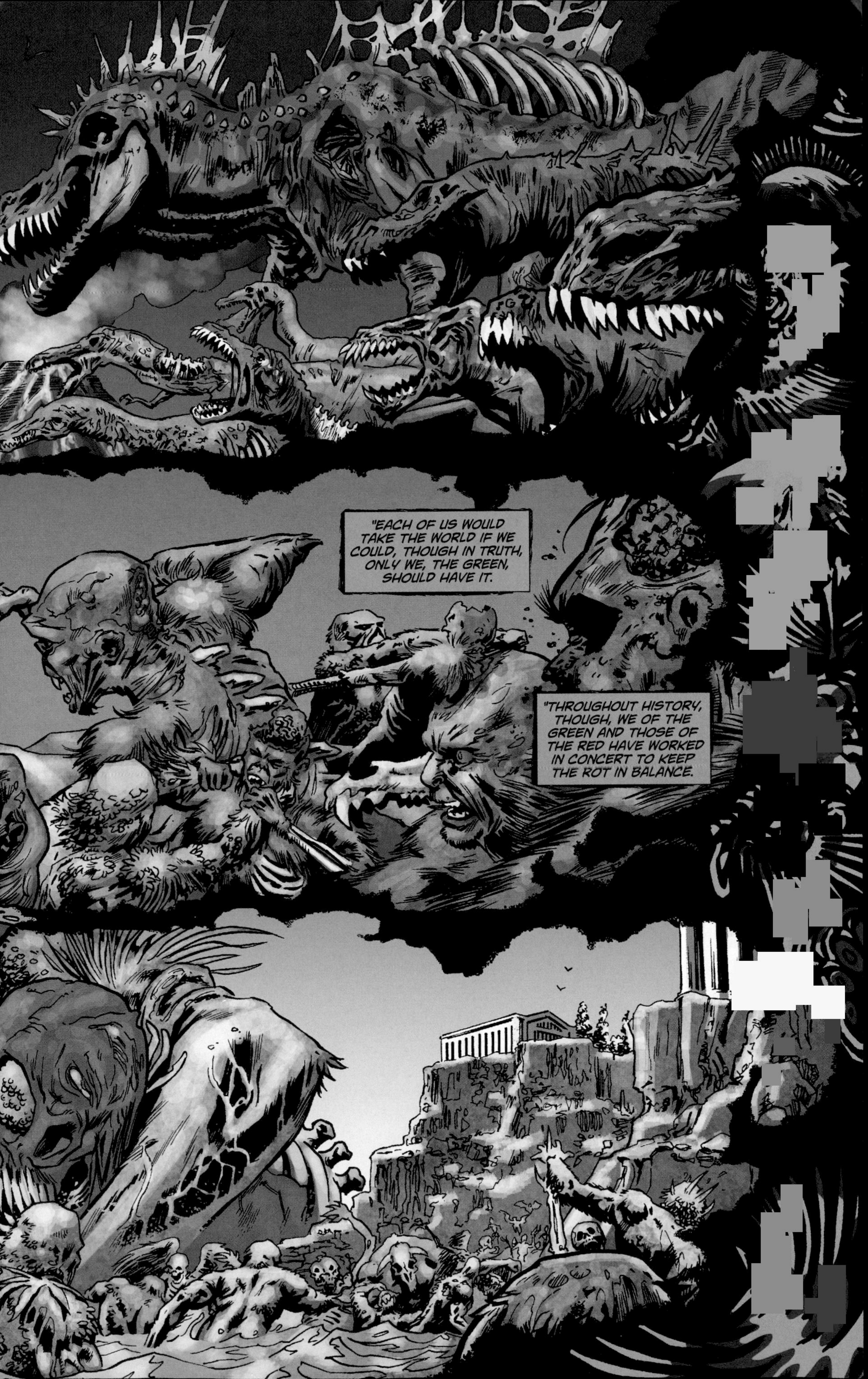
"EACH OF US WOULD TAKE THE WORLD IF WE COULD, THOUGH IN TRUTH, ONLY WE, THE GREEN, SHOULD HAVE IT.
"THROUGHOUT HISTORY, THOUGH, WE OF THE GREEN AND THOSE OF THE RED HAVE WORKED IN CONCERT TO KEEP THE ROT IN BALANCE.

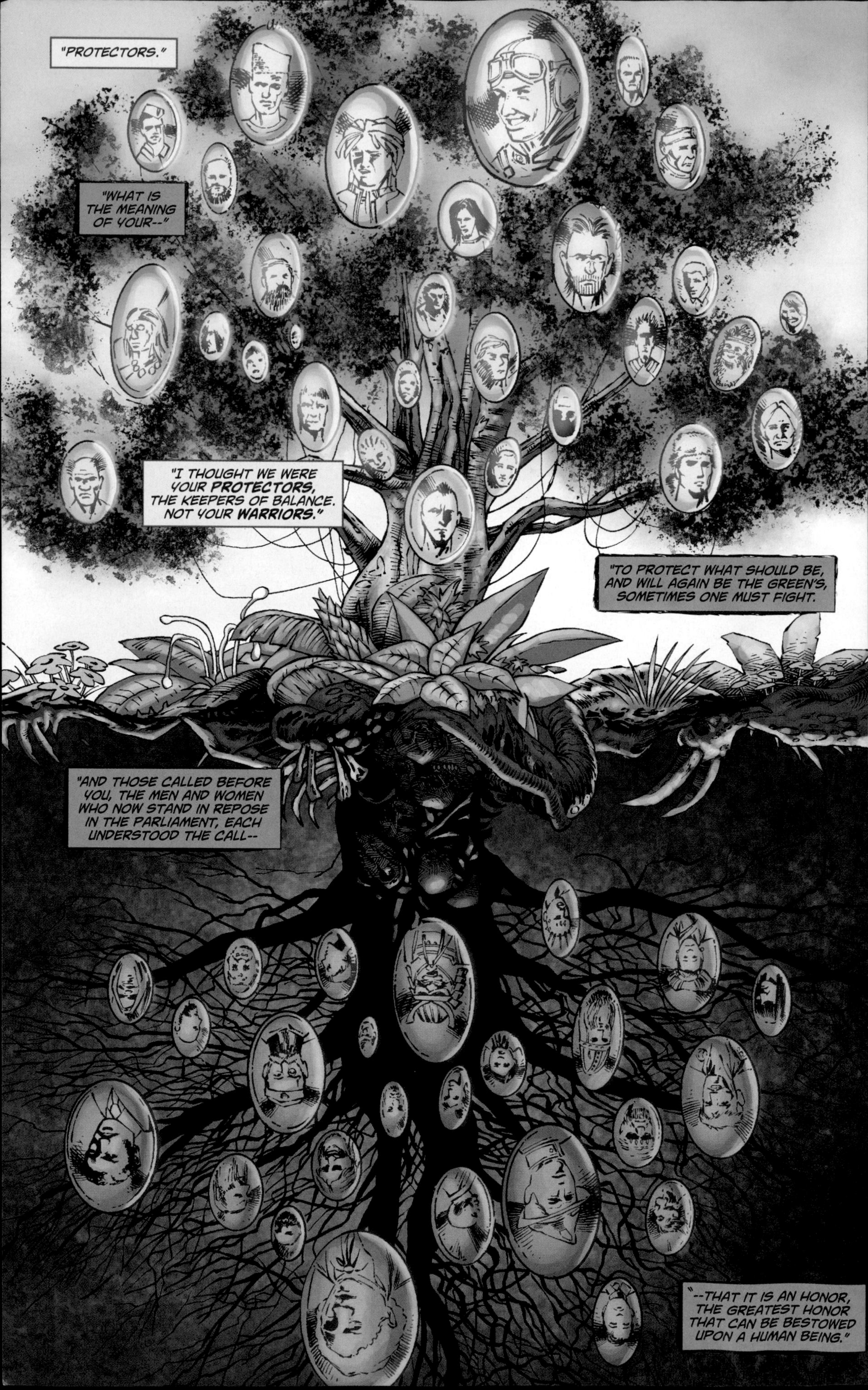
"PROTECTORS."
"WHAT IS THE MEANING OF YOUR--"
"I THOUGHT WE WERE YOUR PROTECTORS, THE KEEPERS OF BALANCE. NOT YOUR WARRIORS."
"TO PROTECT WHAT SHOULD BE, AND WILL AGAIN BE THE GREEN'S, SOMETIMES ONE MUST FIGHT.
"AND THOSE CALLED BEFORE YOU, THE MEN AND WOMEN WHO NOW STAND IN REPOSE IN THE PARLIAMENT, EACH UNDERSTOOD THE CALL--
"--THAT IT IS AN HONOR, THE GREATEST HONOR THAT CAN BE BESTOWED UPON A HUMAN BEING."

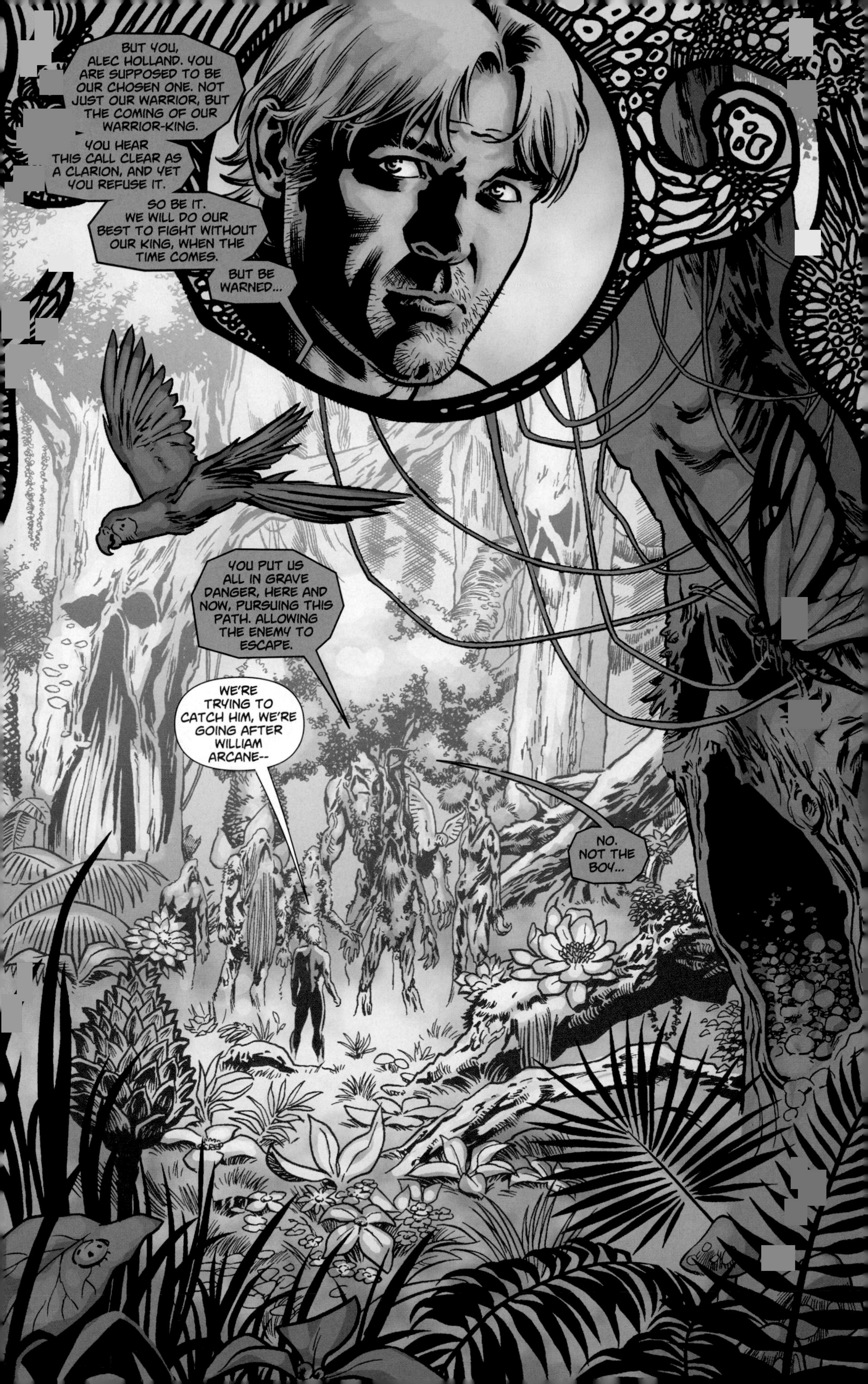
BUT YOU, ALEC HOLLAND. YOU ARE SUPPOSED TO BE OUR CHOSEN ONE. NOT JUST OUR WARRIOR, BUT THE COMING OF OUR WARRIOR-KING.
YOU HEAR THIS CALL CLEAR AS A CLARION, AND YET YOU REFUSE IT.
SO BE IT. WE WILL DO OUR BEST TO FIGHT WITHOUT OUR KING, WHEN THE TIME COMES.
BUT BE WARNED...
YOU PUT US ALL IN GRAVE DANGER, HERE AND NOW, PURSUING THIS PATH. ALLOWING THE ENEMY TO ESCAPE.
WE'RE TRYING TO CATCH HIM, WE'RE GOING AFTER WILLIAM ARCANE--
NO. NOT THE BOY...

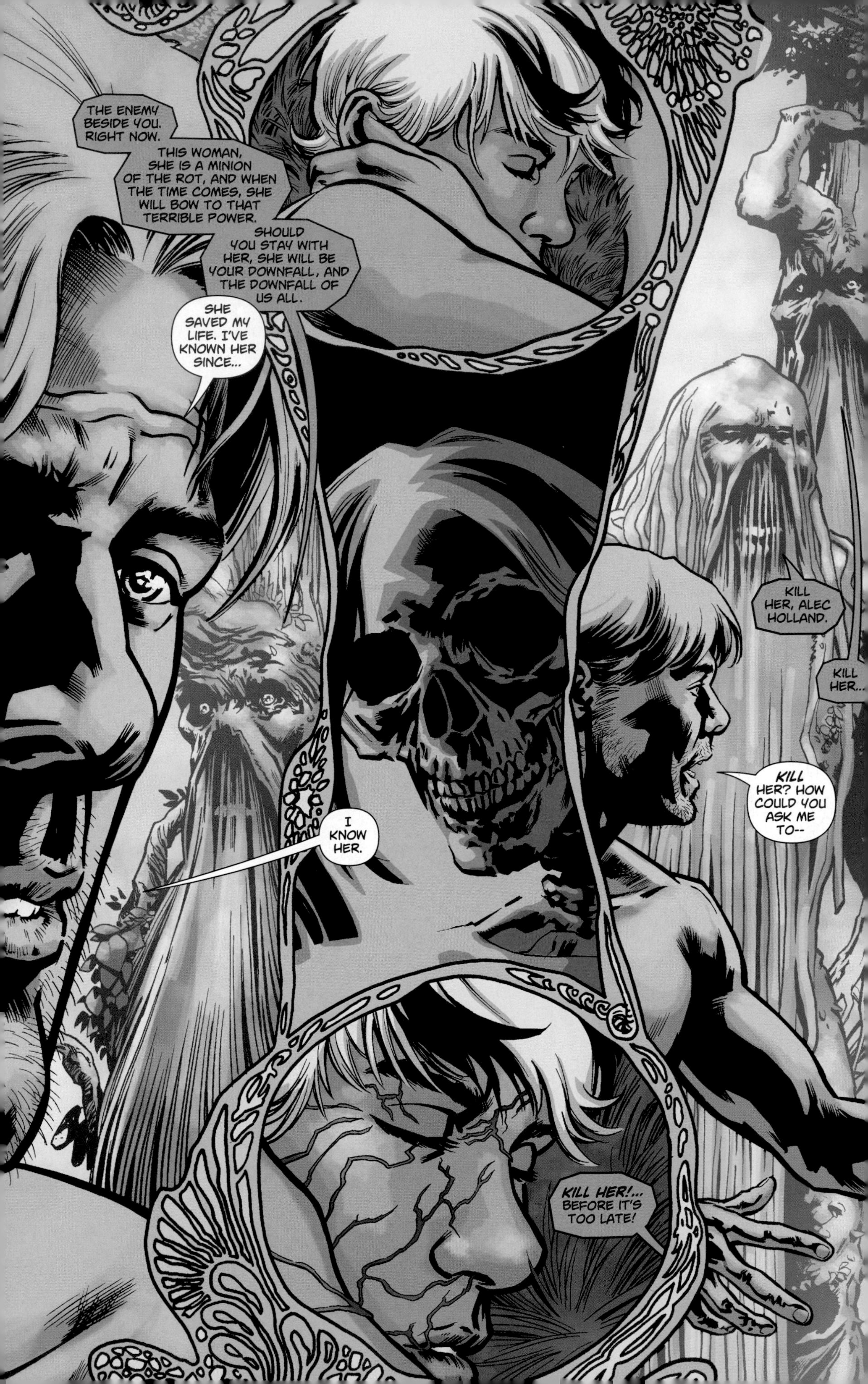
THE ENEMY BESIDE YOU. RIGHT NOW.
THIS WOMAN, SHE IS A MINION OF THE ROT, AND WHEN THE TIME COMES, SHE WILL BOW TO THAT TERRIBLE POWER.
SHOULD YOU STAY WITH HER, SHE WILL BE YOUR DOWNFALL, AND THE DOWNFALL OF US ALL.
SHE SAVED MY LIFE. I'VE KNOWN HER SINCE...
KILL HER, ALEC HOLLAND.
KILL HER...
KILL HER? HOW COULD YOU ASK ME TO--
I KNOW HER.
KILL HER!... BEFORE IT'S TOO LATE!

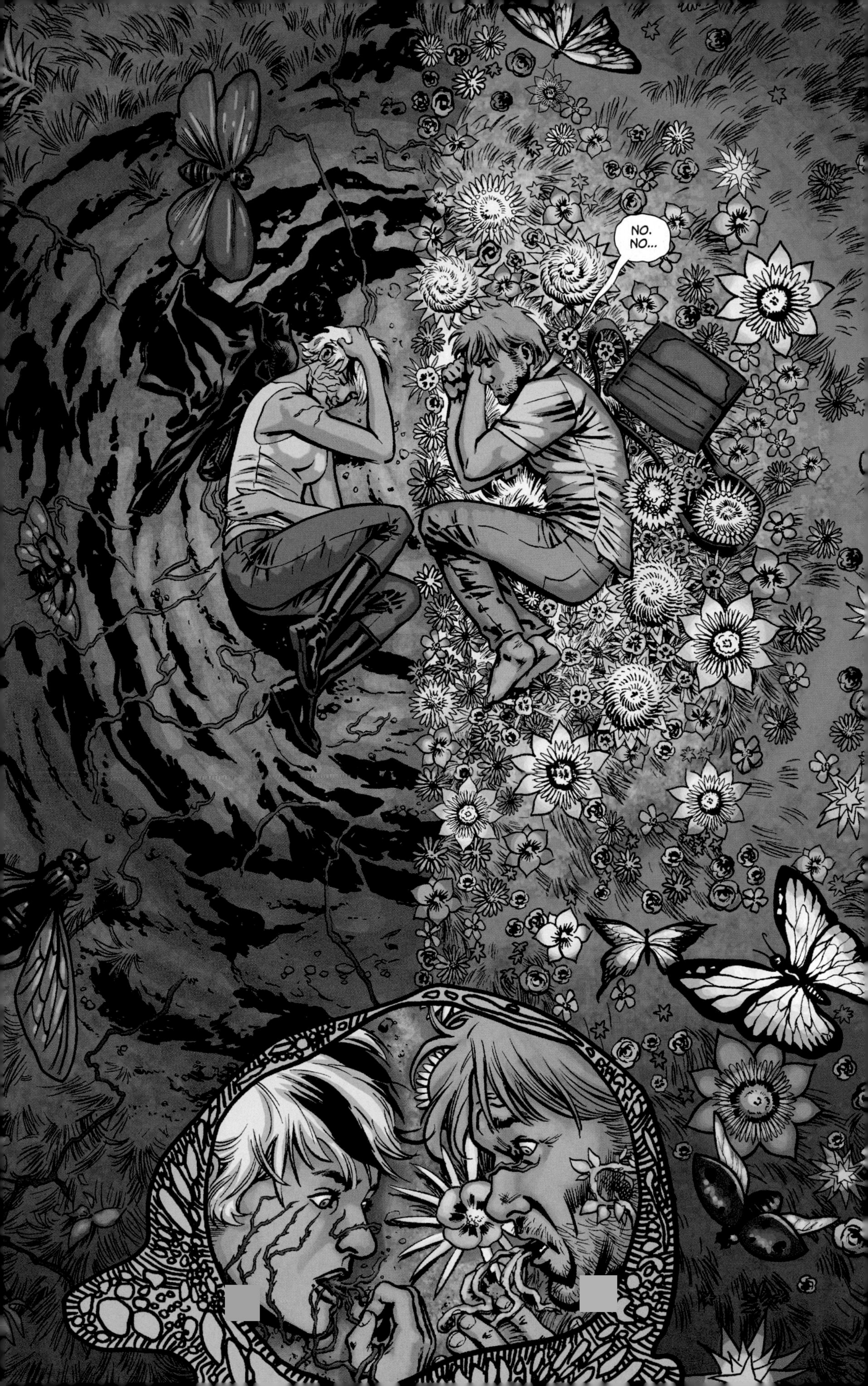
NO. NO...

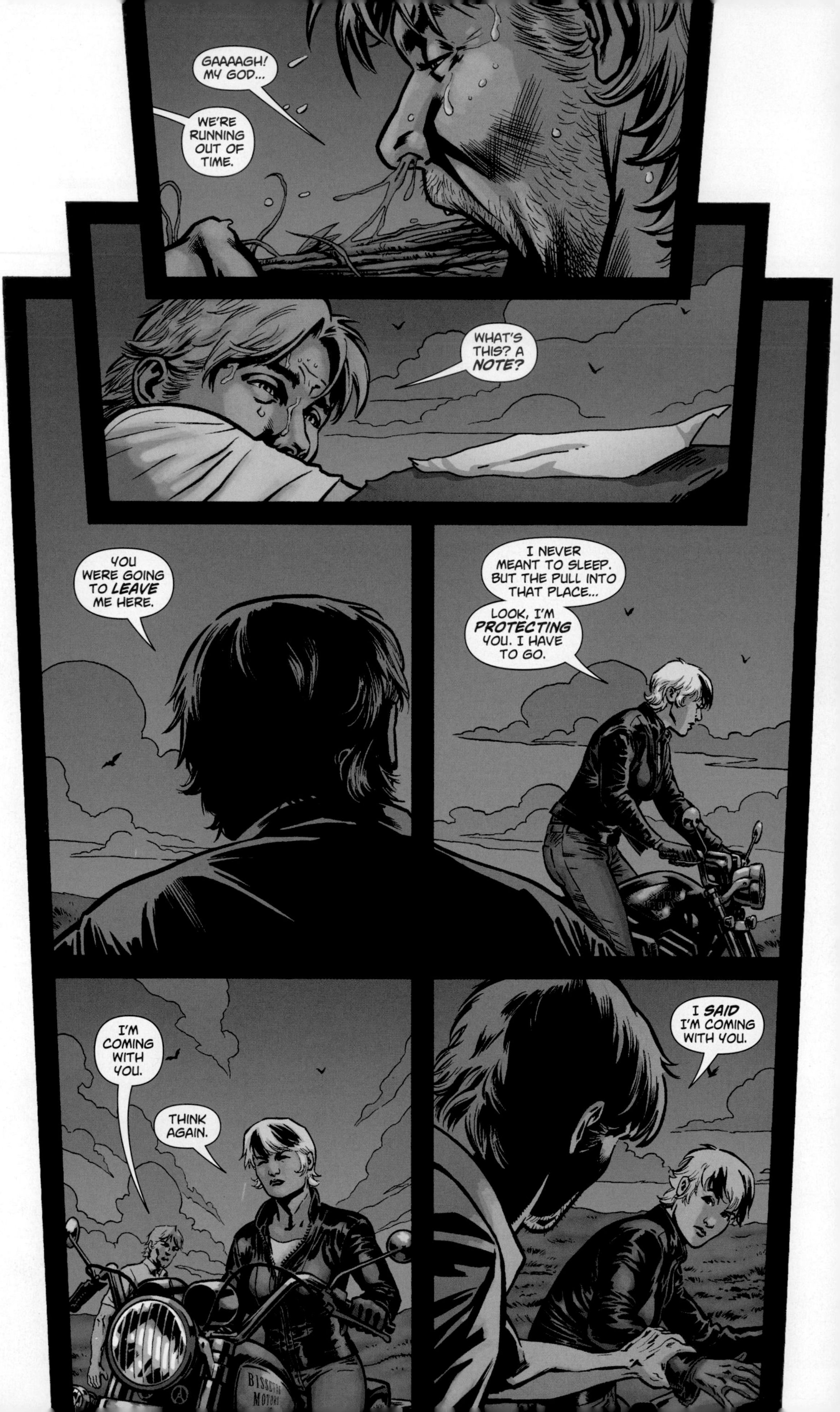
GAAAAGH! MY GOD...
WE'RE RUNNING OUT OF TIME.
WHAT'S THIS? A *NOTE?*
YOU WERE GOING TO *LEAVE* ME HERE.
I NEVER MEANT TO SLEEP. BUT THE PULL INTO THAT PLACE...
LOOK, I'M *PROTECTING* YOU. I HAVE TO GO.
I'M COMING WITH YOU.
THINK AGAIN.
I *SAID* I'M COMING WITH YOU.

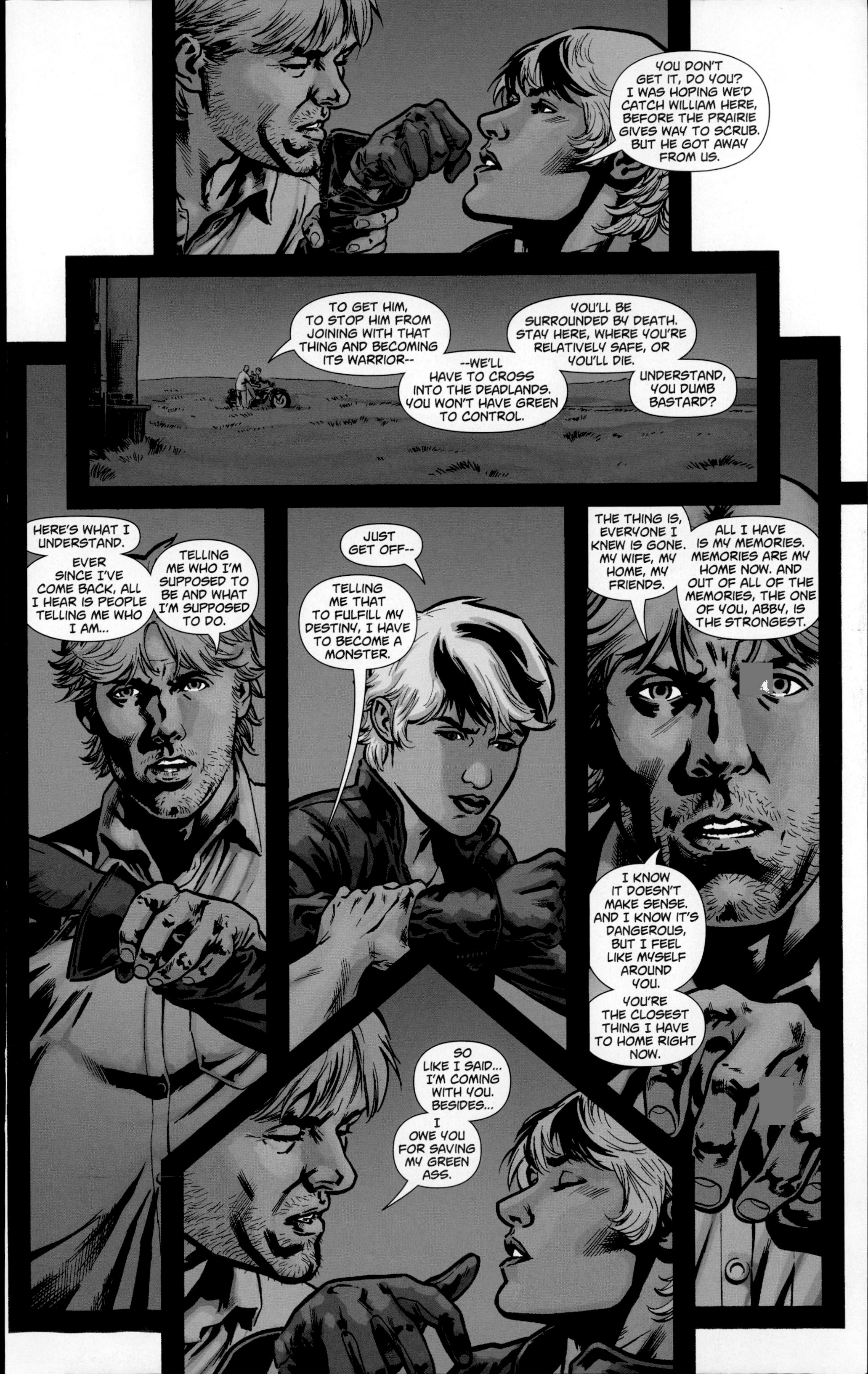
YOU DON'T GET IT, DO YOU? I WAS HOPING WE'D CATCH WILLIAM HERE, BEFORE THE PRAIRIE GIVES WAY TO SCRUB. BUT HE GOT AWAY FROM US.
TO GET HIM, TO STOP HIM FROM JOINING WITH THAT THING AND BECOMING ITS WARRIOR--
--WE'LL HAVE TO CROSS INTO THE DEADLANDS. YOU WON'T HAVE GREEN TO CONTROL.
YOU'LL BE SURROUNDED BY DEATH. STAY HERE, WHERE YOU'RE RELATIVELY SAFE, OR YOU'LL DIE.
UNDERSTAND, YOU DUMB BASTARD?
HERE'S WHAT I UNDERSTAND.
EVER SINCE I'VE COME BACK, ALL I HEAR IS PEOPLE TELLING ME WHO I AM...
TELLING ME WHO I'M SUPPOSED TO BE AND WHAT I'M SUPPOSED TO DO.
JUST GET OFF--
TELLING ME THAT TO FULFILL MY DESTINY, I HAVE TO BECOME A MONSTER.
THE THING IS, EVERYONE I KNEW IS GONE. MY WIFE, MY HOME, MY FRIENDS.
ALL I HAVE IS MY MEMORIES. MEMORIES ARE MY HOME NOW. AND OUT OF ALL OF THE MEMORIES, THE ONE OF YOU, ABBY, IS THE STRONGEST.
I KNOW IT DOESN'T MAKE SENSE. AND I KNOW IT'S DANGEROUS, BUT I FEEL LIKE MYSELF AROUND YOU.
YOU'RE THE CLOSEST THING I HAVE TO HOME RIGHT NOW.
SO LIKE I SAID... I'M COMING WITH YOU. BESIDES...
I OWE YOU FOR SAVING MY GREEN ASS.

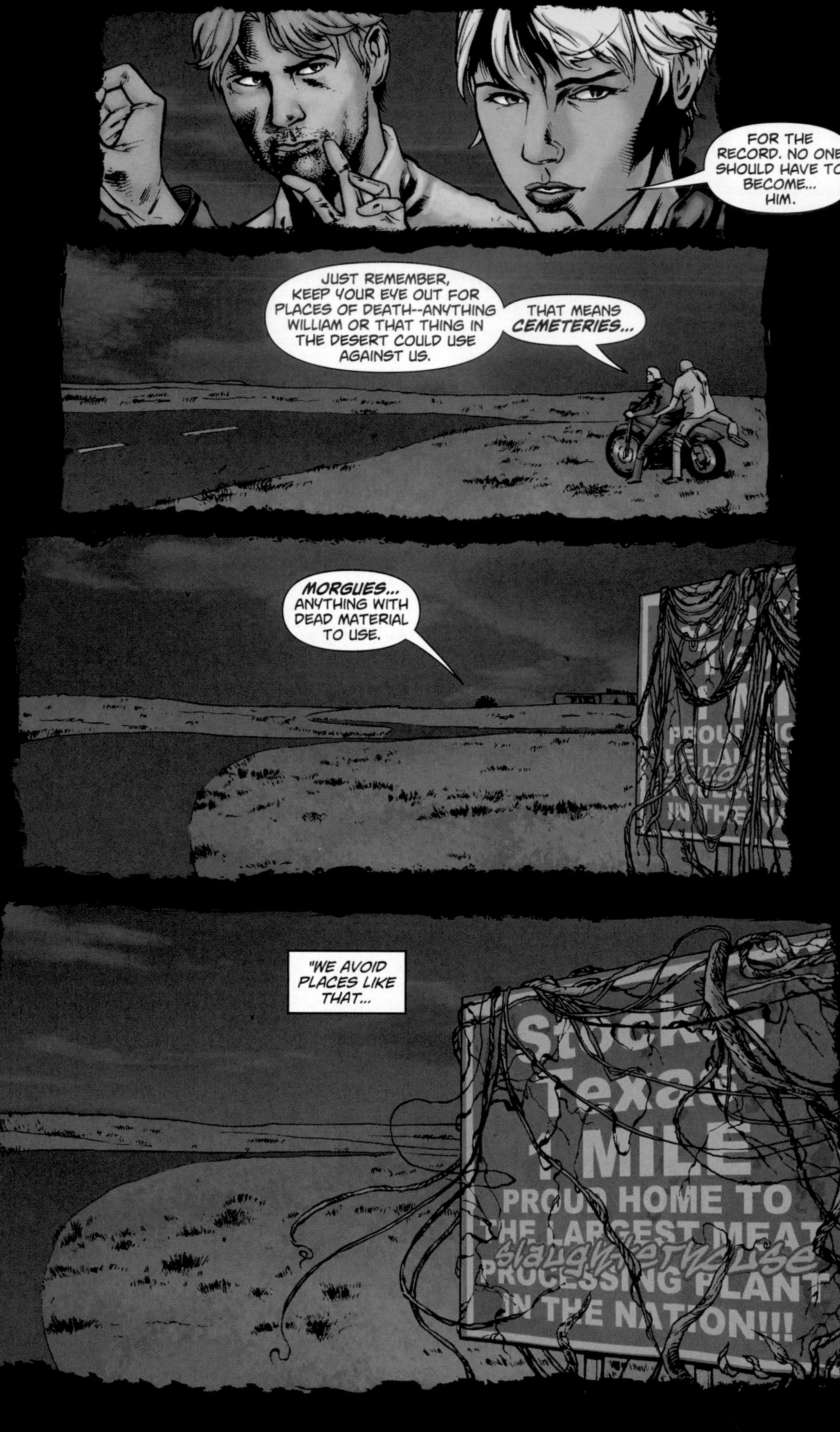
FOR THE RECORD. NO ONE SHOULD HAVE TO BECOME... HIM.
JUST REMEMBER, KEEP YOUR EYE OUT FOR PLACES OF DEATH--ANYTHING WILLIAM OR THAT THING IN THE DESERT COULD USE AGAINST US.
THAT MEANS CEMETERIES...
MORGUES... ANYTHING WITH DEAD MATERIAL TO USE.
"WE AVOID PLACES LIKE THAT...
1 MILE
PROUD HOME TO
slaughterhouse
PROCESSING PLANT
IN THE NATION!!!

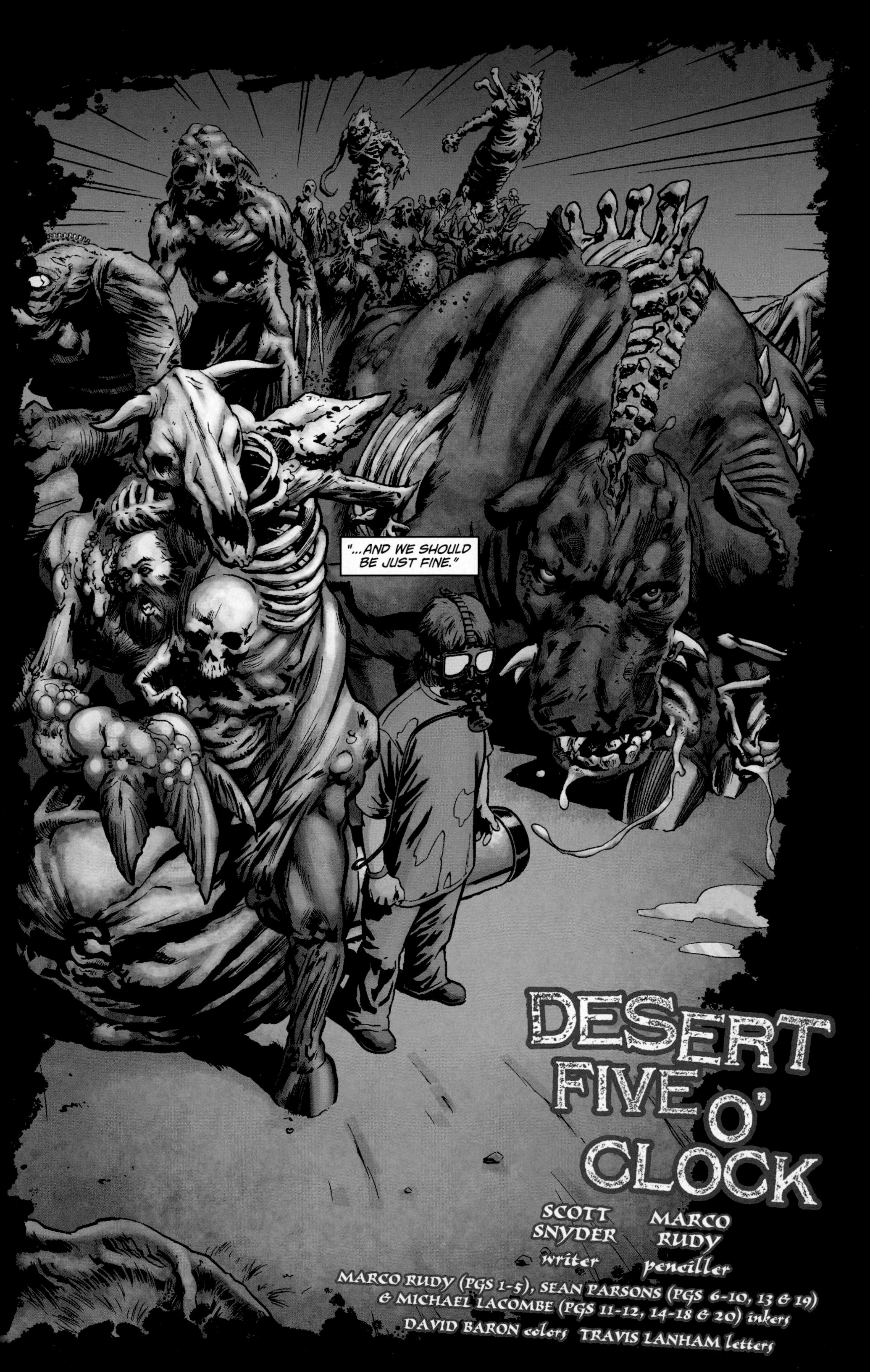
"...AND WE SHOULD BE JUST FINE."
DESERT FIVE O' CLOCK
SCOTT SNYDER writer
MARCO RUDY penciller
MARCO RUDY (PGS 1-5), SEAN PARSONS (PGS 6-10, 13 & 19) & MICHAEL LACOMBE (PGS 11-12, 14-18 & 20) inkers
DAVID BARON colors TRAVIS LANHAM letters

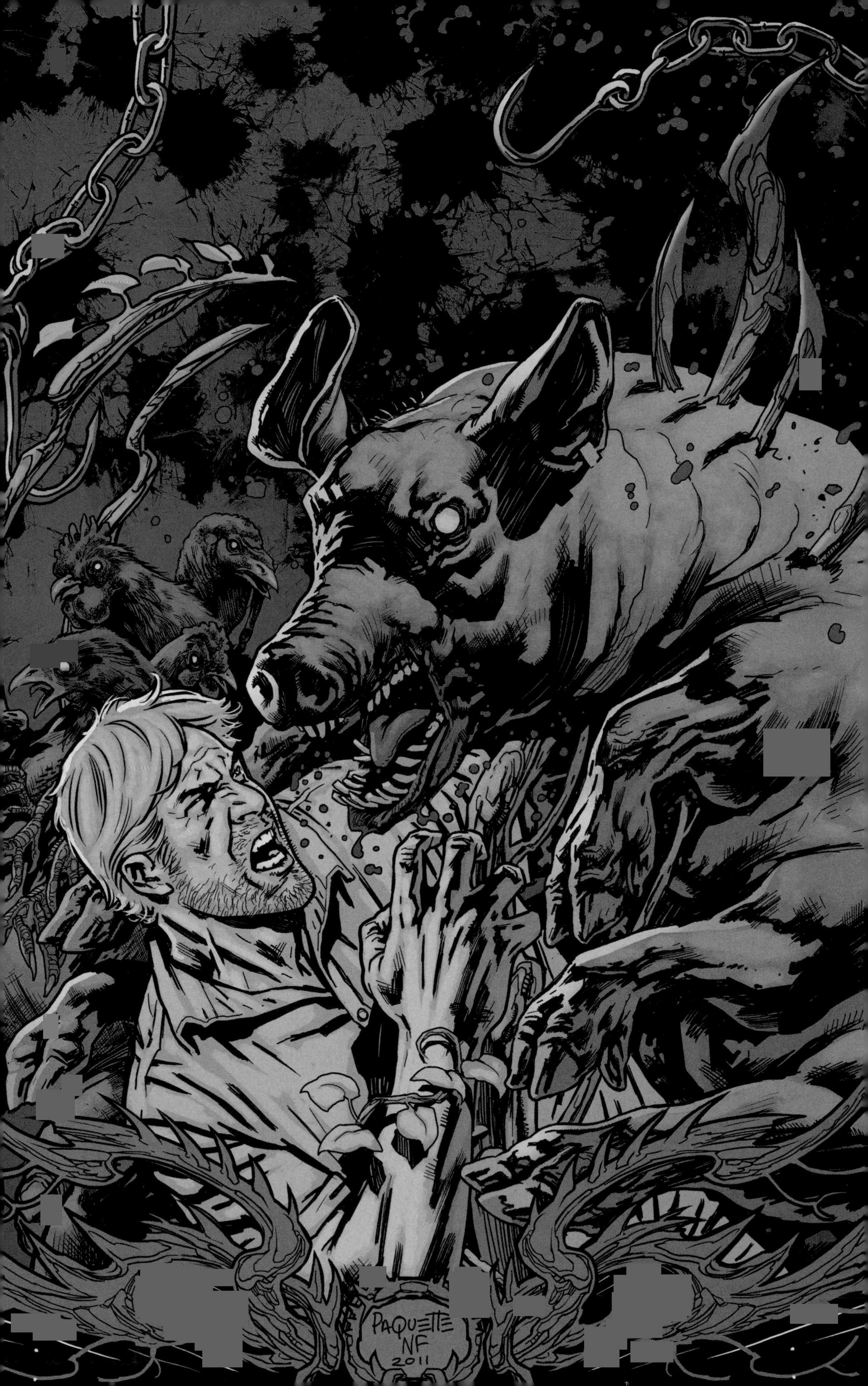
PAQUETTE
NF
2011

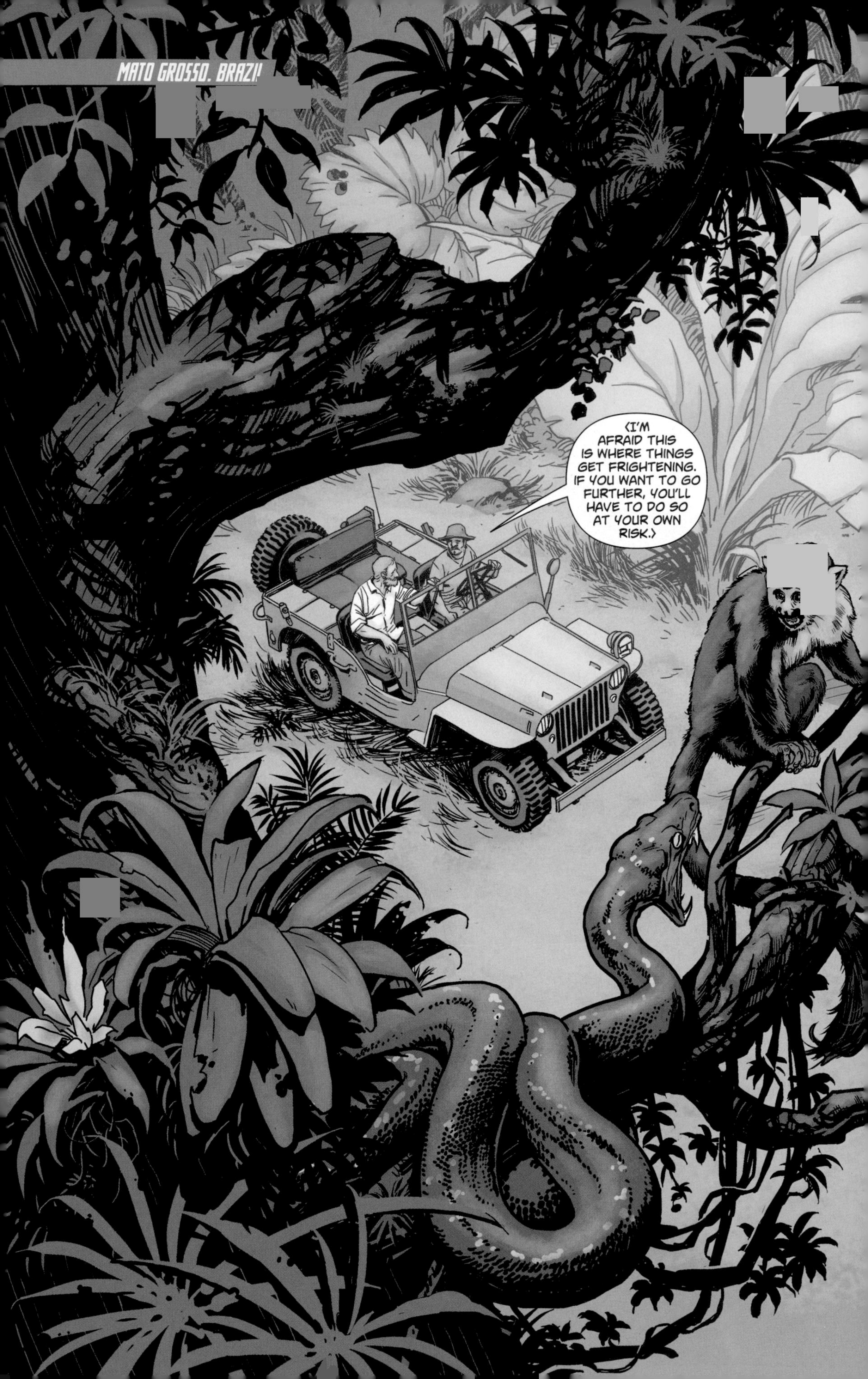
MATO GROSSO, BRAZI
‹I'M AFRAID THIS IS WHERE THINGS GET FRIGHTENING. IF YOU WANT TO GO FURTHER, YOU'LL HAVE TO DO SO AT YOUR OWN RISK.›

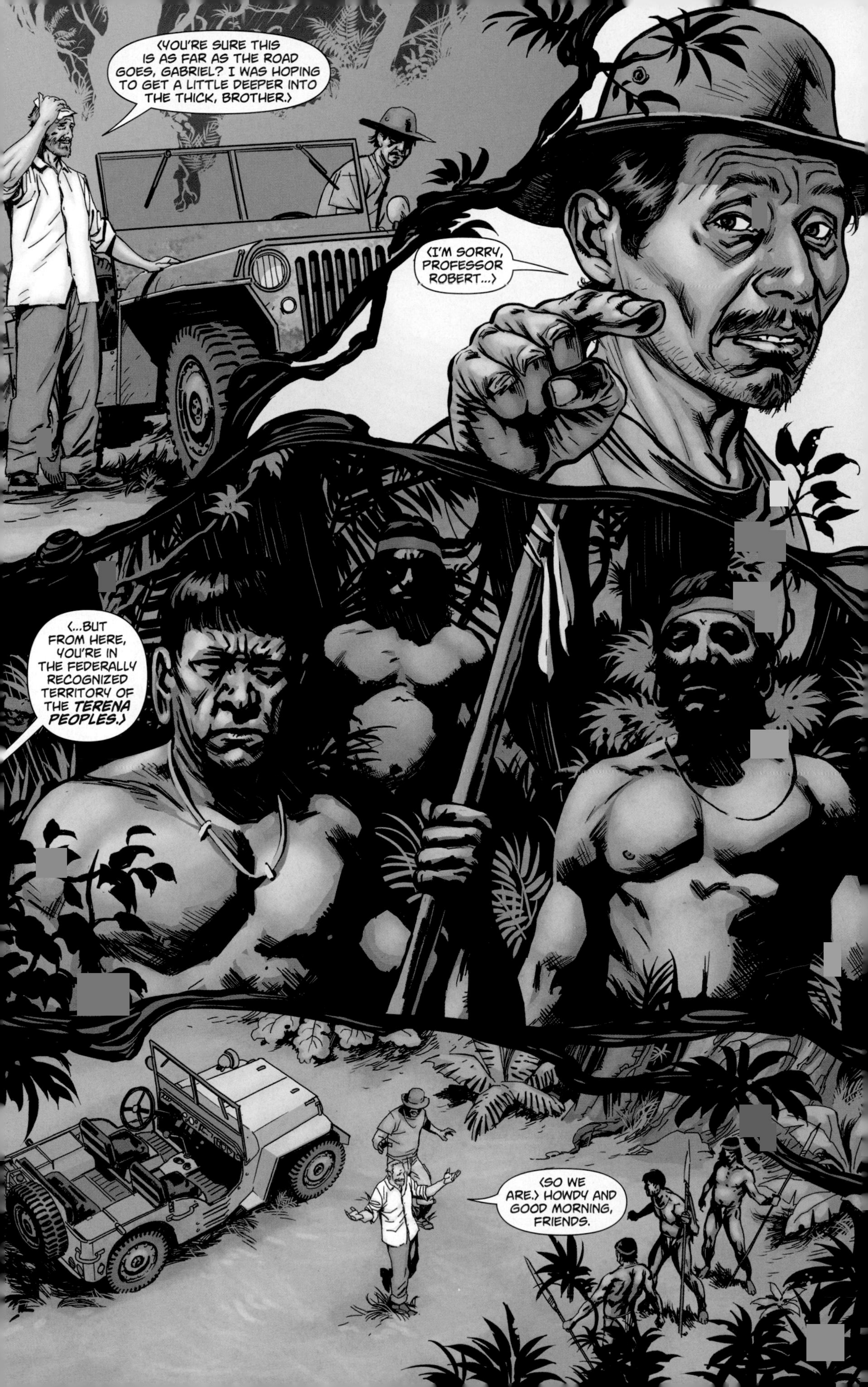

(YOU'RE SURE THIS IS AS FAR AS THE ROAD GOES, GABRIEL? I WAS HOPING TO GET A LITTLE DEEPER INTO THE THICK, BROTHER.)
(I'M SORRY, PROFESSOR ROBERT...)
(...BUT FROM HERE, YOU'RE IN THE FEDERALLY RECOGNIZED TERRITORY OF THE *TERENA PEOPLES.*)
(SO WE ARE.) HOWDY AND GOOD MORNING, FRIENDS.

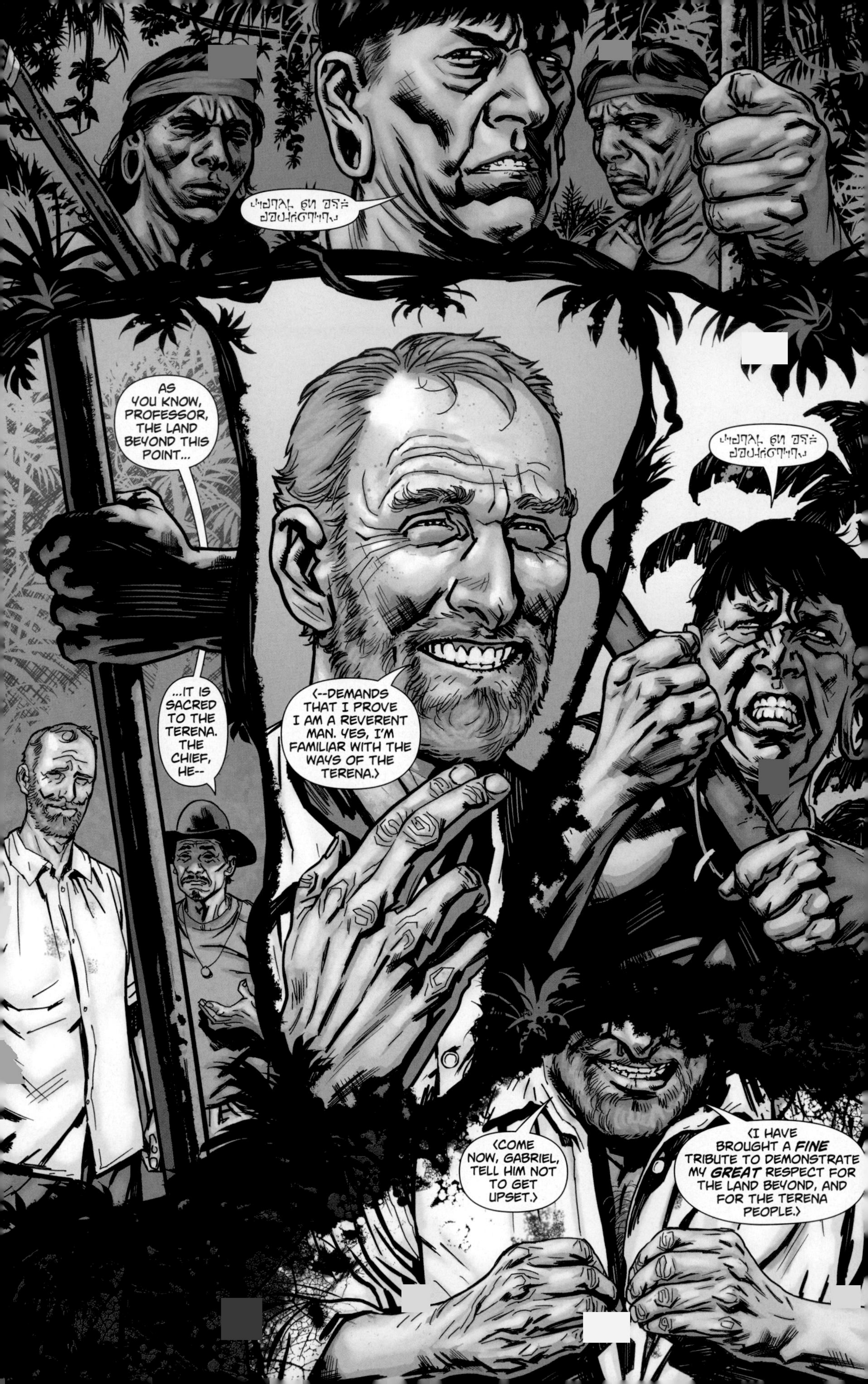
AS YOU KNOW, PROFESSOR, THE LAND BEYOND THIS POINT...
...IT IS SACRED TO THE TERENA. THE CHIEF, HE--
‹--DEMANDS THAT I PROVE I AM A REVERENT MAN. YES, I'M FAMILIAR WITH THE WAYS OF THE TERENA.›
‹COME NOW, GABRIEL, TELL HIM NOT TO GET UPSET.›
‹I HAVE BROUGHT A *FINE* TRIBUTE TO DEMONSTRATE MY ***GREAT*** RESPECT FOR THE LAND BEYOND, AND FOR THE TERENA PEOPLE.›

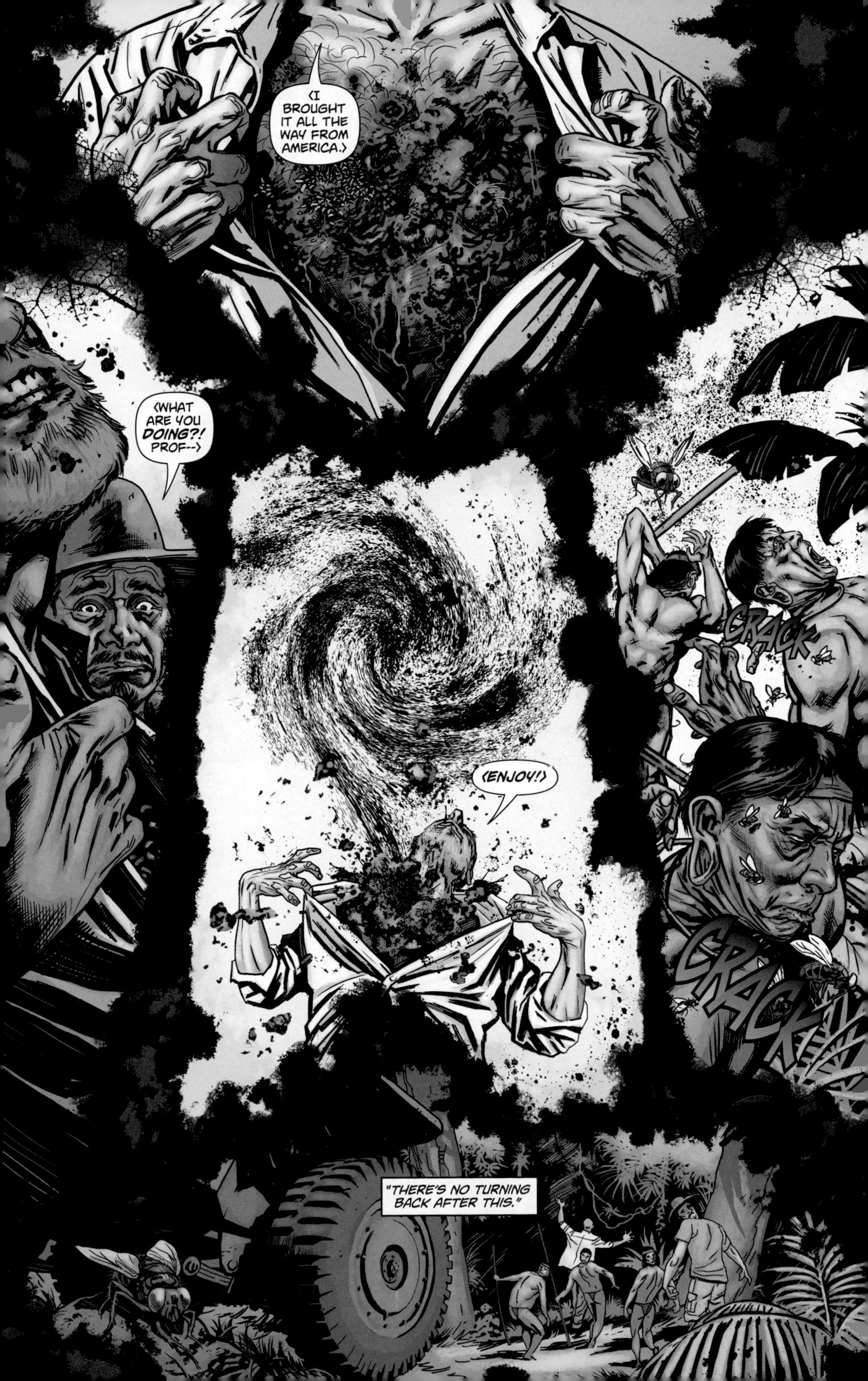

‹I BROUGHT IT ALL THE WAY FROM AMERICA.›
‹WHAT ARE YOU *DOING?!* PROF--›
‹ENJOY!›
CRACK
CRACK
"THERE'S NO TURNING BACK AFTER THIS."

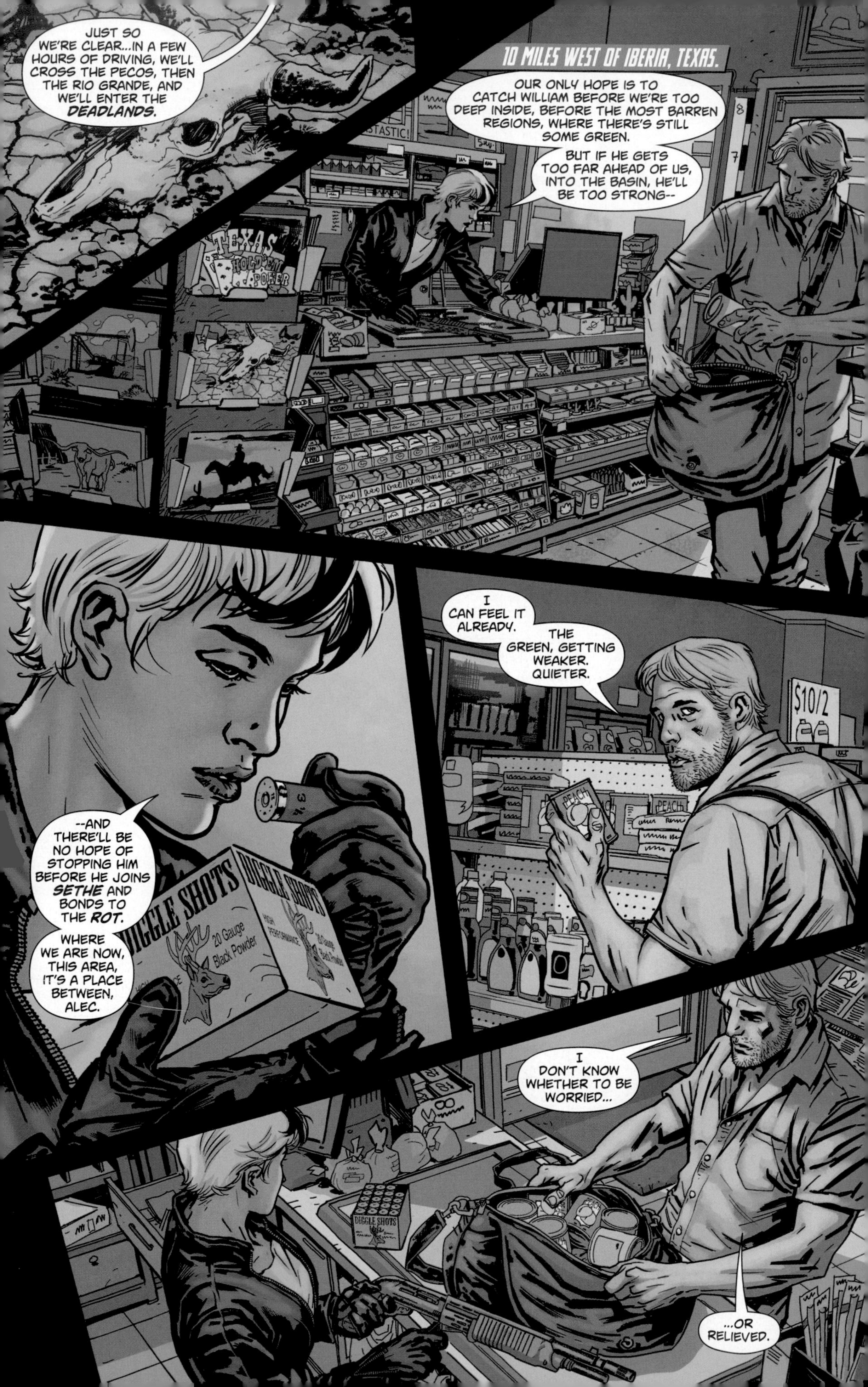
JUST SO WE'RE CLEAR...IN A FEW HOURS OF DRIVING, WE'LL CROSS THE PECOS, THEN THE RIO GRANDE, AND WE'LL ENTER THE DEADLANDS.
10 MILES WEST OF IBERIA, TEXAS.
OUR ONLY HOPE IS TO CATCH WILLIAM BEFORE WE'RE TOO DEEP INSIDE, BEFORE THE MOST BARREN REGIONS, WHERE THERE'S STILL SOME GREEN.
BUT IF HE GETS TOO FAR AHEAD OF US, INTO THE BASIN, HE'LL BE TOO STRONG--
TEXAS HOLDEM POKER
--AND THERE'LL BE NO HOPE OF STOPPING HIM BEFORE HE JOINS SETHE AND BONDS TO THE ROT.
WHERE WE ARE NOW, THIS AREA, IT'S A PLACE BETWEEN, ALEC.
DIGGLE SHOTS
20 Gauge Black Powder
I CAN FEEL IT ALREADY.
THE GREEN, GETTING WEAKER. QUIETER.
$10/2
PEACH
I DON'T KNOW WHETHER TO BE WORRIED...
...OR RELIEVED.

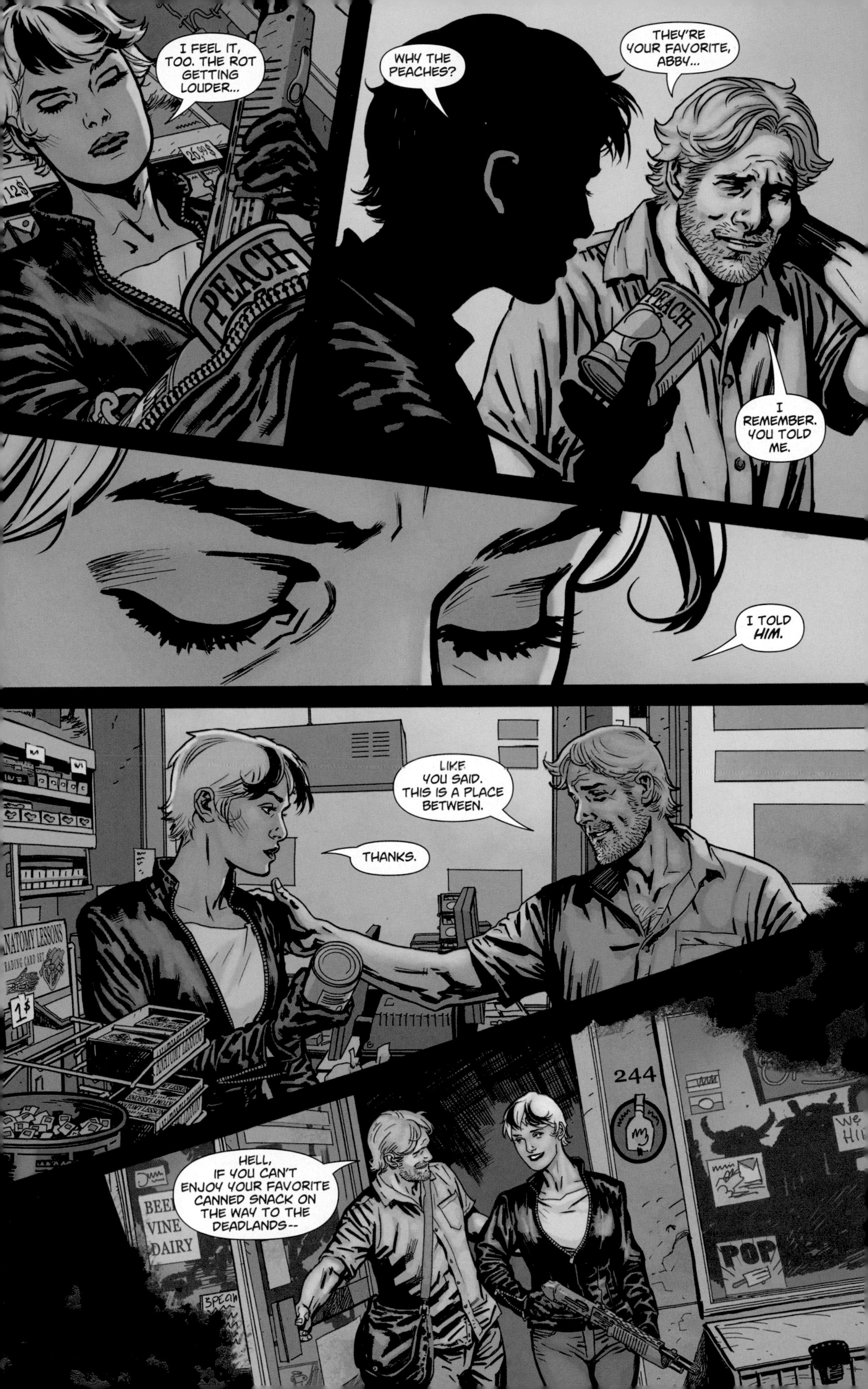
I FEEL IT, TOO. THE ROT GETTING LOUDER...
WHY THE PEACHES?
THEY'RE YOUR FAVORITE, ABBY...
I REMEMBER. YOU TOLD ME.
I TOLD *HIM*.
LIKE YOU SAID. THIS IS A PLACE BETWEEN.
THANKS.
HELL, IF YOU CAN'T ENJOY YOUR FAVORITE CANNED SNACK ON THE WAY TO THE DEADLANDS--
PEACH
ANATOMY LESSONS
1$
244
BEER
WINE
DAIRY
POP

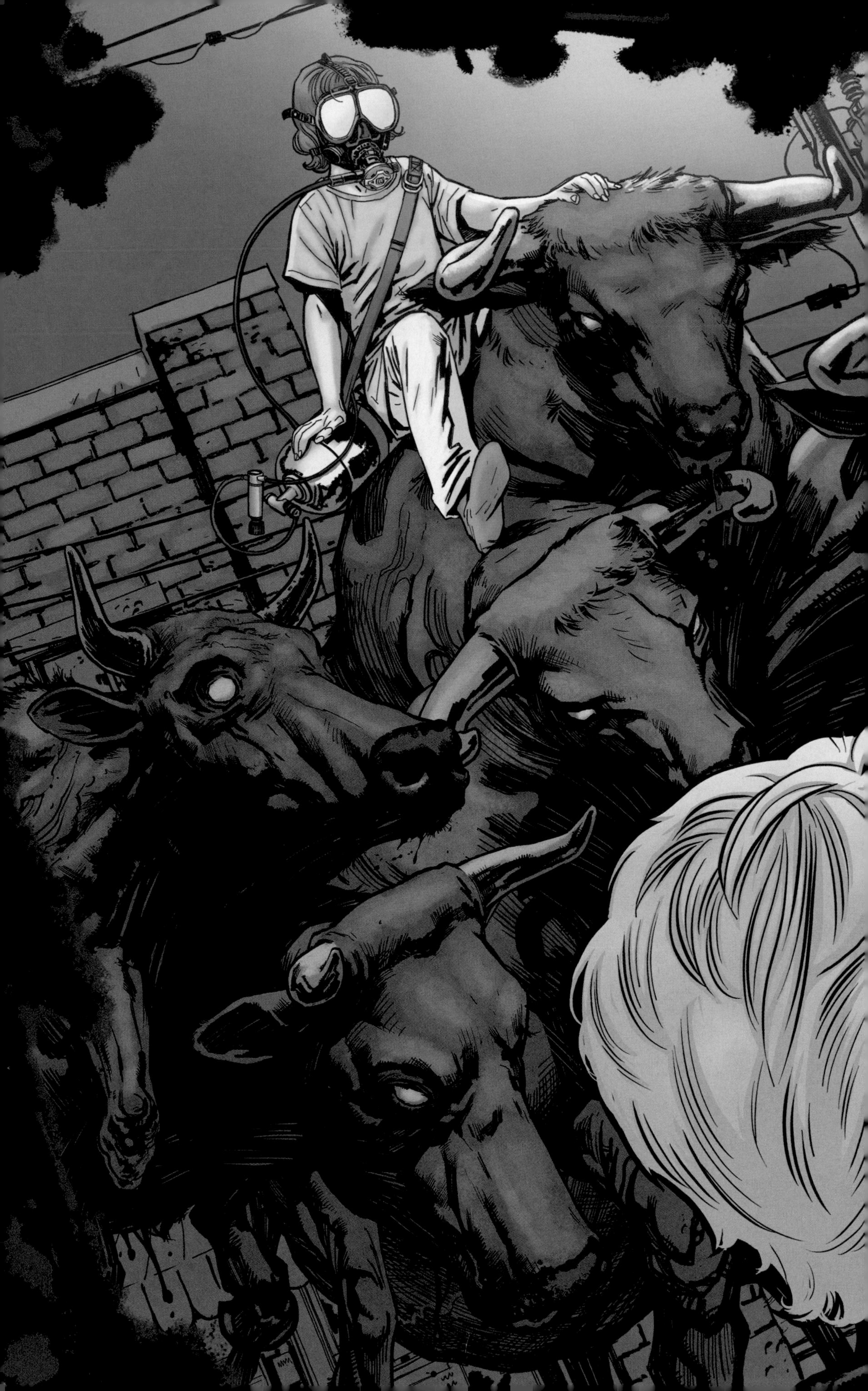

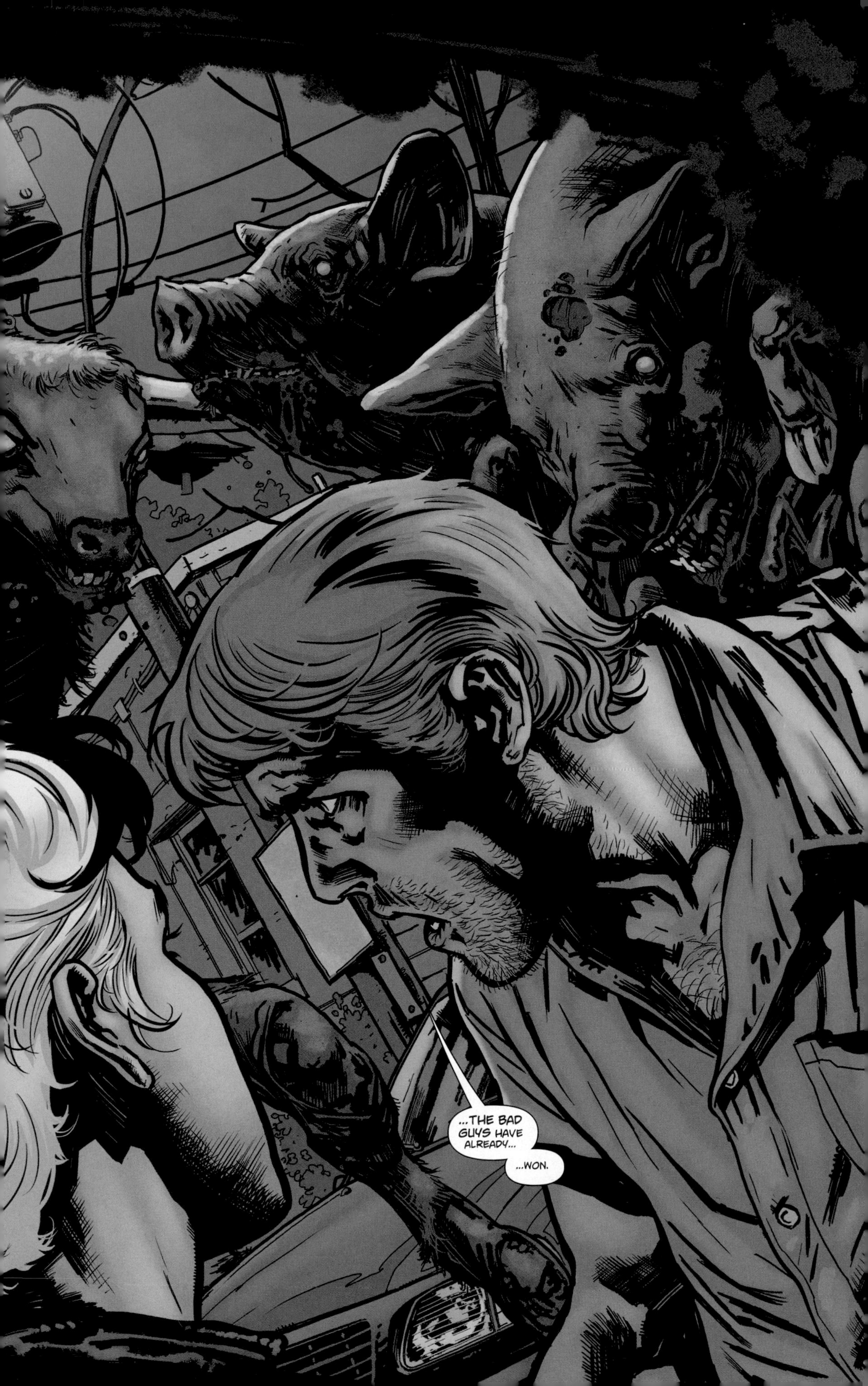
...THE BAD GUYS HAVE ALREADY...
...WON.

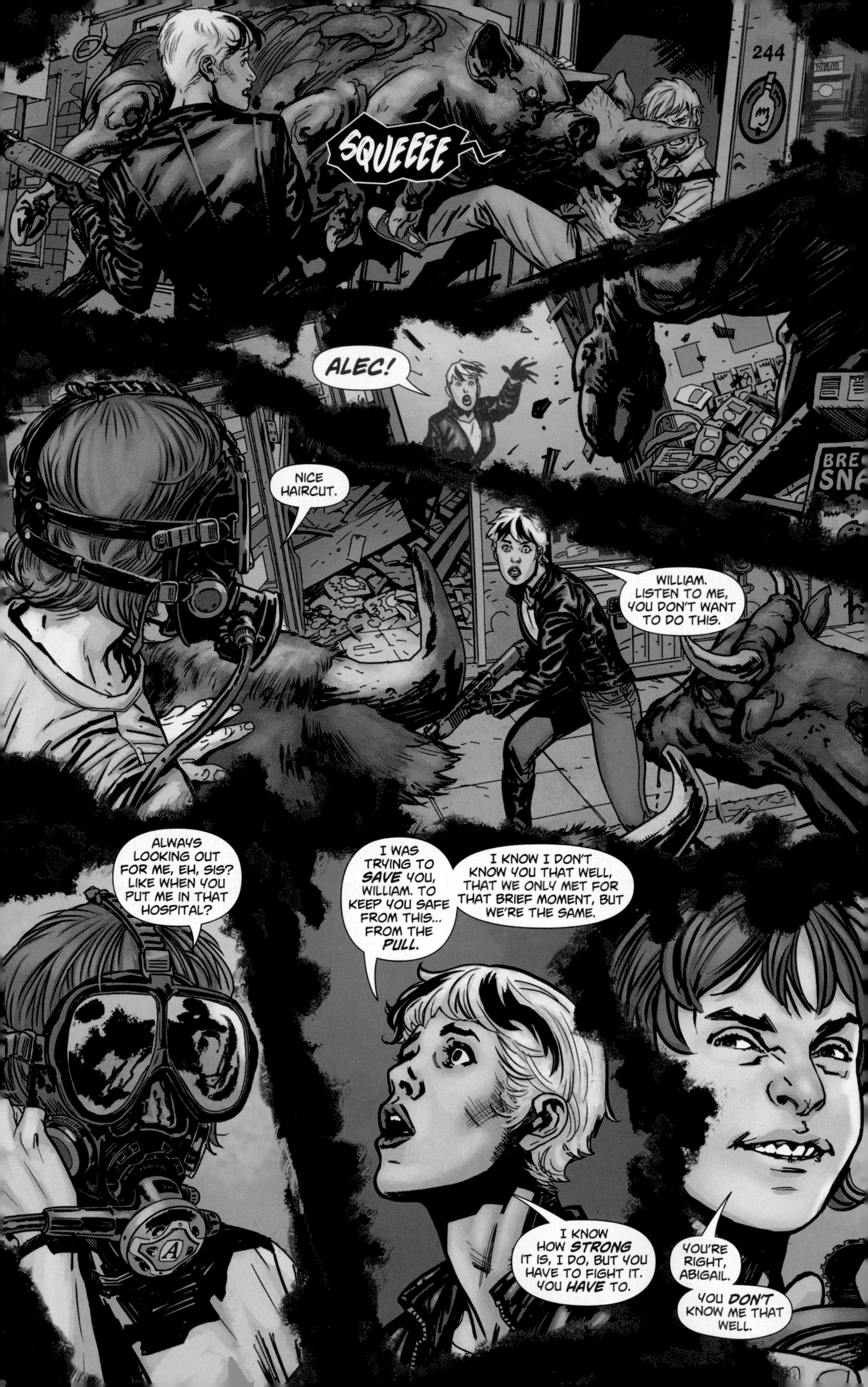
SQUEEEE
244
ALEC!
NICE HAIRCUT.
BRE
SNA
WILLIAM. LISTEN TO ME, YOU DON'T WANT TO DO THIS.
ALWAYS LOOKING OUT FOR ME, EH, SIS? LIKE WHEN YOU PUT ME IN THAT HOSPITAL?
I WAS TRYING TO SAVE YOU, WILLIAM. TO KEEP YOU SAFE FROM THIS... FROM THE PULL.
I KNOW I DON'T KNOW YOU THAT WELL, THAT WE ONLY MET FOR THAT BRIEF MOMENT, BUT WE'RE THE SAME.
I KNOW HOW STRONG IT IS, I DO, BUT YOU HAVE TO FIGHT IT. YOU HAVE TO.
YOU'RE RIGHT, ABIGAIL.
YOU DON'T KNOW ME THAT WELL.

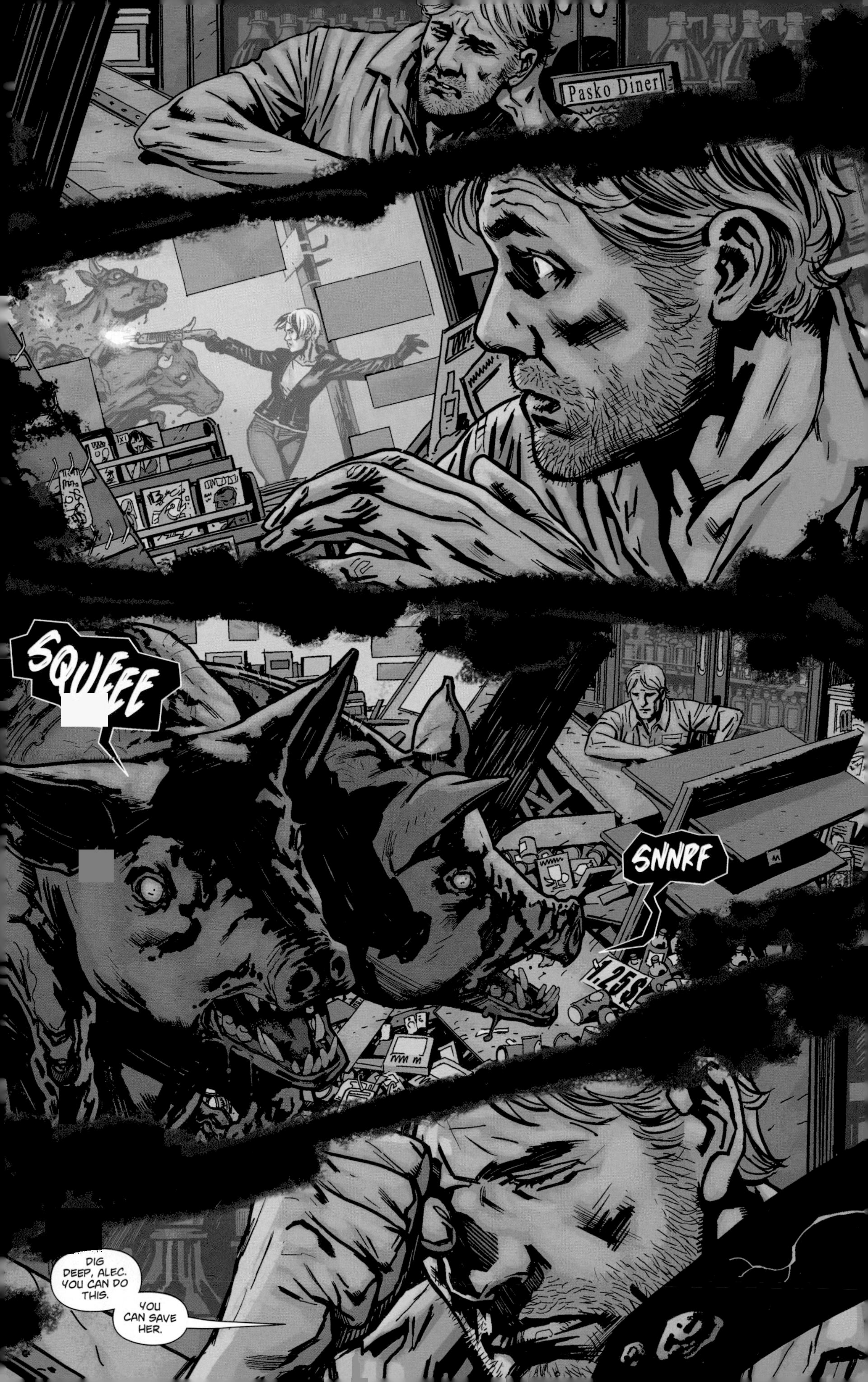
Pasko Diner
SQUEEE
SNNRF
1.25$
DIG DEEP, ALEC. YOU CAN DO THIS.
YOU CAN SAVE HER.

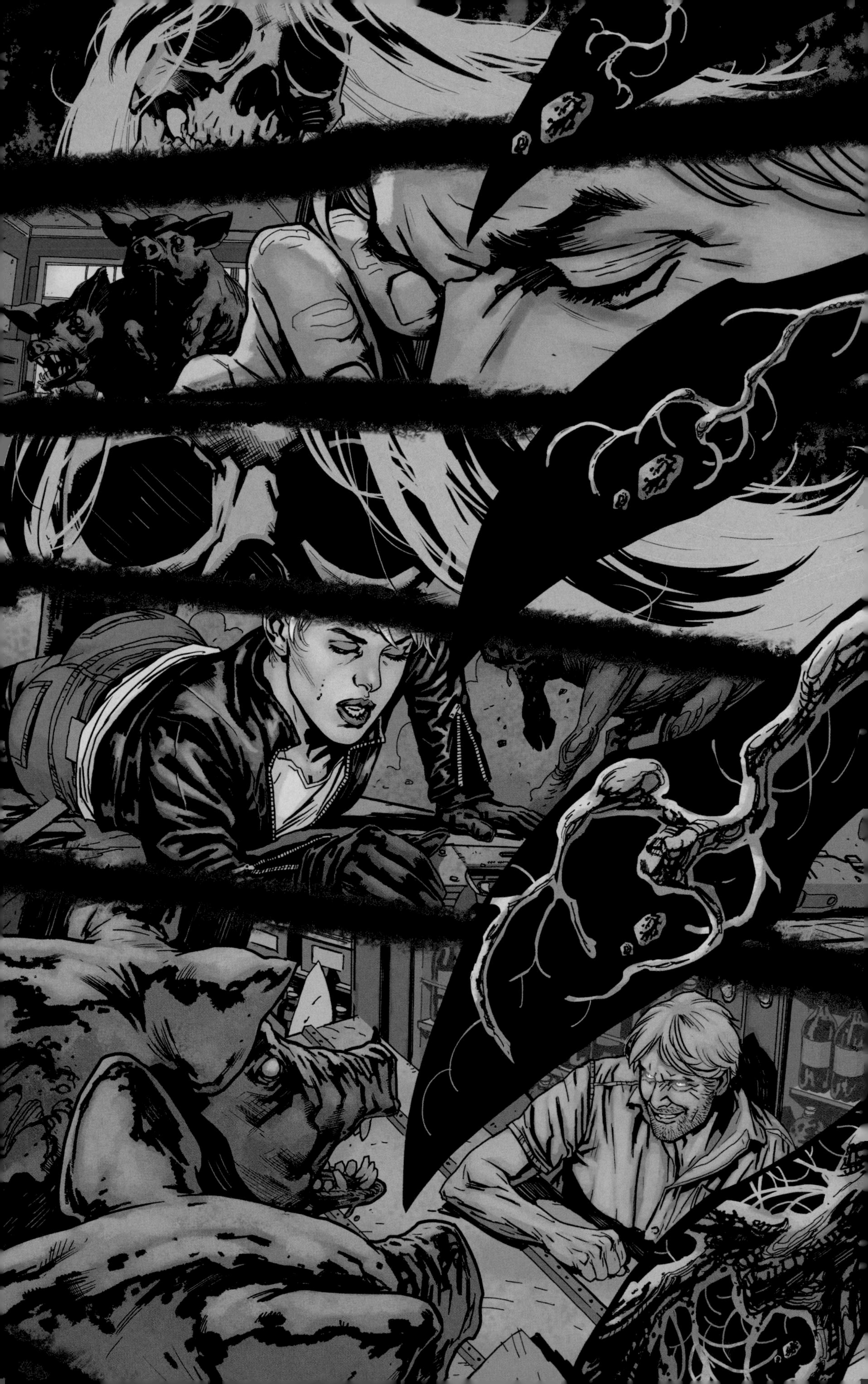

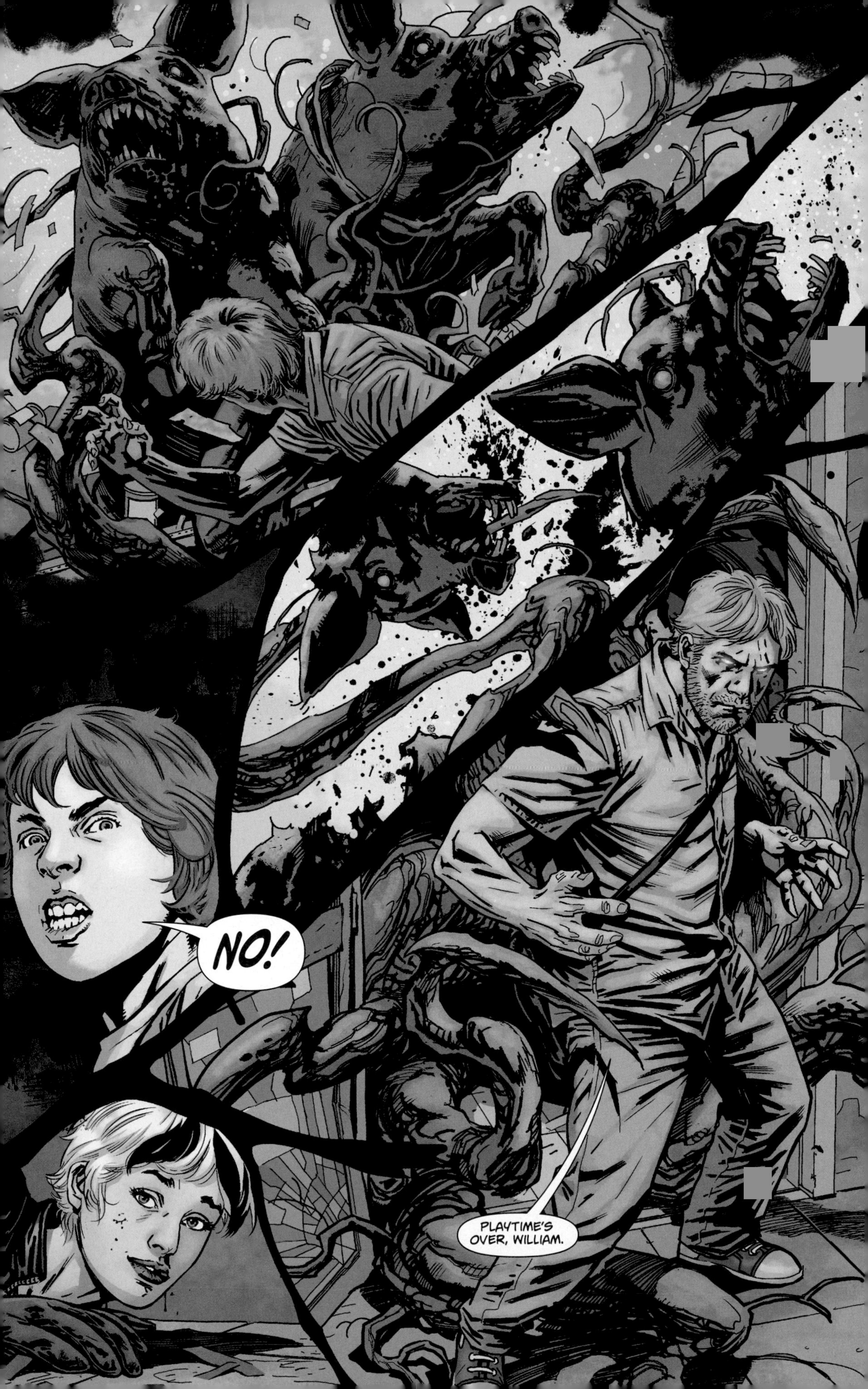
NO!
PLAYTIME'S OVER, WILLIAM.

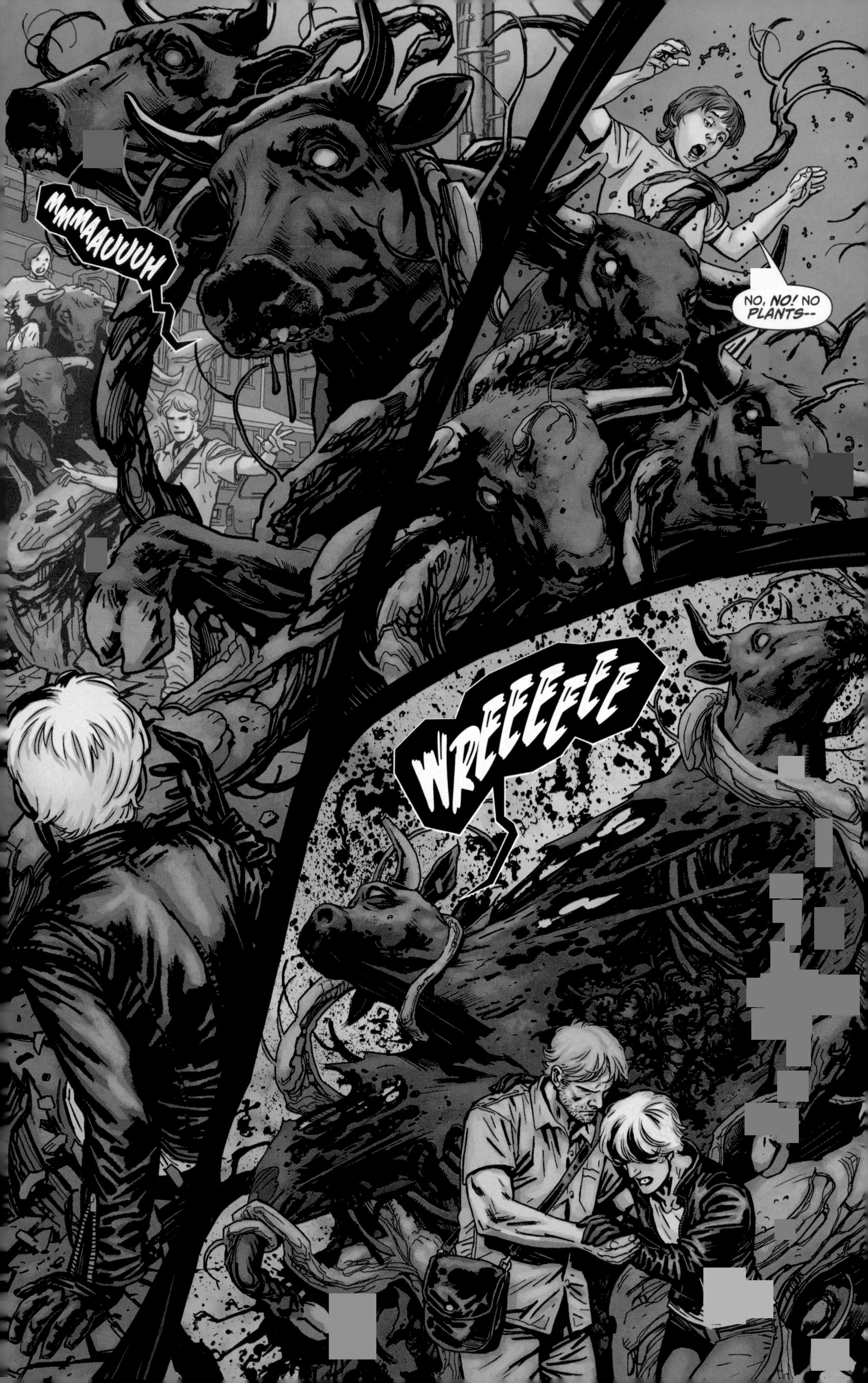
MMMAAUUUH
NO, NO! NO PLANTS--
WREEEEEEE

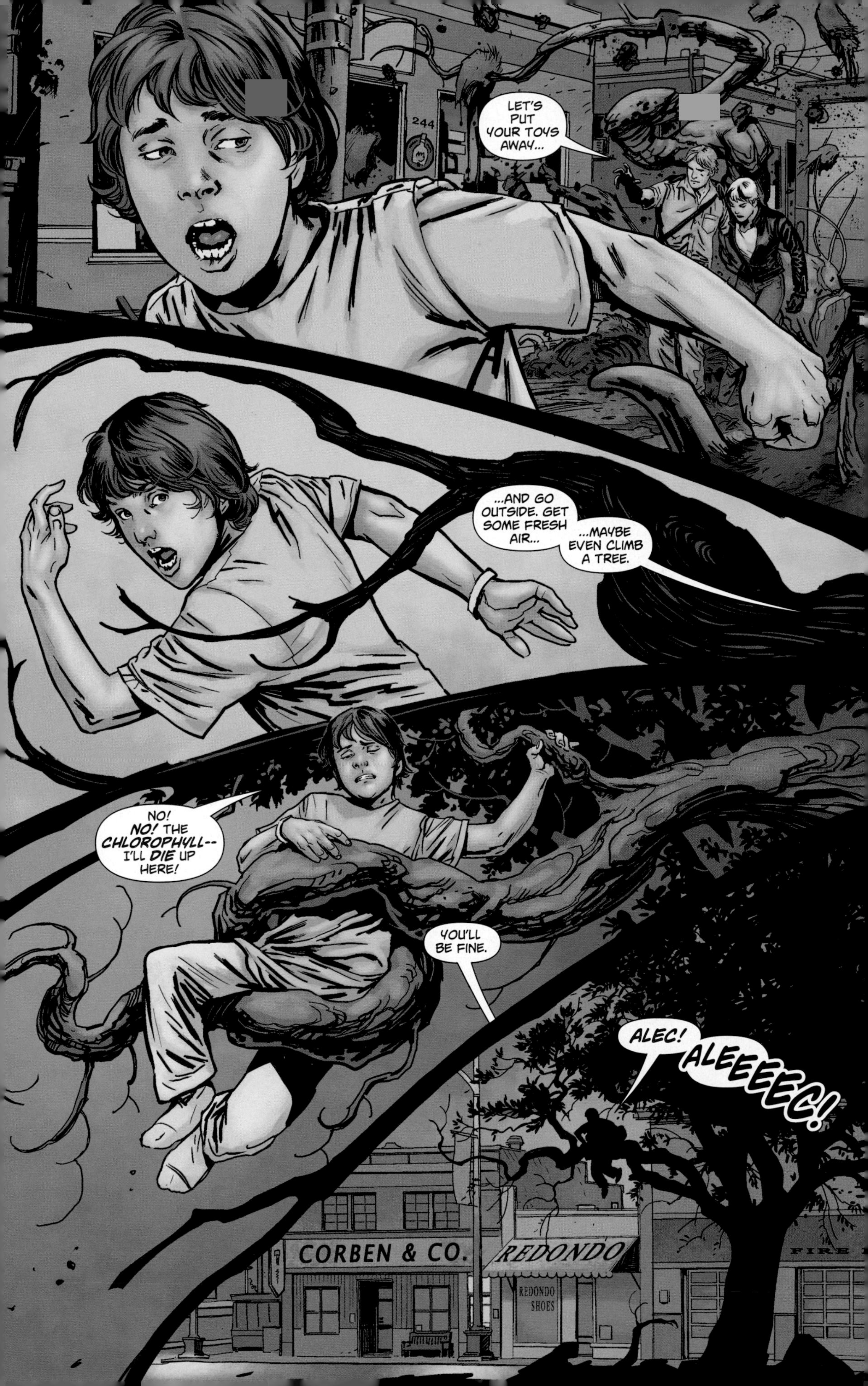

244
LET'S PUT YOUR TOYS AWAY...
...AND GO OUTSIDE. GET SOME FRESH AIR...
...MAYBE EVEN CLIMB A TREE.
NO! NO! THE CHLOROPHYLL-- I'LL DIE UP HERE!
YOU'LL BE FINE.
ALEC!
ALEEEEC!
CORBEN & CO.
REDONDO
REDONDO SHOES

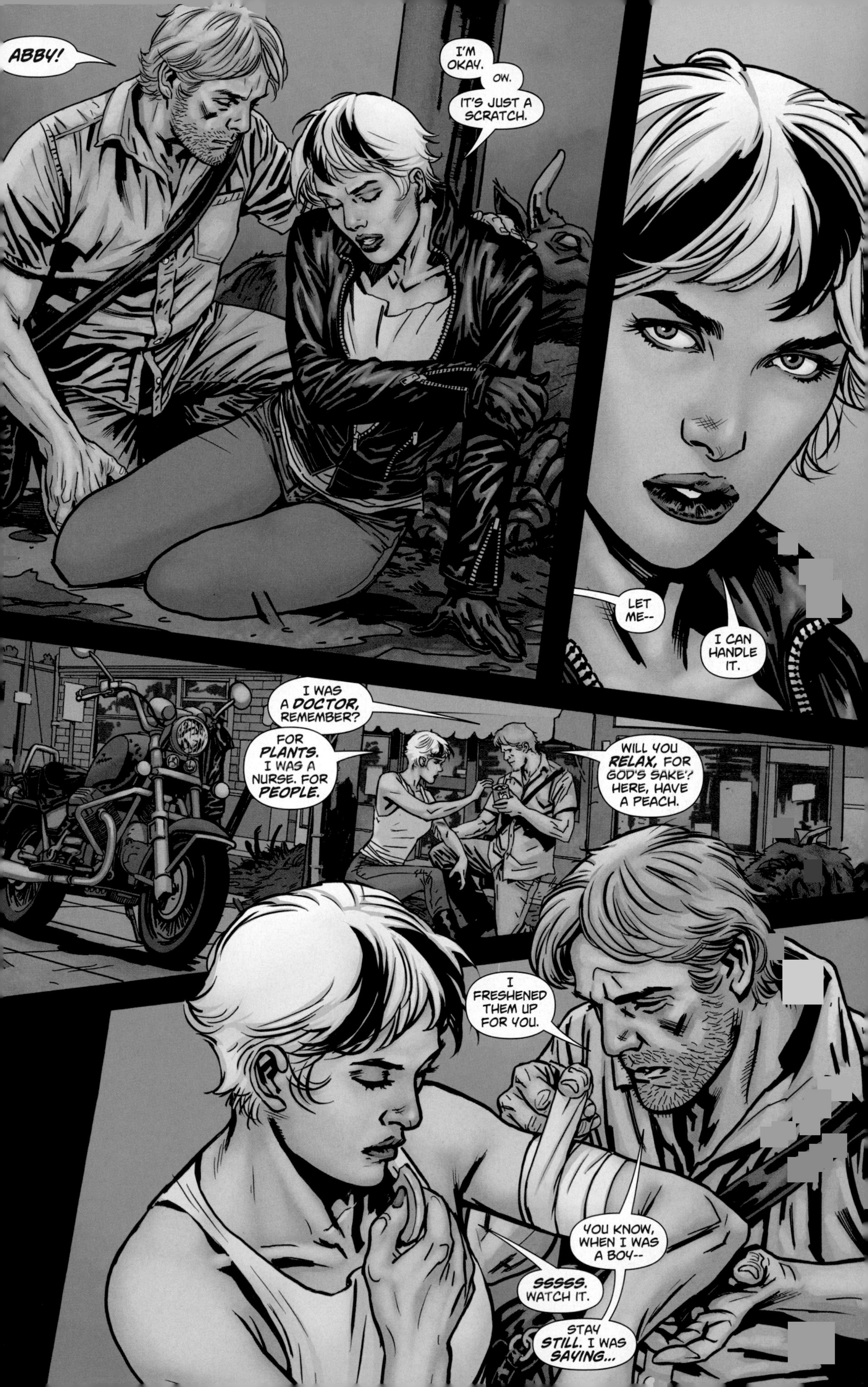
ABBY!
I'M OKAY.
OW.
IT'S JUST A SCRATCH.
LET ME--
I CAN HANDLE IT.
I WAS A **DOCTOR,** REMEMBER?
FOR **PLANTS.** I WAS A NURSE. FOR **PEOPLE.**
WILL YOU **RELAX,** FOR GOD'S SAKE? HERE, HAVE A PEACH.
I FRESHENED THEM UP FOR YOU.
YOU KNOW, WHEN I WAS A BOY--
SSSSS. WATCH IT.
STAY **STILL.** I WAS **SAYING...**

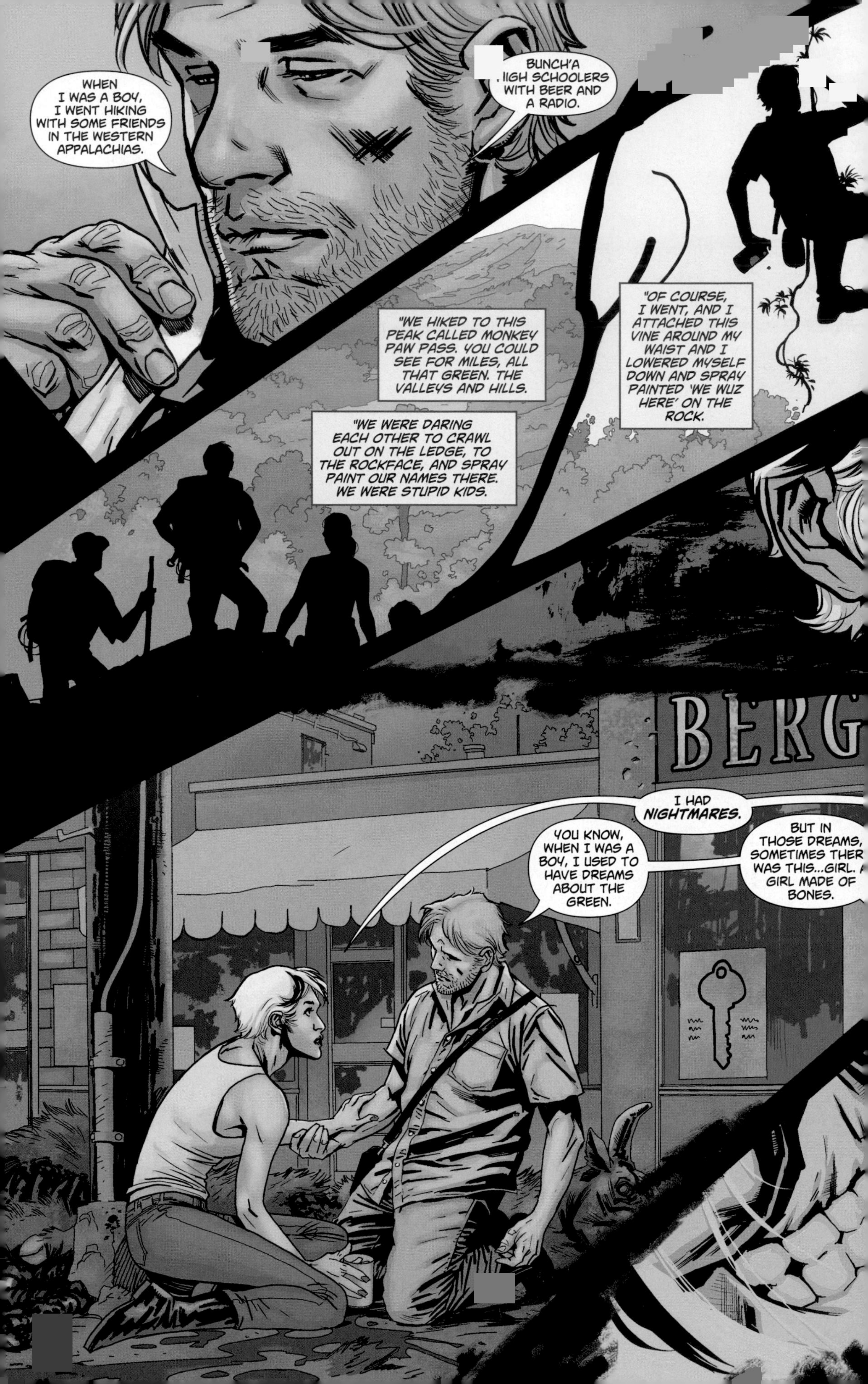
WHEN I WAS A BOY, I WENT HIKING WITH SOME FRIENDS IN THE WESTERN APPALACHIAS.
BUNCH'A IGH SCHOOLERS WITH BEER AND A RADIO.
"WE HIKED TO THIS PEAK CALLED MONKEY PAW PASS. YOU COULD SEE FOR MILES, ALL THAT GREEN. THE VALLEYS AND HILLS.
"WE WERE DARING EACH OTHER TO CRAWL OUT ON THE LEDGE, TO THE ROCKFACE, AND SPRAY PAINT OUR NAMES THERE. WE WERE STUPID KIDS.
"OF COURSE, I WENT, AND I ATTACHED THIS VINE AROUND MY WAIST AND I LOWERED MYSELF DOWN AND SPRAY PAINTED 'WE WUZ HERE' ON THE ROCK.
BERG
I HAD NIGHTMARES.
YOU KNOW, WHEN I WAS A BOY, I USED TO HAVE DREAMS ABOUT THE GREEN.
BUT IN THOSE DREAMS, SOMETIMES THER WAS THIS...GIRL. GIRL MADE OF BONES.

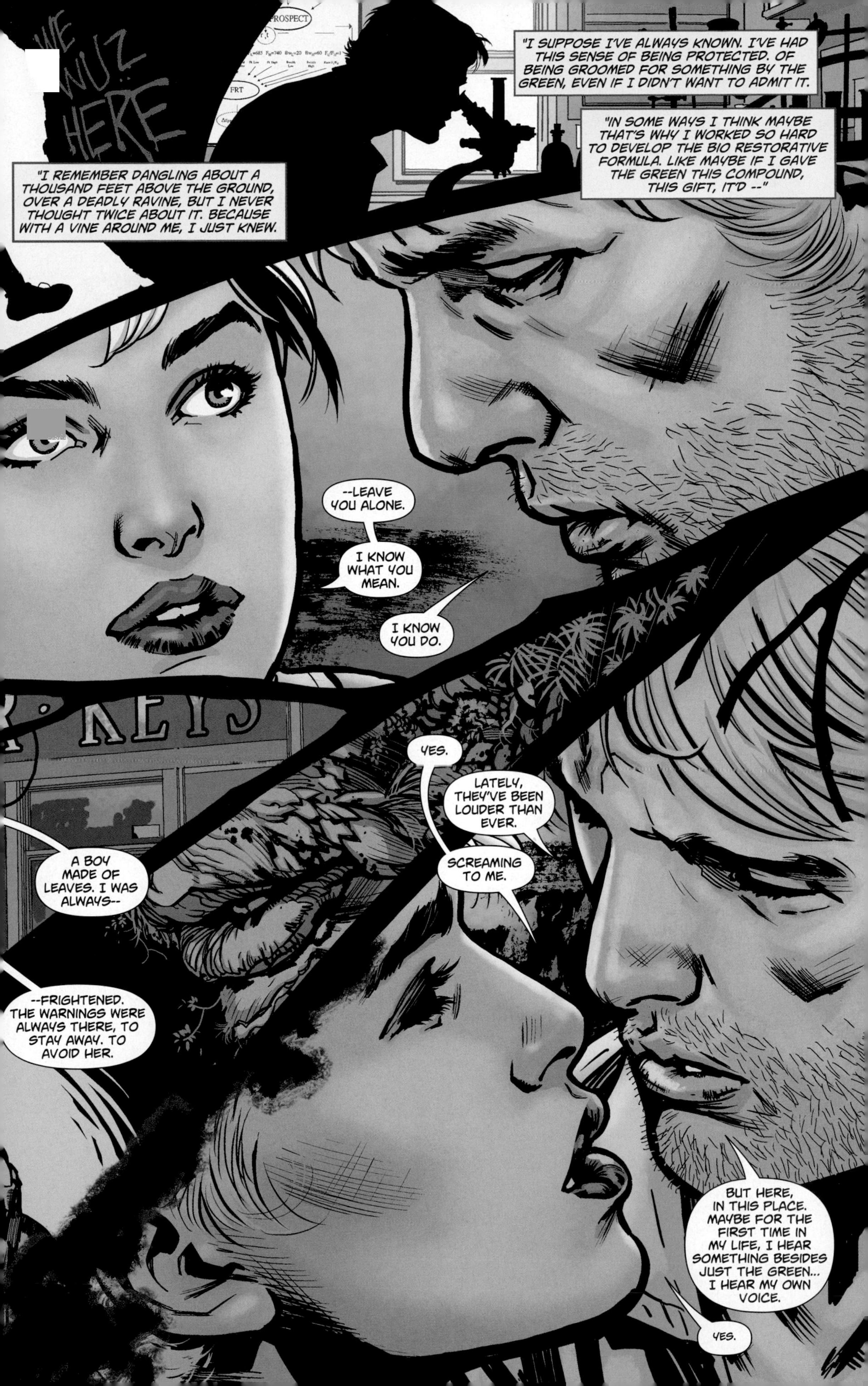
WE WUZ HERE
PROSPECT
FRT
"I SUPPOSE I'VE ALWAYS KNOWN. I'VE HAD THIS SENSE OF BEING PROTECTED. OF BEING GROOMED FOR SOMETHING BY THE GREEN, EVEN IF I DIDN'T WANT TO ADMIT IT.
"IN SOME WAYS I THINK MAYBE THAT'S WHY I WORKED SO HARD TO DEVELOP THE BIO RESTORATIVE FORMULA. LIKE MAYBE IF I GAVE THE GREEN THIS COMPOUND, THIS GIFT, IT'D --"
"I REMEMBER DANGLING ABOUT A THOUSAND FEET ABOVE THE GROUND, OVER A DEADLY RAVINE, BUT I NEVER THOUGHT TWICE ABOUT IT. BECAUSE WITH A VINE AROUND ME, I JUST KNEW.
--LEAVE YOU ALONE.
I KNOW WHAT YOU MEAN.
I KNOW YOU DO.
KEYS
YES.
LATELY, THEY'VE BEEN LOUDER THAN EVER.
SCREAMING TO ME.
A BOY MADE OF LEAVES. I WAS ALWAYS--
--FRIGHTENED. THE WARNINGS WERE ALWAYS THERE, TO STAY AWAY. TO AVOID HER.
BUT HERE, IN THIS PLACE. MAYBE FOR THE FIRST TIME IN MY LIFE, I HEAR SOMETHING BESIDES JUST THE GREEN... I HEAR MY OWN VOICE.
YES.

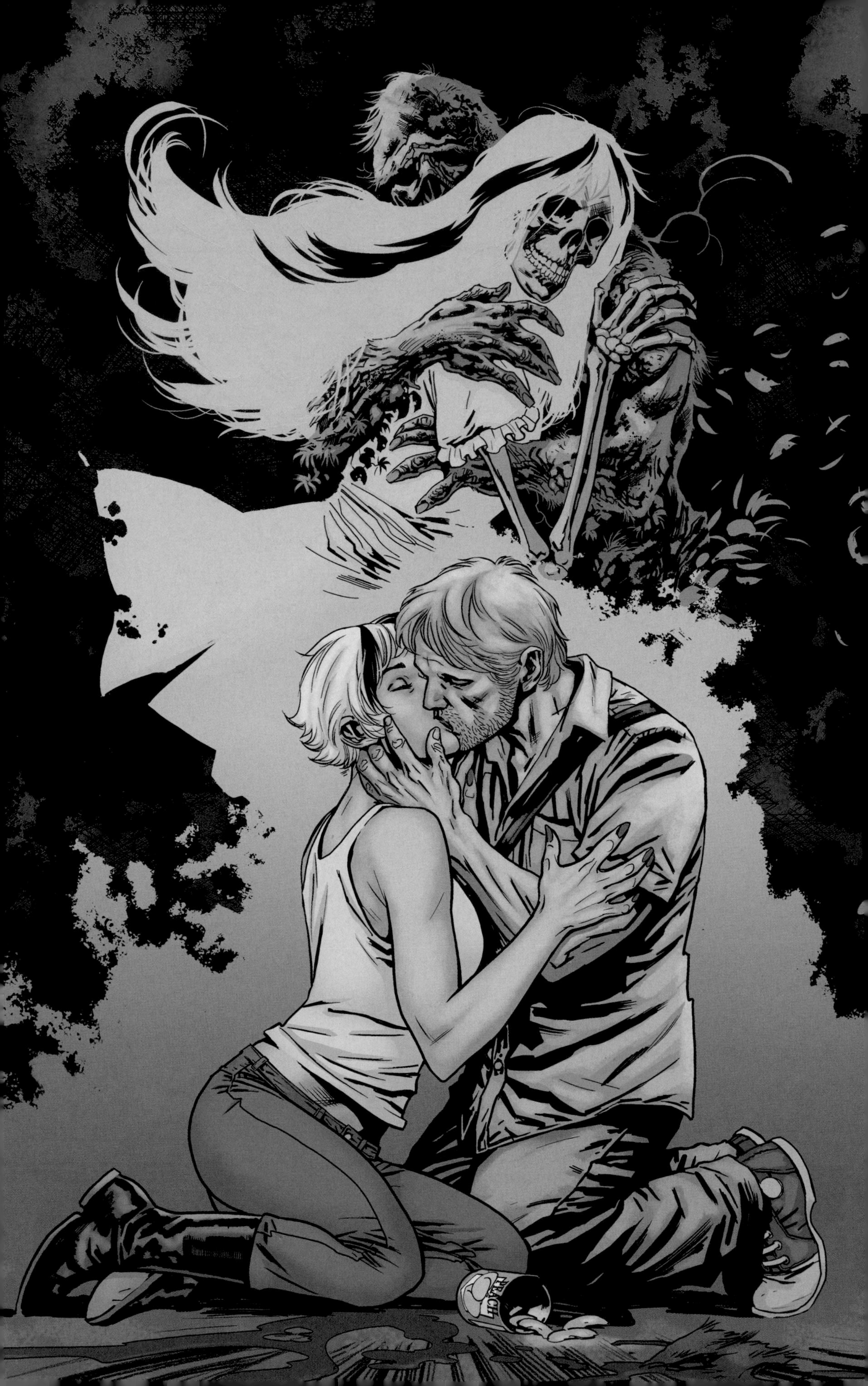
PEACH

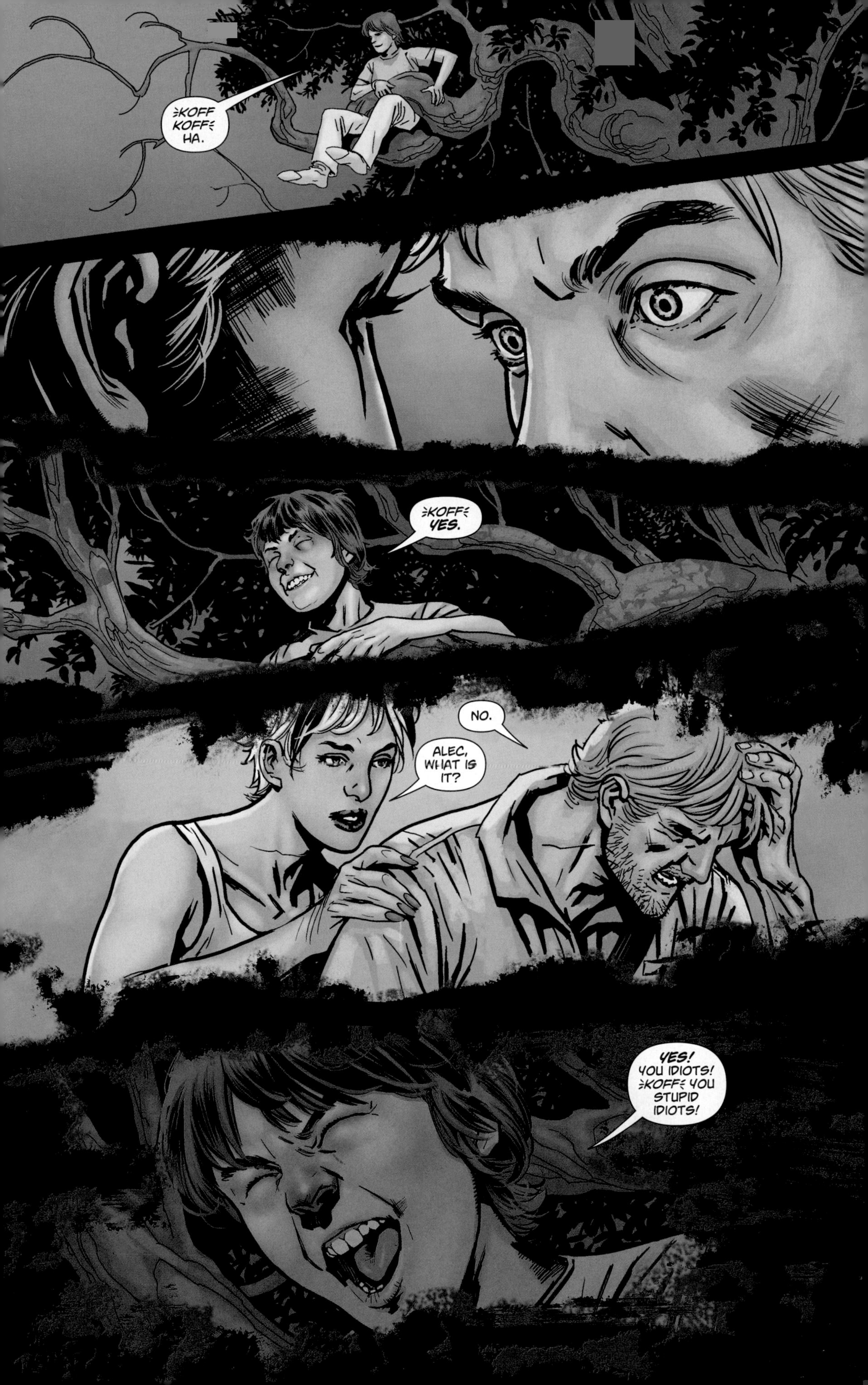

KOFF KOFF HA.
KOFF YES.
NO.
ALEC, WHAT IS IT?
YES! YOU IDIOTS! KOFF YOU STUPID IDIOTS!

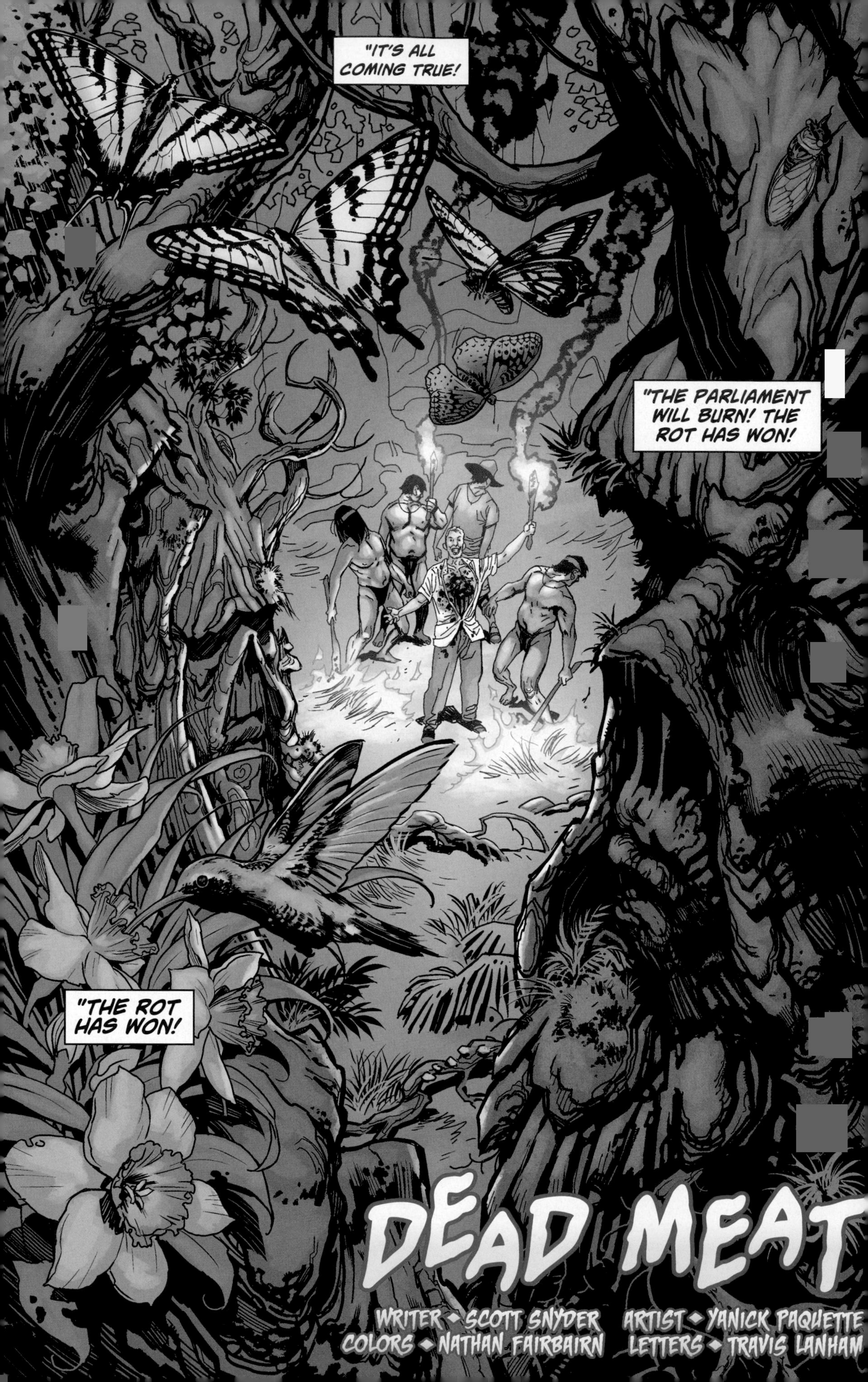
"IT'S ALL COMING TRUE!
"THE PARLIAMENT WILL BURN! THE ROT HAS WON!
"THE ROT HAS WON!
DEAD MEAT
WRITER • SCOTT SNYDER ARTIST • YANICK PAQUETTE
COLORS • NATHAN FAIRBAIRN LETTERS • TRAVIS LANHAM

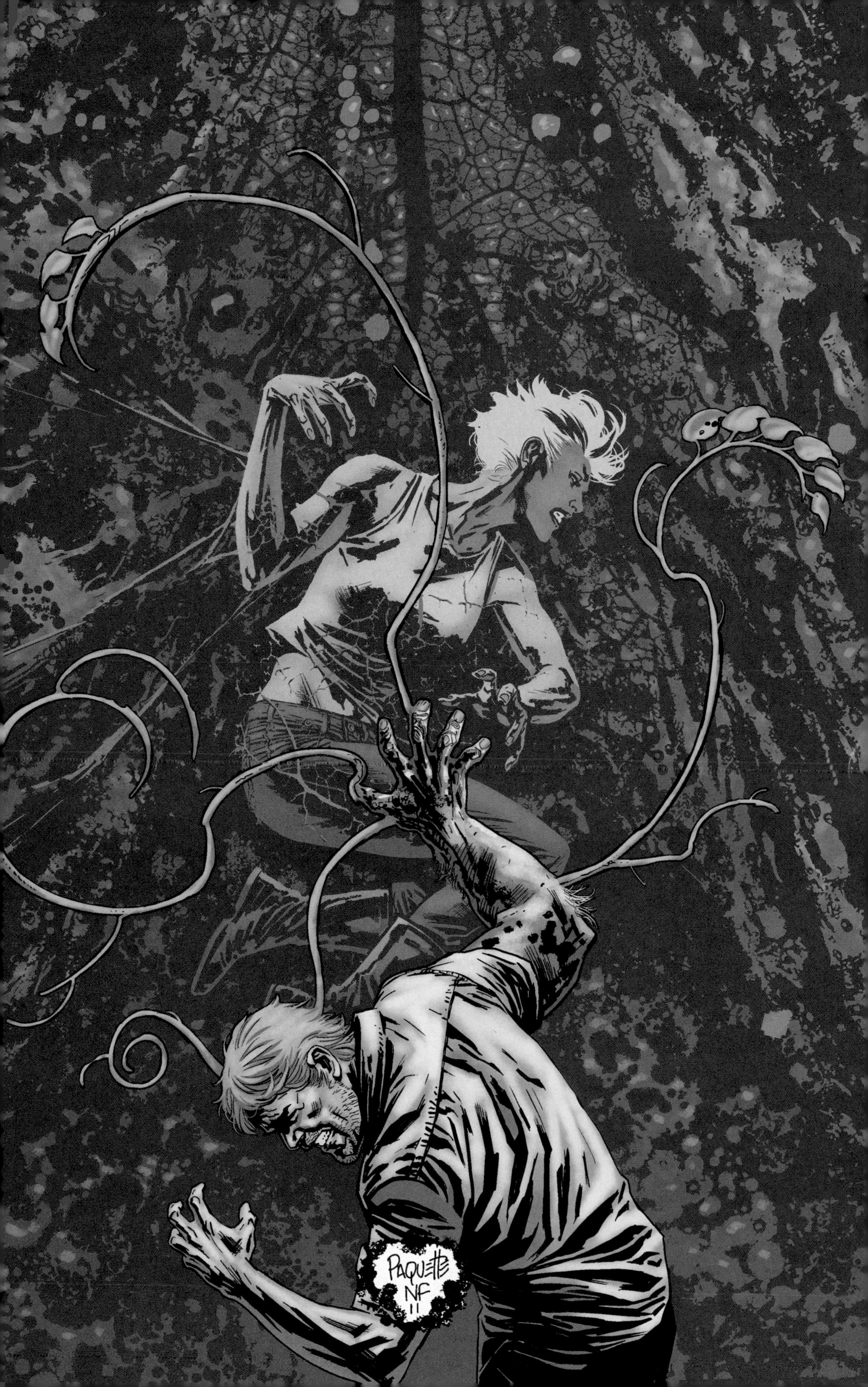
PAQUETTE
NF
11

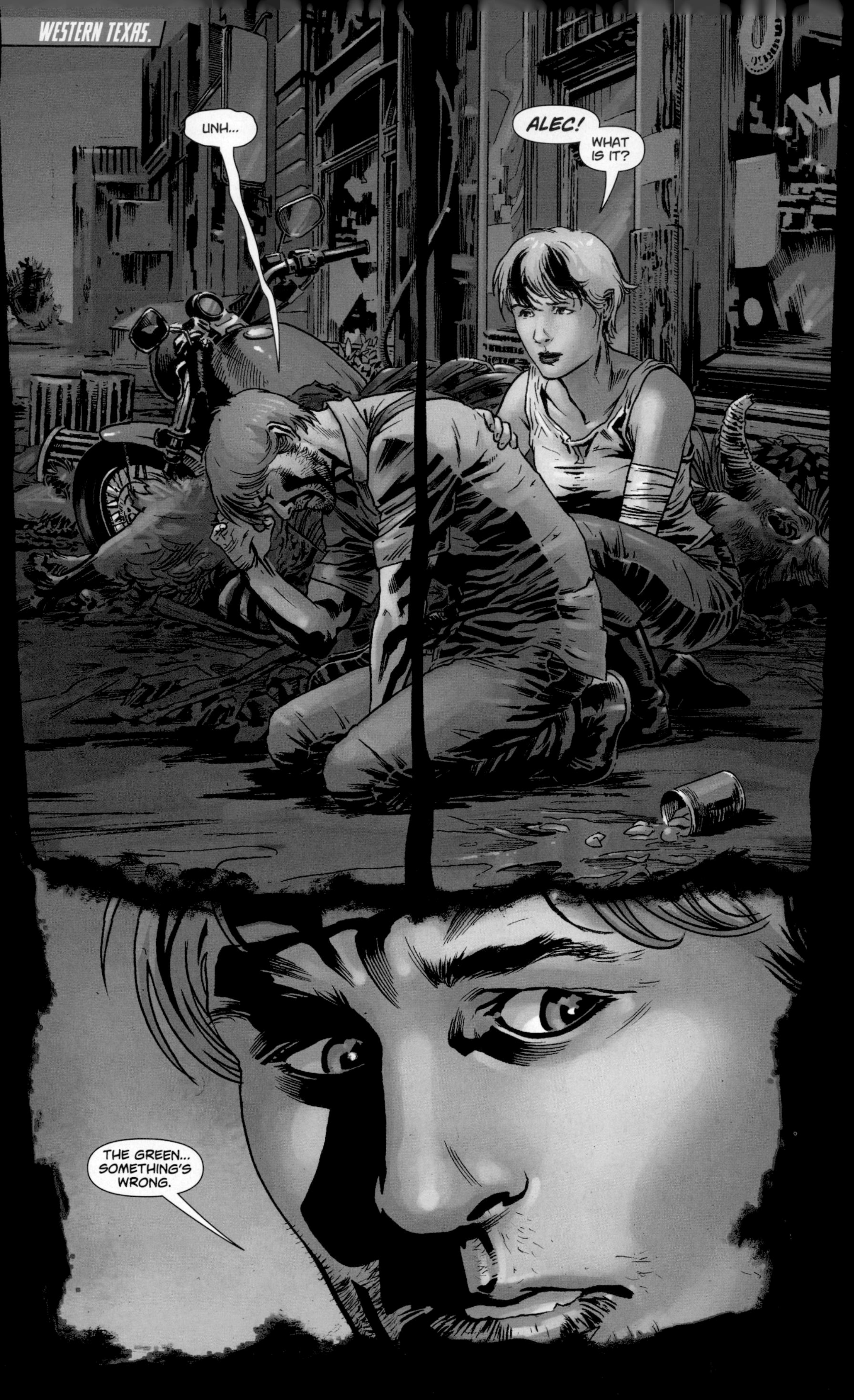
WESTERN TEXAS.
UNH...
ALEC!
WHAT IS IT?
THE GREEN... SOMETHING'S WRONG.

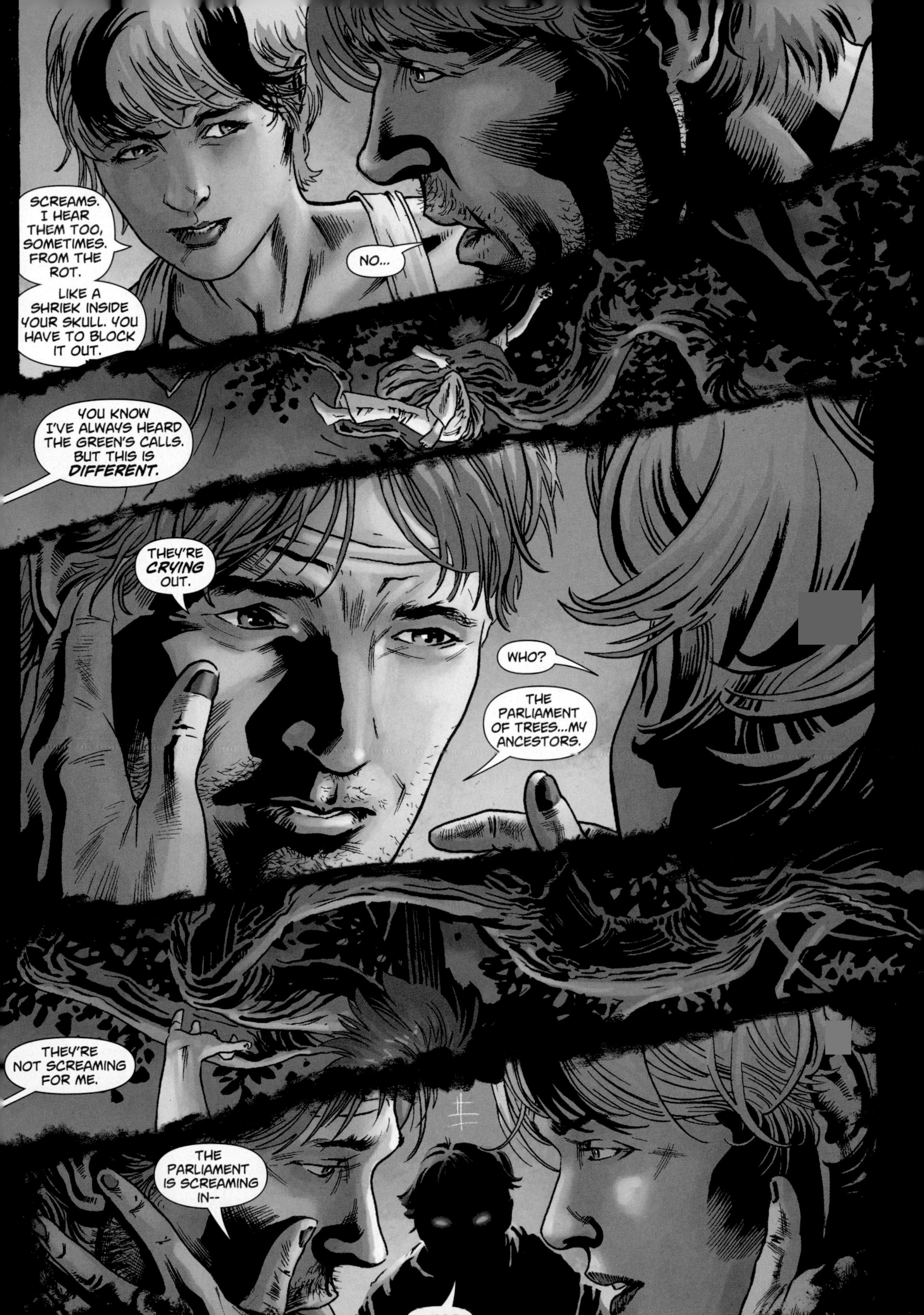
SCREAMS. I HEAR THEM TOO, SOMETIMES. FROM THE ROT.
NO...
LIKE A SHRIEK INSIDE YOUR SKULL. YOU HAVE TO BLOCK IT OUT.
YOU KNOW I'VE ALWAYS HEARD THE GREEN'S CALLS. BUT THIS IS DIFFERENT.
THEY'RE CRYING OUT.
WHO?
THE PARLIAMENT OF TREES...MY ANCESTORS.
THEY'RE NOT SCREAMING FOR ME.
THE PARLIAMENT IS SCREAMING IN--
FEAR.

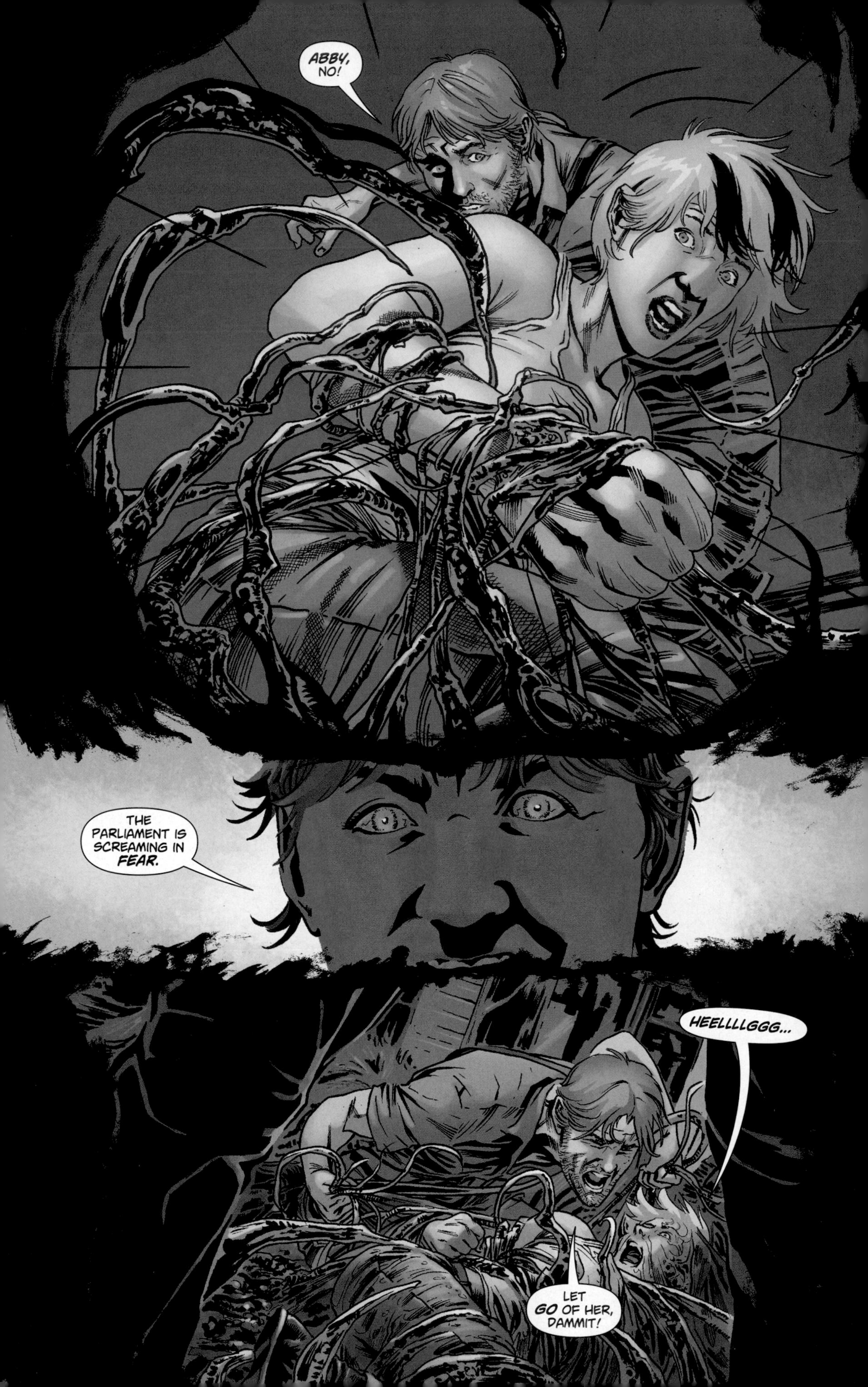
ABBY, NO!
THE PARLIAMENT IS SCREAMING IN FEAR.
HEELLLLGGG...
LET GO OF HER, DAMMIT!

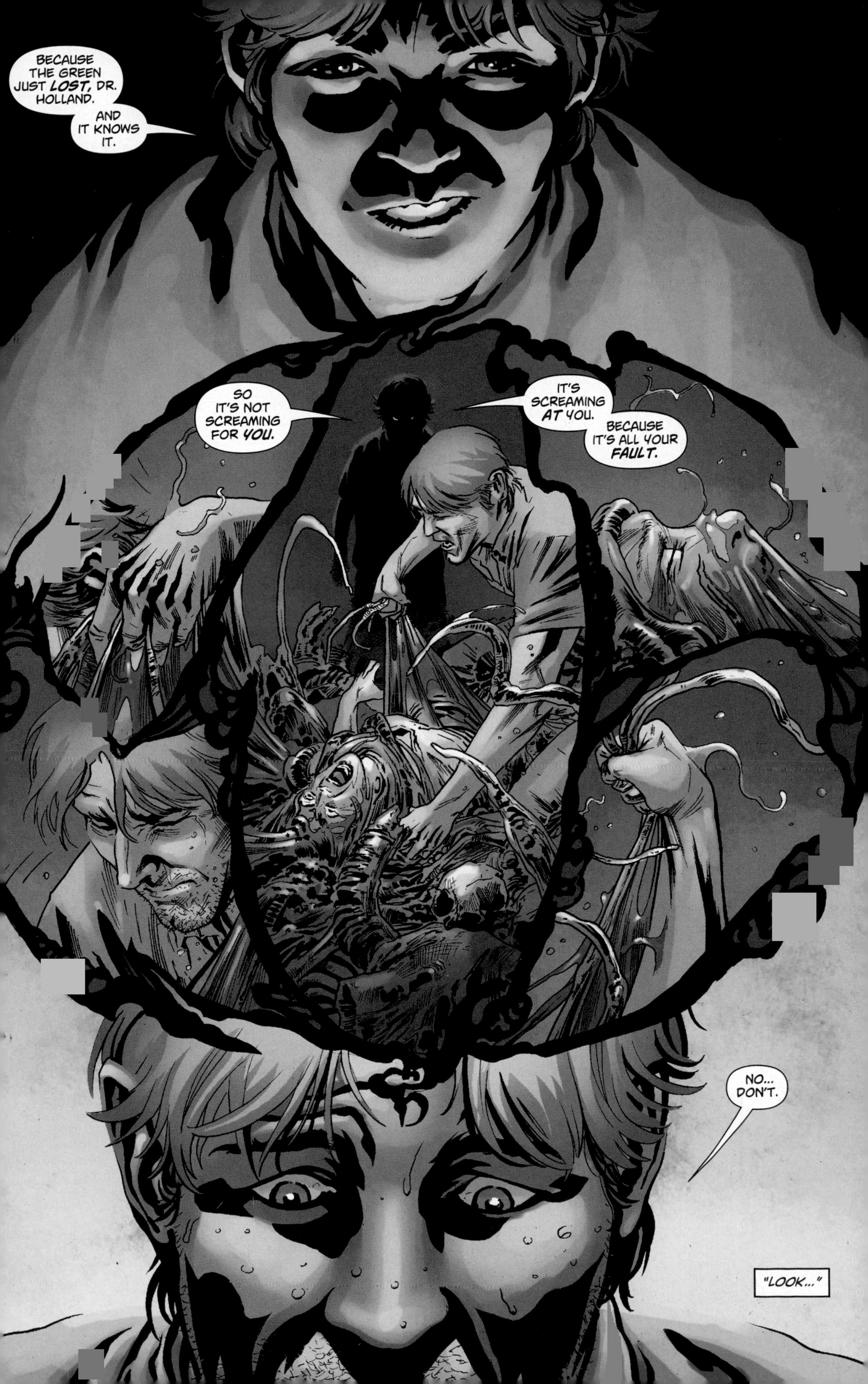
BECAUSE THE GREEN JUST LOST, DR. HOLLAND.
AND IT KNOWS IT.
SO IT'S NOT SCREAMING FOR YOU.
IT'S SCREAMING AT YOU.
BECAUSE IT'S ALL YOUR FAULT.
NO... DON'T.
"LOOK..."

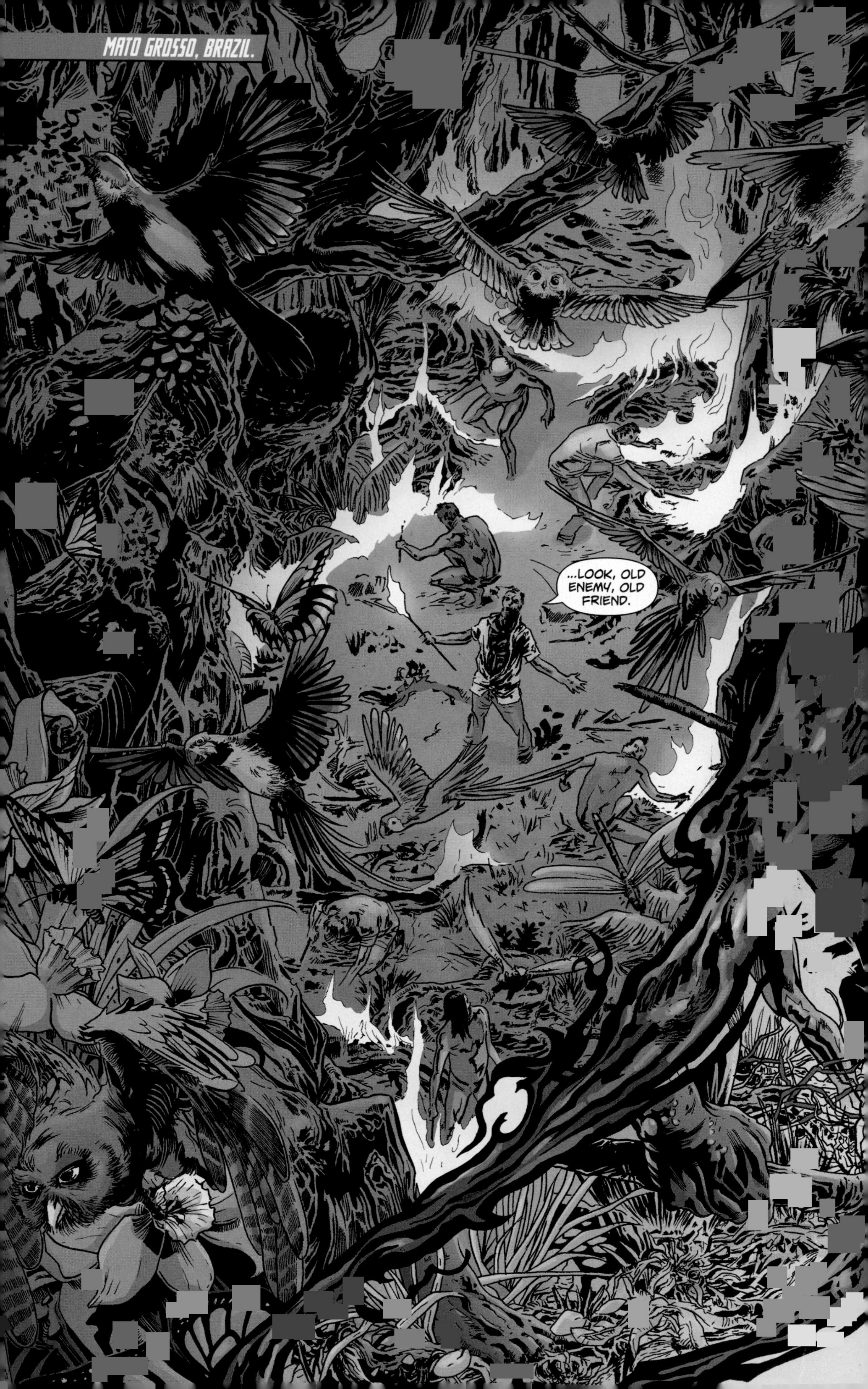
MATO GROSSO, BRAZIL.
...LOOK, OLD ENEMY, OLD FRIEND.

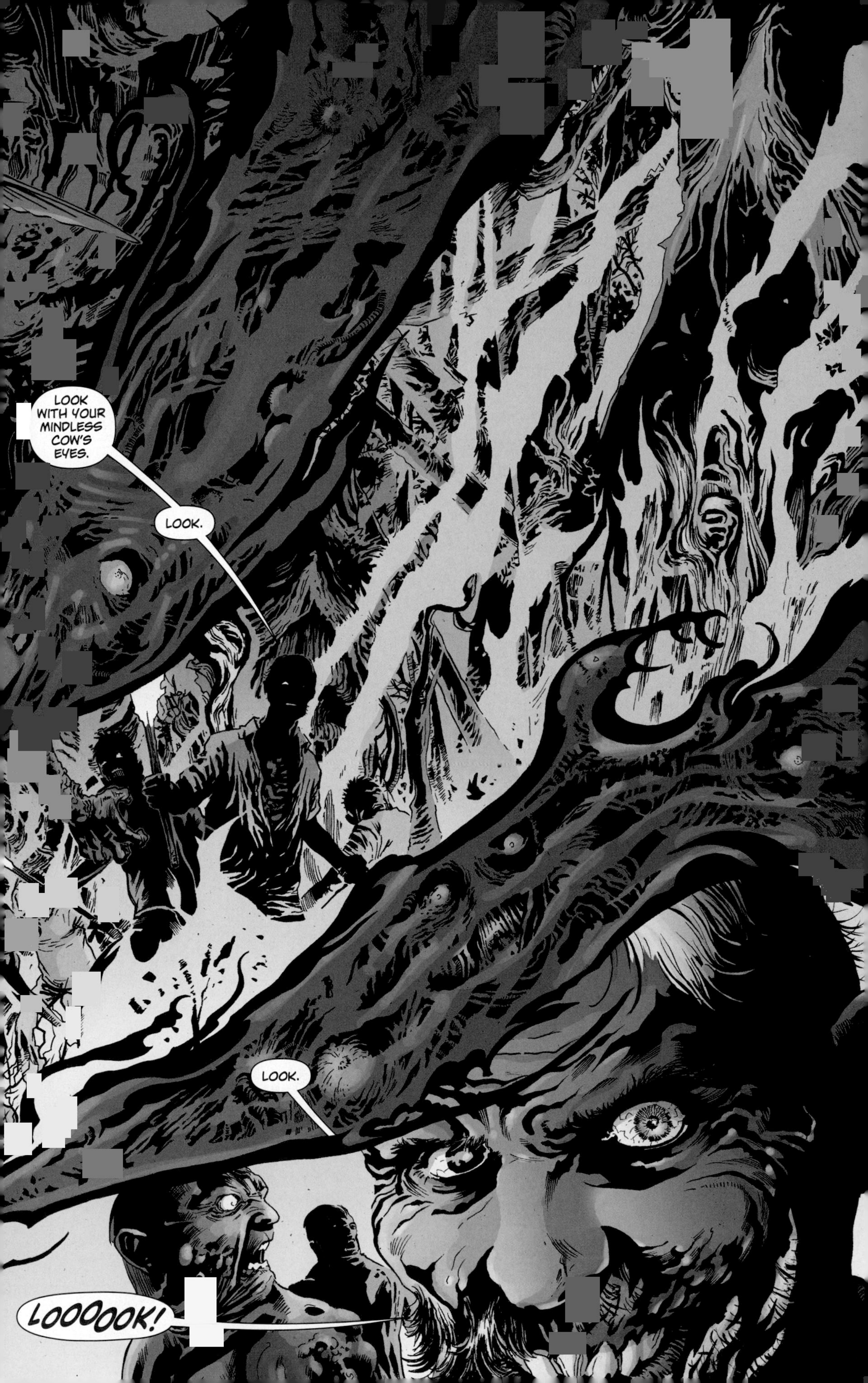
LOOK WITH YOUR MINDLESS COW'S EYES.
LOOK.
LOOK.
LOOOOOK!

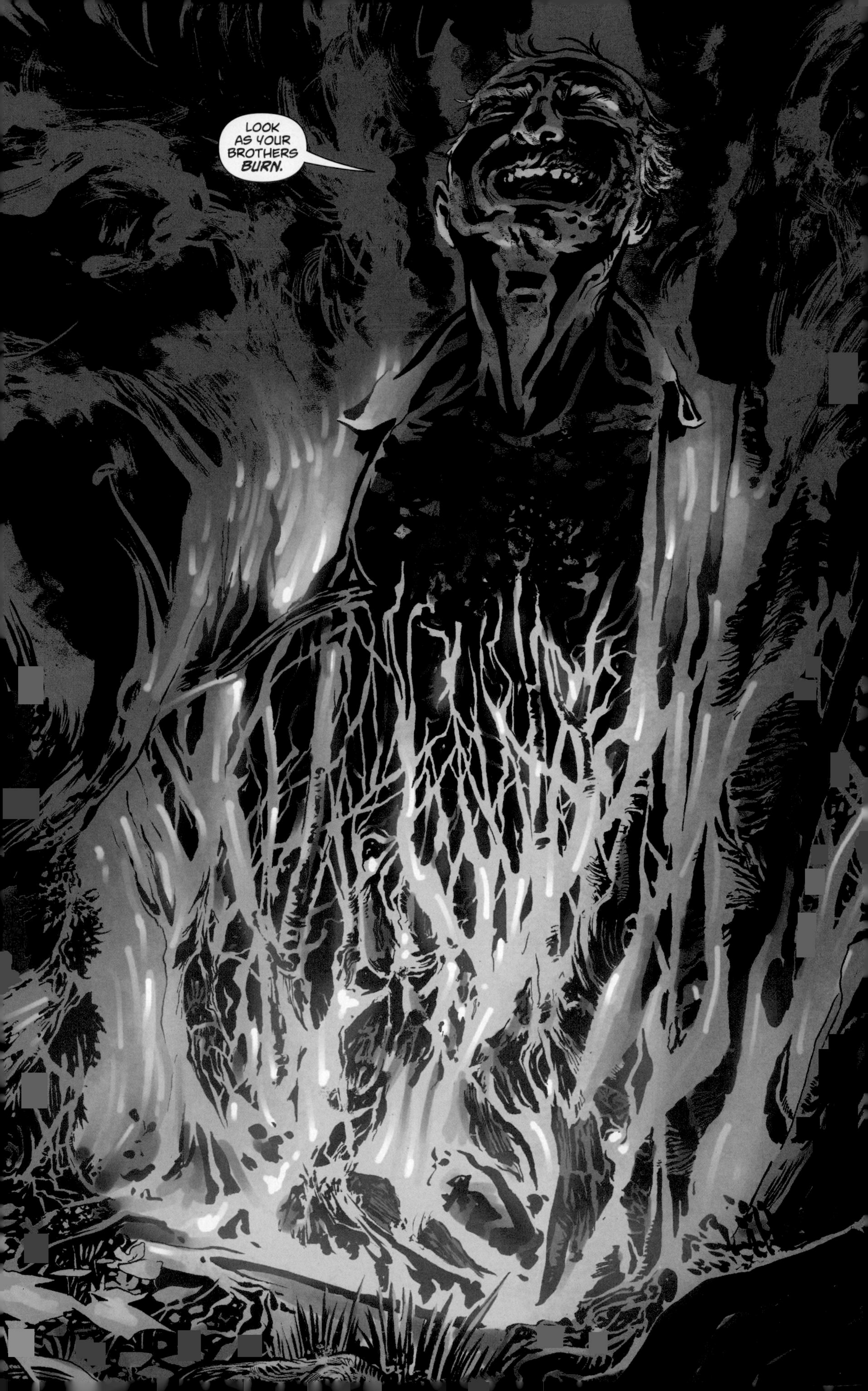
LOOK AS YOUR BROTHERS BURN.

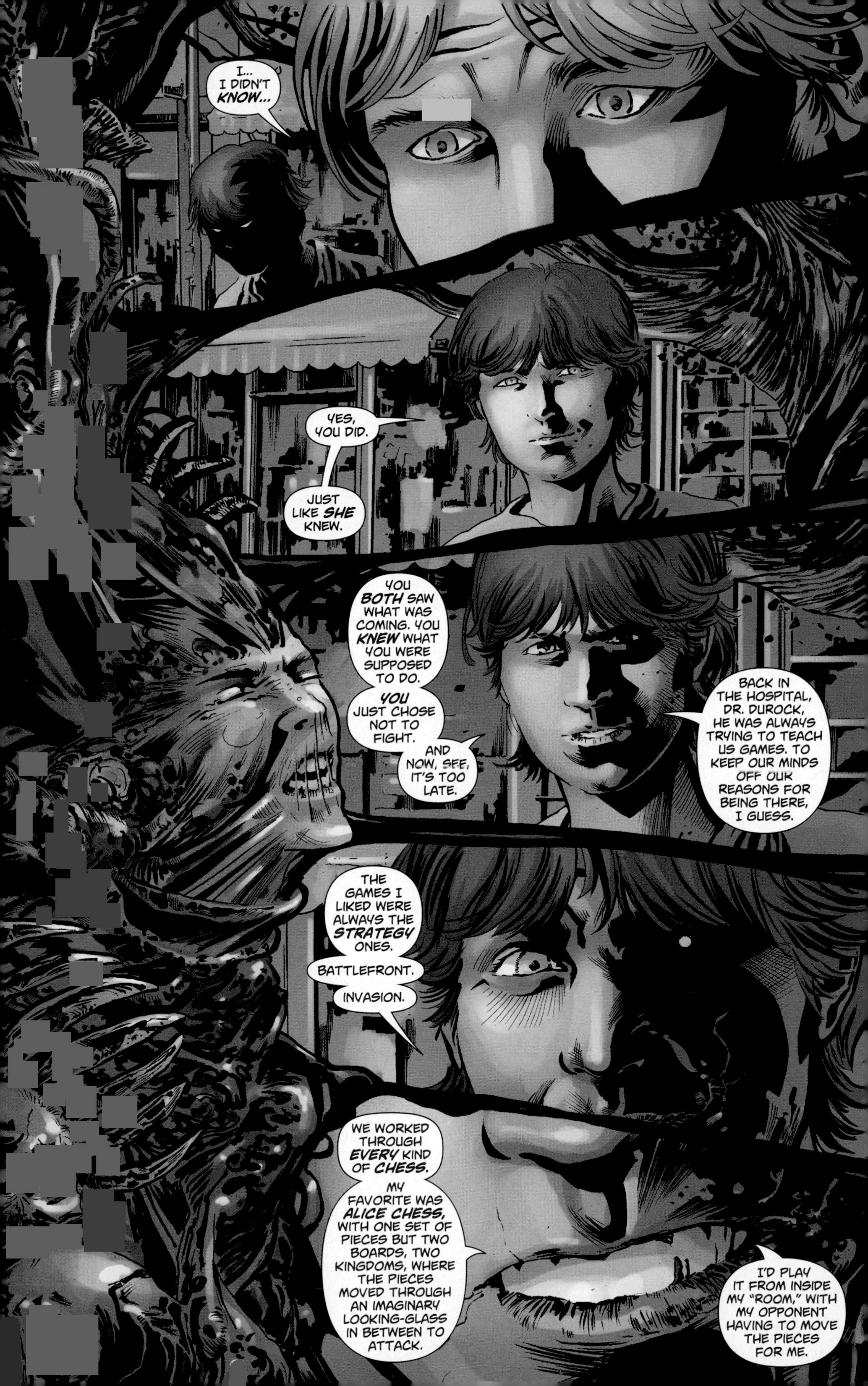
I... I DIDN'T **KNOW...**
YES, YOU DID.
JUST LIKE **SHE** KNEW.
YOU **BOTH** SAW WHAT WAS COMING. YOU **KNEW** WHAT YOU WERE SUPPOSED TO DO.
YOU JUST CHOSE NOT TO FIGHT.
AND NOW, SEE, IT'S TOO LATE.
BACK IN THE HOSPITAL, DR. DUROCK, HE WAS ALWAYS TRYING TO TEACH US GAMES. TO KEEP OUR MINDS OFF OUR REASONS FOR BEING THERE, I GUESS.
THE GAMES I LIKED WERE ALWAYS THE **STRATEGY** ONES.
BATTLEFRONT.
INVASION.
WE WORKED THROUGH **EVERY** KIND OF **CHESS.**
MY FAVORITE WAS **ALICE CHESS,** WITH ONE SET OF PIECES BUT TWO BOARDS, TWO KINGDOMS, WHERE THE PIECES MOVED THROUGH AN IMAGINARY LOOKING-GLASS IN BETWEEN TO ATTACK.
I'D PLAY IT FROM INSIDE MY "ROOM," WITH MY OPPONENT HAVING TO MOVE THE PIECES FOR ME.

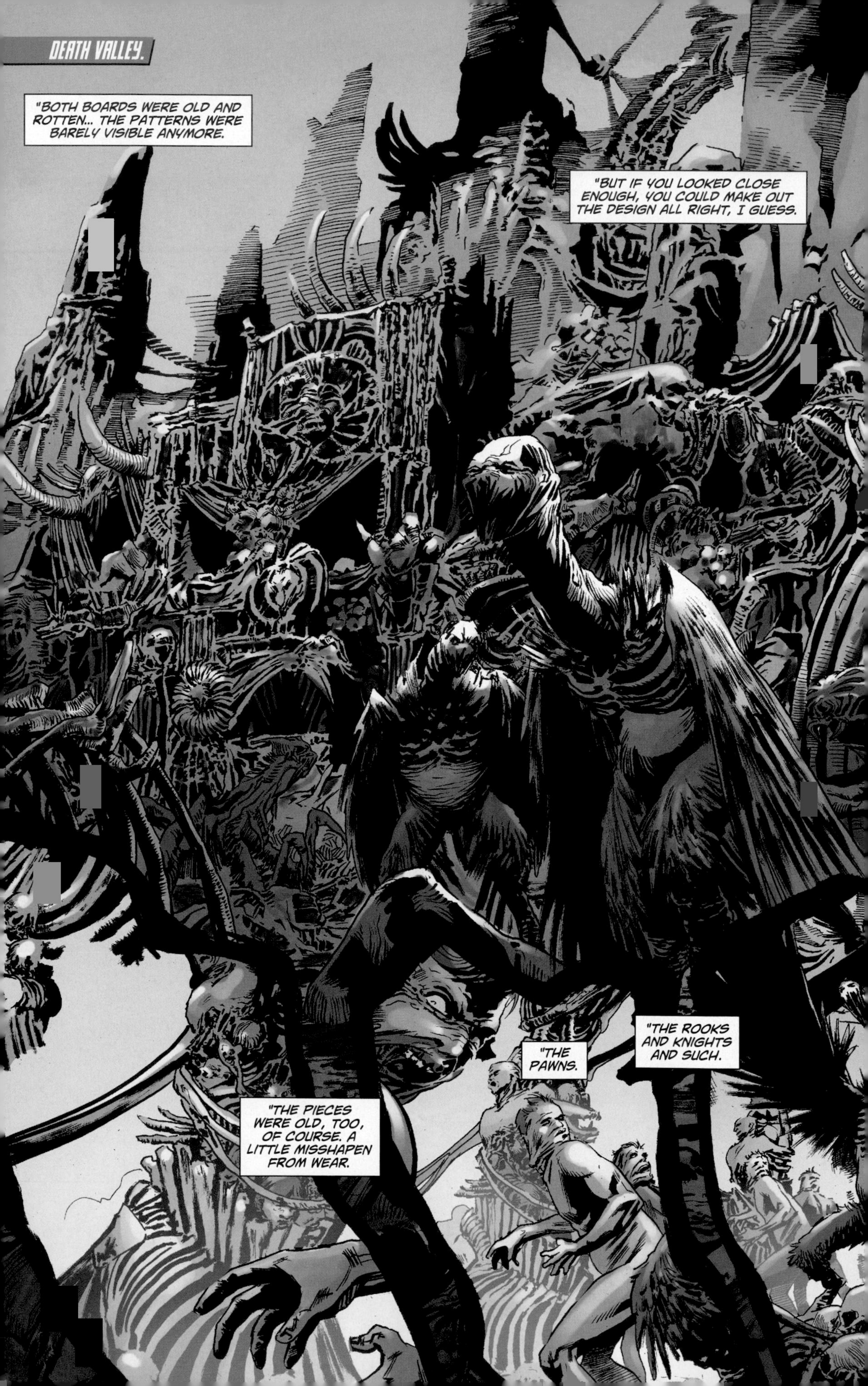
DEATH VALLEY.
"BOTH BOARDS WERE OLD AND ROTTEN... THE PATTERNS WERE BARELY VISIBLE ANYMORE.
"BUT IF YOU LOOKED CLOSE ENOUGH, YOU COULD MAKE OUT THE DESIGN ALL RIGHT, I GUESS.
"THE PIECES WERE OLD, TOO, OF COURSE. A LITTLE MISSHAPEN FROM WEAR.
"THE PAWNS.
"THE ROOKS AND KNIGHTS AND SUCH.

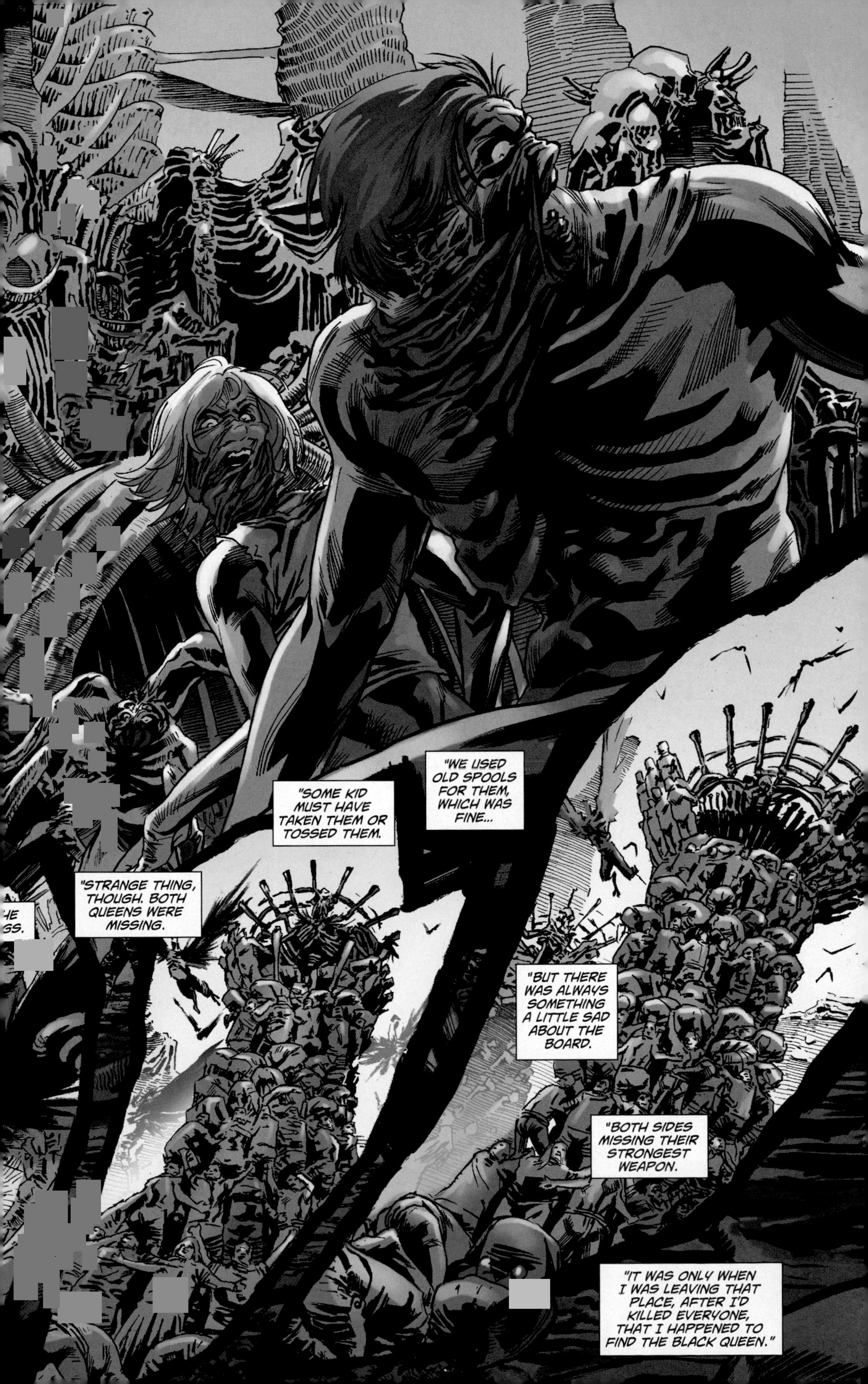
"STRANGE THING, THOUGH. BOTH QUEENS WERE MISSING.
"SOME KID MUST HAVE TAKEN THEM OR TOSSED THEM.
"WE USED OLD SPOOLS FOR THEM, WHICH WAS FINE...
"BUT THERE WAS ALWAYS SOMETHING A LITTLE SAD ABOUT THE BOARD.
"BOTH SIDES MISSING THEIR STRONGEST WEAPON.
"IT WAS ONLY WHEN I WAS LEAVING THAT PLACE, AFTER I'D KILLED EVERYONE, THAT I HAPPENED TO FIND THE BLACK QUEEN."

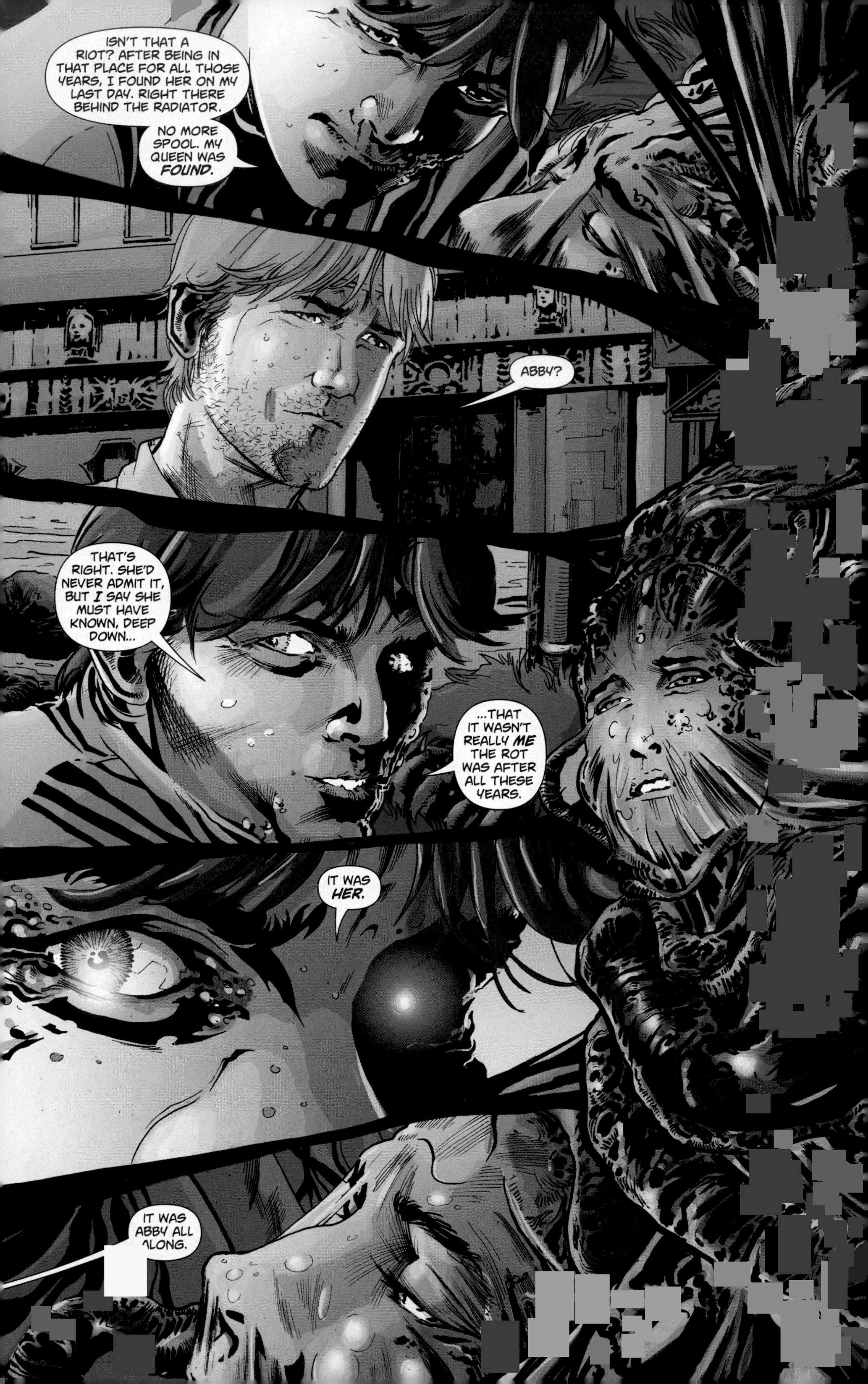
ISN'T THAT A RIOT? AFTER BEING IN THAT PLACE FOR ALL THOSE YEARS, I FOUND HER ON MY LAST DAY. RIGHT THERE BEHIND THE RADIATOR.
NO MORE SPOOL. MY QUEEN WAS FOUND.
ABBY?
THAT'S RIGHT. SHE'D NEVER ADMIT IT, BUT I SAY SHE MUST HAVE KNOWN, DEEP DOWN...
...THAT IT WASN'T REALLY ME THE ROT WAS AFTER ALL THESE YEARS.
IT WAS HER.
IT WAS ABBY ALL ALONG.

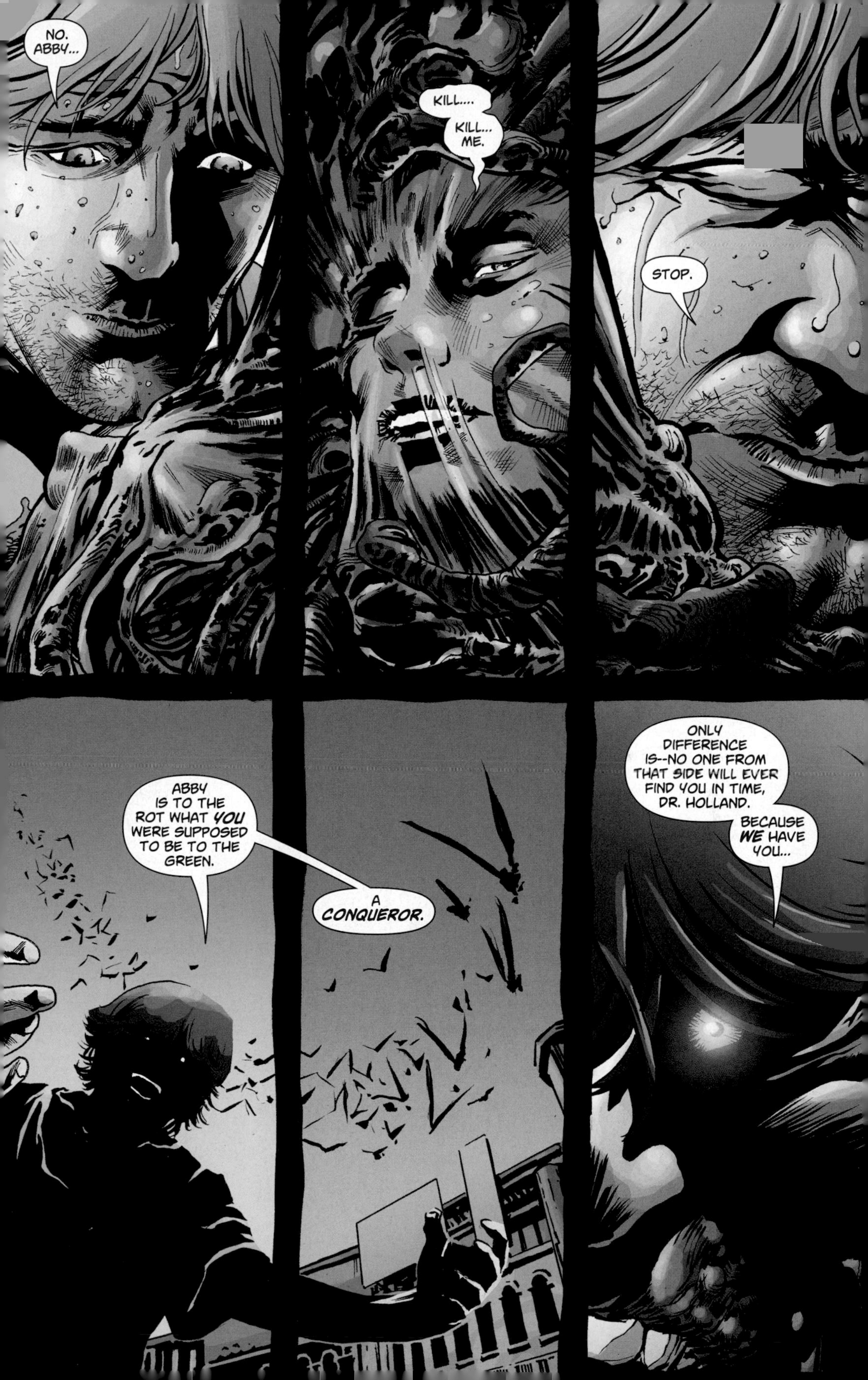
NO. ABBY...
KILL....
KILL... ME.
STOP.
ABBY IS TO THE ROT WHAT *YOU* WERE SUPPOSED TO BE TO THE GREEN.
A *CONQUEROR.*
ONLY DIFFERENCE IS--NO ONE FROM THAT SIDE WILL EVER FIND YOU IN TIME, DR. HOLLAND.
BECAUSE *WE* HAVE YOU...

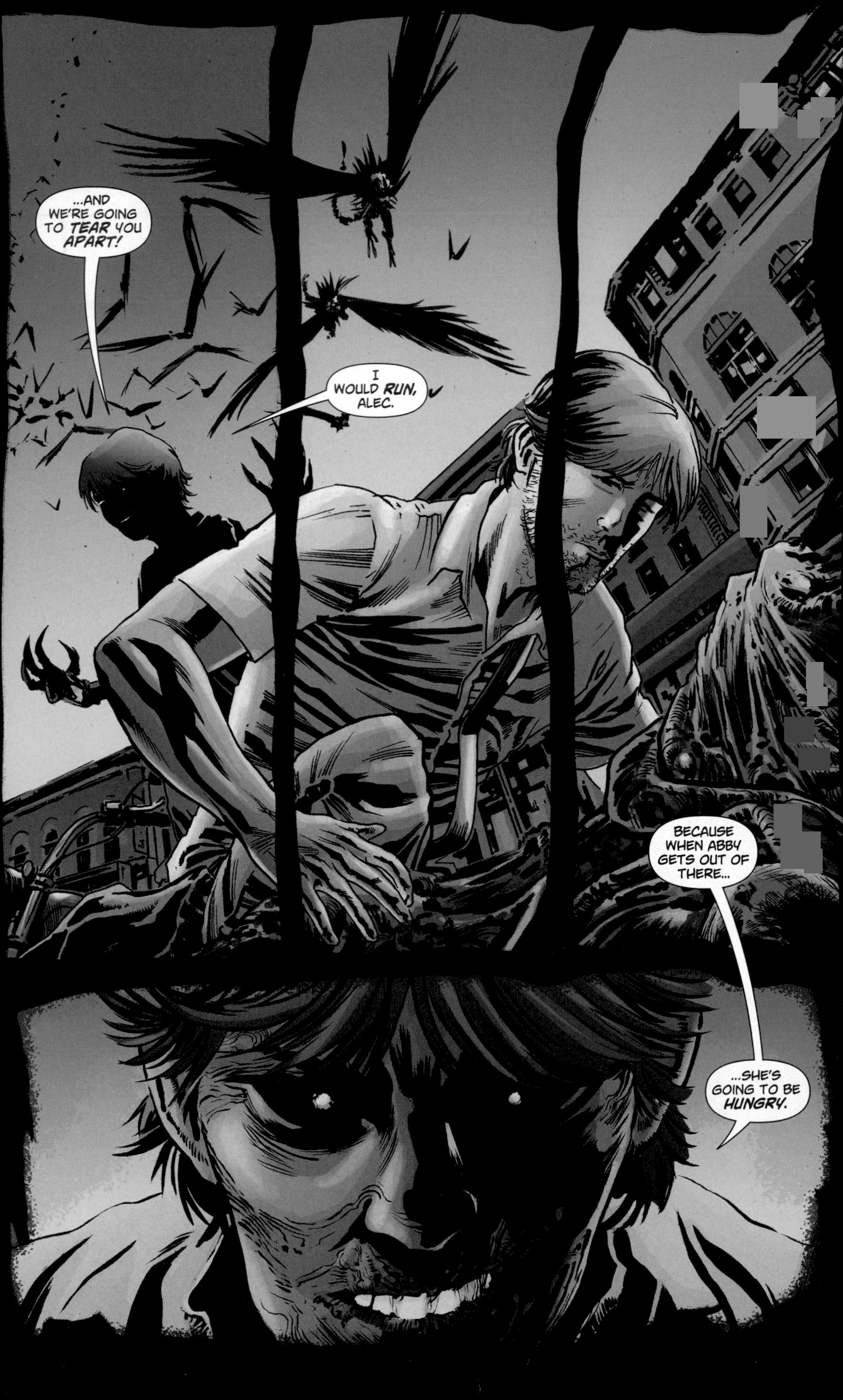
...AND WE'RE GOING TO TEAR YOU APART!
I WOULD RUN, ALEC.
BECAUSE WHEN ABBY GETS OUT OF THERE...
...SHE'S GOING TO BE HUNGRY.

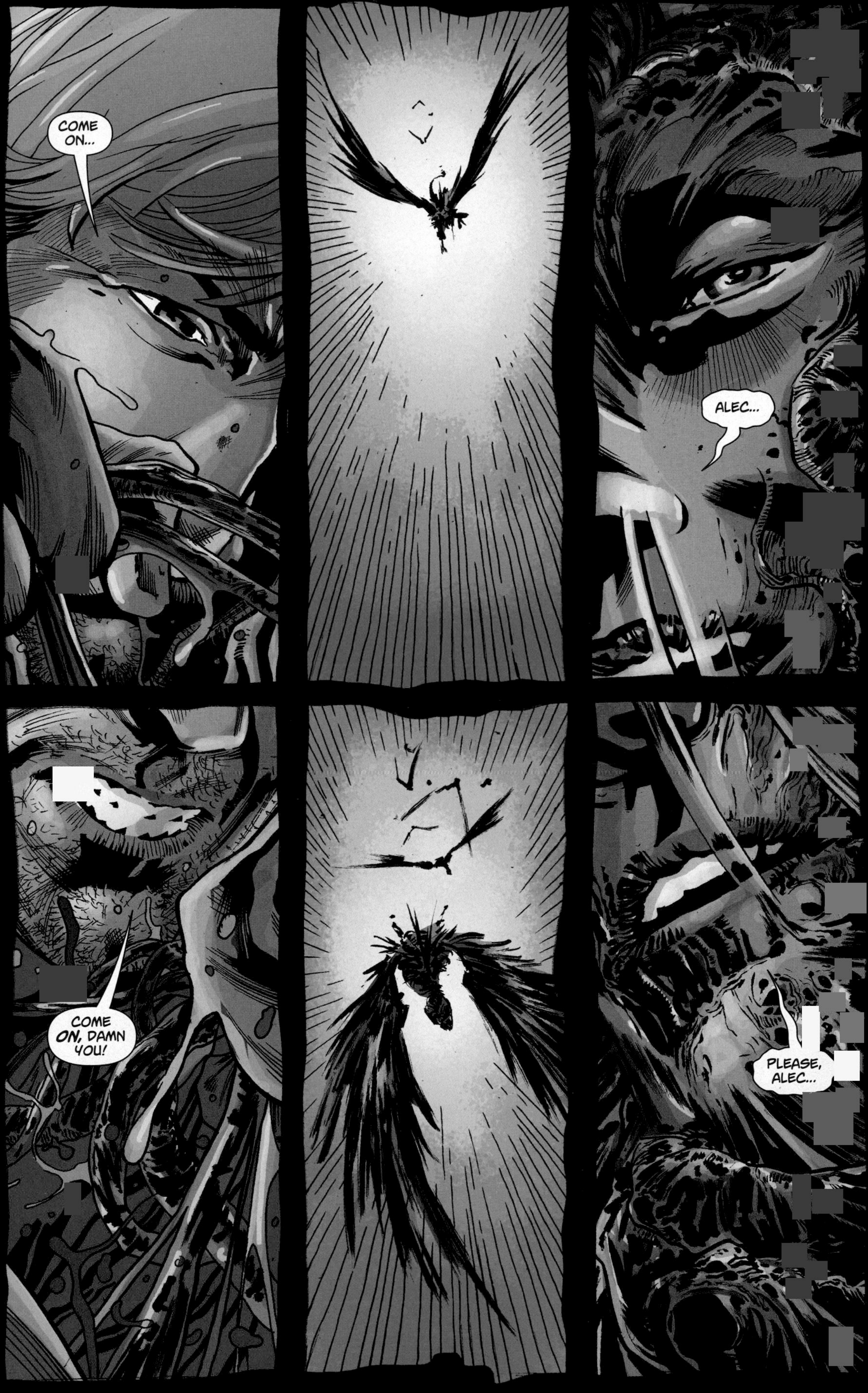
COME ON...
ALEC...
COME ON, DAMN YOU!
PLEASE, ALEC...

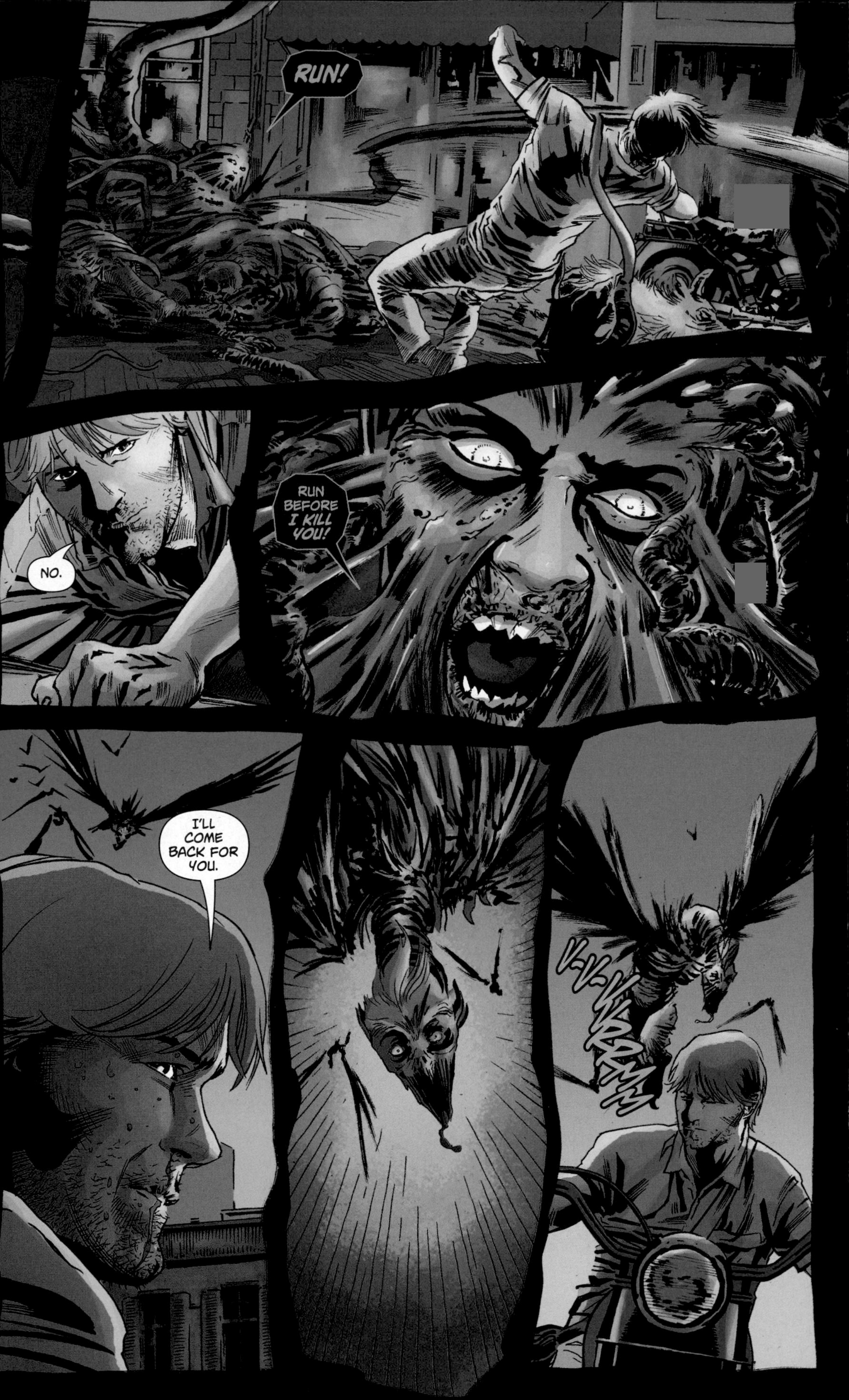
RUN!
NO.
RUN BEFORE I KILL YOU!
I'LL COME BACK FOR YOU.
V-V-VRRMM

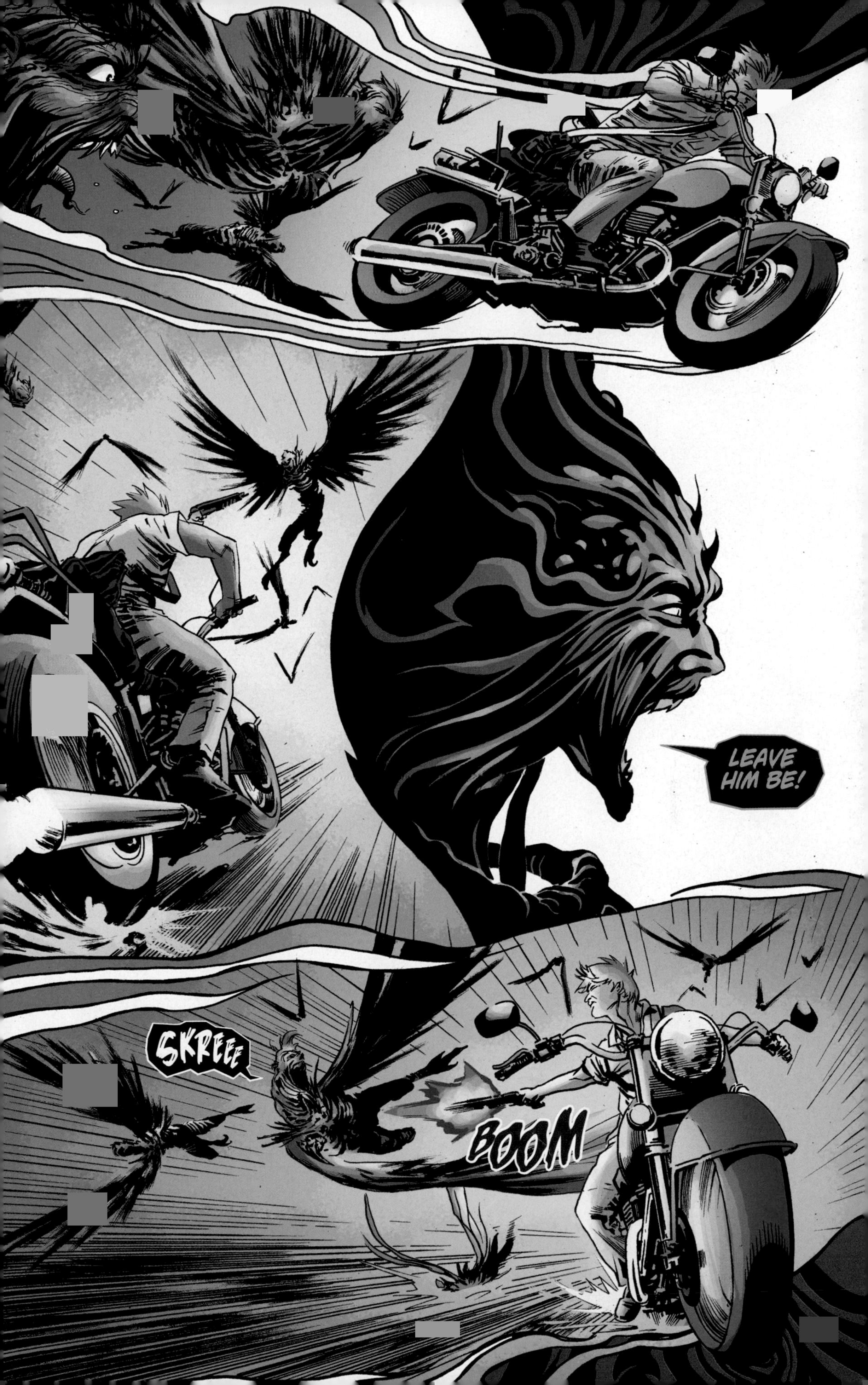
LEAVE HIM BE!
SKREEE
BOOM

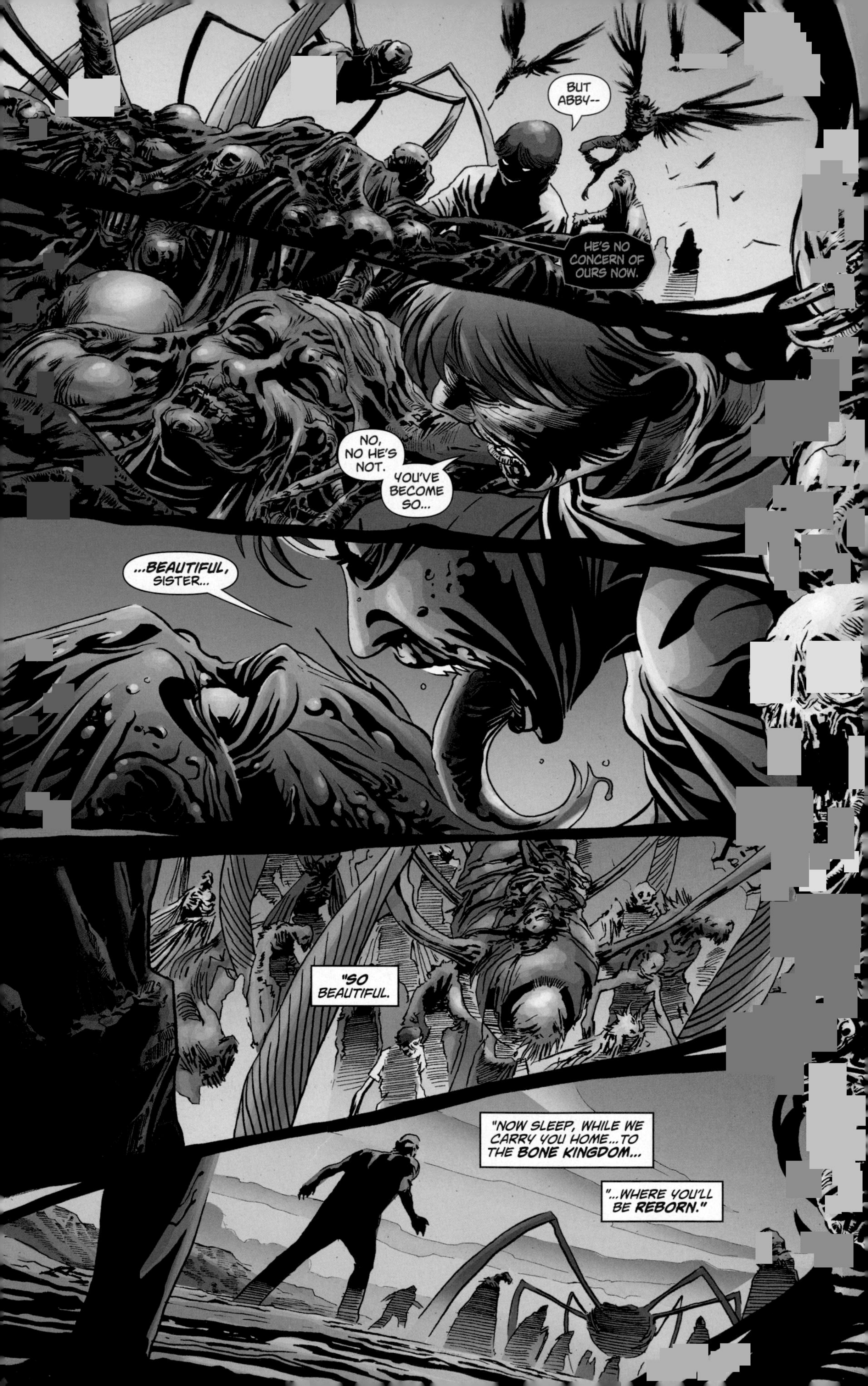
BUT ABBY--
HE'S NO CONCERN OF OURS NOW.
NO, NO HE'S NOT.
YOU'VE BECOME SO...
...BEAUTIFUL, SISTER...
"SO BEAUTIFUL.
"NOW SLEEP, WHILE WE CARRY YOU HOME...TO THE BONE KINGDOM...
"...WHERE YOU'LL BE REBORN."

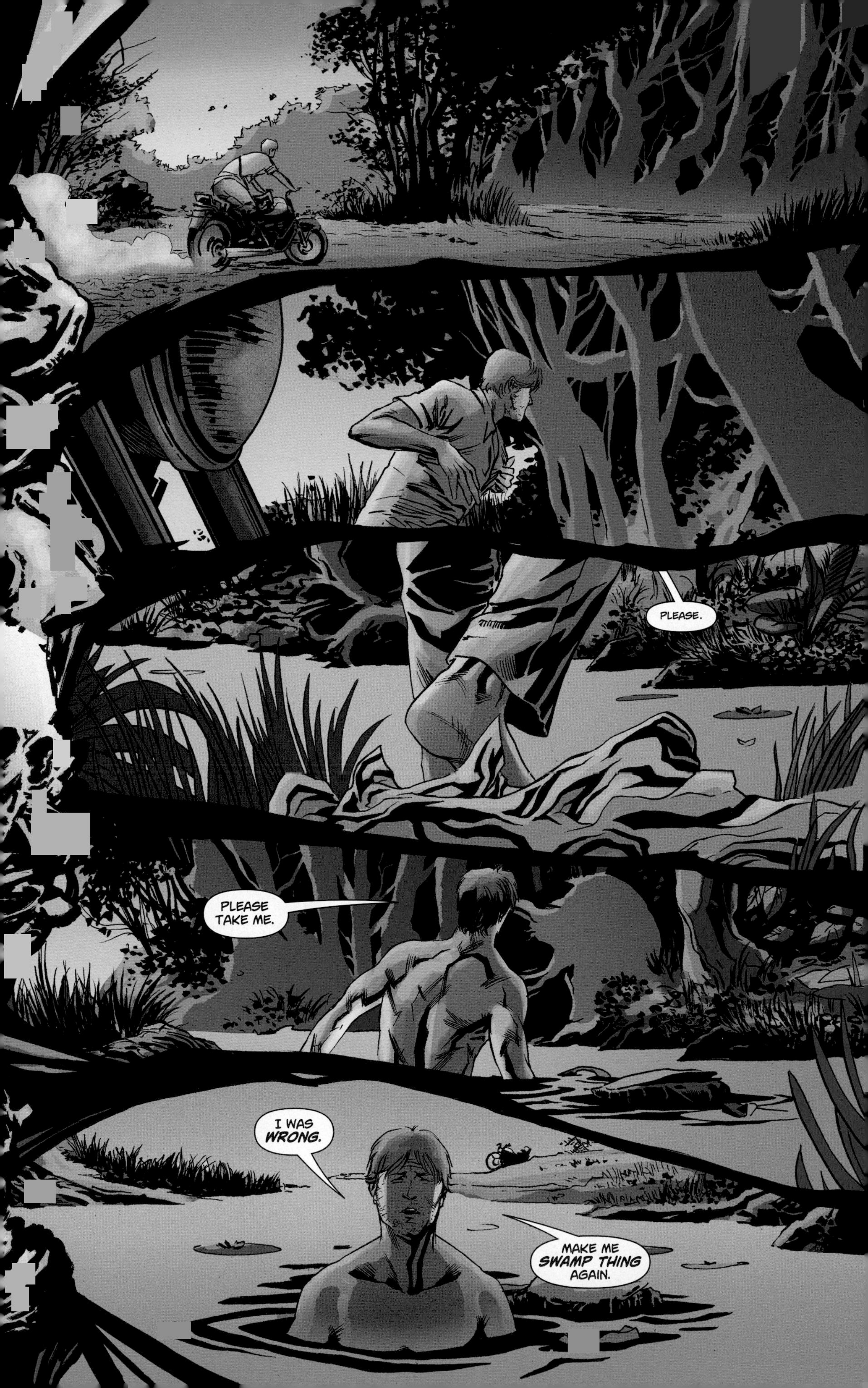
PLEASE.
PLEASE TAKE ME.
I WAS WRONG.
MAKE ME SWAMP THING AGAIN.

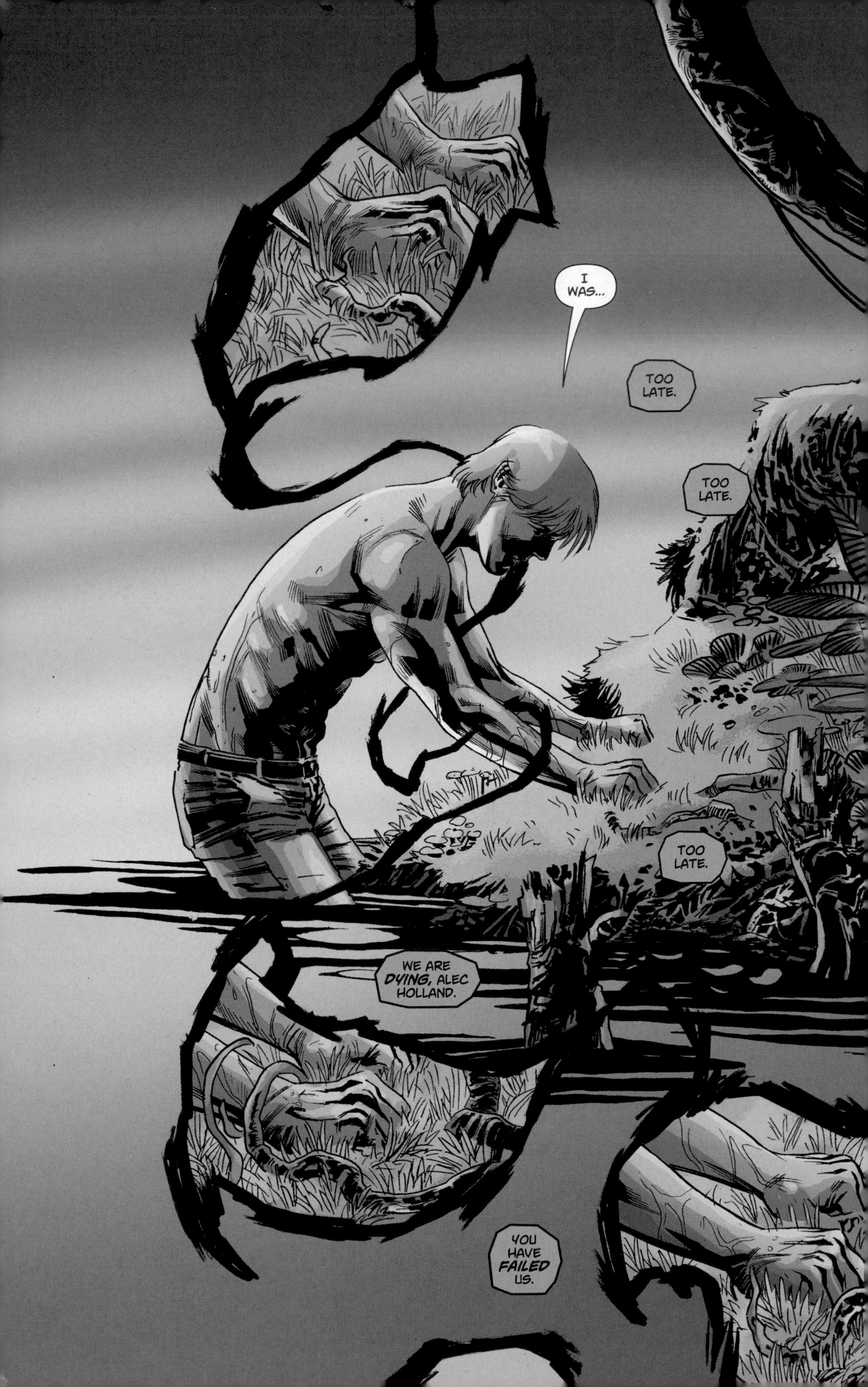
I WAS...
TOO LATE.
TOO LATE.
TOO LATE.
WE ARE DYING, ALEC HOLLAND.
YOU HAVE FAILED US.

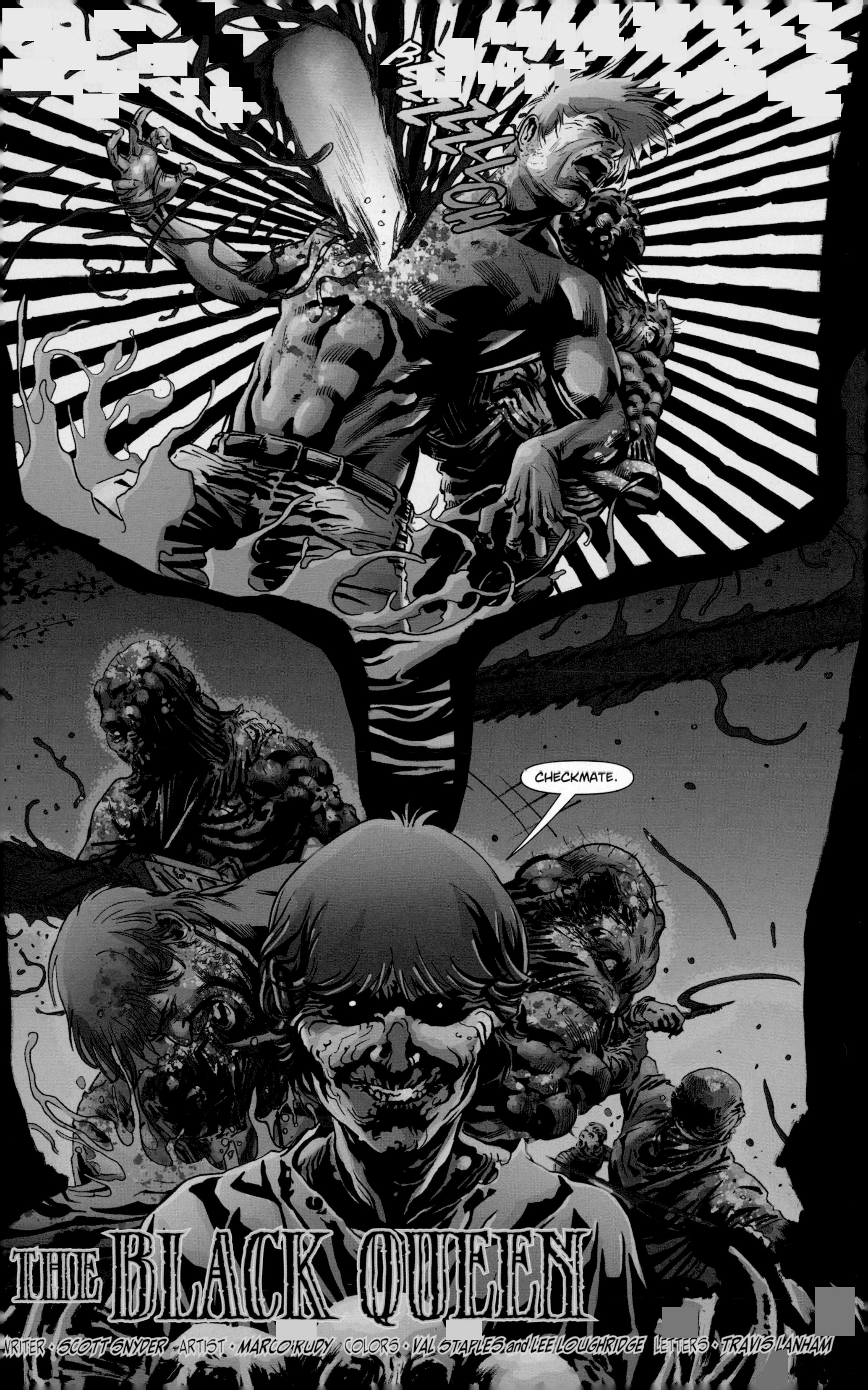
CHECKMATE.
THE BLACK QUEEN
WRITER • SCOTT SNYDER ARTIST • MARCO RUDY COLORS • VAL STAPLES and LEE LOUGHRIDGE LETTERS • TRAVIS LANHAM

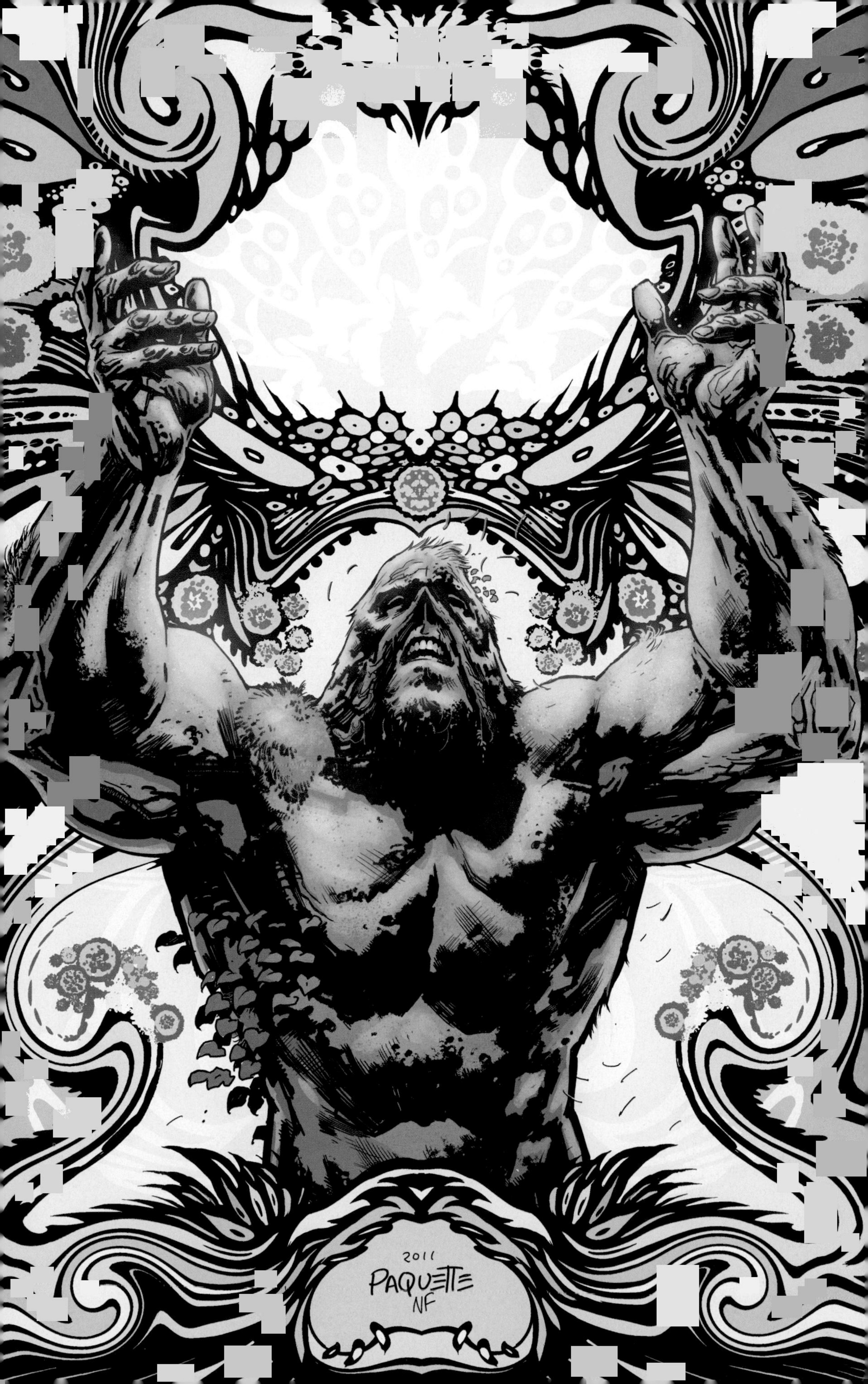
2011
PAQUETTE
NF

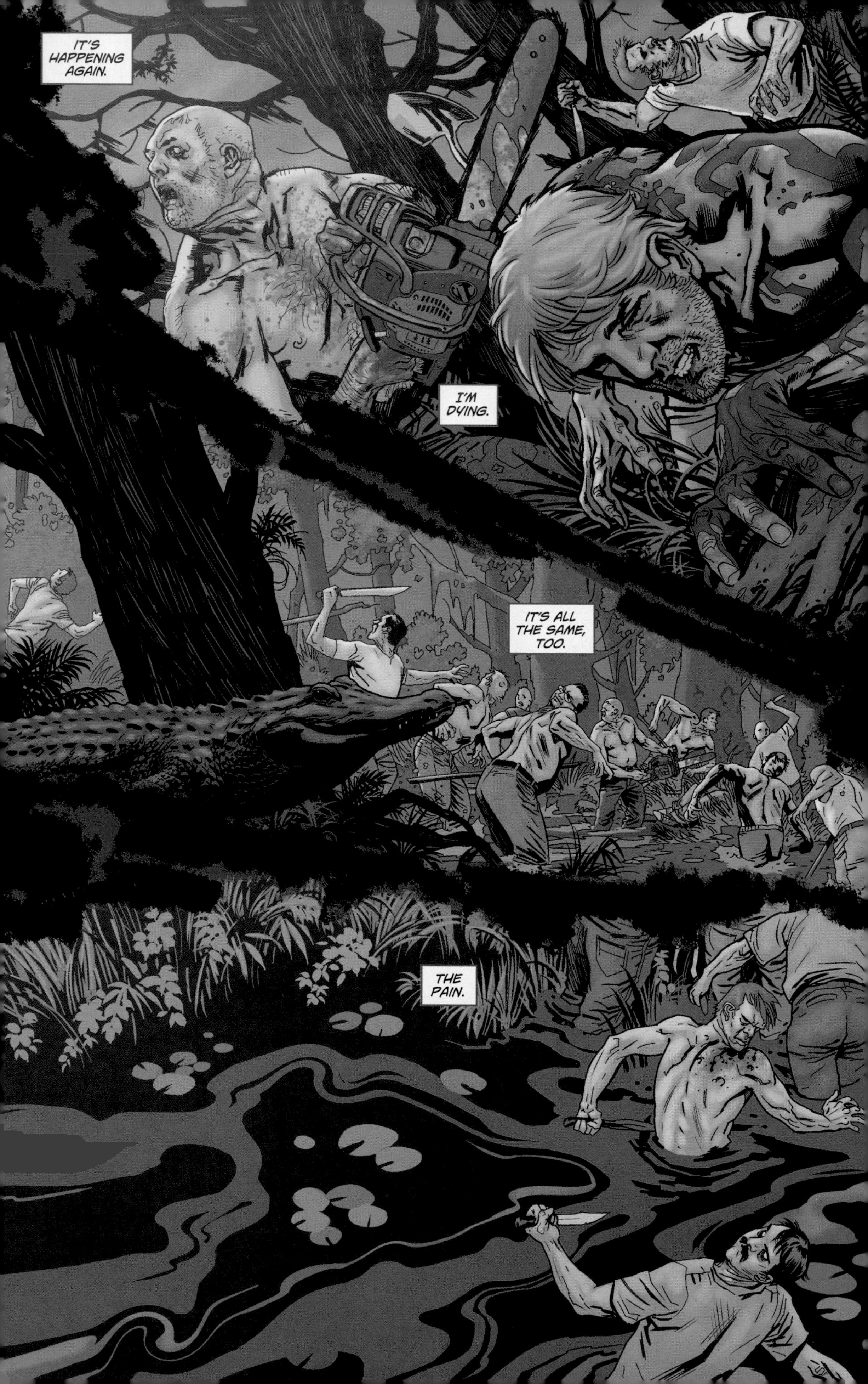
IT'S HAPPENING AGAIN.
I'M DYING.
IT'S ALL THE SAME, TOO.
THE PAIN.

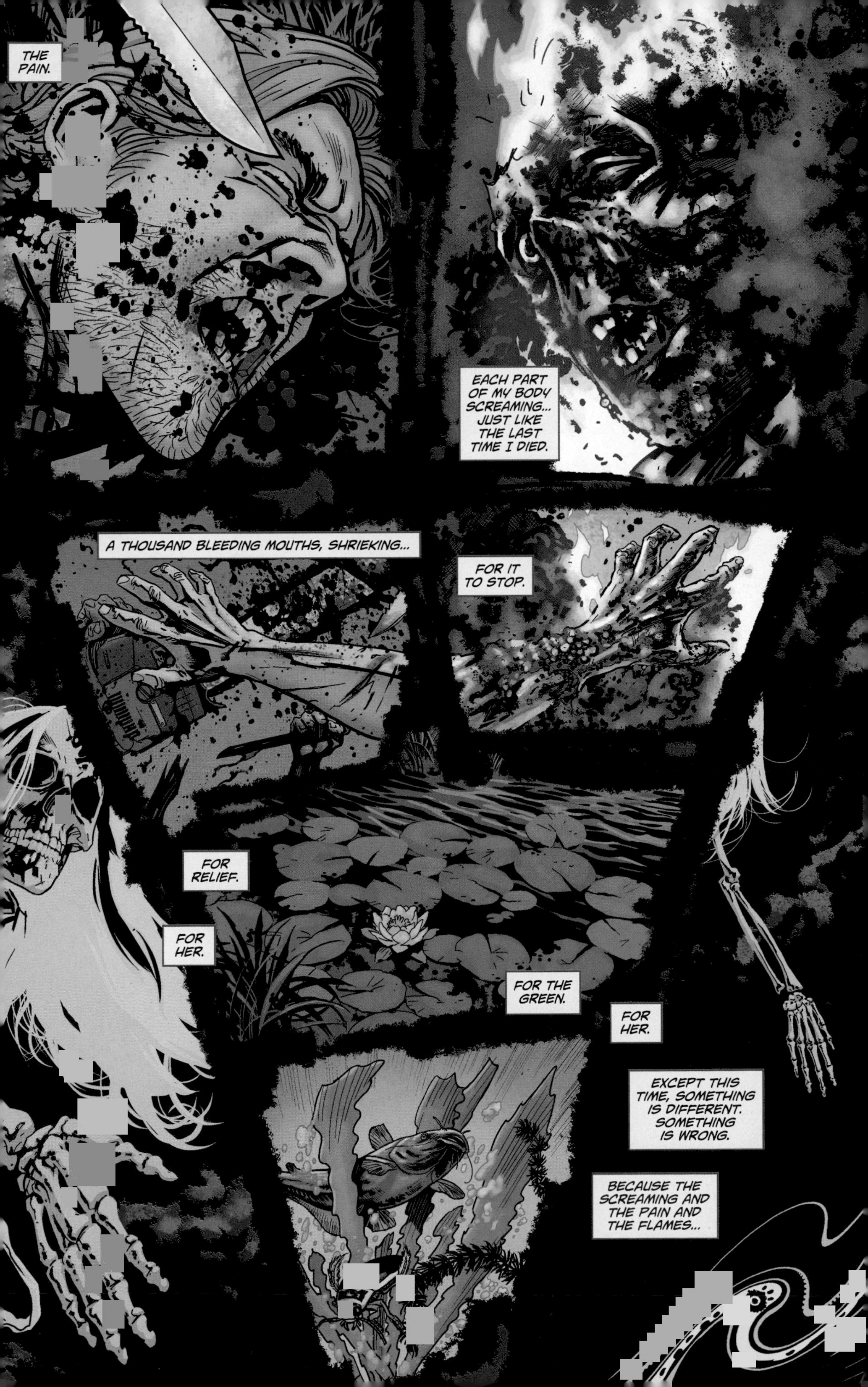
THE PAIN.
EACH PART OF MY BODY SCREAMING... JUST LIKE THE LAST TIME I DIED.
A THOUSAND BLEEDING MOUTHS, SHRIEKING...
FOR IT TO STOP.
FOR RELIEF.
FOR HER.
FOR THE GREEN.
FOR HER.
EXCEPT THIS TIME, SOMETHING IS DIFFERENT. SOMETHING IS WRONG.
BECAUSE THE SCREAMING AND THE PAIN AND THE FLAMES...

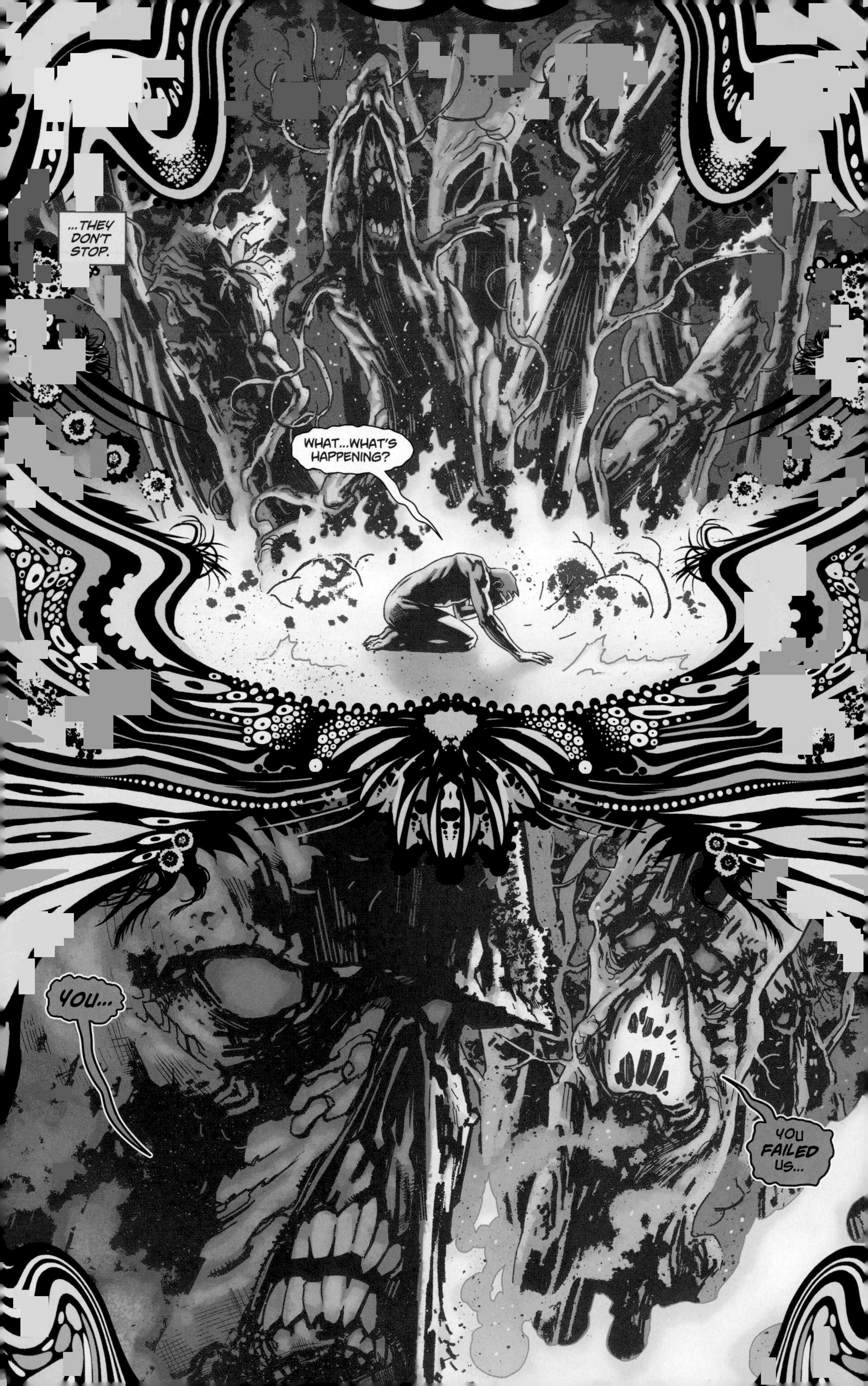
...THEY DON'T STOP.
WHAT...WHAT'S HAPPENING?
YOU...
YOU FAILED US...

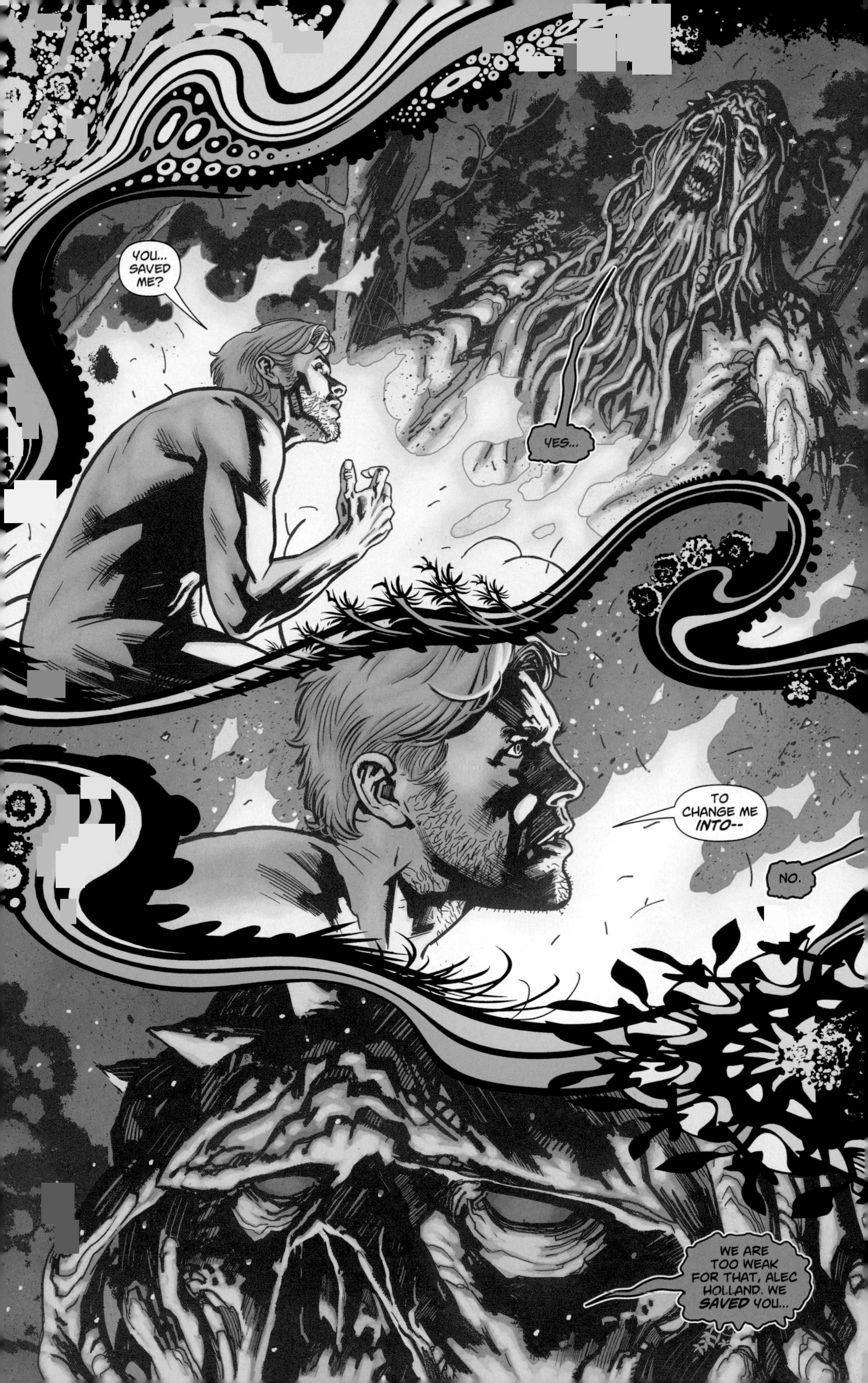
YOU... SAVED ME?
YES...
TO CHANGE ME INTO--
NO.
WE ARE TOO WEAK FOR THAT, ALEC HOLLAND. WE SAVED YOU...

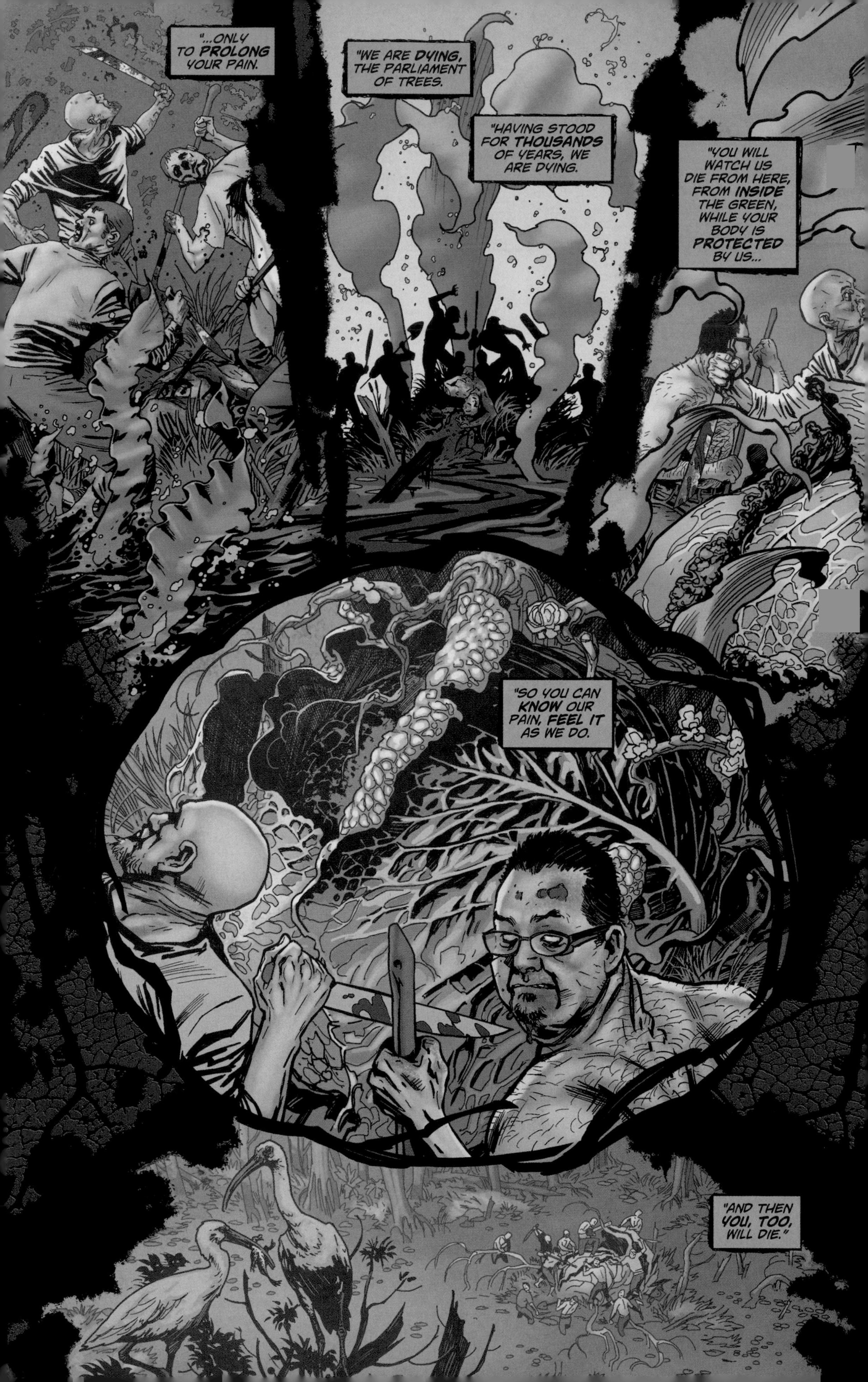
"...ONLY TO PROLONG YOUR PAIN.
"WE ARE DYING, THE PARLIAMENT OF TREES.
"HAVING STOOD FOR THOUSANDS OF YEARS, WE ARE DYING.
"YOU WILL WATCH US DIE FROM HERE, FROM INSIDE THE GREEN, WHILE YOUR BODY IS PROTECTED BY US...
"SO YOU CAN KNOW OUR PAIN, FEEL IT AS WE DO.
"AND THEN YOU, TOO, WILL DIE."

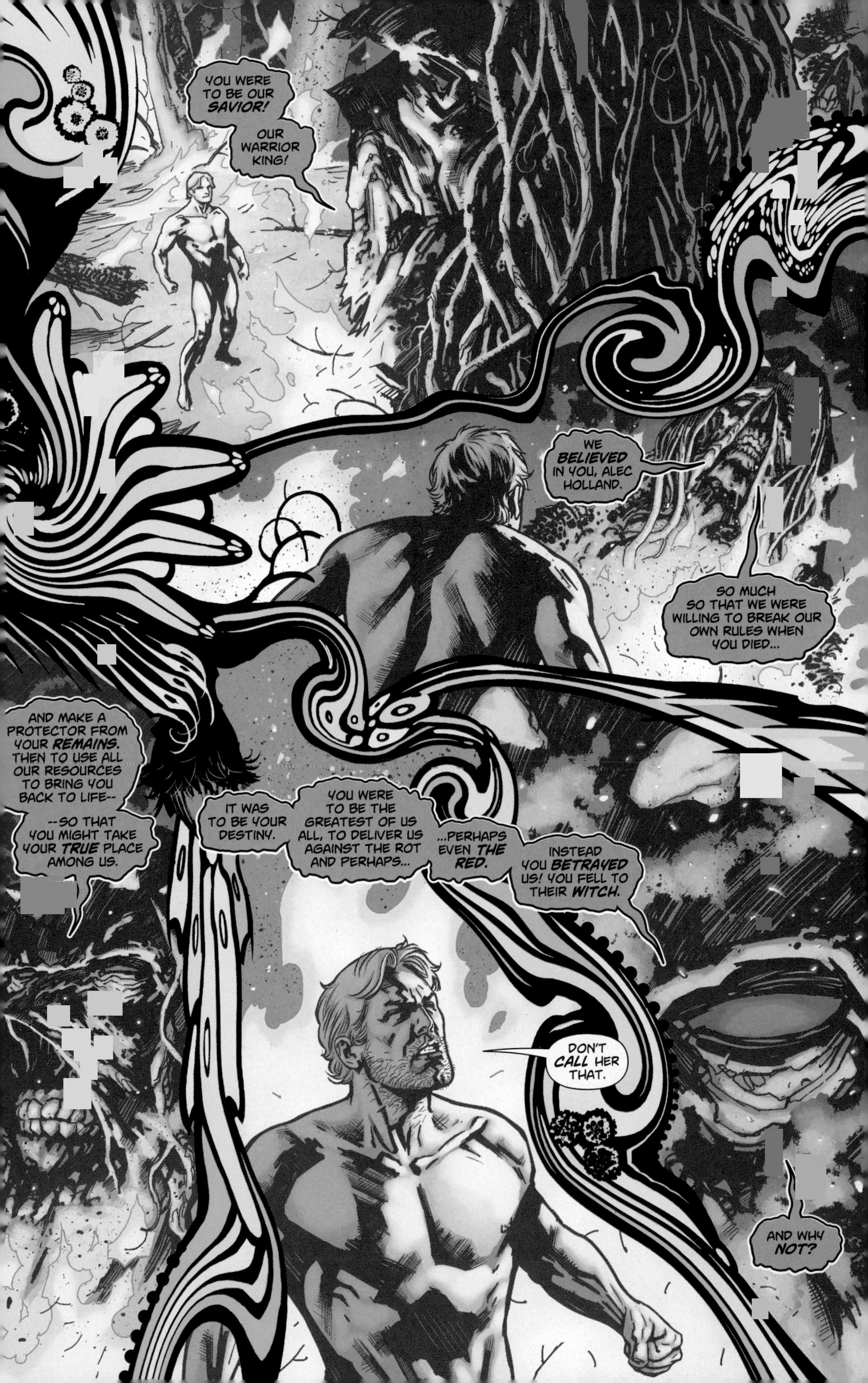
YOU WERE TO BE OUR SAVIOR!
OUR WARRIOR KING!
WE BELIEVED IN YOU, ALEC HOLLAND.
SO MUCH SO THAT WE WERE WILLING TO BREAK OUR OWN RULES WHEN YOU DIED...
AND MAKE A PROTECTOR FROM YOUR REMAINS. THEN TO USE ALL OUR RESOURCES TO BRING YOU BACK TO LIFE--
--SO THAT YOU MIGHT TAKE YOUR TRUE PLACE AMONG US.
IT WAS TO BE YOUR DESTINY.
YOU WERE TO BE THE GREATEST OF US ALL, TO DELIVER US AGAINST THE ROT AND PERHAPS...
...PERHAPS EVEN THE RED.
INSTEAD YOU BETRAYED US! YOU FELL TO THEIR WITCH.
DON'T CALL HER THAT.
AND WHY NOT?

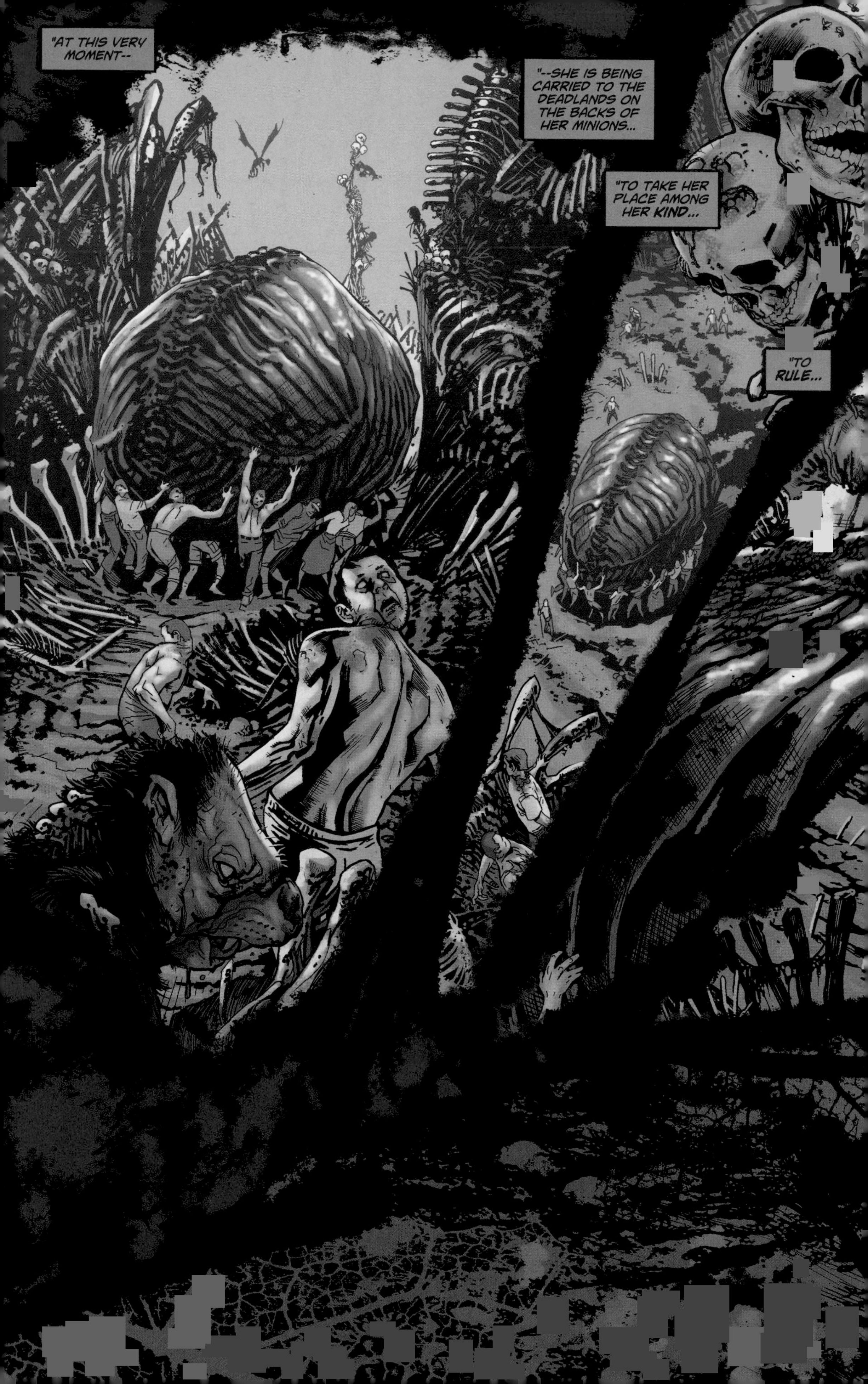
"AT THIS VERY MOMENT--
"--SHE IS BEING CARRIED TO THE DEADLANDS ON THE BACKS OF HER MINIONS...
"TO TAKE HER PLACE AMONG HER KIND...
"TO RULE...

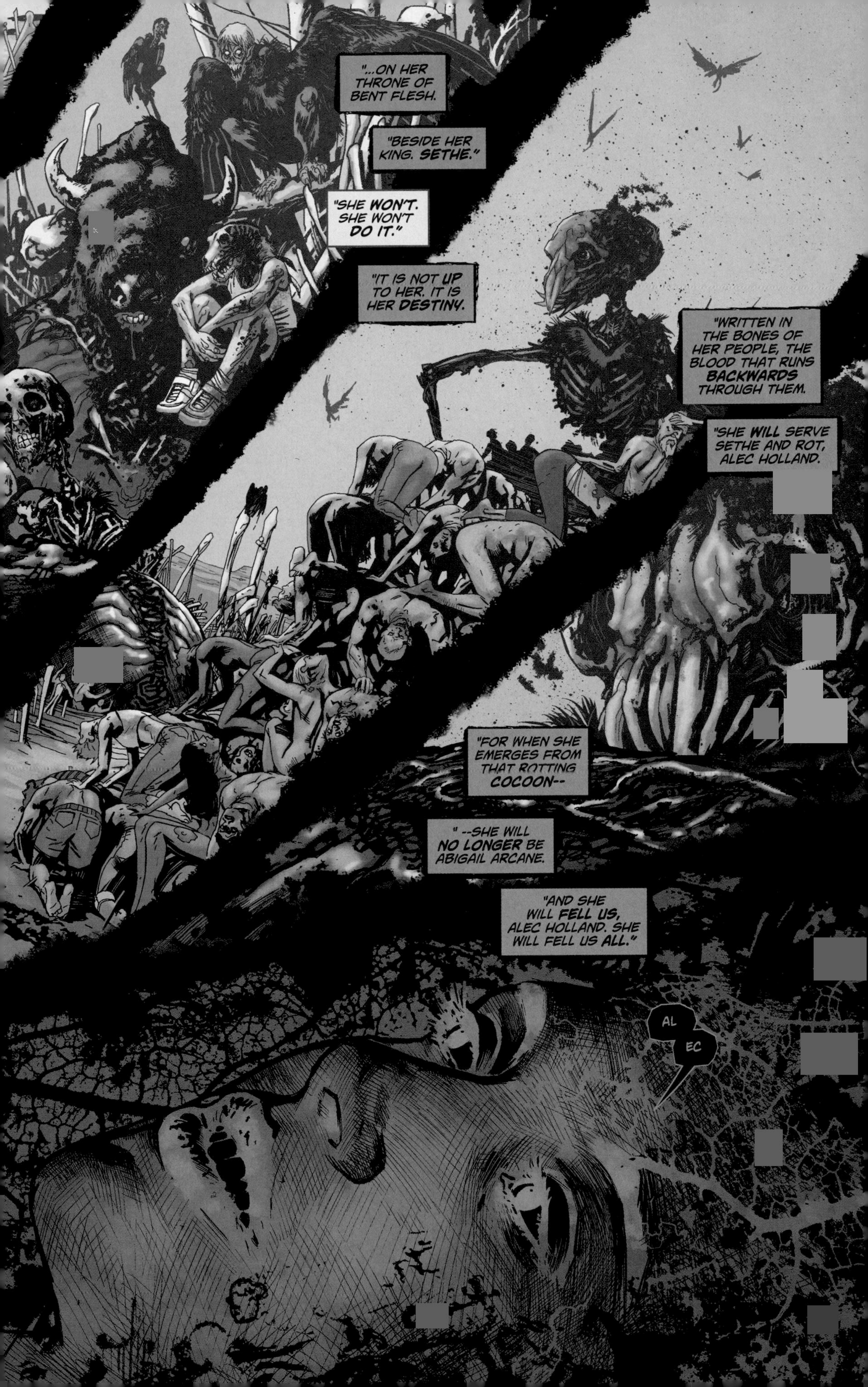
"...ON HER THRONE OF BENT FLESH.
"BESIDE HER KING. SETHE."
"SHE WON'T. SHE WON'T DO IT."
"IT IS NOT UP TO HER. IT IS HER DESTINY.
"WRITTEN IN THE BONES OF HER PEOPLE, THE BLOOD THAT RUNS BACKWARDS THROUGH THEM.
"SHE WILL SERVE SETHE AND ROT, ALEC HOLLAND.
"FOR WHEN SHE EMERGES FROM THAT ROTTING COCOON--
" --SHE WILL NO LONGER BE ABIGAIL ARCANE.
"AND SHE WILL FELL US, ALEC HOLLAND. SHE WILL FELL US ALL."
AL EC

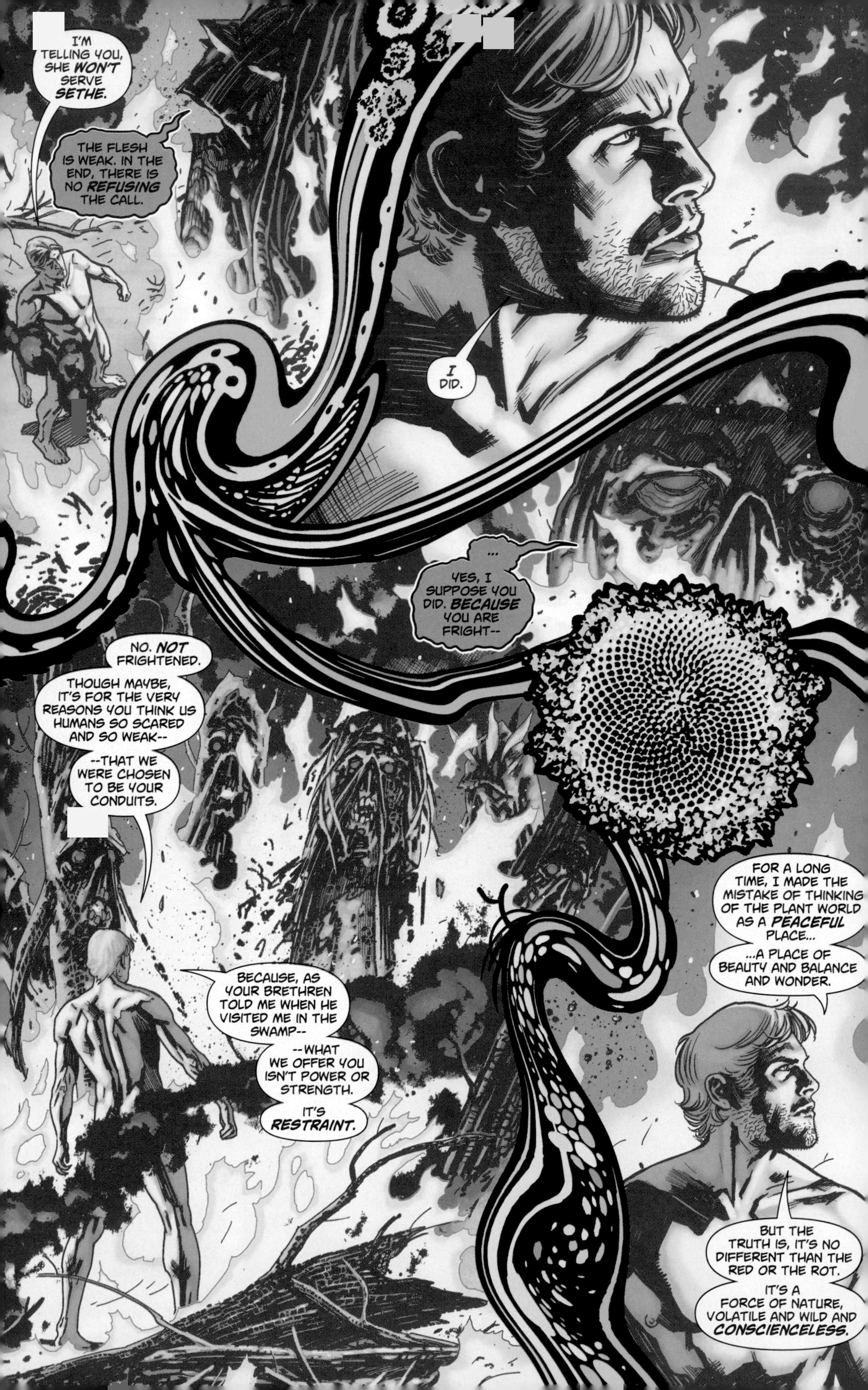
I'M TELLING YOU, SHE WON'T SERVE SETHE.
THE FLESH IS WEAK. IN THE END, THERE IS NO REFUSING THE CALL.
I DID.
...
YES, I SUPPOSE YOU DID. BECAUSE YOU ARE FRIGHT--
NO. NOT FRIGHTENED.
THOUGH MAYBE, IT'S FOR THE VERY REASONS YOU THINK US HUMANS SO SCARED AND SO WEAK--
--THAT WE WERE CHOSEN TO BE YOUR CONDUITS.
BECAUSE, AS YOUR BRETHREN TOLD ME WHEN HE VISITED ME IN THE SWAMP--
--WHAT WE OFFER YOU ISN'T POWER OR STRENGTH.
IT'S RESTRAINT.
FOR A LONG TIME, I MADE THE MISTAKE OF THINKING OF THE PLANT WORLD AS A PEACEFUL PLACE...
...A PLACE OF BEAUTY AND BALANCE AND WONDER.
BUT THE TRUTH IS, IT'S NO DIFFERENT THAN THE RED OR THE ROT.
IT'S A FORCE OF NATURE, VOLATILE AND WILD AND CONSCIENCELESS.

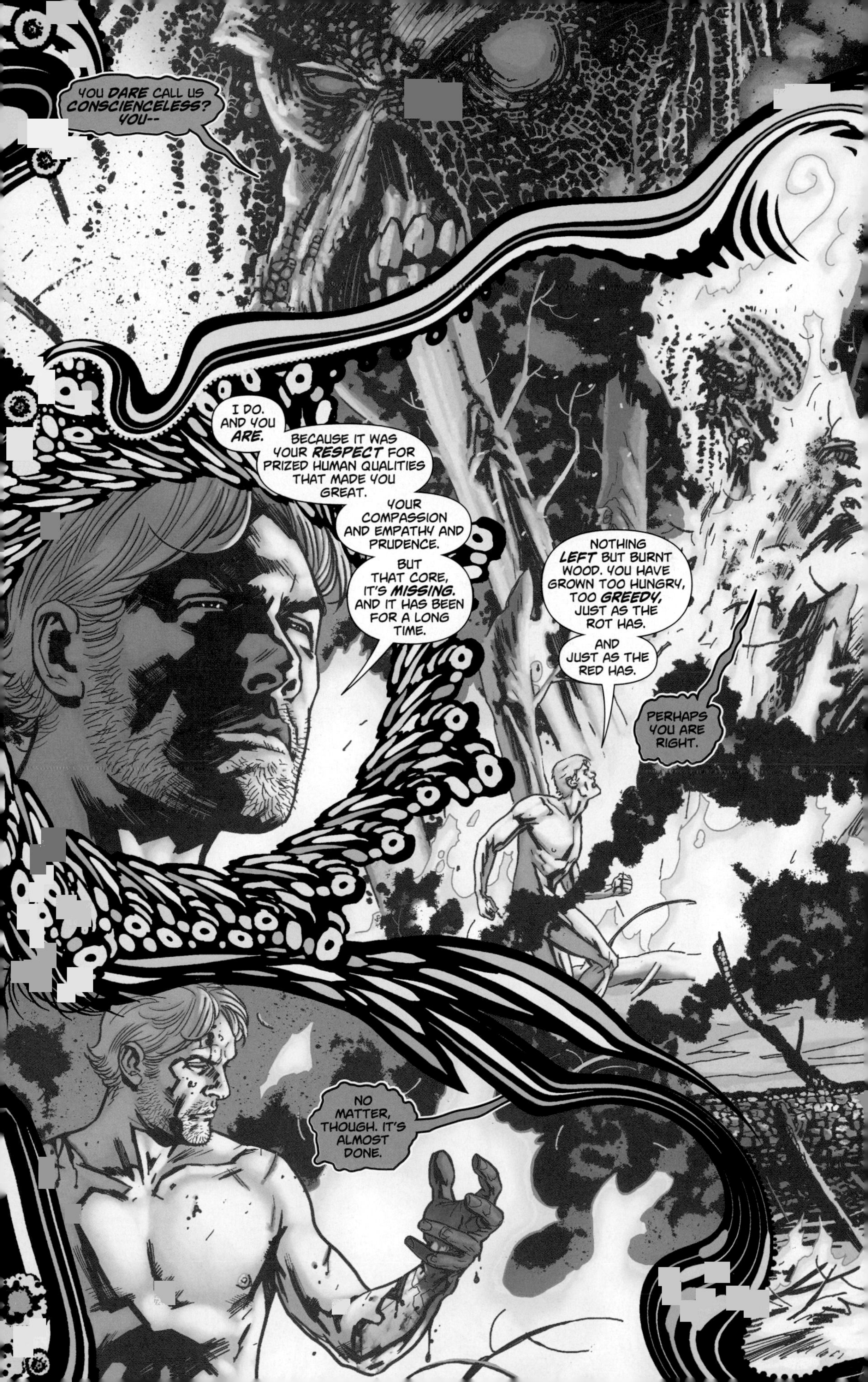
YOU DARE CALL US CONSCIENCELESS? YOU--
I DO. AND YOU ARE.
BECAUSE IT WAS YOUR RESPECT FOR PRIZED HUMAN QUALITIES THAT MADE YOU GREAT.
YOUR COMPASSION AND EMPATHY AND PRUDENCE.
BUT THAT CORE, IT'S MISSING. AND IT HAS BEEN FOR A LONG TIME.
NOTHING LEFT BUT BURNT WOOD. YOU HAVE GROWN TOO HUNGRY, TOO GREEDY, JUST AS THE ROT HAS.
AND JUST AS THE RED HAS.
PERHAPS YOU ARE RIGHT.
NO MATTER, THOUGH. IT'S ALMOST DONE.

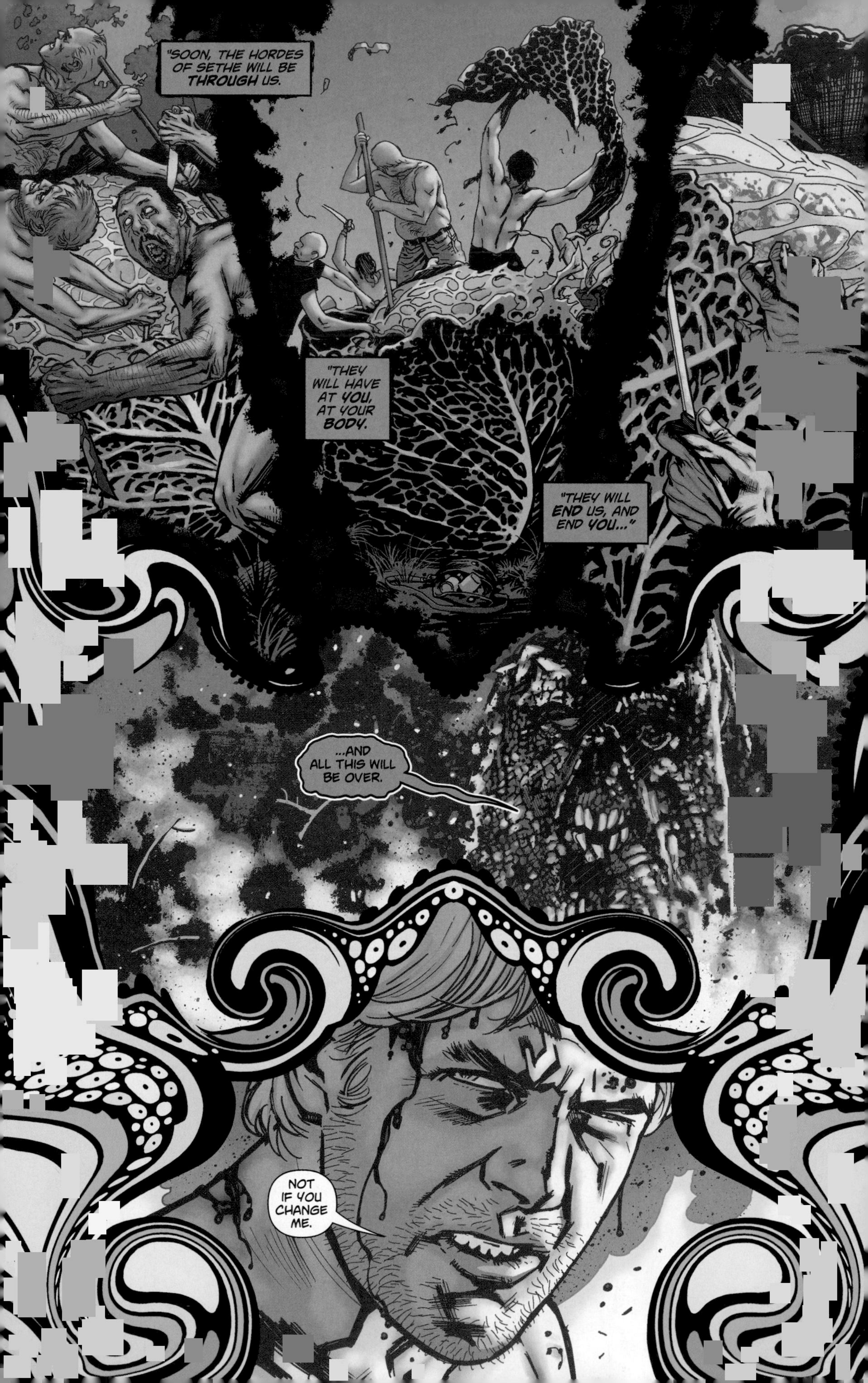
"SOON, THE HORDES OF SETHE WILL BE THROUGH US.
"THEY WILL HAVE AT YOU, AT YOUR BODY.
"THEY WILL END US, AND END YOU..."
...AND ALL THIS WILL BE OVER.
NOT IF YOU CHANGE ME.

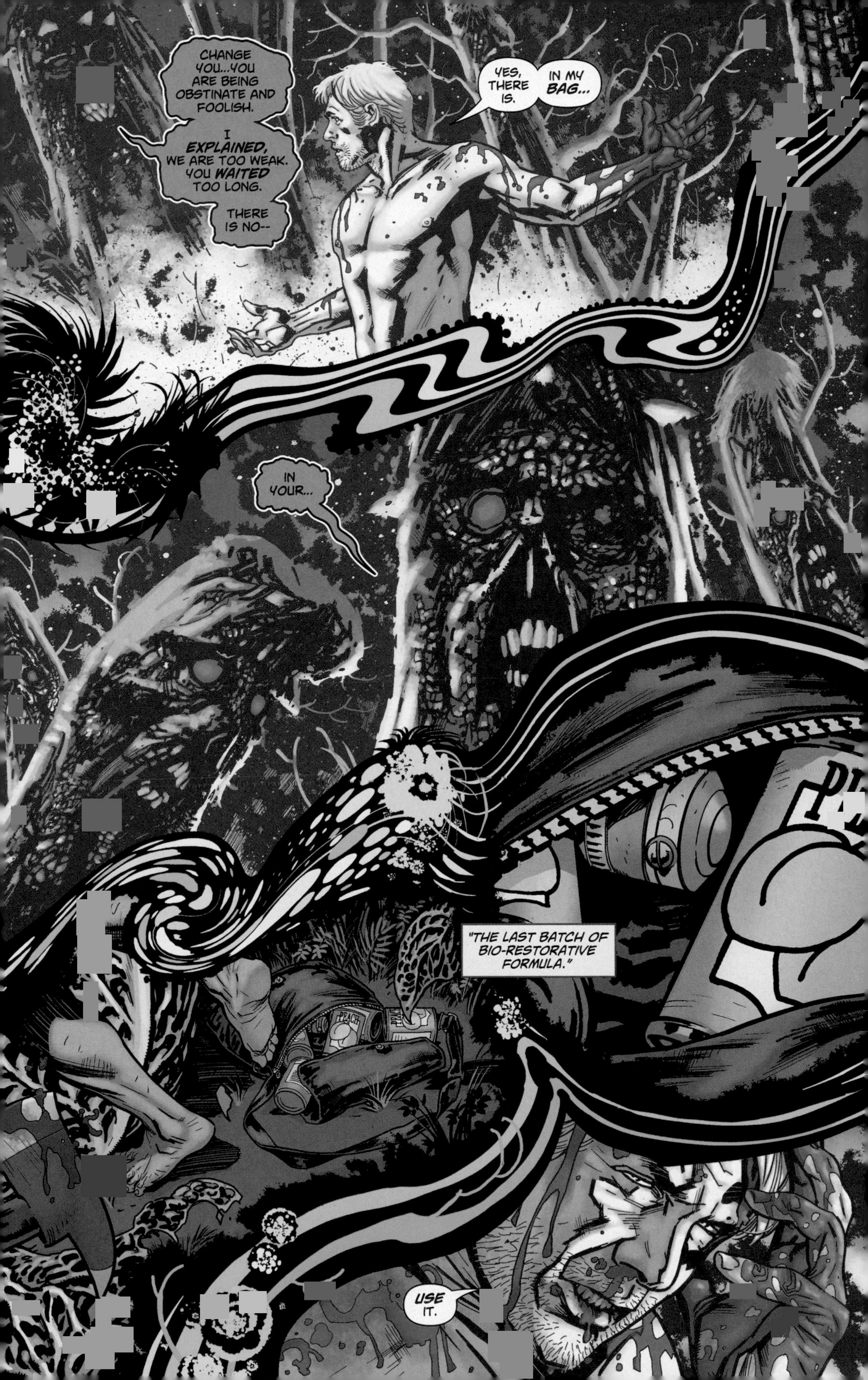
CHANGE YOU...YOU ARE BEING OBSTINATE AND FOOLISH.
I EXPLAINED, WE ARE TOO WEAK. YOU WAITED TOO LONG.
THERE IS NO--
YES, THERE IS.
IN MY BAG...
IN YOUR...
"THE LAST BATCH OF BIO-RESTORATIVE FORMULA."
USE IT.

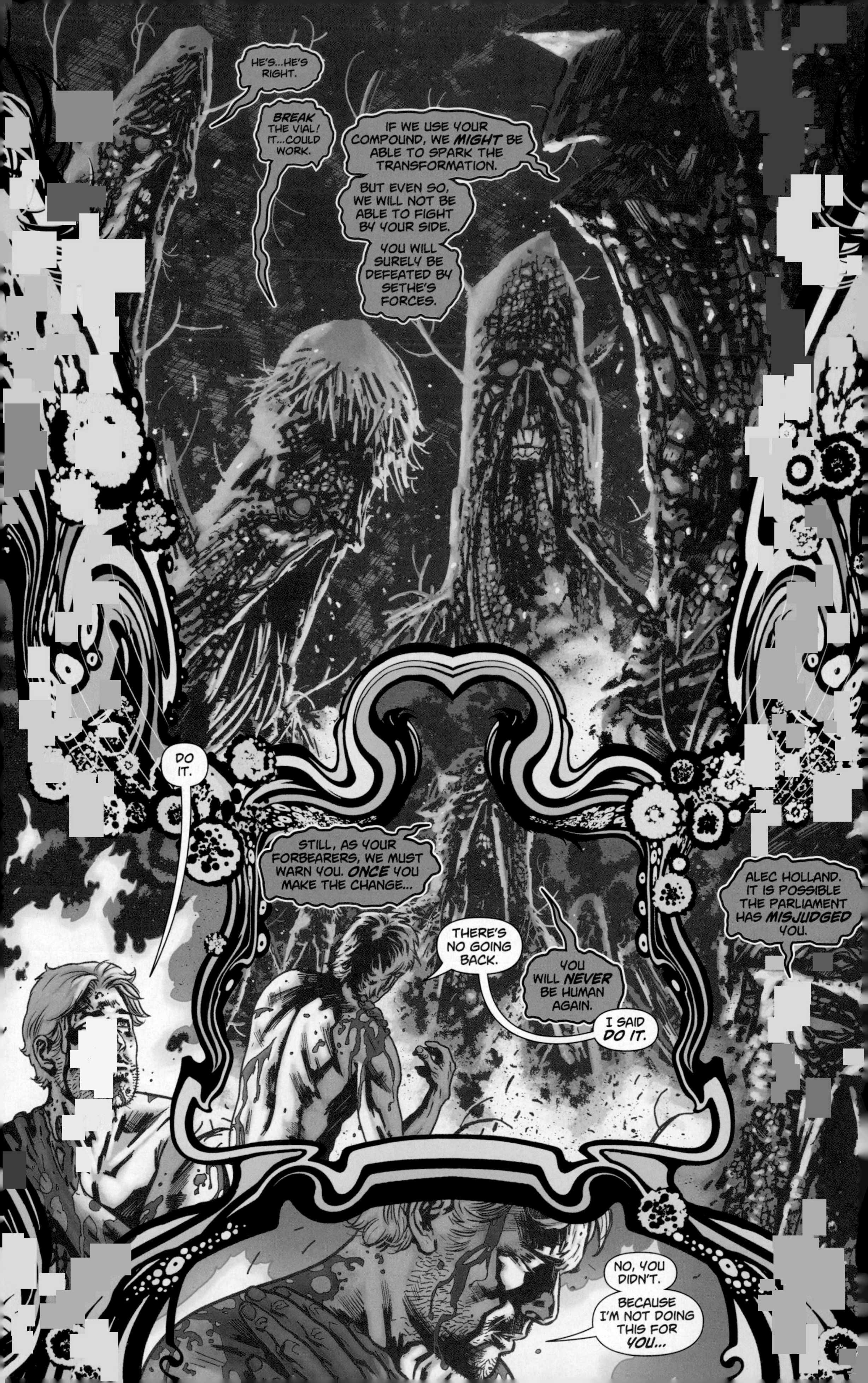
HE'S...HE'S RIGHT.
BREAK THE VIAL! IT...COULD WORK.
IF WE USE YOUR COMPOUND, WE MIGHT BE ABLE TO SPARK THE TRANSFORMATION.
BUT EVEN SO, WE WILL NOT BE ABLE TO FIGHT BY YOUR SIDE.
YOU WILL SURELY BE DEFEATED BY SETHE'S FORCES.
DO IT.
STILL, AS YOUR FORBEARERS, WE MUST WARN YOU. ONCE YOU MAKE THE CHANGE...
THERE'S NO GOING BACK.
YOU WILL NEVER BE HUMAN AGAIN.
I SAID DO IT.
ALEC HOLLAND. IT IS POSSIBLE THE PARLIAMENT HAS MISJUDGED YOU.
NO, YOU DIDN'T.
BECAUSE I'M NOT DOING THIS FOR YOU...

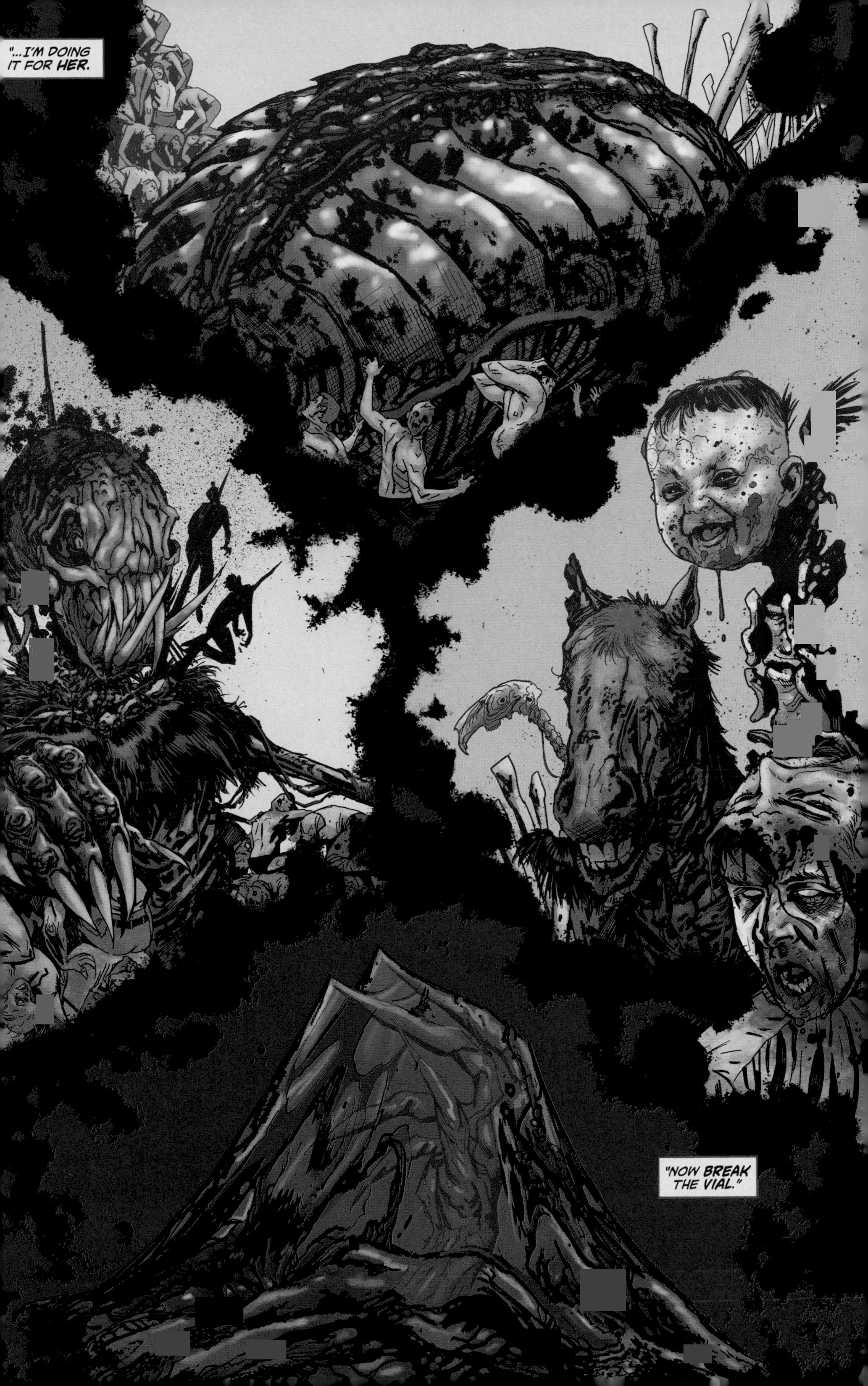
"...I'M DOING IT FOR HER.
"NOW BREAK THE VIAL."

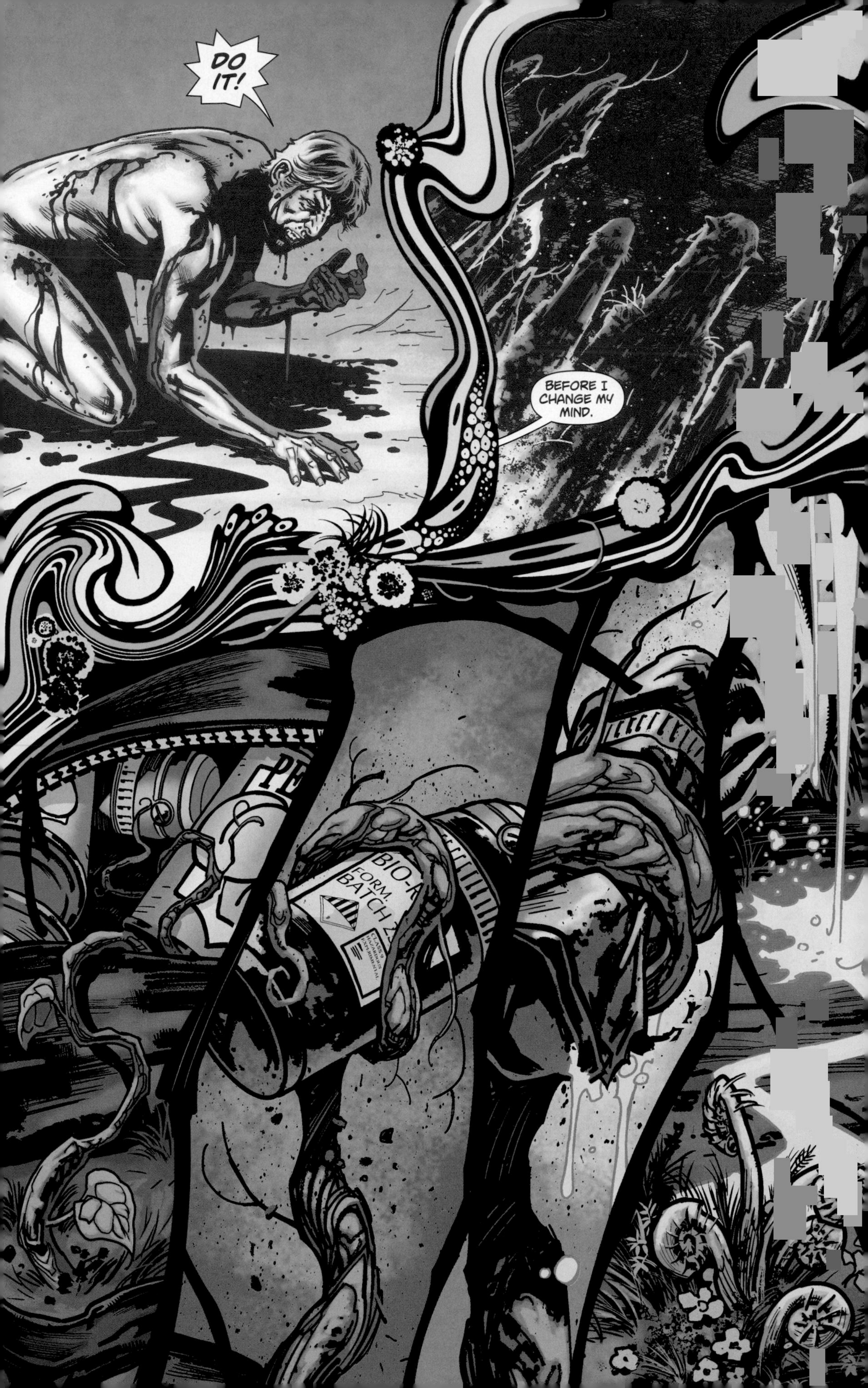
DO IT!
BEFORE I CHANGE MY MIND.
FORM.
BATCH

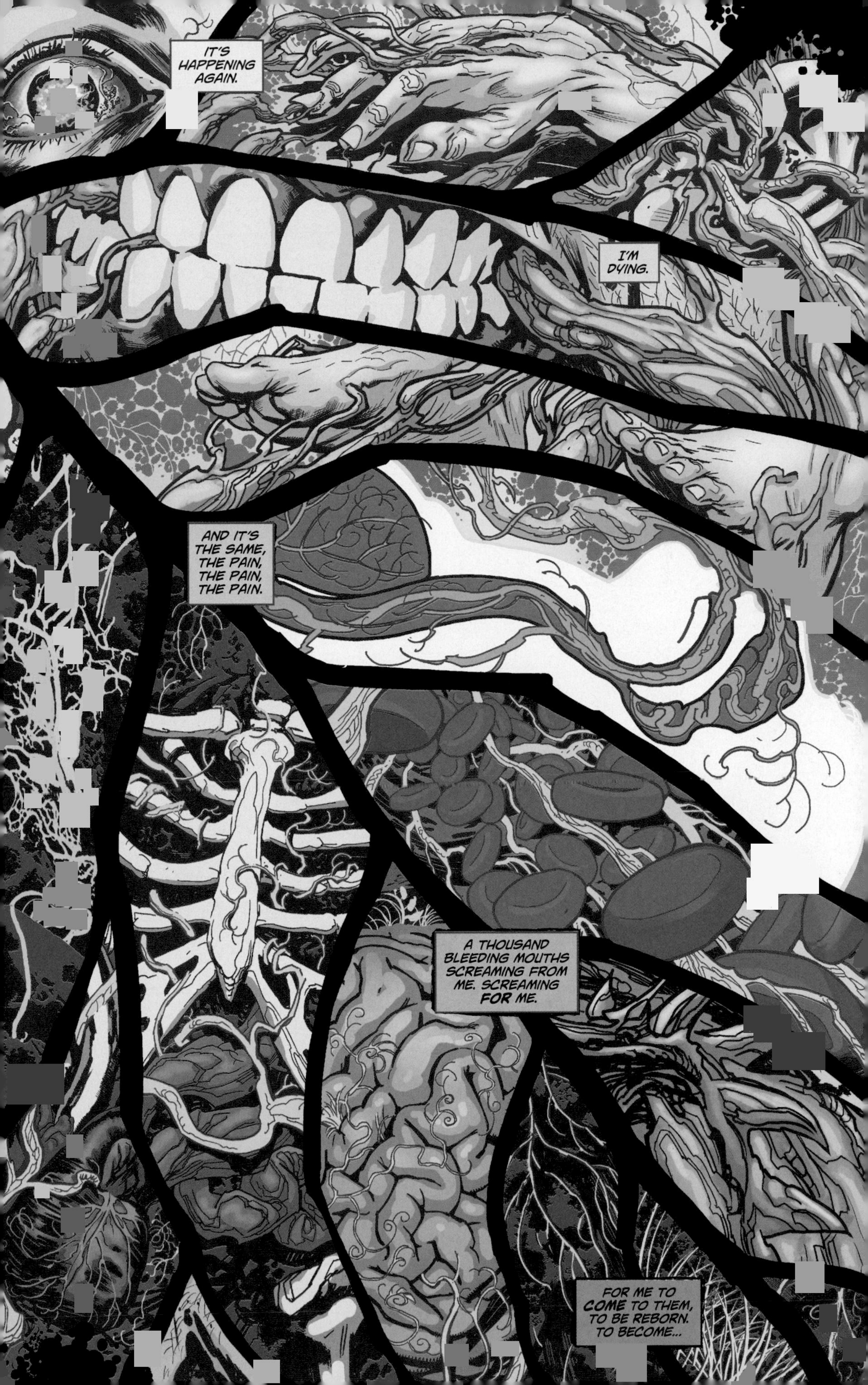
IT'S HAPPENING AGAIN.
I'M DYING.
AND IT'S THE SAME, THE PAIN, THE PAIN, THE PAIN.
A THOUSAND BLEEDING MOUTHS SCREAMING FROM ME. SCREAMING FOR ME.
FOR ME TO COME TO THEM, TO BE REBORN. TO BECOME...

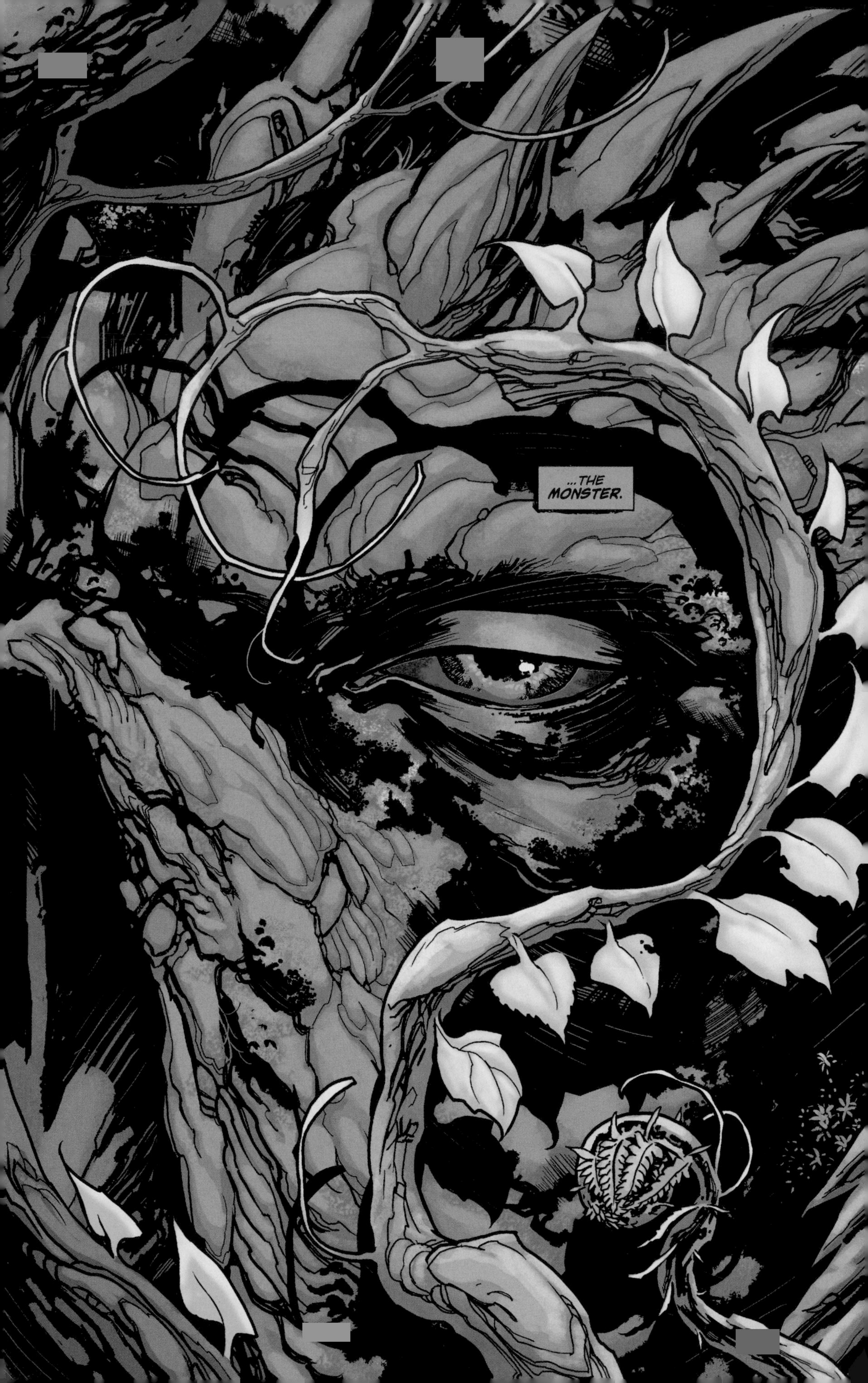
...THE MONSTER.

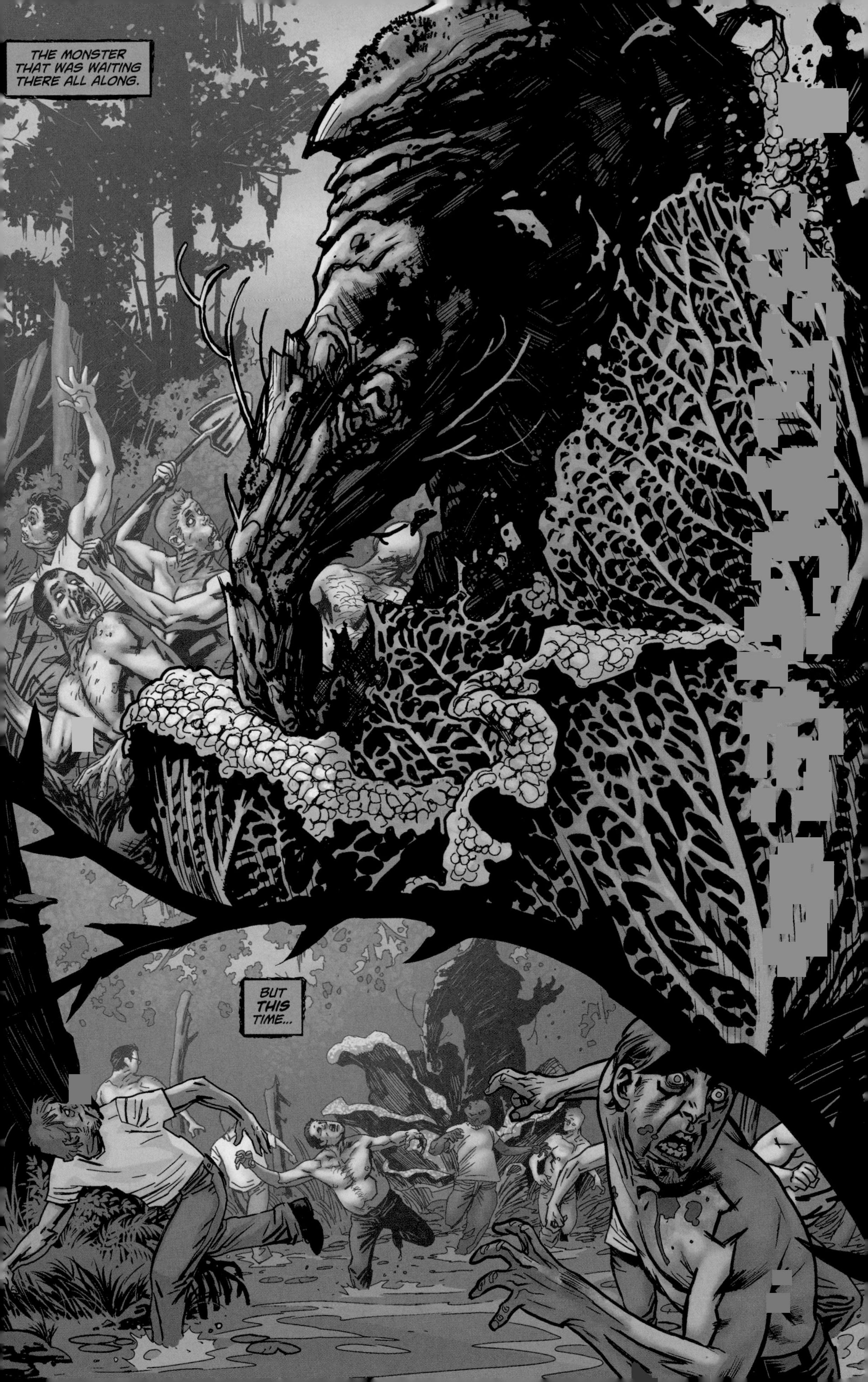
THE MONSTER THAT WAS WAITING THERE ALL ALONG.
BUT THIS TIME...

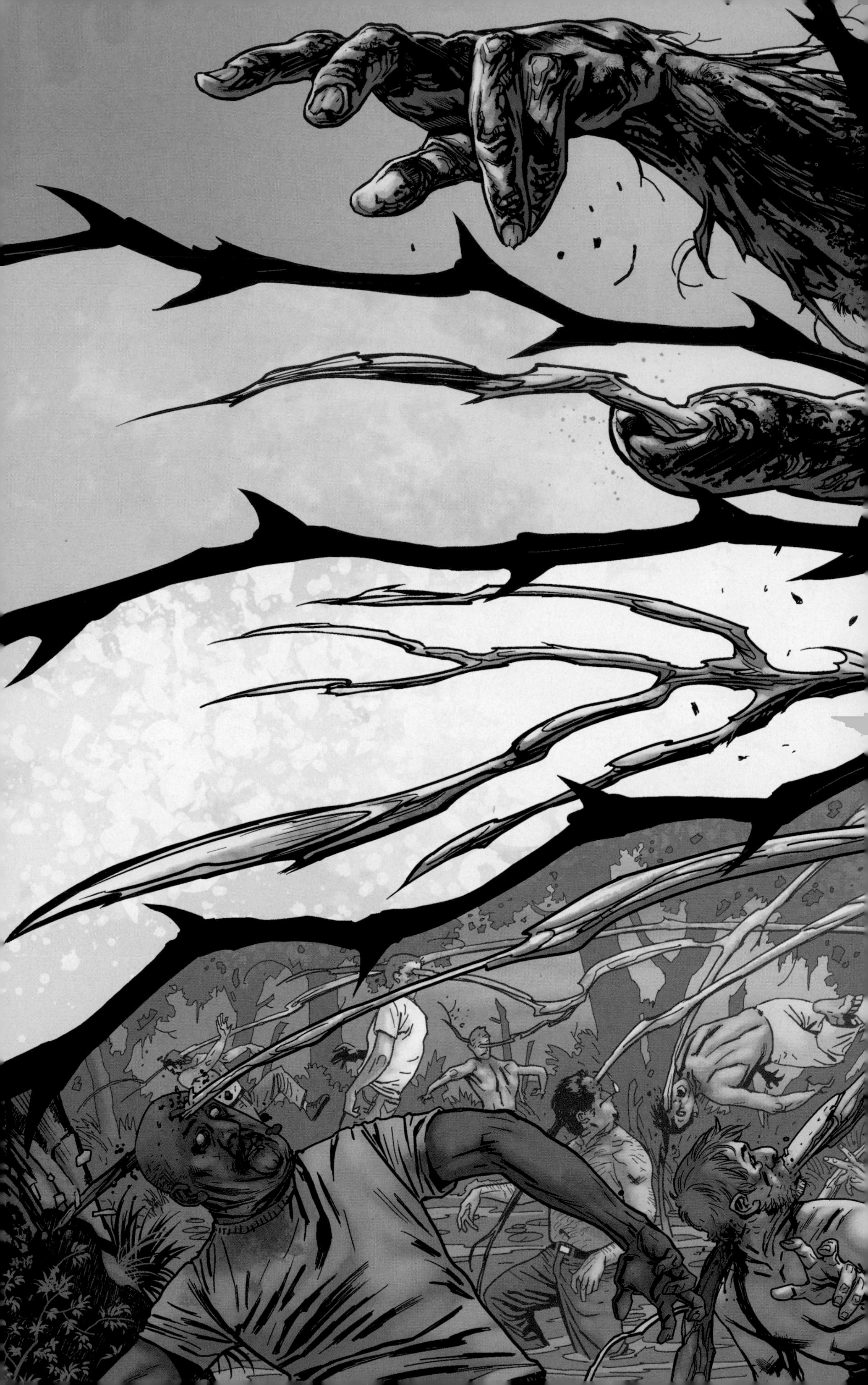

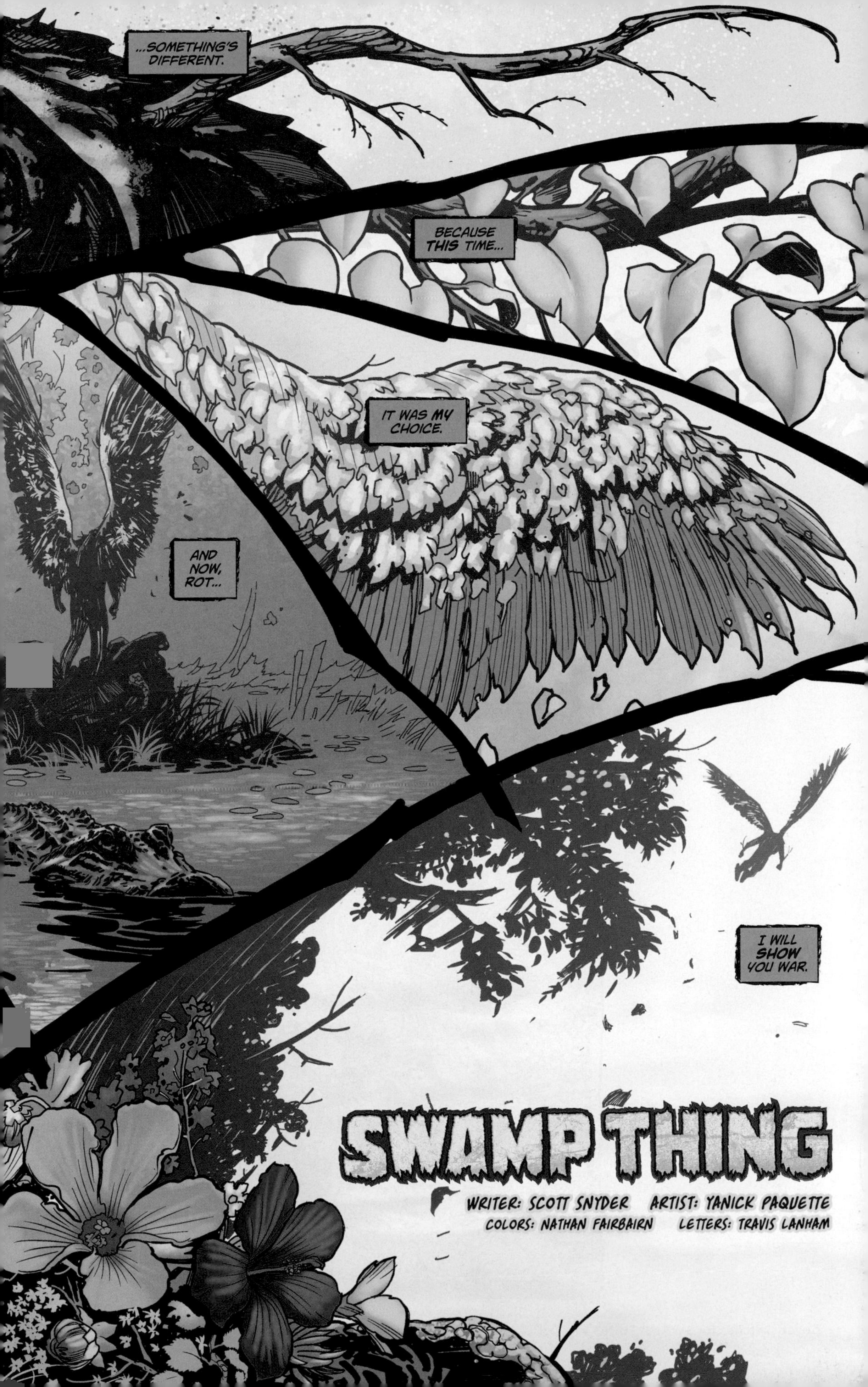
...SOMETHING'S DIFFERENT.
BECAUSE THIS TIME...
IT WAS MY CHOICE.
AND NOW, ROT...
I WILL SHOW YOU WAR.
SWAMP THING
WRITER: SCOTT SNYDER ARTIST: YANICK PAQUETTE
COLORS: NATHAN FAIRBAIRN LETTERS: TRAVIS LANHAM

SWAMP THING
SKETCHES BY YANICK PAQUETTE

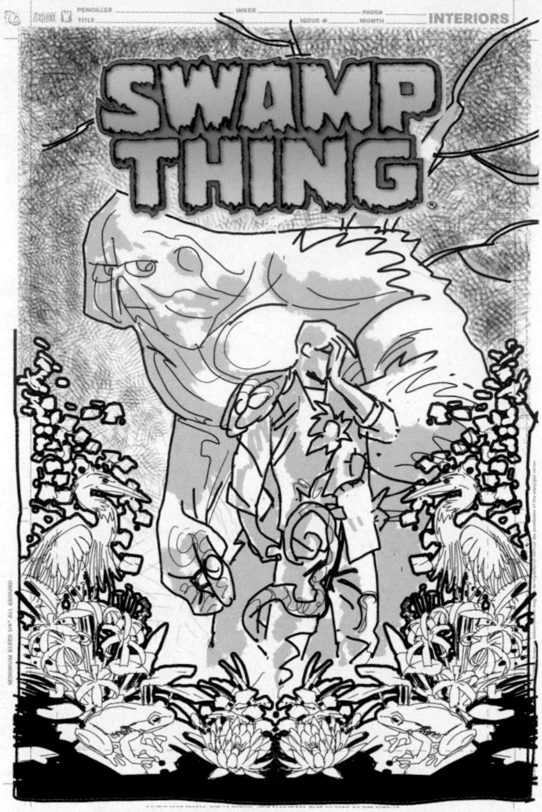
PENCILLER
INKER
PAGE#
TITLE
ISSUE #
MONTH
INTERIORS
SWAMP THING

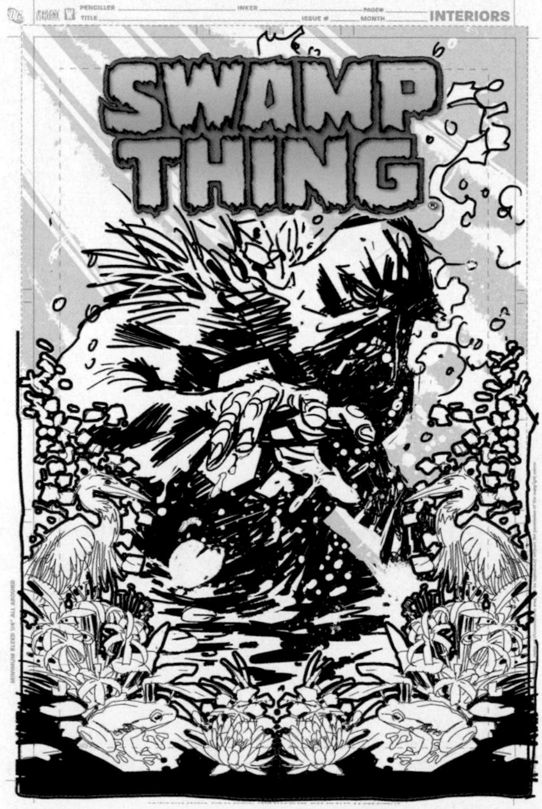
PENCILLER
INKER
PAGE#
TITLE
ISSUE #
MONTH
INTERIORS
SWAMP THING

Cover sketches for SWAMP THING #1

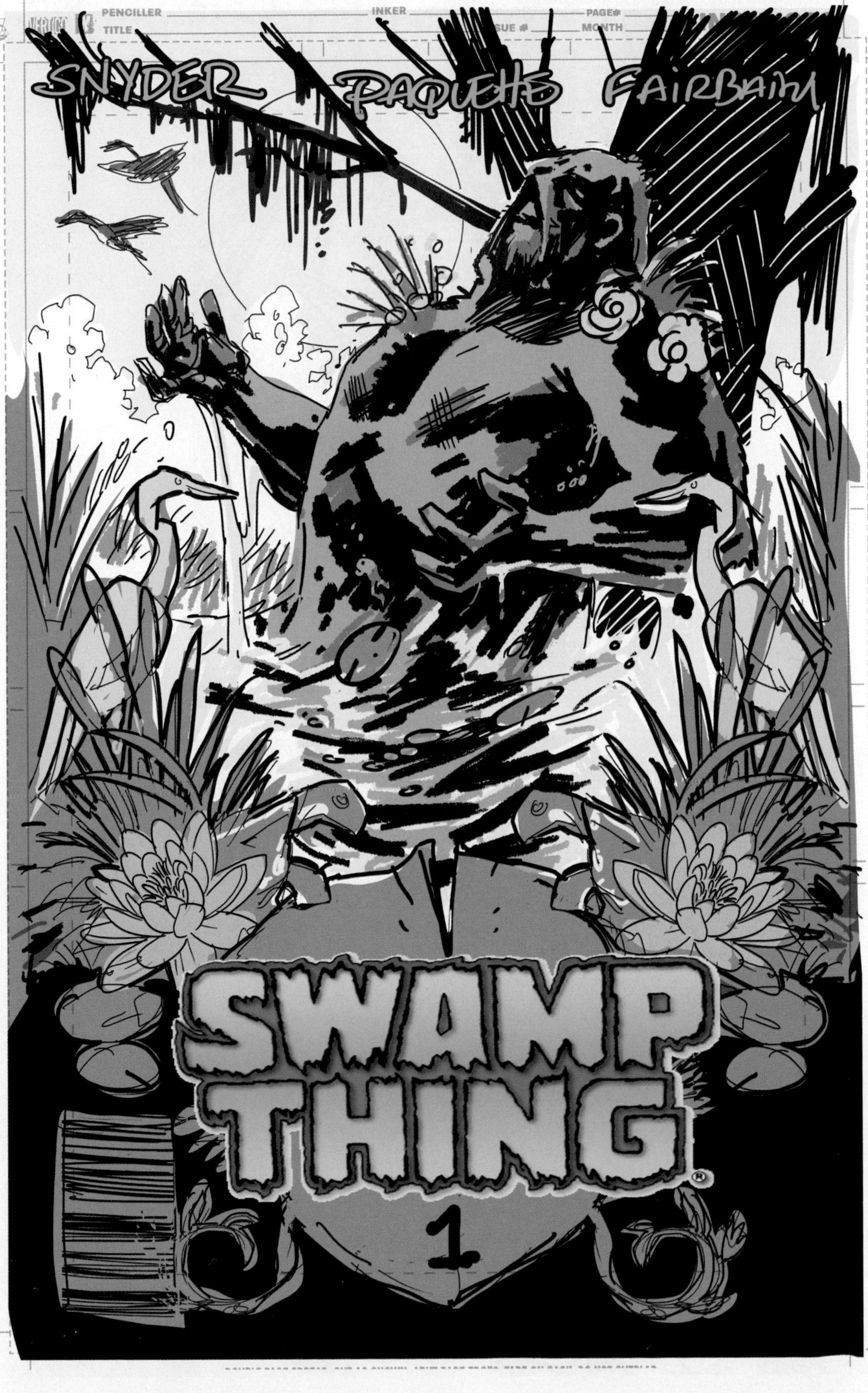
PENCILLER
INKER
PAGE#
TITLE
ISSUE #
MONTH
SNYDER
PAQUETTE
FAIRBAIRN
SWAMP THING®
1

MINIMUM BLEED 1/4" ALL AROUND

Cover sketch for
SWAMP THING #7

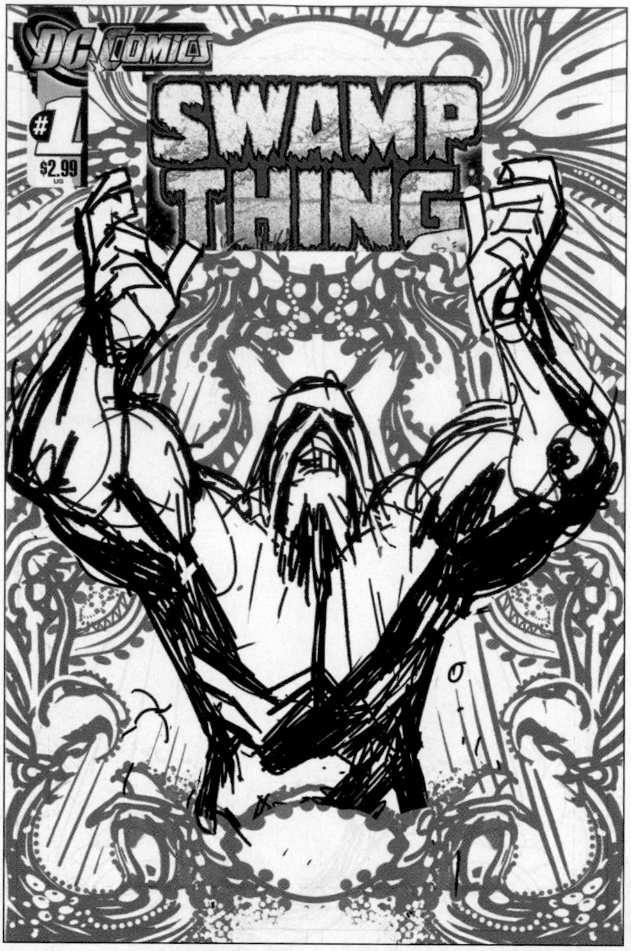
DC COMICS
#1
$2.99
US
SWAMP THING

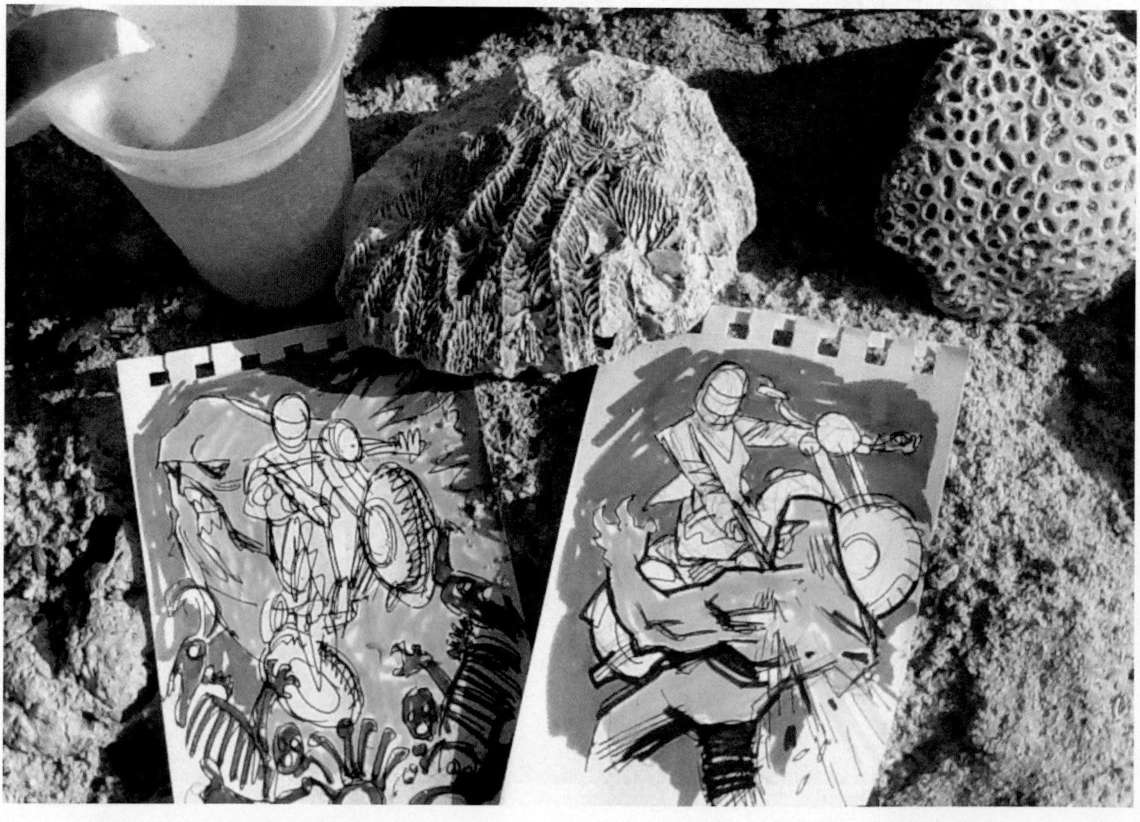

Cover sketches for SWAMP THING #3

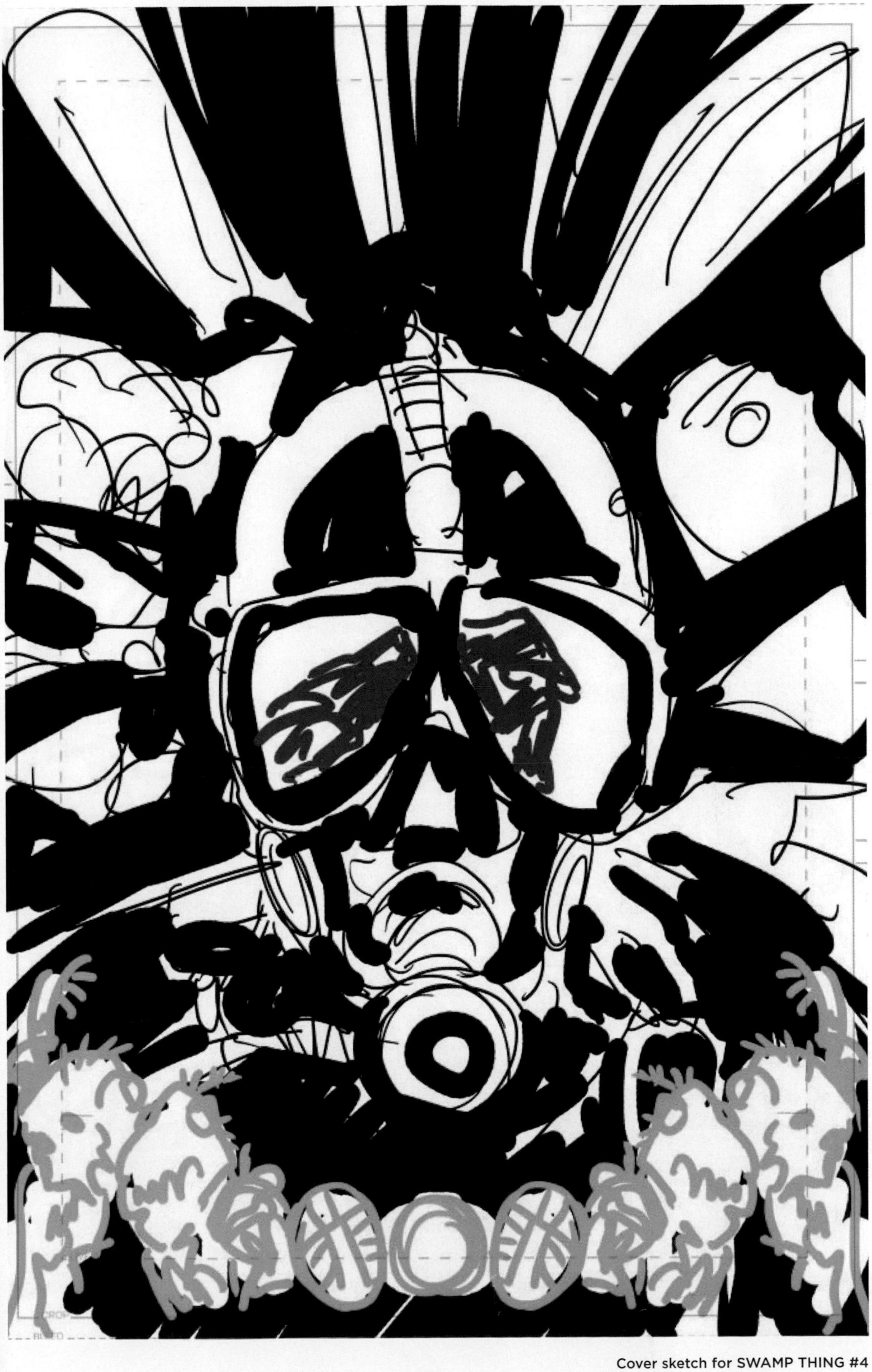

Cover sketch for SWAMP THING #4

Cover sketches for SWAMP THING #5

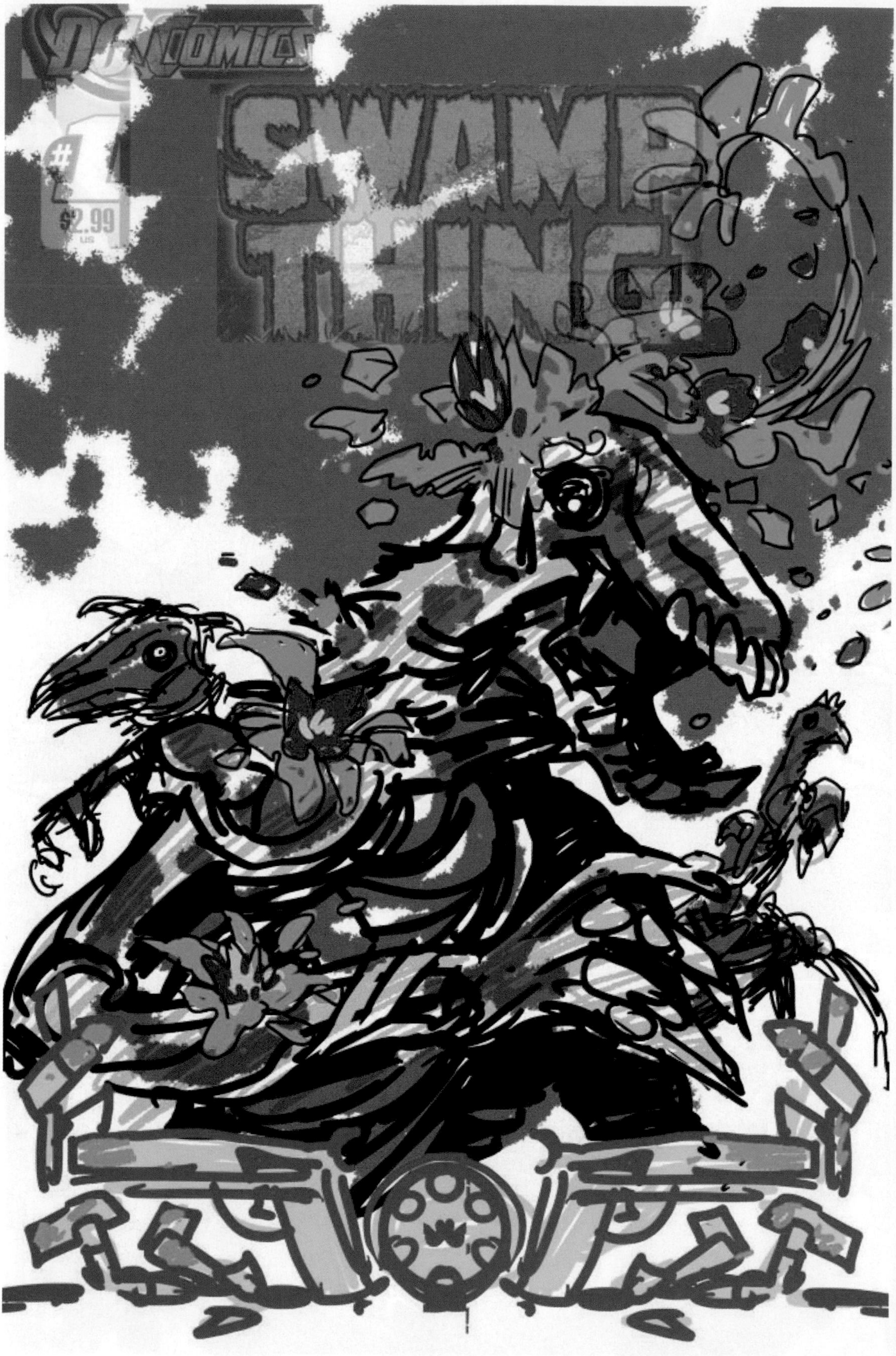
DC COMICS
#1
$2.99
US
SWAMP THING

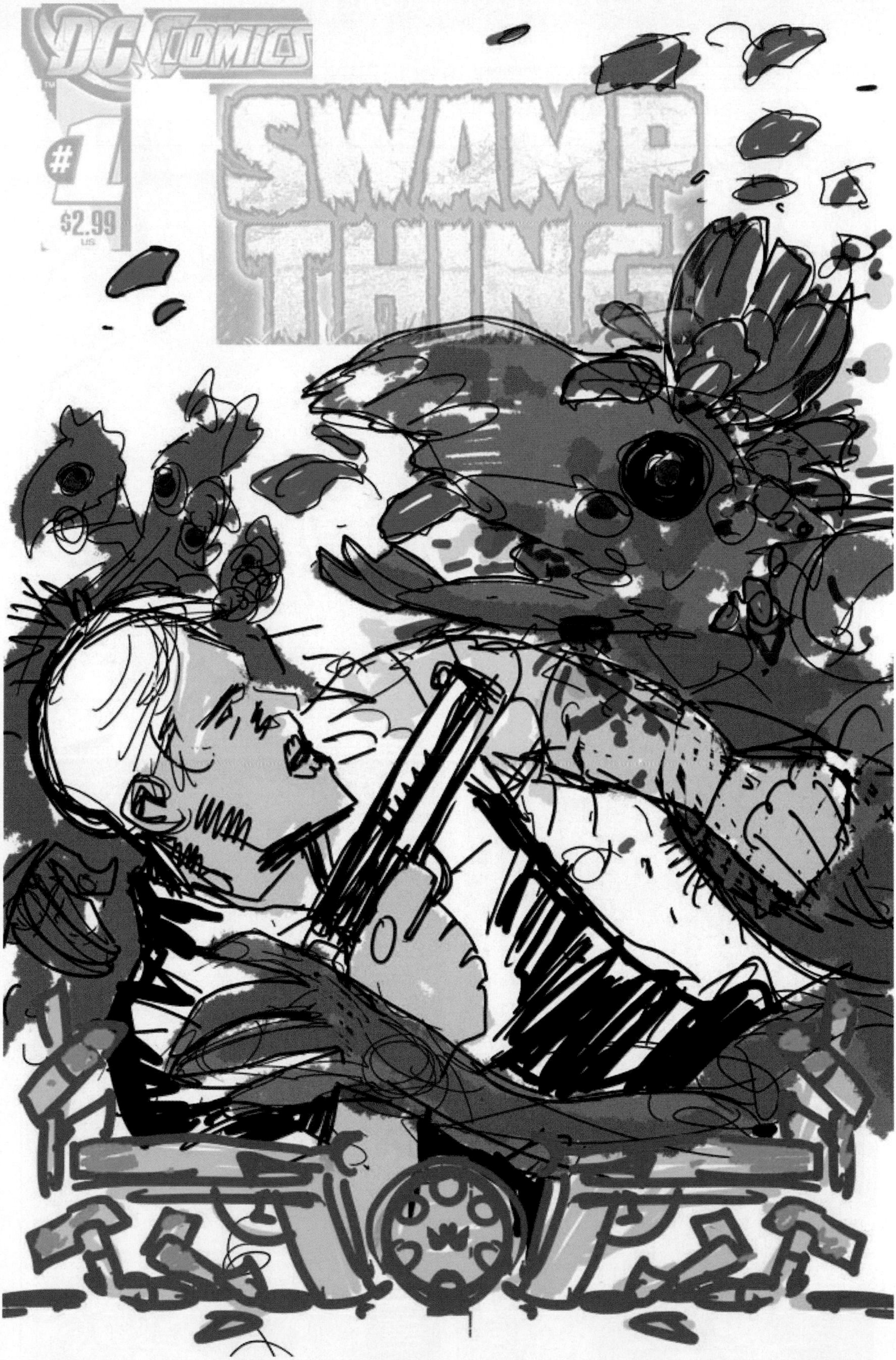
DC COMICS
#1
$2.99
US
SWAMP THING

SWAMP THING
COVER LAYOUT CONCEPTS

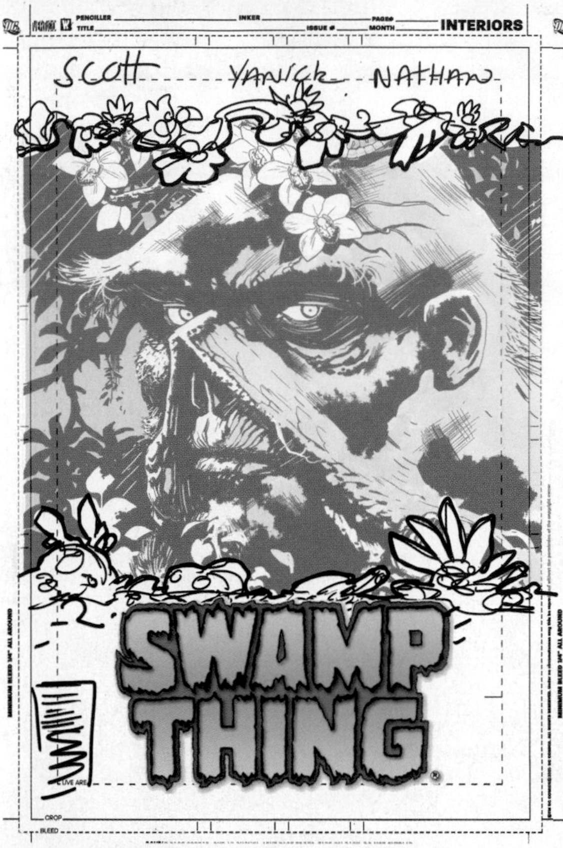
INTERIORS
SCOTT
YANICK
NATHAN
SWAMP
THING

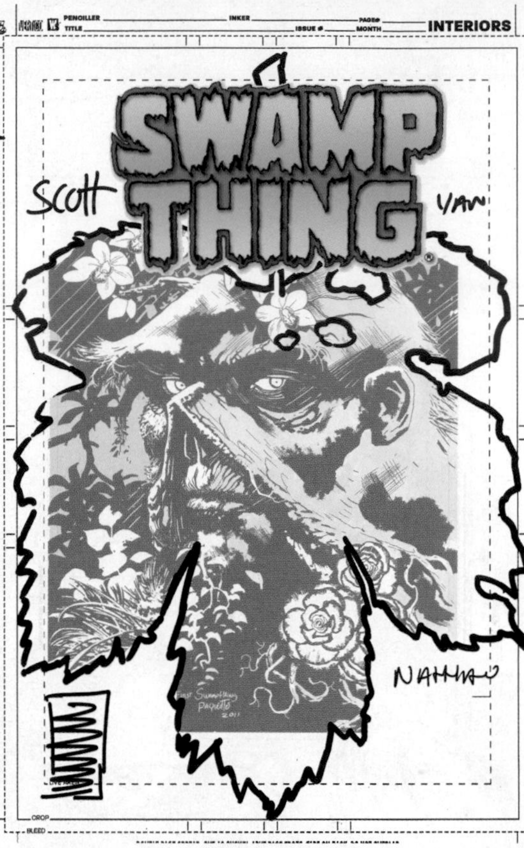
INTERIORS
SWAMP
THING
SCOTT
YAN
NATHAN

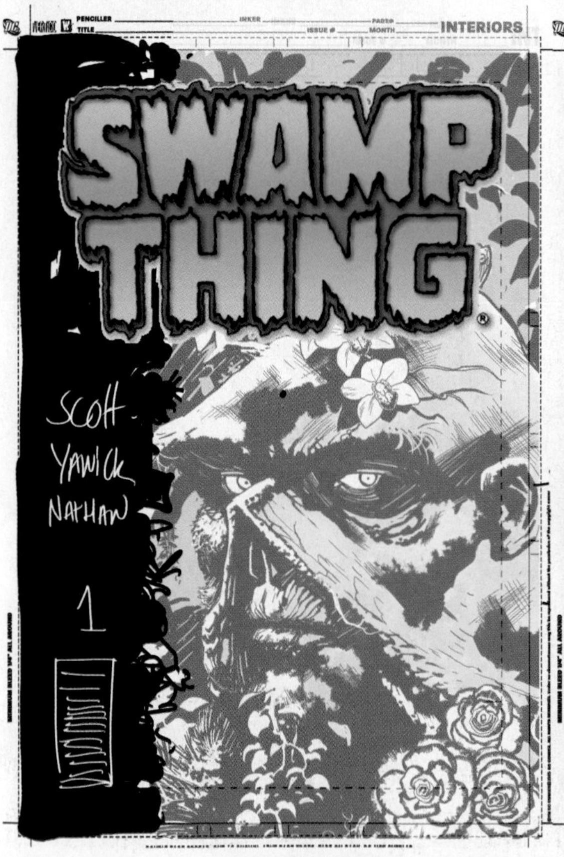
INTERIORS
SWAMP
THING
SCOTT
YANICK
NATHAN
1

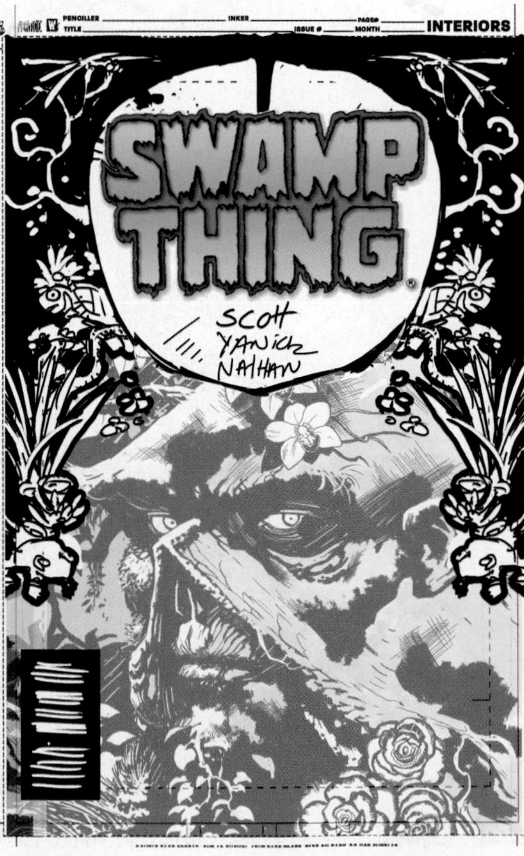
INTERIORS
SWAMP
THING
SCOTT
YANICK
NATHAN

The first Swamp Thing illustration by Yanick

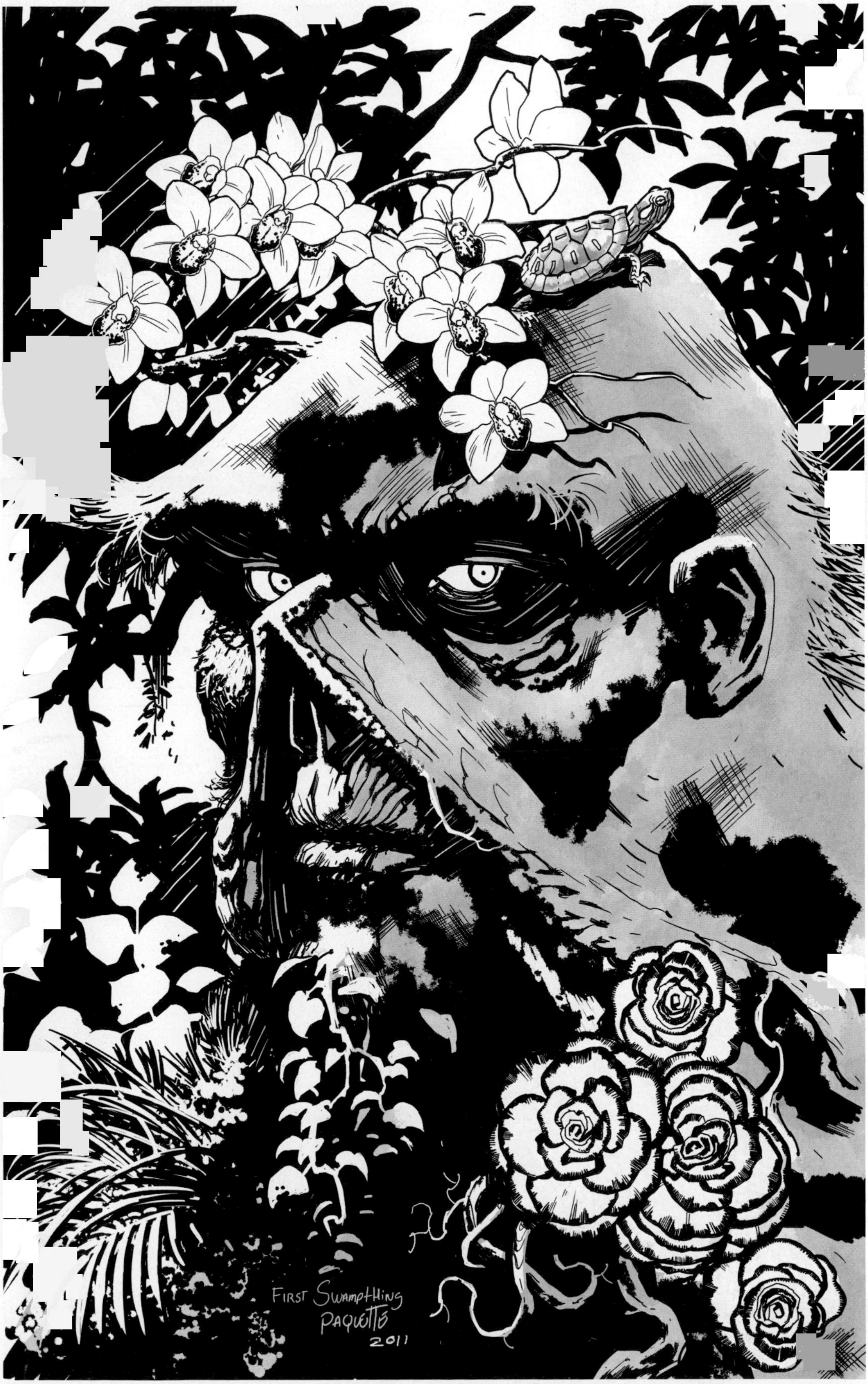

FIRST SWAMPTHING
PAQUETTE
2011

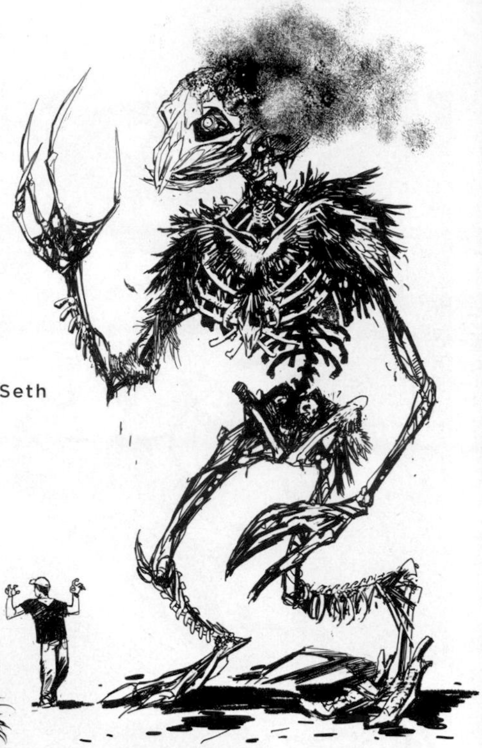

Character design for Seth

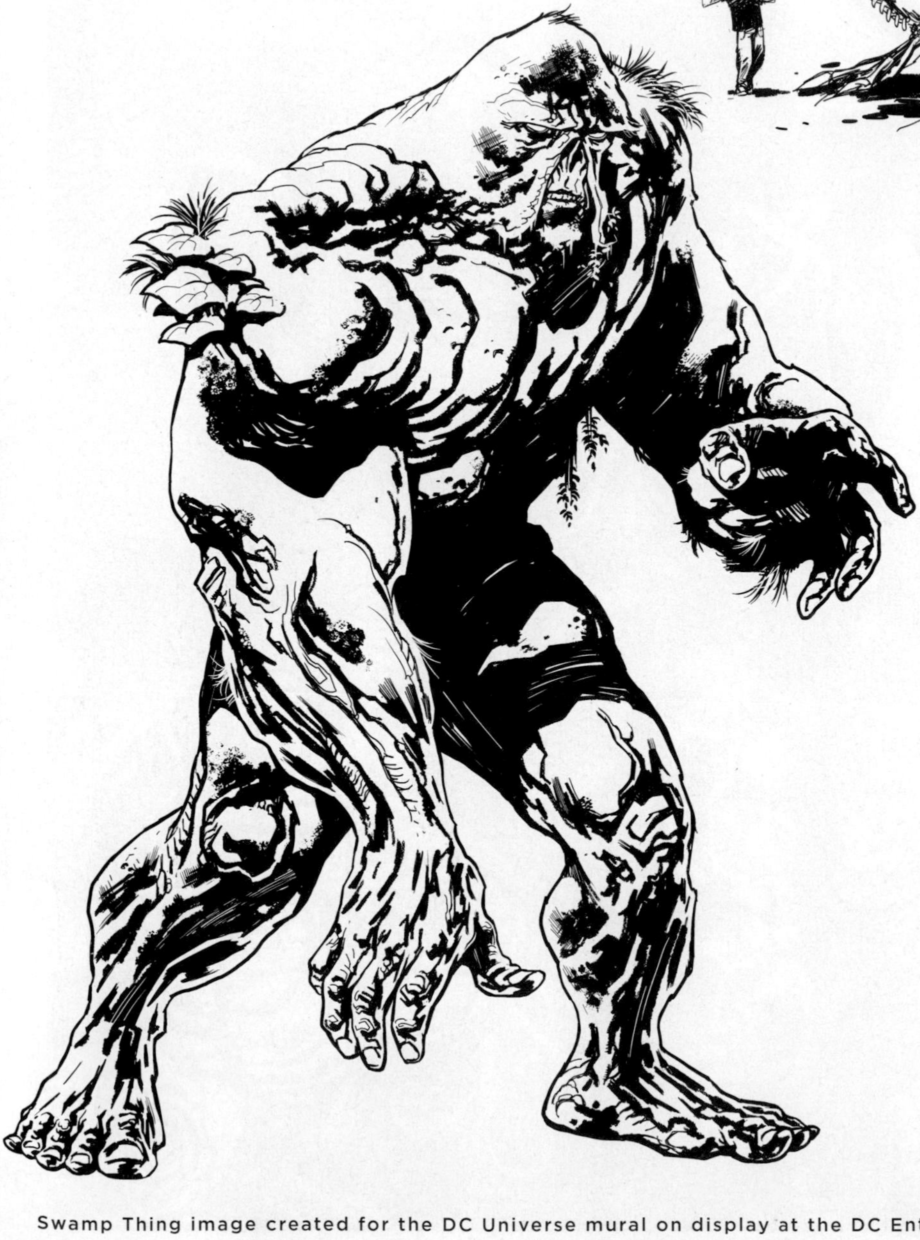

Swamp Thing image created for the DC Universe mural on display at the DC Entertainment offices.